THE LEGACY OF McLUHAN

The Hampton Press Communication Series
MEDIA ECOLOGY
Lance Strate, supervisory editor

THE LEGACY OF McLUHAN

Edited by

Lance Strate
Edward Wachtel
Fordham University

HAMPTON PRESS, INC.
CRESSKILL, NJ 07626

Printed in the United States of America

Library of Congress Cataloging-in-Publication Data

The legacy of McLuhan / edited by Lance Strate, Edward Wachtel.
     p.cm. -- (The Hampton Press communication series)
    Includes bibliographical references and indexes.
    ISBN 1-57273-530-9 -- ISBN 1-57273-531-7
  1. McLuhan, Marshall, 1911- I. Strate, Lance. II. Wachtel, Edward. III. Series.

    P92.5.M3L44 2005
    302.23'092--dc22

                          2005050274

Cover photo: Marshall McLuhan at Fordham University, 1967-68 school year
Archives of Special Collections, Fordham University Library

Hampton Press, Inc.
23 Broadway
Cresskill, NJ 07626

CONTENTS

SECTION SIX: EXTENSIONS

LIST OF ILLUSTRATIONS

ACKNOWLEDGMENTS

We would like to begin by thanking all of our contributors for their efforts and their patience on the long road to publication. This project was born from the Legacy of McLuhan Symposium held at Fordham University on March 27-28, 1998, which would not have been possible without the early and enthusiastic support of Joseph M. McShane, SJ. Thanks are also due to Robert F. Himmelberg, Robert R. Grimes, SJ, and Joseph A. O'Hare, SJ, for their generous contributions to the symposium. And among the many other individuals who helped to make the event a success, we would like to acknowledge Jerome Agel, Robert Albrecht, Albert Auster, Susan B. Barnes, Hopeton Campbell, James Capo, Edmund Carpenter, Sara Floor, Charles Hodulik, Ron Jacobson, Liss Jeffrey, Paul Levinson, Paul Lippert, Bruce Logan, Robert K. Logan, Philip Marchand, Eric McLuhan, Stephanie McLuhan-Ortved, Joshua Meyrowitz, Christine Nystrom, Neil Postman, Meir Ribalow, Douglas Rushkoff, Paul Ryan, Tony Schwartz, Donald Theall, and Amanda Weiss.

We are grateful to Fordham University's Department of Communication and Media Studies for the assistance provided to us in editing this anthology, and special thanks go out to Janet Stemberg, Elizabeth K. Fitzgerald, Audrey Butler, Elaine Miraglia of the Edward A. Walsh Digital Media Lab, and department chair Paul Levinson, And we want to thank Patrice Kane, Head of Archives and Special Collections at the Walsh Library, Fordham University, for her generous efforts on our behalf.

We also need to recognize the ongoing support of the Media Ecology Association, the organization that has done so much to keep McLuhan's spirit and his ideas alive. And a special thank you is required for our publisher, Barbara Bernstein, one of the all time great patrons of media ecology.

We are very grateful for the love, support, and patience of our families, namely Barbara, Benjamin, and Sarah Strate, and Lori Ramos and Henry Wachtel.

Finally, we dedicate this book to the life, the memory, and the legacy of Herbert Marshall McLuhan.

INTRODUCTION

Lance Strate
Edward Wachtel
Fordham University

Media Guru. Sage of Aquarius. Oracle of the Electronic Age. Canada's Intellectual Comet. Patron Saint of *Wired* magazine. This has been the unique public identity of Marshall McLuhan (1911-1980), the scholar who rose to celebrity during the 1960s, and has remained the object of public interest ever since. A controversial figure, infuriating to some, inspiring to many, McLuhan put the study of media on the academic map. In doing so, he became the archetype of the media scholar, joining Descartes, Darwin, Einstein, and Freud in the pantheon of intellectual icons. It is not surprising that dozens of individuals have been anointed "the new McLuhan" over the years (in France there have been a number of critics who have been referred to as the "French McLuhan," see, e.g., Genosko, 1999). Competition for the mantle of McLuhan continues to this day, and his impact as role model is no small part of his legacy.

There is no question that McLuhan combined ideas and image in a singular and unprecedented fashion. It was the media that transformed McLuhan from an obscure academic into an international celebrity. His name has been dropped on television programs from *Laugh-In* to *The*

Sopranos. It has appeared on bumper stickers and in cartoons and comics. It has been used within the fine arts and in serious literature. It has given rise to the terms *McLuhanism* (*Macluhanisme* in France) and *McLuhanesque.* His presence has been seen and felt in the movies: a cameo in Woody Allen's *Annie Hall*; Brian O'Blivion, a character he inspired in David Cronenberg's *Videodrome*; the film title *Medium Cool.* He has been the subject of television and video documentaries, audio recordings, computer software, and web sites. His visage appears on a Canadian postage stamp released on February 17, 2000 (the same day that the Second Annual Marshall McLuhan Fordham University Lecture was given by Camille Paglia). McLuhan's name and ideas are constantly (and countlessly) referenced in articles and books.

As much as the media made McLuhan a popular icon, McLuhan made the media a popular subject. Although others were responsible for the invention of media technology, McLuhan's contribution was the rhetorical invention of THE MEDIA as a phrase and a category that made its way into public discourse. Before McLuhan, there was the press and there was speech, the two modes of communication sanctified by the First Amendment to the Constitution of the United States. Before McLuhan, there were performances and exhibitions, arts and entertainments, spectacles and advertisements. Before McLuhan, there were technologies and techniques, symbols and codes. Before McLuhan, there was mass communication, mass culture, and mass media. The latter was a category generally limited to publishing, broadcasting, motion pictures, and sound recordings; in contrast, McLuhan in *Understanding Media* (1964) examined speech, writing, bicycles, electric light, the telephone, games, clothing, housing, cities, and weapons *as media.* McLuhan revealed the hidden ground that united these and many other phenomena that were previously seen as disparate and unrelated. He helped us to see that language is a technology, that tools and machines are forms of communication, and that all are media. This is part of his legacy.

McLuhan was blessed with a gift for the memorable phrase through which he communicated many of his key insights. His central tenet, "The medium is the message" (McLuhan, 1964, p. 7), has been endlessly quoted, supported, or denied, not to mention modified (even by McLuhan himself, e.g., "the medium is the massage," "the medium is the mass-age;" see, e.g., McLuhan & Fiore, 1967). His metaphor for life in a world dominated by instantaneous telecommunications, "the global village" has proven to be an enduring and evocative neologism. His categories of "hot and cool" (McLuhan, 1964) continue to surface periodically in both popular and scholarly discussions. McLuhan had a quick and agile intellect, and new ideas poured forth in rapid succession—it sometimes seemed as if his mind revolved at 78 RPM while others were stuck at 33 1/3. His speed of thought allowed him to keep up with a swiftly accelerating society, and he came to be known as a futurist and prophet. McLuhan explained, however, that prophets simply describe the present situation while everyone else is preoccupied with the past, looking at life through a "rearview mirror" (see, e.g., McLuhan & Fiore, 1967. In fact, he would have pointed out that our metaphoric use of vinyl record playback speeds—two sentences back—was an example of rearview mirror thinking.)

Speed breeds impatience. McLuhan was too eager an explorer to map fully the territories he had discovered. He referred to his ideas as probes and percepts (as opposed to concepts and precepts). He resisted building coherent theoretical systems, providing elaborated logical explanations or engaging in critical evaluation, leaving such tasks to others. If his reasoning was sometimes hard to follow, many found in him an oracular, Zen-like quality that fit the format of electronic media and electronic culture. Much as he stressed the role of sense perception in understanding cultural trends, McLuhan himself excelled at observation and information processing. And much as he emphasized the need for pattern recognition with data moving at electronic speed, McLuhan discerned the common patterns underlying diverse trends in scholarship, literature and even commerce. He identified the continuities and discontinuities in historical directions and events, and found order in the chaotic *maelstrom* of postwar culture and society. (The *maelstrom*, a metaphor he picked up from the short story by Edgar Allen Poe, was one of McLuhan's favorite metaphors signifying the need for pattern recognition.)

McLUHAN'S MEDIA AND MILIEU

McLuhan viewed media not as tools to be used in different ways, but as part of our environment, often fading into the background, becoming for all intents and purposes invisible, yet influencing and shaping us in highly significant ways. In other words, McLuhan argued that, in effect, the medium is the milieu. In the study of media environments, or media ecology, the first step is to make the invisible milieu visible, to move the background into the foreground, to foster awareness by exchanging the figure and the ground. In this, McLuhan initially was aided by his mother, Elsie, who had a successful career as a monologist and elocutionist. From his mother, Marshall learned to attend to the sound of language and become conscious of communication through speech, his medium of choice. He delighted in dialect, dialogue, and debate, in vocal performance and verbal exchange and in spoken wit and oral word play. He excelled at conversation and lecture, and was a gifted teacher. As a convert to Catholicism, he preferred the aural aesthetics of the Latin

mass to the accessibility of the vernacular version. As a scholar, he emphasized the importance of acoustic modes of communication in the medieval,
ancient, and prehistoric human environments, and their retrieval via electronic technologies.

As much as McLuhan was "the man of the ear," his working medium
was the book. He attended the University of Manitoba from 1928 to 1934,
where he earned bachelor's and master's degrees in English literature. His
studies carried him across the Atlantic to Cambridge University, where he
gained a second bachelor's in 1936, a master's in 1940, and a doctorate in
1943. His thesis, *The Place of Thomas Nashe in the Learning of His Time*,
examined rhetoric in relation to grammar and dialectic. At Cambridge,
McLuhan was trained in the New Criticism of I. A. Richards, William
Empson, and F. R. Leavis. He learned to appreciate the work of modern
writers, such as Eliot, Yeats, Pound, and especially Joyce. In Joyce's experimentation with language, McLuhan found endless inspiration for his study
of the interfaces among the oral, the literate, and the electronic.

McLuhan began work as a teaching assistant in the University of
Wisconsin's English Department in 1936. The product of a Protestant
upbringing, McLuhan became increasingly more attracted to Catholicism,
and was received into the Roman Catholic Church on March 30, 1937.
Seeking an academic environment consistent with his religious beliefs, he
found employment, in 1937, as an instructor in the English Department of
St. Louis University, at that time America's leading Jesuit institution, and
"reputed to be the finest Catholic university in America" (Marchand, 1989,
p. 47). In the summer of 1939, he married Corinne Lewis, and returned with
her to Cambridge to work on his doctoral dissertation; he resumed his
duties at St. Louis in 1940, where he remained until 1944. At St. Louis, he
directed the master's thesis of Walter Ong, S.J., on Gerard Manley Hopkins;
he also directed Ong toward the topic of his Harvard University doctoral
dissertation, the early modern educator Peter Ramus. Ong's subsequent
scholarship was influenced by, and in turn influenced, McLuhan's own
work. During his days at St. Louis University, McLuhan became familiar
with the philosophy of St. Thomas Aquinas, and he subsequently identified
himself as a Thomist. At the same time, McLuhan turned to the study of
technology through the books of Lewis Mumford and Sigfried Giedion, and
arranged a visit for one of his intellectual heroes, the writer and artist
Wyndham Lewis. McLuhan left St. Louis to become head of the English
Department at Assumption College in Windsor, Ontario, in the fall of 1944.
Two years later, he joined the faculty at St. Michael's College, at the
University of Toronto, where he remained for the rest of his academic
career, with the exception of his year (1967-1968) at Fordham University.

At Toronto, he completed the book he had begun writing in St. Louis,
The Mechanical Bride: Folklore of Industrial Man (1951). Drawing on his
background in literary analysis, he turned to the major media forms of the

day, such as advertisements, newspapers, movies, and comics. He argued that popular culture was as deserving of critical attention as high art, but his analysis was grounded in cultural conservatism. McLuhan later disavowed *The Mechanical Bride*'s focus on content in order to emphasize the significance of the medium, and he also distanced himself from the moralistic tone he had adopted for this book, in favor of a more neutral and objective stance. Moreover, McLuhan came to see *The Mechanical Bride*'s highlighting of the mechanical and industrial as rearview mirror thinking, shifting his attention to the electronic to the extent that McLuhan became known as a "post-industrial prophet" (Kuhns, 1971). But the fact that the objects of his study were the products of media and popular culture, and that his analysis was informed by the history of technology is consistent with McLuhan's later work.

It was through the influence of Harold A. Innis, a political economist who took up the study of communications late in his career, and who McLuhan knew as dean of the University of Toronto's School of Graduate Studies, that McLuhan turned to the study of media. And it was through McLuhan's collaboration with a University of Toronto colleague from the Anthropology Department, Edmund Carpenter, that McLuhan began to focus on the relationship between culture and consciousness. McLuhan worked with Carpenter to publish a journal entitled *Explorations*, funded by a grant from the Ford Foundation. Nine issues were published between 1953 and 1959, as well as an anthology (Carpenter & McLuhan, 1960) of the journal's best material. Although modest, the journal was significant in that it brought together anthropologists, art theorists, linguists, and historians to focus on culture and communication. Regardless of their field of expertise, the contributors all shared a concern for the relationship between media *form* and cognitive *effect*. For example, Sigfried Gideon's contribution emphasized the interaction of forms of representation and human space conception, and Dorothy Lee studied how linguistic forms controlled our apprehension of reality (Carpenter & McLuhan, 1960). *Explorations* provided McLuhan with some of the conceptual foundations for his shift from a literary, content orientation to a focus on media structures and their cultural and cognitive implications. The journal was also a forum for McLuhan's earliest forays into the studies of media effects that would reach fruition during the next decade.

McLuhan refined his ideas about media while working on a project for the National Association of Educational Broadcasters, funded by the National Defense Education Act. His goal was to develop a syllabus for the study of communication media for 11th-grade curriculum. It was published under the title *Report on Project in Understanding New Media* (1960), and served as the basis of McLuhan's two major works on media: *The Gutenberg Galaxy: The Making of Typographic Man* (1962), which focused on the roles of the alphabet as the foundation of Western civilization and the printing press as the agent that shifted the West from medievalism to modernity; and *Understanding Media: The Extensions of Man* (1964), which focused on the contemporary media environment, and in particular, on the transformative powers of television. *Understanding Media* was McLuhan's single most important work and it brought him public acclaim.

In his encounter with the foreign cultures of Great Britain and the United States, Canada served as a counter-environment for McLuhan, enabling him to mediate between British tradition in literature and the arts and the American revolution in technology and science. Of the two, it was the United States that consistently pulled at him. His wife was from Texas, and his son Eric was born in St. Louis. New York City had a particular attraction. It is the media capital of the new global village and the center of North America's arts and letters. In New York, McLuhan found kindred academic spirits, such as Louis Forsdale of Columbia University; John Culkin, a Jesuit at Fordham University who later went on to found the Media Studies program at The New School; and Neil Postman, a student of Forsdale's who started the media ecology graduate program at New York University. Moreover, the New York media promoted McLuhan to the general public, including *New York* magazine, which published Tom Wolfe's (1965) famous profile on McLuhan, "What If He is Right?" and *Harper's*, which published Richard Schickel's (1965) article, "Marshall McLuhan: Canada's Intellectual Comet" later that year. In 1966, articles on McLuhan appeared everywhere: in *Fortune, Newsweek, Life, Esquire, Time, The National Review, Partisan Review, Look, The New Yorker, The Nation, The Saturday Review, The New York Times Magazine, Encounter, Family Circle, Vogue, Mademoiselle* — and the list goes on and on. In 1967 alone, the year McLuhan began his tenure at Fordham University, 27 articles about him appeared in *The New York Times* (Molinaro, McLuhan, & Toye, 1987). Additionally, New Yorker Jerome Agel, with his colleague Quentin Fiore, gave McLuhan a bestseller by combining McLuhan quotations and innovative book design. Called *The Medium is the Massage: An Inventory of Effects*, it was published in 1967. It was followed by a CBS Records version of the book (McLuhan, Fiore, Agel, & Simon, 1968) produced by Agel (re-released on compact disc by Sony Music Entertainment in 1998), and an NBC television special, *This is Marshall McLuhan: The Medium is the Massage* (Pintoff, 1967). Agel produced a follow-up book in 1968, *War and Peace in the Global Village* (which McLuhan took a more active role in writing). Agel's two books were often derided as nonbooks, but in fact launched a revolution in graphic design that culminated in the look of *Wired* magazine, launched in 1993 in San Francisco. McLuhan's link to California goes back to the 1960s as well, where his work was brought to public attention by two West Coast business consultants, Gerald Feigen and Howard

Gossage. But it was through the medium of New York City that McLuhan was confirmed as a Media Sage.

McLuhan's New York connection deepened during the 1967 to 1968 school year, spent at Fordham University as the Albert Schweitzer Chair in the Humanities. Recruited by John Culkin, director of Fordham's Center for Communications, McLuhan brought with him Edmund Carpenter, Toronto-based artist Harley Parker, and Marshall's son Eric, who had been assisting his father for several years. They were joined by Paul Ryan, a New York-based film and video artist, and McLuhan came into frequent contact with New York advertising designer/media producer Tony Schwartz. There was also a constant stream of pilgrims and admirers seeking an audience. As Culkin (1988) described it:

> Visitors kept popping in to confer with Marshall. On one occasion, he and Corinne were invited by Stanley Kubrick to a personal, private screening of his unreleased film, *2001*. After ten minutes he told Corinne it was time to leave because he could see which way this one was going. He was coaxed into staying by [his daughter] Teri and he did, if not always in a waking state. (p. 113)

What Culkin termed "Marshall's New York adventure" (p. 106) was marred by the discovery of a brain tumor, necessitating a more than 17-hour operation at Columbia-Presbyterian Hospital, at that time the longest brain surgery ever conducted (dutifully covered by the news media). He recovered in time for Fordham's spring semester. By the end of the school year, Fordham had temporarily lost the Schweitzer Chair (see Culkin, 1988), and McLuhan returned to his professorial position at Toronto, and to the Centre for Culture and Technology that the University had set up for him.

McLuhan's career as an author continued, albeit in nontraditional form, during the late 1960s. In addition to Agel's productions, he reprinted material of his own from *Explorations* as *Verbi-Voco-Visual Explorations* (1967), and contributed extensively to Gerald Stearn's anthology, *McLuhan: Hot and Cool*, published in the same year (a more critical collection, Raymond Rosenthal's *McLuhan: Pro and Con*, was published in 1968). Two other books he published, *Through the Vanishing Point* (1968) and *Counterblast* (1969), were collaborations with the artist Harley Parker. Also in 1969, a collection of articles previously published by McLuhan appeared under the title of *The Interior Landscape: The Literary Criticism of Marshall McLuhan, 1943-1962*, edited by Eugene McNamara. The year 1969 was noteworthy also for the publication of "Playboy Interview: Marshall McLuhan" (reflecting McLuhan's oral bias, the interview is one of the most lucid explanations of McLuhan's thought to appear in print). The following year, McLuhan produced a follow-up to *The Mechanical Bride* (1951) entitled *Culture is Our Business* (1970), and a collaboration with Wilfred Watson, *From Cliché to Archetype* (1970). In 1972 he published *Take Today: The Executive as Dropout*, co-authored with Barrington Nevitt. The last book published during his lifetime was a textbook written with his son Eric and Kathryn Hutchon, by the name of *City as Classroom: Understanding Language and Media*. It was first released in 1977 and reprinted as *Media, Messages, and Language: The World as Your Classroom* in 1980.

In September 1979, McLuhan suffered a stroke that left him unable to speak, read, or write. In June 1980, the University of Toronto closed the Centre for Culture and Technology. According to biographer Phillip Marchand (1989), "For many of McLuhan's friends, the death of the center symbolized and capped the long history of the University of Toronto's antipathy to McLuhan and his works" (p. 273). Marshall McLuhan passed away on December 31, 1980.

McLUHAN'S LEGACY

McLuhan left behind a substantial body of work that has only begun to be explored. Toward the end of the 1980s, new writings by McLuhan, along with reprints, began to appear. A collection of McLuhan's letters (Molinaro et al., 1987) was followed by several of his previously published articles (along with a number of new articles examining his life and work) in a special issue of *The Antigonish Review* (Sanderson, 1988), then reprinted as *McLuhan: The Man and His Message* (Sanderson & Macdonald, 1989). McLuhan was working on "four laws of the media" at the time of his death, and the book was eventually completed by his son Eric and published as *Laws of Media: The New Science* (McLuhan & McLuhan, 1988). Another collaborator, Bruce R. Powers, published a posthumous presentation of McLuhan's tetrad, along with other material, under the title *The Global Village* (McLuhan & Powers, 1989). *The Medium is the Massage* (McLuhan & Fiore, 1967) and *War and Peace in the Global Village* (McLuhan & Fiore, 1968), long out of print, were reissued in 1989, reprinted again in 1996 by *Wired* magazine's book publishing arm, Hardwired, and in 2001 by Gingko Press. A new edition of *Understanding Media,* brought out by the MIT Press in 1994, featured an introduction by the editor of *Harper's* magazine, Lewis H. Lapham, and a critical edition edited by Terrence Gordon was published in 2003 by Gingko Press (which has also announced plans to reprint McLuhan's other books, beginning with *The Mechanical Bride* in 2002).

A number of new volumes came out during the 1990s: Excerpts from McLuhan's books and major articles were collected as *Essential McLuhan* (E. McLuhan & Zingrone, 1995). Numerous quotations were included in *Forward Through the Rearview Mirror: Reflections On and By Marshall McLuhan*, a volume reminiscent of the Agel–Fiore productions (Benedetti & DeHart, 1996). Another anthology collected some of McLuhan's lesser known articles on media under the title *Media Research: Technology, Art, Communication* (Moos, 1997). *The Medium and the Light: Reflections on Religion* (McLuhan, 1999) brought together writings on religion. Through the efforts of Eric McLuhan and others, new publications are planned. They include several volumes of offprints entitled *McLuhan Unbound* (edited by Eric McLuhan), a book of McLuhan's aphorisms and probes (designed by David Carson, edited by Eric McLuhan and William Kuhns), a collection of Marshall and Eric McLuhan's articles on theories of communication, and a revised version of Marshall McLuhan's doctoral thesis on Thomas Nashe. Also, Francesco Guardiani and Eric McLuhan have been editing an online journal entitled *McLuhan Studies* (http://www.chass. utoronto.ca/mcluhan-studies) which has published several short pieces by Marshall McLuhan and analyses, commentary, and reviews by a variety of scholars and critics.

Two biographies of McLuhan have appeared, one by Phillip Marchand (1989), the other by Terrence Gordon (1997a). Gordon also wrote *McLuhan for Beginners* (1997b), a primer in comic book format. Biographical material and personal reflections on McLuhan are found in *Who Was Marshall McLuhan: Exploring a Mosaic of Impressions* (Nevitt & McLuhan, 1995), and elsewhere (e.g., Benedetti & DeHart, 1996; Sanderson & Macdonald, 1989). Introductions to McLuhan's life and thought can be found in audiovisual formats: *McLuhan's Wake*, a video documentary directed by Kevin McMahon, written by David Sobelman, and released in 2002; *The Video McLuhan*, written by Tom Wolfe and produced by McLuhan's daughter, Stephanie McLuhan-Ortved in 1996; and *Understanding McLuhan*, a CD-ROM created by Southam Interactive also published in 1996. Perhaps the strangest of McLuhan's posthumous manifestations comes to us courtesy of *Wired*. McLuhan was featured on the cover of *Wired*'s January 1996 issue. He was the topic of several articles and the subject of an e-mail interview from beyond, conducted by Gary Wolf, and entitled "Channeling McLuhan." (Rumor has it that the part of McLuhan was played by long-time associate Tony Schwartz, but this has not been confirmed.)

Appraisals and critical examinations of McLuhan's thought appeared during the 1960s (e.g., Crosby & Bond, 1968; Finkelstein, 1968; Rosenthal, 1968; Stearn, 1967; West, 1969), and early 1970s (e.g., Kuhns, 1971; Miller, 1971; Theall, 1971), and continue to the present (e.g., Browne & Fishwick,

1999; Fekete, 1977; Neill, 1993; also see later). A special issue of the *Journal of Communication* (Gerbner, 1981), planned as a celebration of McLuhan, was published as a memorial, and as noted, he was the subject of a special issue of the *Antigonish Review* (Sanderson, 1988). A number of scholars have examined McLuhan and Harold Innis as the main representatives of the "Toronto School," often comparing and contrasting the two scholars' perspectives (e.g., Carey, 1989, 1997; Czitrom, 1983; Heyer, 1988; Kroker, 1984; Patterson, 1990). Recently, there have been attempts to analyze McLuhan in comparison to the Frankfurt School (Stamps, 1995), French post-structuralism (Genosko, 1999), postmodernism (Willmott, 1996), Marxism (Grosswiler, 1998), cultural studies (Stevenson, 1995), and cultural geography (Cavell, 2002). Others have placed McLuhan in the context of journalism (e.g., Altschull, 1990;) and environmentalism (e.g., Dale, 1996; DeLuca, 1999). Perhaps the most compelling recontextualization of McLuhan is in terms of the current revolution in computing, online communications, and digital media (see, e.g., Biro, 1999; Bolter & Grusin, 1999; Dery, 1996; Horrocks, 2000; Johnson, 1997, 2001; Kroker & Kroker, 1997; Lanham, 1993; Landow, 1997; Levinson, 1999; Moos, 1997; Provenzo, 1986; Theall, 2001).

McLuhan's legacy lives on at the University of Toronto. It replaced his Centre for Culture and Technology with the McLuhan Program in Culture and Technology, under the directorship of Derrick de Kerckhove. McLuhan remains the most prominent member of the so-called Toronto School, which also includes Harold Innis (e.g., 1951, 1972), Eric Havelock (e.g., 1963, 1986), Edmund Carpenter (e.g., 1973; Carpenter & Heyman, 1970), and Barrington Nevitt (1982). The school lives on, largely in the work of contemporary Canadian scholars and artists such as de Kerckhove (1995), Eric McLuhan (1998), Donald Theall (1971, 1995, 1997, 2001), Frank Zingrone (2001), Robert Logan (1986, 1997, 2000), R. Murray Schafer (1977), David R. Olson (1994), Scott Eastham (1990), Ronald Deibert (1997), Arthur Kroker (1984; Kroker & Cook, 1987; Kroker & Kroker, 1997), Judith Stamps (1995), Bruce R. Powe (1995), and Liss Jeffrey (1989). Across the Atlantic, his perspective has been shared by the anthropologist Jack Goody (1977, 1986, 1987) and the film and media scholar Anthony Smith (1980, 1993, 1996), among others.

In the United States, McLuhan's work has been carried forward by many scholars, including the media critics and theorists Neil Postman (e.g., 1979, 1982, 1985), Joshua Meyrowitz (e.g., 1985), Tony Schwartz (e.g., 1974), Gary Gumpert (e.g., 1987), James Curtis (e.g., 1978, 1987), David L. Altheide and Robert P. Snow (e.g., Altheide, 1985, 1995; Altheide & Snow, 1979, 1991; Snow, 1983) Jay David Bolter (1984, 1991; Bolter & Grusin, 1999), Paul Levinson (e.g., 1988, 1997, 1999), James W. Chesebro and Dale A. Bertelsen (1996), Scott McCloud (1993, 2000), Casey Man Kong Lum

(1996), Paul Grosswiler (1998), Ray Gozzi, Jr. (1999), and Lance Strate, Ron L. Jacobson, and Stephanie B. Gibson (1996); literary theorists Susan Sontag (e.g., 1977), Camille Paglia (e.g., 1990), Richard Lanham (e.g., 1993), and Walter Ong (e.g., 1982); psychologists such as Kenneth Gergen (e.g., 1991), and Robert Romanyshyn (e.g., 1989); and a variety of other scholars, such as the historian Elizabeth Eisenstein (e.g., 1980), the archeologist Denise Schmandt-Besserat (e.g., 1992), art historian Ellen Lupton (1993), the philosopher Mark Taylor (Taylor & Saarinen, 1994), the physician Leonard Shlain (1998), and our leading theorist of management and business, Peter F. Drucker (e.g., 1969, 1970, 1979, 1989, 1993). McLuhan's influence is also felt among poststructuralist, postmodernist, and cultural studies writers in France, including Jean Baudrillard (e.g., 1981, 1983), Paul Virilio (e.g., 1986, 1991), and Regis Debray (e.g., 1996); in Britain, including Anthony Smith (1980, 1993, 1996), Raymond Williams (1975) and Nick Stevenson (1995); in Italy, including Umberto Eco (e.g., 1986); and in the United States, including Fredric Jameson (1991) and Mark Poster (1990, 1995).

McLuhan's ideas and approaches have been incorporated into curricula throughout the world. His influence is felt most directly in the field of communication, and in the growth of cultural studies, media studies, and *media ecology,* the latter being a term that he either coined or inspired. The scholarship that he pioneered has been brought into the 21st century through the introduction of *Explorations in Media Ecology,* the journal of the Media Ecology Association, in 2002; both the journal and the association itself stress the interdisciplinary nature of McLuhan's perspective. McLuhan has affected virtually every field and discipline in the humanities and social sciences, in education, business, and legal studies—even the sciences. His thought has had an impact on artists, musicians, and novelists, media practitioners and policymakers; and his work has been studied by politicians, public officials, activists, entrepreneurs, CEOs, and clergy.

Tom Wolfe (1965) originally posed the question, "What if he's right?" Time has proven McLuhan right about a great many facets of the electronic media environment, and this is why so many are turning to his work today. Indeed, from our current perspective in a world of global markets and global gossip, which is instantly and multisensuously connected, McLuhan's work can seem positively prescient.

But whether his answers are right or wrong, McLuhan asked the right questions, as Postman (1985) noted, and therefore pointed others in the right direction. The significance of any individual's brilliance is not so much in what it sheds light upon, but what that light enables others to see. McLuhan's light has made visible the invisible environments of media, of communication, culture and technology. He has extended our powers of perception and our capacity for understanding.

ABOUT THIS BOOK

The turn of the century has been accompanied by a kind of McLuhan revival or renaissance. Perhaps this is due to millennial fever. Perhaps it is due to the decline of empiricism and quantitative methodologies in the humanities and social sciences. Perhaps it is due to the rise of cultural studies, post-structuralism, and postmodernism (which McLuhan helped to launch and which make his often dense writing seem entirely accessible by contrast). Perhaps it is due to the explosion of personal computers, online communications, and digital media. Perhaps it is a matter of a generational changing of the guard and a paradigm shift of the sort Kuhn (1970) described. Perhaps it is simply the natural cycle of intellectual interests and fads. Perhaps it is simply a perceptual illusion, a matter of shifting figure and ground.

To the extent that we are in the midst of a rebirth of McLuhanism, it is part of the context of this book, and the publication of the *Legacy of McLuhan* in turn contributes to the renewal of interest in Marshall McLuhan and his work. Fordham University played a part in the McLuhan Renaissance by hosting "The Legacy of McLuhan: A Symposium," held on March 27 and 28, 1998, in honor of the 30th anniversary of McLuhan's tenure as Albert Schweitzer Professor of the Humanities, and featuring more than 40 scholars, artists, and media professionals. One of the two editors of this volume, Lance Strate, was the symposium coordinator, the other editor, Edward Wachtel, served on the symposium committee, and the 27 chapters that make up this volume all had their origins in that event. It will perhaps serve to capture some of the spirit of the event by quoting from the welcoming remarks:

> Over the next 2 days Marshall McLuhan will be the subject of discussion and debate, his work will be reviewed and examined, his ideas will be evaluated and critiqued, and his probes will be refined and extended. The focus of this symposium is McLuhan's content, the body of work he has left behind. But to speak of a legacy is to speak of a continuity, from the past to the present, with an eye to the future. What this means is that this symposium itself is a part of his legacy, and we who are gathered here today are a part of his legacy. . . . Like all of us McLuhan is also a metonym, a part standing for a greater whole, a figure denoting a hidden ground, an individual representing a larger community. That is to say that, as all visionaries have done, McLuhan stood on the shoulders of giants. Like all innovators, he benefited from the contributions and criticisms of contemporaries, colleagues, and collaborators. And like all true teachers, he learned his greatest lessons from his students. It

is the community of McLuhan that we all honor by this symposium, and it is the present-day community of McLuhan that is his legacy. (Strate, 1998)

It is impossible to capture in this typographic medium the sense of good will and, yes, the enchantment that reigned at the McLuhan Symposium. But we believe that the enormous intellectual ferment that characterized the event has been enhanced by the process of editing, revision, and publication. This volume is best understood, then, not as the proceedings of the symposium, but as an original anthology that emerged from that singular moment.

The book begins with "McLuhan's Message," a section with four chapters providing a general discussion of McLuhan's work. In chapter 1, Lance Strate discusses *media* as McLuhan's god term and argues that he developed a transcendent conception of media, and viewed media as the vehicle of transcendence. Joshua Meyrowitz discusses one of McLuhan's major contributions, a theory of history based on changes in media and technology, in chapter 2. In chapter 3, Frank Zingrone considers McLuhan's emphasis on media and art as environments, and how they anticipate current notions of virtual reality and cyberspace. Donald Theall, in chapter 4, places McLuhan in the context of the humanities and literary studies, and assesses his relevance for a postliterate poetics.

Section II, "The Media on McLuhan," presents the reactions of five media professionals to Marshall McLuhan and his work. Chapter 5, by Neil Hickey, author, former editor of *TV Guide*, and Editor-At-Large of the *Columbia Journalism Review*, is entitled "McLuhan in the Digital Age: Where Are You Now That We Need You?" Hickey provides his personal reflections on McLuhan, and considers his relevance in light of current events. A similar note is sounded in chapter 6 as Michael J. O'Neill, author and former editor of *The New York Daily News* points to contemporary social and political developments that validate McLuhan's arguments. Television critic Marvin Kitman provides a humorous reflection on McLuhan in chapter 7. Chapter 8 can be appreciated purely for its extreme McLuhanesque style or as a postmodern satire, as well as an example of how McLuhan's writings worked their way into contemporary counterculture. The author, Bob Dobbs, has been a radio personality, a recording artist, a writer for the alternative press, and the inspiration for the Church of the SubGenius (see, e.g., http://www.subgenius.com). Taking a critical stance, author and cultural commentator Mark Dery argues that McLuhan, despite his futuristic appeal, is rooted in 19th-century Romanticism in chapter 9.

Part III, "Art and Perception," explores a topic that goes to the heart of McLuhan's theories. In chapter 10, archeologist and art historian Denise

Schmandt-Besserat discusses the origins of writing in Mesopotamia, and how McLuhan's observation concerning the linearity of written communication holds true even as primitive art evolved into protowriting. Edward Wachtel, in chapter 11, explores McLuhan's perspective on perception as it is reflected in artistic expression. Video artist Paul Ryan explains how McLuhan influenced his own work and led him to construct his own system of media semiotics in chapter 12.

Section IV, "Letters and Laws," emphasizes the humanistic basis of McLuhan's thought and its applications. In chapter 13, Italian literary theorist Elena Lamberti explores McLuhan's background in English and literary studies. James M. Curtis, a professor of Russian, discusses the value of McLuhan's perspective to the discipline of history in chapter 14. In chapter 15, Neil Kleinman considers the criminal status of usury as a product of the medieval media environment. Activist Stephanie Gibson discusses McLuhan in relation to the campaign to ban capital punishment in chapter 16. In chapter 17, Robert Lewis Shayon suggests that McLuhan is best understood as a Christian apologist.

Section V, "Communication and Culture," covers the sector of scholarship that McLuhan is best known for. In chapter 18, Barbara Jo Lewis brings us back to McLuhan's first book, and looks at it in light of recent explorations of the concept of the cyborg. In an ambitious project entitled "Why Print is Cool, and Oral is Body Temperature," Ray Gozzi, Jr. (chapter 19) returns to one of McLuhan's most problematic probes, his theory of hot and cool media, revising it in light of contemporary metaphor theory. Gary Gumpert provides both personal and professional reflections on McLuhan and the field of communication in chapter 20. In a critical assessment of McLuhan as a media theorist, Donna Flayhan (chapter 21) places him in the context of the Toronto School and Harold Innis. In chapter 22, Paul Grosswiler recontextualizes McLuhan, arguing that McLuhan's work is not inconsistent with neo-Marxist approaches to the study of media and society. And sounding a warning note in chapter 23, Frederick Wasser and Harris Breslow argue against appropriations of McLuhan that ignore his grounding in the materialities of culture.

Section VI, "Extensions," examines McLuhan's work in light of theory and research on the new media of the past two decades. Paul Levinson applies the categories of hot and cool to digital media in chapter 24. Susan B. Barnes, in chapter 25, looks at the Internet in light of McLuhan's concept of a return to tribalism and village life on a global scale. Chapter 26 highlights the new medium of hypertext: Michel Moos argues that McLuhan anticipated the new form in both style and content. Jay David Bolter and Richard Grusin (chapter 27) return to one of McLuhan's (1964) insights, that the content of a medium is always another medium, and apply it to current technologies.

McLuhan's legacy lives on in the contributors to this volume, even those who take him to task. And for those of us who find his ideas truly exciting and inspiring, it is indeed a pleasure to be the medium, and spread the message.

REFERENCES

Altschull, J. H. (1990). *From Milton to McLuhan: The ideas behind American journalism*. New York: Addison-Wesley.

Altheide, D. L. (1985). *Media power*. Beverly Hills, CA: Sage.

Altheide, D. L. (1995). *An ecology of communication: Cultural formats of control*. New York: Aldine de Gruyter.

Altheide, D. L., & Snow, R. P. (1979). *Media logic*. Beverly Hills, CA: Sage.

Altheide, D. L., & Snow, R. P. (1991). *Media worlds in the postjournalism era*. New York: Aldine de Gruyter.

Baudrillard, J. (1981). *For a critique of the political economy of the sign* (C. Levin, Trans.). St. Louis, MO: Telos Press.

Baudrillard, J. (1983). *Simulations* (P. Foss, P. Patton & P. Beitchman, Trans.). New York: Semiotext (e).

Benedetti, P., & DeHart, N. (Eds.). (1996). *Forward through the rearview mirror: Reflections on and by Marshall McLuhan*. Cambridge, MA: MIT Press.

Biro, G. M. (1999). *Marshall McLuhan meets the millennium bug: The first 100 years of computers, and how we can make it*. Kingston, ON: Uplevel.

Bolter, J. D. (1984). *Turing's man: Western culture in the computer age*. Chapel Hill: University of North Carolina Press.

Bolter, J. D. (1991). *Writing space: The computer, hypertext, and the history of writing*. Hillsdale, NJ: Erlbaum.

Bolter, J. D., & Grusin, R. (1999). *Remediation: Understanding new media*. Cambridge, MA: MIT Press.

Browne, R. B., & Fishwick, M. W. (Eds.). (1999). *Global village: dead or alive?* Bowling Green, OH: Bowling Green State University Popular Press.

Carey, J.W. (1989). *Communication as culture: Essays on media and society*. Boston: Unwin Hyman.

Carey, J.W. (1997). *James Carey: A critical reader* (E. S. Munson & C. A. Warren, Eds.). Minneapolis: University of Minnesota Press.

Carpenter, E. (1973). *Oh, what a blow that phantom gave me!* New York: Holt, Rinehart & Winston.

Carpenter, E., & Heyman, K. (1970). *They became what they beheld*. New York: Outerbridge and Dienstfrey.

Carpenter, E., & McLuhan, M. (Eds.). (1960). *Explorations in communication*. Boston: Beacon Press

Cavell, R. (2002). *McLuhan in space: A cultural geography*. Toronto: University of Toronto Press.

Chesebro, J. W., & Bertelsen, D. A. (1996). *Analyzing media: Comuunication technologies as symbolic and cognitive systems*. New York: Guilford Press.

Crosby, H. H., & Bond, G. R. (1968). *The McLuhan explosion: A casebook on Marshall McLuhan and understanding media*. New York: American Book.

Culkin, J. (1988). Marshall's New York adventure. *The Antigonish Review, 74-75*, 106-116.

Curtis, J. M. (1978). *Culture as polyphony: An essay on the nature of paradigms*. Columbia: University of Missouri Press.

Curtis, J. M. (1987). *Rocker eras: Interpretations of music and society, 1954-1984*. Bowling Green, OH: Bowling Green State University Popular Press.

Czitrom, D. J. (1983). *Media and the American mind: From Morse to McLuhan*. Chapel Hill: University of North Carolina Press.

Dale, S. (1996). *McLuhan's children: The Greenpeace message and the media*. Toronto: Between the Lines.

Debray, R. (1996). *Media manifestos: On the technological transmission of cultural forms* (E. Rauth, Trans.). Verso Books.

de Kerckhove, D. (1995). *The skin of culture: Investigating the new electronic reality*. Toronto: Sommerville.

Deibert, R. J. (1997). *Parchment, printing, and hypermedia: Communication in world order transformation*. New York: Columbia University Press.

DeLuca, K. M. (1999). *Image politics: The new rhetoric of environmental activism*. New York: Guilford Press.

Dery, M. (1996). *Escape velocity: Cyberculture at the end of the century*. New York: Grove Press.

Drucker, P. F. (1969). *The age of discontinuity: Guidelines to our changing society*. New York: Harper & Row.

Drucker, P. F. (1970). *Technology, management & society*. New York: Harper & Row.

Drucker, P. F. (1979). *Adventures of a bystander*. New York: Harper & Row.

Drucker, P. F. (1989). *The new realities: In government and politics, in economics and business, in society and world view*. New York: Harper & Row.

Drucker, P. F. (1993). *Post-capitalist society*. New York: Harperbusiness.

Eastham, S. (1990). *The media matrix: Deepening the context of communication studies.* Lanham, MD: University Press of America.

Eco, U. (1986). *Travels in hyperreality* (W. Weaver, Trans.). San Diego: Harcourt Brace Jovanovich.

Eisenstein, E. L. (1980). *The printing press as an agent of change*. New York: Cambridge University Press.

Fekete, J. (1977). *The critical twilight: Explorations in the ideology of Anglo-American literary theory from Eliot to McLuhan*. London: Routledge.

Finkelstein, S. (1968). *Sense and nonsense of McLuhan*. New York: International

Genosko, G. (1999). *McLuhan and Baudrillard: Masters of implosion*. London: Routledge.

Gerbner, G. (1981). The living McLuhan (Special Issue). *Journal of Communication, 31*(3).

Gergen, K. J. (1991). *The saturated self*. New York: Basic Books.

Goody, J. (1977). *The domestication of the savage mind*. Cambridge, UK: Cambridge University Press.

Goody, J. (1986). *The logic of writing and the organization of society*. Cambridge, UK: Cambridge University Press.

Goody, J. (1987). *The interface between the written and the oral.* Cambridge, UK: Cambridge University Press.

Gordon, W. T. (1997a). *Marshall McLuhan: Escape into understanding.* New York: Basic Books.

Gordon, W. T. (1997b). *McLuhan for beginners.* New York: Writers & Readers.

Gozzi, R., Jr. (1999). *The power of metaphor in the age of electronic media.* Cresskill, NJ: Hampton Press.

Grosswiler, P. (1998). *Method is the message: Rethinking McLuhan through critical theory.* Montreal: Black Rose Books.

Gumpert, G. (1987). *Talking tombstones and other tales of the media age.* New York: Oxford University Press.

Havelock, E.A. (1963). *Preface to Plato.* Cambridge, MA: The Belknap Press of Harvard University Press.

Havelock, E.A. (1986). *The muse learns to write: Reflections on orality and literacy from antiquity to the present.* New Haven, CT: Yale University Press.

Heyer, P. (1988). *Communications and history: Theories of media, knowledge, and civilization.* New York: Greenwood Press.

Horrocks, C. (2000). *Marshall McLuhan and virtuality.* Duxford, Cambridge, UK: Icon Books.

Innis, H.A. (1951). *The bias of communication.* Toronto: University of Toronto Press.

Innis, H.A. (1972). *Empire and communication* (rev. ed.). Toronto: University of Toronto Press.

Jameson, F. (1991). *Postmodernism, or, the cultural logic of late capitalism.* Durham, NC: Duke University Press.

Jeffrey, L. (1989). The heat and the light: Towards a reassessment of the contribution of H. Marshall McLuhan. *Canadian Journal of Communication, 14,* 1-29.

Johnson, S. (1997). *Interface culture: How new technology transforms the way we create and communicate.* New York: HarperEdge.

Johnson, S. (2001). *Emergence: The connected lives of ants, brains, cities, and software.* New York: Simon & Schuster.

Kroker, A. (1984). *Technology and the Canadian mind: Innis/McLuhan/Grant.* New York: St. Martin's Press.

Kroker, A., & Cook, D. (1987). *The postmodern scene: Excremental culture and hyper-aesthetics.* New York: St. Martin's Press.

Kroker, A., & Kroker, M. (Eds.). (1997). *Digital delerium.* New York: St. Martin's Press.

Kuhn, T. (1970). *The structure of scientific revolutions* (2nd ed.). Chicago: University of Chicago Press.

Kuhns, W. (1971). *The post-industrial prophets: Interpretations of technology.* New York: Weybright & Talley.

Lanham, R. A. (1993). *The electronic word: Democracy, technology, and the arts.* Chicago: University of Chicago Press.

Landow, G. P. (1997). *Hypertext 2.0: The convergence of contemporary critical theory and technology.* Baltimore, MD: Johns Hopkins University Press.

Lapham, L. H. (1994). Introduction to the MIT Press Edition: The eternal now. In M. McLuhan, *Understanding media: The extensions of man.* Cambridge, MA: MIT Press.

Levinson, P. (1988). *Mind at large: Knowing in the technological age.* Greenwich, CT: JAI Press.

Levinson, P. (1997). *The soft edge: A natural history and future of the information revolution.* London & New York: Routledge.

Levinson, P. (1999). *Digital McLuhan: A guide to the information millennium.* London & New York: Routledge.

Logan, R. K. (1986). *The alphabet effect: The impact of the phonetic alphabet on the development of Western civilization.* New York: William Morrow.

Logan, R. K. (1997). *The fifth language: Learning a living in the computer age.* Toronto: Stoddard.

Logan, R. K. (2000). *The sixth language: Learning a living in the internet age.* Toronto: Stoddard.

Lum, C. M. K. (1996). *In search of a voice: Karaoke and the construction of identity in Chinese America.* Mahwah, NJ: Erlbaum.

Lupton, E. (1993). *Mechanical brides: Women and machines from home to office.* New York: Cooper Hewitt National Museum of Design Smithsonian Institution & Princeton Architectural Press.

Marchand, P. (1989). *Marshall McLuhan: The medium and the messenger.* New York: Ticknor & Fields.

McCloud, S. (1993). *Understanding comics: The invisible art.* New York: Paradox Press.

McCloud, S. (2000). *Reinventing comics.* New York: Paradox Press.

McLuhan, E. (1998). *Electric language: Understanding the message.* New York: Buzz Books.

McLuhan, E., & Zingrone, F. (1995). *Essential McLuhan.* New York: Basic Books.

McLuhan, M. (1951). *The mechanical bride: Folklore of industrial man.* New York: Vanguard.

McLuhan, M. (1960). *Report on project in understanding new media.* Washington, DC: U.S. Department of Health.

McLuhan, M. (1962). *The Gutenberg galaxy: The making of typographic man.* Toronto: University of Toronto Press.

McLuhan, M. (1964). *Understanding media: The extensions of man.* New York: McGraw-Hill.

McLuhan, M. (1967). *Verbi-voco-visual explorations.* New York: Something Else Press.

McLuhan, M. (1969, March). Playboy interview: Marshall McLuhan. *Playboy,* pp. 53-74, 158.

McLuhan, M. (1970). *Culture is our business.* New York: McGraw-Hill.

McLuhan, M. (1999). *The medium and the light: Reflections of religion* (E. McLuhan & J. Szklarek, Eds.). Toronto: Stoddart.

McLuhan, M., & Fiore, Q. (1967). *The medium is the massage: An inventory of effects.* New York: Bantam.

McLuhan, M., & Fiore, Q. (1968). *War and peace in the global village : An inventory of some of the current spastic situations that could be eliminated by more feed-forward.* New York: Bantam.

McLuhan, M., Fiore, Q., Agel, J., & Simon, J., (1968). *The medium is the massage with Marshall McLuhan.* [LP]. Columbia.

McLuhan, M., Hutchon, K., & McLuhan, E. (1977). *City as classroom: Understanding language and media*. Agincourt, ON: Book Society of Canada.

McLuhan, M., Hutchon, K., & McLuhan, E. (1980). *Media, messages, and language: The world as your classroom*. Skokie, IL: National Textbook Co.

McLuhan, M., & McLuhan, E. (1988). *Laws of media: The new science*. Toronto: University of Toronto Press.

McLuhan, M., & Nevitt, B. (1972). *Take today: The executive as dropout*. New York: Harcourt Brace Jovanovich.

McLuhan, M., & Parker, H. (1968). *Through the vanishing point: Space in poetry and painting*. New York: Harper & Row.

McLuhan, M., & Parker, H. (1969). *Counterblast*. New York: Harcourt, Brace & World.

McLuhan, M., & Powers, B. R. (1989). *The global village: Transformations in world life and media in the twenty-first century*. New York: Oxford University Press.

McLuhan, M., & Watson, W. (1970). *From cliché to archetype*. New York: Viking Press.

McLuhan-Ortved, S. (Producer), & Wolfe, T. (Writer). (1996). *The video McLuhan* [Video]. (Available from Video McLuhan Inc., 73 Sighthill Avenue, Toronto Ontario M4T 2H1 Canada)

McMahon, K. (Director), & Sobelman, D. (Writer). (2002). *McLuhan's Wake* [video]. (Available from National Film Board of Canada Library, 22-D Hollywood Avenue, Ho-Ho-Kus, NJ, 07423)

McNamara, E. (Ed.). (1969). *The interior landscape: The literary criticism of Marshall McLuhan, 1943-1962*. New York: McGraw-Hall.

Meyrowitz, J. (1985). *No sense of place*. New York: Oxford University Press.

Miller, J. (1971). *Marshall McLuhan*. New York: Viking.

Molinaro, M., McLuhan, C., & Toye, W. (Eds.). (1987). *Letters of Marshall McLuhan*. New York: Oxford University Press.

Moos, M. A. (Ed.). (1997). *Media research: Technology, art, communication*. Amsterdam: G+B Arts International.

Neill, S. D. (1993). *Clarifying McLuhan: An assessment of process and product*. Westport, CT: Greenwood Press.

Nevitt, B. (1982). *The communication ecology: Re-presentation versus replica*. Toronto: Butterworths.

Nevitt, B., & McLuhan, M. (Eds.). (1995). *Who was Marshall McLuhan: Exploring a mosaic of impressions*. Toronto: Stoddart.

Olson, D. R. (1994). *The world on paper: The conceptual and cognitive implications of writing and reading*. Cambridge, UK: Cambridge University Press.

Ong, W. J. (1982). *Orality and literacy*. London: Methuen.

Paglia, C. (1990). *Sexual personae: Art and decadence from Nefertiti to Emily Dickinson*. New Haven, CT: Yale University Press.

Patterson, G. (1990). *History and communications: Harold Innis, Marshall McLuhan, and the interpretation of history*. Toronto: University of Toronto Press.

Pintoff, E. (Producer). (1967, March 19). *This is Marshall McLuhan: The medium is the massage* [television broadcast]. National Broadcasting Co.

Poster, M. (1990). *The mode of information*. Chicago: University of Chicago Press.

Poster, M. (1995). *The second media age.* Polity Press.

Postman, N. (1979). *Teaching as a conserving activity.* New York: Delacorte.

Postman, N. (1982). *The disappearance of childhood.* New York: Delacorte.

Postman, N. (1985). *Amusing ourselves to death.* New York: Viking.

Powe, B. R. (1995). *Outage: A journey into electric city.* Hopewell, NJ : Ecco Press

Provenzo, E. F., Jr. (1986). *Beyond the Gutenberg galaxy: Microcomputers and the emergence of post-typographic culture.* New York: Teachers College Press.

Romanyshyn, R. D. (1989). *Technology as symptom and dream.* London: Routledge.

Rosenthal, R. (Ed.). (1968). *McLuhan: Pro and con.* New York: Funk & Wagnalls.

Sanderson, G. (1988). Marshall McLuhan (Special Issue). *The Antigonish Review,* 74–75.

Sanderson, G., & Macdonald, F. (Eds.). (1989). *McLuhan: The man and his message.* Goldon, CO: Fulcrum.

Schafer, R. M. (1977). *The tuning of the world.* New York: Alfred A. Knopf.

Schickel, R. (1965, November). Marshall McLuhan: Canada's intellectual comet. *Harper's,* 62–68.

Schmandt-Besserat, D. (1992). *Before writing : From counting to cuneiform.* Austin: University of Texas Press.

Schwartz, T. (1974). *The responsive chord.* Garden City, NY: Anchor Books.

Shlain, L. (1998). *The alphabet versus the goddess: The conflict between word and image.* New York: Viking.

Smith, A. (1980). *Goodbye, Gutenberg: The newspaper revolution of the 1980s.* New York: Oxford University Press.

Smith, A. (1993). *Books to bytes: Knowledge and information in the postmodern era.* London: British Film Institute.

Smith, A. (1996). *Software for the self: Technology and culture.* New York: Oxford University Press.

Snow, R. P. (1983). *Creating media culture.* Newbury Park, CA: Sage.

Sontag, S. (1977). *On photography.* New York: Farrar, Straus & Giroux.

Southam Interactive. (1996). *Understanding McLuhan* [CD-ROM]. New York: Voyager.

Stamps, J. (1995). *Unthinking modernity: Innis, McLuhan, and the Frankfurt School.* Montreal & Kingston: McGill-Queens University Press.

Stearn, G. E. (Ed.). (1967). *McLuhan: Hot and cool.* New York: The Dial Press.

Stevenson, N. (1995). *Understanding media cultures: Social theory and mass communication.* London: Sage.

Strate, L. (1998, March 25). *Welcoming remarks.* Presented at The Legacy of McLuhan: A Symposium, New York.

Strate, L., Jacobson, R. L., & Gibson, S. B. (Eds.). (1996). *Communication and cyberspace: Social interaction in an electronic environment.* Cresskill, NJ: Hampton Press.

Taylor, M. C., & Saarinen, E. (1994). *Imagologies: Media philosophy.* London: Routledge.

Theall, D. F. (1971). *The medium is the rear view mirror.* Montreal: McGill-Queens University Press.

Theall, D. F. (1995). *Beyond the word : Reconstructing sense in the Joyce era of technology, culture, and communication.* Toronto: University of Toronto Press.

Theall, D. F. (1997). *James Joyce's techno-poetics.* Toronto: University of Toronto Press.

Theall, D. F. (2001). *The virtual Marshall McLuhan.* Montreal & Kingston: McGill-Queens University Press..

Virilio, P. (1986). *Speed and politics: An essay on dromology* (M. Polizzotti, Trans.). New York: Semiotext(e).

Virilio, P. (1991). *The lost dimension* (D. Moshenberg, Trans.). New York: Semiotext(e).

West, R. (1969). *McLuhan and the future of literature.* London: English Association.

Williams, R. (1975). *Television: Technology and cultural form.* New York: Schocken Books.

Willmott, G. (1996). *McLuhan, or modernism in reverse.* Toronto: University of Toronto Press.

Wolf, G. (1996, January). Channeling McLuhan. *Wired,* p. 128.

Wolfe, T. (1965, November 21). What if he is right? *New York, The Sunday Herald Tribune Magazine,* pp. 6-9, 22, 24, 27.

Zingrone, F. (2001). *The media symplex: At the edge of meaning in the age of chaos.* Toronto: Stoddart.

SECTION I

McLuhan's Message

1 MEDIA TRANSCENDENCE

Lance Strate

Fordham University

Of course, McLuhan began *in medias res*, in the middle of things. This is what Horace says of the blind poet Homer, that he "hastens into the action and precipitates the hearer into the middle of things" (cited in Ong, 1982, p. 142). For Homer, who was the product of a nonliterate, oral culture, beginning in the middle was common sense. Not only would it grab the attention of his audience, but it also matched their experience as listeners. As McLuhan taught us, sound comes to us from all directions at once, surrounding us. The hearing subject is therefore situated in the center of acoustic space, in the middle of the aural ecosystem, or in this case echo system. The experience of the reader is entirely different. The fixed gaze can only focus on one fragment of the visual field at a time. We move from letter to letter, word to word, line to line. And we learn to read our environment as if it were a book. We become voyeurs, outsiders looking in, occupying an objective position and objectifying what we see. With the power of this alien vision, we can reorder the world, impose a linear structure on phenomena, and thereby begin at the beginning, move through the middle, to at last reach the end. In this way, McLuhan could determine that the shift in emphasis from the ear to the eye began with the development of writing more than five millenia ago, reached its peak following the invention of the printing press more than five centuries ago, and comes to an end with the ascent of television about five decades ago.

The history of civilization is the story of the war between the ear and the eye. It is an epic tale that Homer would have been proud to sing of, a narrative of biblical proportions—it is the story of civilization. McLuhan would no doubt have been amused to learn that one small skirmish in this war is being fought by Fordham University, the battle lines drawn along Southern Boulevard in the Bronx. There, a stone's throw from his old office stands our half-completed WFUV radio tower, its construction halted by legal action on the part of our neighbor, the Bronx Botanical Gardens. The tower is an electronic extension of the ear, a mass hearing aid. But to the Botanical Gardens it is also an eyesore, a tower of babble marring their picture perfect landscape. Their concern is understandable, given that the garden in Western cultures is a visual medium. It presents us with nature, that is, with the biological environment as other, objectified, mastered, and made available for the elite eye's appreciation. McLuhan (1988) suggested that the concept of *nature* has become obsolescent in the electronic era, reduced to an art form, relegated to the status of content for the garden medium. Nature has been replaced by the idea of ecology, which situates us in the middle of our environment, as active participants. Were McLuhan available to comment on our dilemma, he might playfully suggest that the Botanical Gardens somehow sense the threat that electronic media such as radio pose to their worldview. No doubt, he would also conclude that this is hardly a Homeric tragedy comparable to the wrath of Achilles, but rather an Ovidian tale of metamorphosis, a modern day Echo and Narcissus. The courts have supported our case, so it seems that our radio tower will not fade from view; but Fordham and the Gardens are presently in the midst of negotiations, and so I must end this story in the middle.

Of course, beginning and ending in the middle is part of the human condition. We are born somewhere between the alpha and the omega, the big bang and the heat death of the universe. Darwin situates us somewhere between evolution and extinction, making us nothing more than monkeys in the middle. As individuals, we come into conscious awareness gradually, remembering little or nothing of our first few years; we experience our own lives as if we were walking into a movie that has already begun. And we are born into a moment bordered by memory and anticipation. We are born into history, and McLuhan, like us all, was a product of his times. Had he been born in an earlier era, he no doubt would have taken up philosophy. Had he been born more recently, I am confident that he would have become a communication and media studies major. But he was born in 1911, and like many of his contemporaries, he found the most agreeable form of general education in the study of literature. But he was not content with the literary focus on the fixed text, on the written word as a stable object, on creative production as a body of work waiting to be dissected. He therefore turned early in his career to the study of the communication process, specifically the ancient art of rhetoric, defined by Aristotle (1850) as the "faculty of considering all the possible means of persuasion on every subject" (p. 11). And the analysis of the possible *means* of persuasion and expression, which in Aristotle's day was limited to the techniques used in public speaking, in McLuhan's time led to the investigation of the growing number of media of communication.

McLuhan found himself in the middle of a major change in the media environment, and this unique vantage point, situated between two worlds, made it possible for him to gain his understanding of media. McLuhan explained media, and his explanation, his media ecology, also explained McLuhan. He was the product of hybrid energy, much like Homer was some 27 centuries ago. Homer was a singer of tales whose songs were recorded in writing, who was thereby transformed by the power of the alphabet into an author. McLuhan was a literate scholar transmogrified into a media celebrity. Figures such as these, emerging when worlds collide, are often admired as archetypes. But they may also be shunned as anomalies. To be in the middle may also mean to be in the margins, and an anomaly is a phenomenon that exists between categories, that defies classification. Perhaps because he was one himself, McLuhan did not shun anomalies. He was not bound by Aristotle's laws of logic, not by the law of noncontradiction, and most certainly not by the law of the excluded middle. In developing his laws of media, McLuhan gave names to anomalies, using the technique of oxymoron to coin the term *global village*, for example (see McLuhan, 1962). The village is the smallest unit of human habitation, the globe the largest; the two terms are nearly polar in their opposition, but their fusion illuminates with the intensity of the sun.

McLuhan understood media by including the middle and mediating contradictory concepts. He combined the word *medium* with its near opposite to give us his archetypical aphorism, "the medium is the message" (see McLuhan, 1964). These five words are enduring and endearing, and yet, I cannot tell you how many times I have seen someone say: "Of course, the medium is *not* the message." As one of the editors of the anthology *Communication and Cyberspace* (Strate, Jacobson, & Gibson, 1996), I dealt with an article that would otherwise have made McLuhan proud, but that included in the first paragraph the phrase: "Of course, the medium is *not* the message." I told the author that I personally detested that sentence, that it was a cliché and a bore, an insult to the reader and an embarrassment for the writer. I am pleased to tell you that you will not find that phrase in that particular chapter, or anywhere in *Communication and Cyberspace*. The problem with that sentence is not that it opens up discussion, but rather that it closes it down. It is a form of dismissal, not debate. And it misses the point. It makes no sense to say that "the medium is the message" unless you already know that the medium is *not* the message, that is, unless you can begin with the conventional categories of medium and message; this is the unspoken first premise in McLuhan's paradoxical enthymeme. McLuhan builds on this basic understanding, working toward a more complex conception of media and technology. He reverses the commonsense relationship between medium and message, and blurs their boundaries. You might say that he deconstructs the popular conceptions of message and medium in order to gain new insight. Saying that the medium is not the message does not refute McLuhan's aphorism, it simply returns us to square one. Must we always begin at the beginning? The answer is no so far as McLuhan is concerned. He hastens into the action and plunges into the middle of things, and all he asks of us is to meet him halfway.

The medium is the message is a wake up call, alerting us to the fact that although content tends to monopolize our attention, media function as an invisible environment shaping the way we communicate, think, perceive, and organize ourselves. McLuhan's media ecology approach is in part a kind of materialism, grounded in the analysis of the physical environment, including artifacts and technologies, and the analysis of the human body and its extensions. In contrast to Marx's dialectical materialism, however, McLuhan gives us a rhetorical and grammatical materialism. But McLuhan's perspective is also grounded in the grand North American tradition of pragmatism. By medium, McLuhan refers not only to the material, but also to the means, modes, and methods by which we operate on the material world. The medium is the message expresses with perfect economy the idea that how we do something has much to do with the results we obtain, no matter what our original intent may be. It is the idea that when you ask a silly question, you get a silly answer, and that the way we make our beds determines how we sleep. It is present in Henry David Thoreau's (1980) observation on the building of the railroads, that "we do not ride on the railroad; it rides on us" (p. 67) and in Mark Twain's wonderful quip, that when you have a hammer in your hand, everything looks like a nail (cited in Eastham, 1990, p. 17). It is entirely absent, however, from the slogan of the National Rifle Association, that "guns don't kill people, people do." If you believe that guns themselves have increased the potential for violence, then you are with McLuhan.

The medium is the message implies that different media give us different messages, different worldviews, different ways of life. This focus on difference has a history, and in one direction can be traced back to the semiotics of Charles Saunders Peirce (1972), and the distinction between index, icon, and symbol. This pragmatic approach is distinct from the broader trend toward universal theories and explanations in both the humanities and the social sciences. Even in semiotics, particularly among the French semiologists, the tendency has been to abandon categorical differences and universalize, to treat all signs as symbols. The drive to universalize, a product of alphabetic abstraction, is so powerful that even when differences are discovered, this often gives rise to a new form of universalism. Take the case of the French deconstructionist Jacques Derrida (1976). Influenced by McLuhan, he discovers that most discussions of language universalize the spoken word and ignore what is unique to the medium of writing. But rather than accept the difference, he proceeds to universalize writing, even arguing that speech is a form of writing. Although Derrida and deconstruction have a contribution to make, here the project falls short. And yes, universalism has been widely rejected in recent years, in favor of multiculturalism, social construction, and postmodernism. But the result has been a particularism so extreme as to reverse into a new form of universalism: We are all the same in our difference. In contrast, McLuhan is concerned with difference, but only with those "differences that make a difference," to invoke Gregory Bateson's (1972) happy phrase. Between the poles of the universal and the particular, McLuhan's approach seeks a middle ground.

The medium is the message implies that we must begin in the middle, with the medium. The medium comes first. Before the sculpture, there is the stone and the chisel. Before the painting, there is the paint and the canvas. Before the song, there is the instrument and voice. And consider the process of language acquisition. First, the newborn cries and screams. Later, he or she begins to babble. And out of this babble eventually emerges speech. Before meaningful words can be uttered, we learn how to recognize and produce the sounds of our language. The medium of speech precedes the messages formed through language. Once this process is complete, the medium may then become content for another medium. Thus, speech becomes the content of writing, writing the content of printing, printing the content of word processing. As a medium becomes content, it is reduced to an element of style, and relegated to the role of semiotic signifier. Failure to account for this hidden ground is the fatal flaw that runs through much of semiotics, structuralism, deconstruction, and postmodernism. Signs and signifiers may be socially constructed, but they are constructed out of the raw material of a medium, and with the aid of the tools and techniques that are also part of the medium.

Of course, in declaring that the medium is the message, McLuhan was doing nothing more than carrying out the ancient injunction to seek "media in all things, including media." He began with the media of communication, but stretched the concept of medium to cover all technology. In *Understanding Media* (McLuhan, 1964) he includes under the heading of media such items as clothing, housing, money, clocks, transportation, weapons, and automation. All technologies are media because they go between ourselves and our environment. They extend our bodies and minds, but they also shield and numb them. Thus, Max Frisch (1959) maintains that "technology is the art of never having to experience the world" (p. 178). As buffer zones, media become our environment, and in using them, we are at the same time used by them. This is as true for speech as it is for tools. Some object to the characterization of language as a technology, arguing that speech comes naturally to our species. But why should the products of opposable thumbs be seen as any more artificial than the products of opposable tongues? Why this distinction between labor and dialogue, mechanical invention and rhetorical invention? McLuhan saw through to the middle ground between them, and he continued to expand that common ground. In his later work he arrived at his four laws of the media (McLuhan & McLuhan, 1988; McLuhan & Powers, 1989), that any given medium enhances or intensifies some pre-existing element, renders obsolescent another, retrieves yet another element that had been previously obsolesced, and when taken to extremes reverses into its opposite. In applying his tetrad, McLuhan treated as media various forms of communication and technology, but also such disparate phenomena as the Copernican Revolution, the periodic table, crowds, hermeneutics, semiotics, pollsters, romanticism, and Aristotelian causality. Truly media in all things, including media.

Implicit in McLuhan's work is a General Media Theory that can be used to understand any phenomenon, be it cultural or biological, physical or metaphysical. The idea of media is present even when he used other terms such as gaps and intervals, resonances and the total field; it is there in the notion of cliché in relation to archetype, or ground in relation to figure. It is particularly useful for reframing concepts that are otherwise presented as opposing forces or irreconcilable ideas. For example, let me quote from one of McLuhan's televison interviews, circa 1970: "Affluence creates poverty as a form of complementarity just as without the white man there are no colored people—it's a figure ground relationship. . . . And there are many forms of it: learning creates ignorance. Literally, during the Depression nobody talked about poverty, they talked about hardship. But there was no affluence. And so affluence is the ground that creates the figure of poverty, and makes it noticeable" (Southam Interactive, 1996, p. 1). In other words, affluence and poverty are not equivalent terms that define each other. Rather, affluence is the medium, and poverty is its message. By the same token, learning is the medium and ignorance its message—is this not why Socrates so self-consciously professed his lack of knowledge? And the concept of the "White race" as McLuhan put it, is a medium whose message is the other of non-White races.

Let us look at some other examples. Instead of a conflict between mind and body, we can understand the body as the medium from which the mind is born. The mind is not the body, but it emerges out of the body, is contained within the body, is dependent on the body, but may also affect and alter the body. From another point of view, the content of the body is another medium: In a physical sense it is the ocean that we carry in our circulatory systems, whereas in a metaphysical sense it is the spirit. Along the same lines, technology is the content and biology is the medium. Technology is produced by the biological, extends the biological, and also acts on the biological. Of course, technology as a medium itself can in turn use the biological as its content. To return to the mind, instead of a polar opposition between the conscious and unconscious, we can see the conscious mind as the message and the unconscious its medium. This is consistent with Jung's (1968) understanding of the psyche, and by the same token we can interpret Jung's notions of a collective unconscious and of synchronicity as references to a hidden ground, a medium that may not yet be identified. Or to plug in St. Augustine's (1961) commentary on the experience of time, we can identify the present as the medium whose contents include the past and the future. Along similar lines, the concept of permanence is a medium that precedes and gives rise to the concept of change (Watzlawick, Weakland, & Fisch, 1974). And chaos is the medium out of which order may emerge (Kauffman, 1995; Prigogine & Stengers, 1984; Waldrop, 1992). Also, we might well say that evil is only the content that all too often monopolizes our attention, whereas good is the medium that constitutes our invisible environment.

Marshall McLuhan is best described by the very phrase he used to characterize G.K. Chesterton: "a practical mystic" (see McLuhan, 1999, p. 3). He was practical because his work was grounded in the materialities of communication and the pragmatics of technology. And he was a mystic because his work was building toward a concept of media transcendence. That is, on the one hand, he was developing a transcendent concept of the media, and on the other hand he understood that media are the bridge to transcendence. The key to mysticism is the encounter with a medium without content, light and sound, for example. Ritual incantations and prayers, by their repetition, lose their meaning as messages and move toward the state of pure medium. This is aided by the use of tongues that are unfamiliar, and therefore communicate primarily in a paralinguistic mode. Meditation takes the process a step further through the technique of repeating a nonsense syllable, a sound entirely devoid of meaning—we might call it transcendental mediation. Religions based on the written word also tend to treat the writing system as sacred, for example in the Cabalistic contemplation of the aleph-bet. In the tradition of Judaism, Christianity, and Islam, God communicates through the medium of the word, both spoken and written. It is significant that Genesis describes His first act as taking the form of speech, the message being "Let there be light." Speech and sound precede light and vision, just as orality comes before literacy. In this tradition, God also uses human beings as media, in the form of prophets or in the Christian belief of Divine Incarnation. To see ourselves as a medium is humbling, whether we are the medium of God's will, or the medium through which the spirit of an age expresses itself, or the medium through which our genes reproduce themselves. When we see ourselves as the message, we stray into Narcissism. When we see ourselves as the medium, we become like Echo, an invisible environment.

In the tradition of Judaism, Christianity, and Islam, the beginning is God's act of creation. Creation, then, comes after the beginning—it exists in the middle, and it is God's medium. The natural philsophers, for example Francis Bacon, Isaac Newton, and Giambattista Vico sought to move closer to the divine through this medium, by reading and studying the book of nature. Their successors continue to unravel the complexities of the universe, and there is no indication that the task will ever be complete. But when we consider the properties of the universe, we can discern a few basic messages inherent in this medium. They are embarassingly simple, but nonetheless worth stating. They are existence and life, relationship and communication, and consciousness and understanding. McLuhan moved us far along the path of understanding. He could not help but leave us still in the middle of things, and most likely he would have it no other way.

REFERENCES

Aristotle. (1850). *Treatise on rhetoric* (T. Buckley, Trans.). London: Henry G. Bohn.

St. Augustine. (1961). *Confessions* (R.S. Pine-Coffin, Trans.). New York: Penguin.

Bateson, G. (1972). *Steps to an ecology of mind.* New York: Ballantine Books.

Derrida, J. (1976). *Of grammatology* (G. Chakravorty, Trans.). Baltimore, MD: Johns Hopkins University Press. (Original work published in 1967)

Eastham, S. (1990). *The media matrix: Deepening the context of communication studies.* Lanham, MD: University Press of America.

Frisch, M. (1959). *Homor faber: A report* (M. Bulloock, Trans.). San Diego: Harcourt Brace Jovanovich.

Jung, C.G. (1968). *The archetypes and the collective unconscious* (2nd ed., R.F.C. Hull, Trans.). Princeton, NJ: Princeton University Press.

Kauffman, S. (1995). *At home in the universe: The search for the laws of self-organization and complexity.* New York: Oxford University Press.

McLuhan, M. (1962). *The Gutenberg galaxy: The making of typographic man.* Toronto: University of Toronto Press.

McLuhan, M. (1964). *Understanding media: The extensions of man.* New York: McGraw-Hill.

McLuhan, M. (1988). At the moment of Sputnik the planet became a global theatre in which there are no spectators but only actors. *The Antigonish Review, 74-75,* 78-87.

McLuhan, M. (1999). *The medium and the light: Reflections on religion* (E. McLuhan & J. Szklarek, Eds.). Toronto: Stoddart.

McLuhan, M., & McLuhan, E. (1988). *Laws of media: The new science.* Toronto: University of Toronto Press.

McLuhan, M., & Powers, B. R. (1989). *The global village: Transformations in world life and media in the twenty-first century.* New York: Oxford University Press.

Ong, W. J. (1982). *Orality and literacy: The technologizing of the word.* London: Methuen.

Peirce, C. S. (1972). *Charles S. Peirce: The essential writings* (E. C. Moore, Ed.). New York: Harper & Row.

Prigogine, I., & Stengers, I. (1984). *Order out of chaos: Man's new dialogue with nature.* New York: Bantam.

Southam Interactive. (1996). Probes/figure/ground. *Understanding McLuhan* [CD-ROM]. New York: Voyager.

Strate, L., Jacobson, R., & Gibson, S.B. (1996). *Communication and cyberspace: Social interaction in an electronic environment.* Cresskill, NJ: Hampton Press.

Thoreau, H. D. (1980). *Walden or, life in the woods and on the duty of civil disobedience.* New York: Signet.

Waldrop, M. M. (1992). *Complexity: The emerging science at the edge of order and chaos.* New York: Simon & Schuster.

Watzlawick, P., Weakland, J., & Fisch, R. (1974). *Change: Principles of problem formation and problem resolution.* New York: Norton.

2 FROM TRIBAL TO GLOBAL

A BRIEF HISTORY OF CIVILIZATION
FROM A McLUHANESQUE PERSPECTIVE

Joshua Meyrowitz
University of New Hampshire

I had the great pleasure of meeting Marshall McLuhan a few times. And I felt his spirit upon me when I first proposed the title for this chapter. But I suspect that Marshall never composed on a computer, because when I tried to summon back his spirit for advice on exactly how to do justice to a "history of civilization" in a brief essay, all I got was a blinking cursor on a blank screen.

Nevertheless, I pressed on because I knew that although McLuhan's penchant for making sweeping claims drove his critics crazy, this tendency also made his contributions to our understanding of media and social change much more enduring than the contributions of the more widely embraced social-scientific media studies carried out by McLuhan's number-crunching and content-coding contemporaries.

I refer to a "McLuhanesque perspective," rather than "McLuhan's perspective," because I don't think that the brief history I attempt here would be precisely the one that McLuhan himself would offer. Yet, it draws on McLuhan's major argument that the influence of a medium cannot be reduced to the content of its messages. I've called this perspective "medium theory." I use the singular, "medium," because this approach views each communication technology as a unique type of environment that encourages certain forms of interaction and discourages other forms of interaction. My historical overview also draws on the work of additional medium theorists, such as Harold Adams Innis, Walter Ong, Eric Havelock, Elizabeth Eisenstein, H.L. Chaytor, and others, as well as on my own role-system medium theory. Role-system medium theory suggests that roles, "places," and situations are not static entities but fluid "information systems," whose structure changes with changes in forms of communication.

Taken together, these medium-theory works suggest the view that human civilization has been marked by three major phases—traditional, modern, and postmodern—each linked in many important ways to a dominant mode of communication: traditional to oral communication, modern to literate communication, and postmodern to electronic communication.

Obviously, I have space here to sketch these three phases only in the very broadest of strokes. I do not discuss any of their subphases and other qualifications. And I do not review the key limits of this approach that I have described elsewhere (Meyrowitz, 1994, 2003). For brevity and simplicity, I focus on how each major evolution in communication forms has involved a shift in social boundaries and hence a shift in the relationship between self and others.

ORAL CULTURE:
FAMILIAR INSIDERS AND DISTANT OUTSIDERS

In the first phase, traditional oral societies are characterized by very familiar insiders and very distant outsiders. In oral societies, the preservation of ideas and practices depends on the living memory of people. This form of "living library" ties people closely to those who live around them.

In a traditional oral society, almost every person one sees on a regular basis is familiar. Compared with other social forms, there is not a high degree of social differentiation in roles and experiences. "Strangers" are not an explicit part of everyday encounters. But in a sense, strangers play a more important role in traditional oral societies than in any other form of social organization. There is, after all, an underlying awareness of a vast, mysterious external world filled with faceless "others." In fact, the often subliminal awareness of a larger world of strangers is one of the nearly constant forces that keeps members from leaving the community, both physically and psychologically. The boundary that keeps strangers out also keeps insiders in. A distant world of strangers helps to bind this form of society together.

LITERATE SOCIETIES:
HOMOGENIZED SEGREGATION

In the second phase, modern literate societies offer a new form of association that might be called "homogenized segregation." With the rise of the modern, urban-oriented industrial society there is increasing contact with, and more explicit awareness of, "strangers." In other words, it is a common experience to see and have at least limited interaction with people from very different social worlds.

The rise of such a modern society is supported by, and further supports, the spread of literacy. Print factories serve as the prototypes of all mechanized production. Printed documents help to disseminate widely the plans for and ideals of industrialization, as well as advertisements and catalogs for mass-produced goods.

In Western culture, the relatively wide availability of printed materials further undermines the importance of the oral community. For the literate, there is a retreat from the web of local community life and from extended kinship ties in favor of greater isolation for the nuclear family.

While printing creates smaller units of interaction at the expense of the oral community, it also bypasses the local community in the other direction by creating larger political, spiritual, and intellectual units. For example, the ability to see on a printed page what were once only spoken folk languages fosters a sense of unity among all those who use the same language, wherever they are (not just among those who speak it at the same time in the same place). Conceptions of *them* versus *us* change. Feudal societies based on face-to-face loyalties and oral oaths begin to give way to nation states and to nationalism, which are based in large part on a shared printed language. Printed constitutions literally help to "constitute" each nation, as do printed laws, printed national histories, and printed national myths.

Similarly, religious cohesion no longer depends exclusively on shared rituals with those one can see, hear, and touch. The potential for religious unity across great distances (along with *dis*unity among those in the same place) is fostered by the patterns of sharing (and not sharing) holy *texts*.

The spread of print supports compartmentalization of social roles. The new emphasis on reading as a source of wisdom and religious salvation widens the gap between those who can read and those who cannot. And distinctions in levels of reading ability come to be seen as tied to "natural" differences in rank and identity.

The young and illiterate are excluded from all printed communication and are increasingly seen as different from literate adults. Modern conceptions of both "childhood" and "adulthood" are invented in Western culture in the 16th century, and their spread follows the spread of literacy and schooling. The multi-age behaviors and dress characteristic of oral societies begin to splinter into separate behaviors and distinct dress for people of different ages and reading abilities. In the literate middle and upper classes, children are more frequently isolated from adults a year or two younger or older. Literate adults use books as a private context within which to discuss what topics and books are—and are not—appropriate for children. With the help of such books, children are shielded from much information—and from the adult conspiracy to control their knowledge. In a sense, people of different ages become strangers to each other. The same occurs for other roles.

As printing spreads, women are told by men that only men need to become fully literate, and men use restricted literacy to enhance their positions relative to women. The public male realm is increasingly isolated from the private female realm. Minimally literate women are given more of the responsibility of caring for the increasingly dependent preliterate children.

For men, identities splinter into a multitude of separate spheres based on distinct specialties and on mastery of field-specific stages of literacy. The new grading of texts serves as a barrier to straying from one field into another, because a man would have to start all over again—as if he were a child.

Unlike oral societies with oral vows of allegiance, print societies develop a form of leadership organized from a distance and based on inaccessibility, delegated authority, and tight control over public image. Machiavelli's *The Prince*—written at the start of the print age—is an early "public relations manual" for political leaders. Machiavelli advises that what a leader does in private doesn't matter that much, as long as the public image is controlled. And because leaders are rarely seen closeup even when in public, they are advised to hide their emotions, hide their intimate behaviors, and to offer in public an idealized display of "majesty."

Separate training and etiquette manuals are published for each sex and for people of different ages. Indeed, every category of age, sex, and class begins to be increasingly isolated from the information and experiences of others.

Separate information systems foster distinct uses of separate places, with increasingly particular rules of access to these places and distinctions in appropriate behavior within them. People pass from role to role many times a day and change status many times in a lifetime through various rites of physical and social passage. Print leads to an emphasis on stages, levels, and ranks. The world comes to seem naturally layered and segmented. There is a distinct place for everything and everybody.

The boundaries around prisons, hospitals, military barracks, factories, and schools thicken over several hundred years leading up to the 20th century. Birth, death, education, mental illness, and celebrations are increasingly removed from the home and put into isolated institutions. People are increasingly separated into distinct places in order to homogenize them into groups with single identities ("students," "workers," "prisoners," "mentally ill," etc.). The individuals within these bounded categories are, in a sense, interchangeable parts. And the groups themselves are elements of a hierarchically organized social machine.

ELECTRONIC CULTURE: GLOBAL IDIOSYNCRASIES

Postmodern electronic societies entail what might be called "global webs of individual idiosyncrasy." As the membranes around spatially segregated institutions have become more informationally permeable through electronic media, the notion of a special sphere for each type of person and for each type of activity has been diminishing. Unlike modern literate society, which highlights differences between groups and the interchangeability of people within social categories, the current, postmodern trend is toward integration of members of all groups into a relatively common sphere of experiential options. This is accompanied by a new recognition of the special needs and idiosyncrasies of *individuals*.

As detailed in *No Sense of Place* (Meyrowitz, 1985), electronic media differ from print media along a number of significant dimensions. With electronic media, public and private behaviors tend to blur. Those who hide their personal emotions seem stiff and phony. We are encouraged to value personal revelation, exposure, intimacy—even in the public realm. The evaluation of figures in the public realm shifts from résumé criteria ("What is his training?" "What has she accomplished?") to dating criteria ("What is she like? Do I like him?"). Machiavelli's teachings fail the postmodern prince. On television, Princess Diana—the seductive and self-revelatory charmer who had struggled to graduate from high school—easily triumphs over the highly educated, but aloof Prince Charles. Machiavelli yields to Oprah.

Differences among media also interact with the structures of group identity, socialization, and hierarchy. Printed texts tend to divide audiences into groups based on education, age, class, and gender, but a great deal of electronic information and experience is shared across these demographic categories.

In the postmodern electronic society, the social functions of physical locations become fuzzier. The family home, for example, is now a less bounded and unique environment as family members have access to others and others have access to them. We go to the oddly named "family room" to watch television—and thereby to ignore our family members. We can stay at home and yet travel—via TV, VCR, DVD, and Internet—through dozens of psychological video spaces in the course of a few minutes.

We continue to live in physical settings and to be dependent in many ways on local geography and community. Yet, we increasingly share information with and about distant others. In a sense, the world is becoming a collection of what I have called "glocalities" (Meyrowitz, 1991)—places that are shaped both by their local uniqueness and by global trends and global consciousness.

Metaphors aside, of course, it is not possible to experience the whole world as one's neighborhood or village. Even apart from the numerous political, religious, economic, and cultural barriers that remain, there is a limit to the number of people with whom one can feel truly connected. Electronic media, therefore, foster a broader, but also a shallower, sense of "us."

The effect of these boundary changes is both unifying and fractionating. The forms of group identities and place-defined roles characteristic of modern societies are bypassed in both directions: Members of the whole society—and the world—are growing more alike, but members of particular families, neighborhoods, and traditional groups are growing more diverse.

On the macro-level, the world is becoming more homogeneous. Our leaders try to act more like the person next door, even as our real neighbors want to have more of a say in local, national, and international affairs—and, for that matter, in the affairs of presidents. In a print culture, it somehow made sense to carve the heads of presidents into a mountain. In a TV era, in contrast, we often find ourselves dwelling on the nature of other parts of the president's anatomy. Thus, we have a blurring of leaders and average citizens. We also see more adultlike children and more childlike adults. And we see more career-oriented women and more family-oriented men.

Along with macro-level blurring, comes micro-level fragmentation. On the micro-level, individuals experience more choice, more variety, and more idiosyncrasy. Just as there is now greater sharing of behaviors among people of different ages and different sexes and different levels of authority, there is also greater variation in the behaviors of people of the same age, same sex, and same level of authority.

CONCLUSION

Medium theory, of course, does not provide a complete picture of our current social landscape or of any prior period. Medium theory tends to pay insufficient attention to the role played by powerful political and economic interests in the development of communication technologies and in the way media are employed. Medium theory tends to downplay the significance of cultural and individual differences in the use of and reaction to communication technologies. And medium theory tends to be overly linear and causal in its structure. Nevertheless, medium theory offers insights into general patterns of social change that are often invisible within other schema.

Taking a broad view, medium theory suggests that human civilization has been characterized by three different "worlds of familiars and strangers"—traditional oral societies, modern literate cultures, and postmodern electronic societies:

1. Each traditional oral society has a relatively thick boundary separating it from every other oral community. Each oral society is a small world of "familiars" separated from a vast and mysterious world of strangers.

2. Modern print societies mix together formerly distinct oral communities. There is a new, larger boundary around the nation state, but there are also new internal boundaries around social categories (of age, sex, class, ethnicity, etc.) within the society. Members of the modern nation state move in and out of the internal boundaries on a regular basis, and the encountering of strangers within the boundaries of the nation is a frequent occurrence.

3. The postmodern, electronic matrix leads to more permeable boundaries between different nation states and more permeable boundaries around social categories within nations. There is a sense of global familiarity, as well as a greater sense of individual idiosyncrasy and the strangeness of local others.

Indeed, I argue that there has never been a time in human civilization when it has been more difficult than it is now to predict the activities and behavior and knowledge of a person based on his or her age, gender, physical location, and other demographic categories. And many of the daily social roles that were once unthinkingly enacted are now the subject of constant doubts and negotiations.

Even in our homes, experience is splintered: A son may walk around the house with an Apple iPod, a daughter's eyes may dart between a parent's face and a computer screen, and a spouse may leave an intimate embrace to respond to a cell-phone call. More than ever before, therefore, the postmodern, electronic era is one in which everyone else, foreigners and family members, seems somewhat familiar—and somewhat strange.

REFERENCES

Meyrowitz, J. (1985). *No sense of place: The impact of electronic media on social behavior.* New York: Oxford University Press.

Meyrowitz, J. (1991). *The changing global landscape.* Atlanta: Quest.

Meyrowitz, J. (1994). Medium theory. In D. Crowley & D. Mitchell (Eds.), *Communication theory today* (pp. 50-77). Cambridge, UK: Polity Press.

Meyrowitz, J. (2003). Canonic anti-text: Marshall McLuhan's *Understanding Media.* In E. Katz, J. Peters, T. Liebes, & A. Orloff (Eds.), *Canonic texts in media research: Are there any? Should there be any? How about these?* (pp. 191-212). Cambridge, UK: Polity Press.

3 VIRTUALITY AND McLUHAN'S "WORLD AS ART FORM"

Frank Zingrone

York University

To no one type of mind
is it given to discern the totality of the truth.

William James

How accessible is McLuhan's work to the newly enthusiastic but basically casual reader? Will the dilettante cybernaut who has sampled an insight here, an aphorism there, who "digs the whole vibe" of McLuhan's prescient and timely spin on electric reality actually engage his ideas at deeper levels ? This matter is more complex than simply wondering if the microserfs can digest big Mac.

McLuhan has always produced a partially virtual audience, one that senses his value in effect but makes too small an effort in fact to read him. He complained to me about this. Reading McLuhan is hard work, takes time, and involves some fairly complex sourcing. Ironically, those least likely to read him are most interested in understanding him—media people, artists, and semi-serious students of electric culture. This sets up what George Steiner (1972), calls "a crisis of relationship between traditional literacy and

43

the hypnotic mendacities of the mass media [which] are exactly those to which McLuhan . . . applies his . . . often penetrating attention" (p. 251).

A scholarly gap may exist between the insiders and the outsiders in McLuhan studies that does not turn wholly on the question of whether or not you knew the man, or attended his seminars in Eliot or Joyce or somehow have gained a topographic feel for the map of his intellect. It may be that the elitist divide has more to do with whether you haven't read or can't read *Finnegans Wake* and less with whether you think that's important in understanding virtual reality (VR). Less a matter of age or acquaintance, it is more a matter of seeing how Joyce uniquely configures the literate ground for advanced communication theory. It's the vision that goes with the technology.[1]

Don Theall's (1992) foundation article, "Beyond Orality and Literacy: James Joyce and the Pre-History of Cyberspace," positions the challenge: "Understanding the social and cultural implications of VR and cyberspace requires a radical reassessment of the inter-relationships between Gibson's cyberspace, McLuhan's modernist influenced vision of the development of electric media and the particular impact that Joyce had on . . . McLuhan" (p. 4). His article offers such as reassessment. (I recommend it as essential.)

"Nobody could pretend serious interest in my work," McLuhan warned, "who is not completely familiar with the works of James Joyce and the French Symbolists" (E. McLuhan, 1996, pp. 151–157). According to Eric McLuhan (1996), in *The Antigonish Review*, "he intended such statements to be taken quite literally" (p. 157). It appears that the prerequisite of a doctorate in literature is not merely "provocative hyperbole" (p. 157). But Eric cannot be unaware that his dad was a gifted put-on artist dedicated to hyperbole as an attention-getting strategy. If only obsessive-compulsive English majors can adequately read McLuhan what are the rest doing who are not members of the Pythagorean fraternity of wonderworking *Wake* fakirs? And what has that got to do with VR and the contemporary obsession with the computerization of experience?

If, as Theall suggests, the work of McLuhan, William Gibson, and MIT's Media Lab, and, I would add, Jean Baudrillard's (1983) *Simulations*, Michael Heim's (1993) VR work in which he pairs McLuhan and Heidegger, the enlightened balance of Richard Lanham (1993) in *The Electronic Word*, and Arthur Kroker (1994) who expertly exposes the exclusionary practices of "high-tech capitalism" in denying to the informationally deprived underclass

---

[1]Many scholars, young and old, especially those who have read McLuhan's Cambridge University doctoral dissertation, have come to McLuhan as if Hermetically through the hieratic steps of the agenda of "The Ancient" grammarians and Joyce's transformed consciousness of the world. McLuhan was implicitly on track to arrive at Chaos and Complexity theory.

access to the "Utopian visionary space" of the "Virtual Class," if all these arbiters of VR are working against a Joycean ground and his vision of electronic reality, we should pay attention and get beyond our trivial satisfaction with virtual surgery and the myriad of training simulations and social games that VR creates.

I bring you instead an example of McLuhan using Joyce to produce metaphysical insight into the VR process. In a long lost tape of his presentation to the Buffalo Spring Festival of the Arts in 1965 in discussing media as environments, McLuhan outlined the thesis that electric process transforms all the arts and sciences into anti-environments and thus the world through media into art forms. During the 1960s he was stressing the word *merge* as a fundamental term. (This is not the same notion as the often denigrated term *emergence*, the accidental appearance of unexplained evolutionary novelties, like consciousness. *Mergence* is an inhibitive adaptation or, a desensitizing dumbing down process that pushes experience out of conscious awareness into a sort of preconscious or subliminal state.)

In describing how electric process transforms rational literate space into something close to a primitive idea of the world and art, McLuhan sets up a compelling distinction between the creation by new technologies of anti-environments, which are art forms that produce new percepts for probing old concepts: and the tendency, on the other hand, to "merge" experience with a new technology in order to inhibit awareness of perceptual change.

This adaptation of new perceptions to old forms is an attempt to quell turbulent changes that threaten the equilibrium of established consciousness and its particular reality. For example, if a person sees the opening of a rose by time-lapse cinematic technique that reveals the hidden beauty of the implicate unfolding process of a flower, that person may never again experience flowers in a vase or garden in a simple way. But awareness of the meaning of this new perception is generally suppressed. McLuhan refers to such actions as the "disadvantages of using art merely as a way of merging" that is, as adaptive assimilation of a Disney-like, virtualized view of nature. Michael Heim (1993), discusses the ontological significance of the virtual reality shift of the late 1980s to the digital psychic framework. "The reality shift I saw was not a highly visible surface break, but a deep, underlying, slow-moving drift in the underground techtonic plates of our awareness" (p. 140).

McLuhan, as we know, thinks of anti-environments as artistic probes for training perception to reveal new meanings and new roles for us and to enable us to see the world as a "museum without walls"—full of art, being art itself. If, however, art is used merely to *merge*, he says rather than to create or *express* new meaning, we will remain ignorant of the patterns of change that would reveal to us the new world and new strategies of survival. We can become victims of that power, mere specimens in the game of managing public consciousness. Mergence is either a deliberate sort of blindness or perhaps evidence of a universal technological syncretism, the pairing or combining of technologies in ever more complex arrangements, new art forms for conquering newer realities.

For a Joycean like McLuhan, *merge* would also suggest the panoplied word "reamalgamerge" from *Finnegans Wake* (Joyce, 1959), a reference to the Identity of Indiscernibles of Leibniz (1992).

> *Now let the centuple celves of my egourge . . . by the coincidance of their contraries reamalgamerge in that indentity of indiscernible.* (pp. 49-50)

This phrase refers to a canny analysis by Leibniz of effect to cause relations between his living monads that enunciates the "principle that there cannot be two things (monads) in the universe that are exactly alike" (p. 424). This is implicit recognition that there can never be exact duplication of initial conditions for human experience in general and science in particular. Leibniz, then, has intuited Chaos theory. VR and Chaos are inextricably linked in, for example, animatronic imagery. The film, *Jurassic Park* signals the end of the stone age and the birth of the fractal image as medium of the simulated future.

VR that merges real with artificial moves toward the preservation of sameness, the established order of perception. It's ironic that redundancy (sameness) is also the heart of pattern recognition that allows us to communicate in the first place. VR that always articulates differences moves toward art and thus communicates new dimensions of awareness. But true art is revolutionary, too different, if not merged gradually into perception.

In *Finnegans Wake,* Joyce is using Chaos as if to create of the *Wake* a gigantic strange attractor that only simulates the general tendency of language to order, the neg-entropy of Norbert Wiener. Using Leibniz, he shows that no word in *Finnegans Wake* is ever the same. Even a word that seems the same is different in its nature by occupying, like particles, a different spatio-temporal position. That's what Leibniz says about his infinitely varied monads. Every line of *Finnegans Wake* is about *Finnegans Wake* as new medium transformed by Joyce's spectacular structural adventure with grammar and words into a simulated extension of unconscious reality. In the *Wake*, meaning is lodged simultaneously in both the medium and its apparent content.

An "Identity of Indiscernibles" may be the best description of what the reader of *Finnegans Wake* must try relentlessly to discover in its portmanteau language imploded by electric process into an encyclopedia of preconscious utterance. McLuhan's word *merge* carries hermetic implications that lurk in the term *amalgam*, a complex alchemical and grammarian allusion and that leaves us to wonder just how hermetic McLuhan's imagination was, since most great grammarians, like himself, tended toward arcane views of reality?

McLuhan was insisting in 1965 that his reality was composed of "many spaces" like Leibnizian "possible worlds," not just rational visual space, but also acoustic space, proprioceptive space, audile/tactile space and, though he didn't use the term *cyberspace* with the structure of each space and its psychic state depending on specific media simulations.

He said in 1965 that automation puts all the senses back together again, though he would now probably add "in a virtual arrangement." He is referring to the defeat of the eye's tyranny and the reintegration of the sensorium by electric process. He did say, "the extension of our nervous system electrically enables us to put sight and sound outside as total environments." The electrification of the arts and sciences creates a "need for them to become anti-environments," an ever intensifying need as media proliferate.

Finnegans Wake is a grand experiment in simulating unconscious language for conscious appreciation that generates keys to unlock the deepest levels of mind, a cultural psychotherapy of sorts. The *Wake* is a technique for merging prehistoric orality with postmodern orality using deconstructed literacy as an analytical tool for reworking perception. Despite there being no word in the *Wake* the same as any other, which ought to defeat meaningful communication, together, as a simulation of language, the words cohere as pattern and not by line, a primary effect of electric process.

Also apropos cyberspace, McLuhan (1965) says on the Buffalo tape: "We have as a world gone through the looking glass. At the other side of the looking glass you are in a new kind of space, one in which the human observer creates his own space and his own time" (or virtual reality?) This is the technologically induced condition of, he says in the Buffalo talk, "world as artifact, world as art form, world as programmed experience." Furthermore, he then invokes the archetypal fears of William Burroughs for our reprogramming the environment "as a cannibalistic assault on our whole existence, of just eating us alive of just turning technology loose to chew us to bits—and I think there's ample evidence that this does happen," McLuhan says. What protection do we have against such brutal changes? "Media do create these new environments and they do require new anti-environments, new art forms do make us competent to handle the new environmental forces" (McLuhan, 1965). So we have to learn to use VR to enable us to bring humane stability to our turbulent world by overturning complacent and entrenched assumptions about how things mean.

Art as anti-environmental is bifurcating, fissionable, and complexifying, whereas mergence is simplifying uncritical assimilation through media of subliminal effects on perception. Media in their simplifying action defeat the higher purpose of effecting a true transformation of human consciousness. Apropos the management of public consciousness through perceptual controls by media, mergence suggest the complicity of the subjects in their own seduction. Go into any up-to-date VR parlor and watch the young men grimacing intensely, fixated like psychopaths manqué on ethereal goals of puerile scoring. The realization of thousand-petalled lotus heaven through VR is a long way off.

REFERENCES

Baudrillard, J. (1983). *Simulations* (P. Foss, P. Patton, & P. Beitchman, Trans.). New York: Semiotext(e).

Heim, M. (1993). *The metaphysics of virtual reality*. New York: Oxford University Press.

Joyce, J. (1959). *Finnegans wake*. New York: Viking Press.

Kroker, A., & Weinstein, M. (1994). *Data trash*. Montreal: New World Perspectives.

Lanham, R. A. (1993). *The electronic word: Democracy, technology, and the arts*. Chicago: University of Chicago Press.

Leibniz, G.W. (1972). *The encyclopedia of philosophy* (Vol. 4). New York: Macmillan, The Free Press.

McLuhan, E. (1996). Joyce and McLuhan. *The Antigonish Review, 106*.

McLuhan, M. (1965, March). *New media and the arts*. Buffalo Spring Festival of the Arts, State University of New York. (The author holds the rights to this tape which was never published. Copies may be arranged on special request. E-mail the author at zingf@yorku.ca)

Steiner, G. (1972). *Language and silence: Essays on language, literature and the inhuman*. New York: Atheneum.

Theall, D. (1992). Beyond the orality/literary dichotomy: James Joyce and the prehistory of cyberspace. *Post Modern Culture, 23*. [an electronic journal; available at gopher://jefferson.village.virginia.EDU/O/pubs/ pmc/issue.592/theall.592].

4 BEYOND McLUHANISM

McLUHAN AND THE DIGITAL AGE

Donald F. Theall

Trent University

A recent "official" biography of Marshall McLuhan asserts that he is simple and easy to understand (Gordon, 1997). Yet more than 40 years since the publication of *The Gutenberg Galaxy* (McLuhan, 1962), scholars have only just begun to understand his relevance to the emergence of informatics and cyberculture. Somehow his simplicity has not been all that obvious. Certainly since the 1960s there have been attempts to simplify McLuhan—which unfortunately he often failed to discourage—but his work, although not conventionally academic, nevertheless exhibits its own unique and complex intellectuality—the often unrecognized intellectuality of the learned artist and satirist. McLuhan's strength in understanding the contemporary and future implications of the emerging technoculture depended on his complexity and his ambivalence. But ambivalence, compounded by his desire to exercise the power of influence, not only blocked any "easy" understanding of his work, but also obscured his sources. His writings have been further obscured by the critical debates about his value.

My exploration of McLuhan and beyond may at times seem foreign to the social scientific commitment of communication studies, yet it will be an exploration with its roots in the very foundations of humanism—a journey consistent with Fordham University and Father Culkin's invitation to McLuhan in 1967, which exhibited the understanding that his deepest insights into the history and nature of human communication and technologies came from ancient, classical, pagan, and medieval roots. Beginning with McLuhan's relation to modernism, to its artists and writers, and to the aftermath of modernism, I explore the implications of what he considered to be the "poetic" scientific yet anti-theoretical method he developed. McLuhan's development of a method which is both social scientific (in the sense of a human science) and poetic—the poetics of a new science—indicates the possibility of moving "beyond McLuhan" by enhancing his method and retrieving his radical modernist roots, thus reversing his pietistic Catholicism and obsolescing his conservatism—for on McLuhan's own assertion, such positing of value inhibits understanding.

McLuhan's frequent citation of Joyce—a relationship that might be described as moving in modernity's wake—is most illuminating, for the wake of modernity is then the assemblage of literary, theoretical and artistic works that precede or succeed *Finnegans Wake* (Joyce, 1939/1960), which creates its own flotsam and jetsam and illuminates the history of mental and physical artifacts, such as codes and cables or signals and telephones. Adapting this concept—"modernity's wake"—in order to assist in understanding McLuhan provides a precise index for speaking both about going "Beyond McLuhanisms" and even going "Beyond McLuhan." It emphasizes how McLuhan's work demonstrates that the process of understanding media implied going beyond media, so that in *Laws of Media* all artifacts become media, and also that the force and energy of such quasi-poetic work, like that of Joyce, necessarily implied that those who try to follow McLuhan should always already be moving beyond him. This suggests why the more interpretative "poetic" work of commentators such as Jean Baudrillard (1976/1995, 1981) or Arthur Kroker (1984) provide greater insight for moving beyond McLuhan than does the work of those such as Ong (1982) and de Kerckhove (1995). Because McLuhan always insisted on associating his work with Joyce's poetry and with modernist art and literature, so doing provides an understanding of why McLuhan emphasized the probe and the percept, rather than theory and the concept.

As Ted Carpenter (2000) recently pointed out, McLuhan "picked up" (or as T.S. Eliot said of great poets, "stole") concepts and insights from others. That is, items such as: Dorothy Lee's "linearity"; Sigfried Giedion's "time, space and mechanization"; anthropologist Ashley Montagu's "medium as message" and the Toronto millionaire art collector Sam Zack's "medium is the massage"; Edward Hall's "extensions of man" (which Hall said he had borrowed from Buckminster Fuller); Wyndham Lewis' "global village"; Ezra Pound's "artist as the antennae of the race," an early warning system; and Joyce's numerous puns. McLuhan's poetic essays transformed these "borrowed" phrases into ambivalent, consequently mysterious, visionary epiphanies of an emerging future.

Carpenter (2000) describes his life long friend and colleague as:

> Rainmaker, sorcerer, trickster, juggler, poet, punster, magician, scientist.
> It was no accident he teamed up with an ethnologist. The main differ-
> ence between us was that he'd long ago crossed over to the other side.
> What I studied he lived. Forget art imitates life/life imitates art; for him,
> life was art, art was life. (p. 248)

Although McLuhan's quest was directed at understanding those social,
cultural, and material changes resulting from the impact of contemporary
electrification and digitalization after World War II, his poetic method—in
the Baconian or Viconian sense—was grounded in the history of the trivium—the study of grammar, rhetoric, literature, and the arts—from its recognized roots in Greece and Rome and from its esoteric and occult roots in
Egypt and the hermetic tradition. This is not incidental to McLuhan's project, for along with Francis Yates' (1974) developing important historical
work on the art of memory and its extension into contemporary poetic history, her exploration of the rise of modern science from the alchemical and
the occult also influenced him.

Rarely were there artists who spoke as perceptively about McLuhan as
the Québécois multimedia artist, novelist, dramatist and broadcaster,
Jacques Languirand (1972), in *From McLuhan to Pythagoras*. Having participated in designing the theme pavilions at McLuhan's World Fair—
Montréal's Expo67—he knew how McLuhan's writings, like those of Joyce
and modernist artists, reflected the New Age affiliation of technology, art,
mysticism, and alchemy with its historical thrust from the future to the past.
The digital world is in one of its aspects, as we now know, the new age world
of Pythagoras, Leonardo, hermeticism, Eastern mysticism, and
Gnosticism—all phenomena in which McLuhan was immersed and from
which he felt he could learn, as long as he could reconstruct their theories
and practices within Catholicism and the contemporary scholastic revival.
Although my going behind McLuhan into the historic past, particularly his
new age fascination with the occult, the esoteric and the cabalistic, may seem
far from going beyond McLuhan, it is an essential preliminary because it
uncovers the keys to the core of McLuhan's project. McLuhan had a *method*
not a *theory*; he was a poetic empiricist and as such a poetic empiricist, similar to the literary and occult aspects of Francis Bacon, a futurist and
prophet. Although he disguised himself in the pose of a scientist, McLuhan's
project would have failed without his poetic method, for he deliberately
positioned himself as the prophet of the automated, wired, digitalized world
of the coming millennium.

To move beyond McLuhan requires still another momentary short
biographical diversion, for his poetic insight was problematized by an

essential schizoid vacillation between his pietistic commitment to a conservative Catholic, pseudo-Jansenism, whereas as modernist artist he was
attracted by the post-Nietzschean visions of modernist art and literature.
This vacillation permeates McLuhan's project—a vacillation that he can sus-
tain, because his method eschews value judgments and promotes disinterested observation as the strategy for coping with continuous technological
transformations. So the paradox of his supporting censorship, and opposing
birth control and abortion can go hand in hand with his utilizing the sen-
sate, hedonistic, erotic culture of the 20th century the way he does in *The
Medium Is the Massage*—his first commercially published *essai concréte* (a
term I introduced in 1971)—or in his interview on 1960s sexuality in *Look*
magazine.

This problematic schizoid streak in McLuhan also affects the way he
interpreted and applied modernist poetics. As his correspondence reveals,
different poetic practices—for example, what he describes as the vertical,
space-oriented Wyndham Lewis and the horizontal, time-oriented, T.S.
Eliot, or Joyce—were shaped by disguised, conflicting theologies of occult
secret societies (Theall, 2000). For McLuhan, the postliterate media world is
demonic, ensnared between these contesting occult camps, which in the
process nevertheless provide insights into new technologies by using a poetic history to develop an ecological view of artifacts—an ecology of sense.
McLuhan's social scientific poetics in prose are his strategy for repossessing
for the contemporary Christian—read *Catholic*—world, the "wisdom of the
ancients" concealed in such occultism. McLuhan is a pre-postmodernist like
Joyce; but he is a *counterimage*, who, as a convert, embraced Catholicism,
just as Joyce, born a Catholic, rejected it as an apostate.

Going beyond McLuhan involves confronting this problematic by partially revising his reading of modernism, particularly of Joyce's poetic, to
render successful his attempt to develop the genuine post-Joycean poetic
ecology of sense, which complemented and supplemented Bateson's (1972)
ecology of mind, thus developing a genuine artifactual ecology, built on the
Viconian foundation of *The Gutenberg Galaxy* (McLuhan, 1962), *Laws of
Media* (McLuhan & McLuhan, 1988) from which McLuhan's approach to
history/communication evolves and thus provides a necessary foundation
for a "media ecology." Speaking of an ecology of mind and of sense, and
ultimately of an artifactual ecology, grounds the transformation of environment in the tri-partite relation of technologies to the human person, the
extension of the central nervous system (CNS), and the human processes of
making, building or constructing cultural productions, from fashion and
roadways to multimedia happenings and personal computers.

To underline further the importance to McLuhan of modernist art and
poetry, note that in the formative 1950s many well-recognized cultural producers were included in his agenda: artists: Kepes, Moholy-Nagy, Lewis,

Picasso, Leger, Klee; symbolist and postsymbolist poets: Baudelaire, Rimbaud, Laforgue, Mallarmé, Valéry, Yeats, Pound and Eliot; architects, town planners, and art historians: Le Corbusier, Giedion, Gropius and the Bauhaus; representatives of the lively arts: Eisenstein, Chaplin, Al Capp, Walt Kelly; classical and Renaissance theorists of language, literature, and education: from Aristotle, Cicero, and Quintilian to Erasmus, Bacon, and Vico; and finally major figures of medieval universalism and scholasticism: from the makers of cathedrals to Dante and Thomas Aquinas. His was a world of art, poetry, alchemy, mysticism and the history of the articulation and transmission of knowledge—a world from which he crafted what he knew to be his Viconian-Joycean artifactual history, which shapes the *Laws of Media* (McLuhan & McLuhan, 1988).

In this context, McLuhan created what some have denominated as his highly successful "presentation of post-literacy in anti-book format"—actually a book-oriented technique for indicating how postliteracy will lead to the synaesthetic and coenaesthetic emergence of a multisensory, all inclusive, hyper-transformation of the book as the culmination of the long march from telegraphy and photography to the merger of information processing with the making of artificial realities and with global telecommunications, producing a postelectronic book in which sounds, movements, images, speech, and typography intermix. It has been suggested that atlthough his so-called anti-book successfully presages the implications of the postliterate, his use of postliterate methods for historical analyses was far less successful. Yet, his best and most historically oriented book, *The Gutenberg Galaxy* (McLuhan, 1962) is grounded in the history of literature, education and the theory of the arts, with strong biases toward a modernized revision of Renaissance commitments to history and literature. Whatever his weaknesses—and there were many—McLuhan has quite rightly left his impact on communication history—a more deep and intuitive one than that of Harold Innis.

Modernist poetics and posthumanist history rooted in the classical world, the middle ages, the Renaissance and Enlightenment are the ground of McLuhan's project—a ground, which, provided him as it did Joyce, with a unique vision of the emerging post-literate, digital telecosm. Since, according to Stuart Brand (1987), computer programming unites the modes of art, technology, and science in the writing of the architect and technologist, Nicolas Negroponte and his associates in the MIT Media Lab, he can invoke McLuhan as a kindred spirit. Andy Hertzfeld, co-designer of the Macintosh, in his book, *Programmers at Work,* noted that programming is "the only job where I get to be both an engineer and an artist" (cited in Brand, 1987, p. 58). McLuhan's vision of the remarriage of art, science, and technology through the evolution of telecommunications and computerization both shapes his method and indicates how a new poetic genealogy and ecology of the artifact pave the road to the telecosmic "global village" and beyond, just as *The Gutenberg Galaxy* had mapped, as its working title proclaimed, the "Road to *Finnegans Wake*." McLuhan well knew that Joyce (1939/1960), who shared with H.G. Wells (1920) an interest in contemporary technologies and their evolution, had made it abundantly clear that in the *Wake* (1939) he was writing a history of the world, as Wells had attempted in his *Outline of History*. But like the *Wake* as an "outline of history" — or natural history of the technological ascent of humanity — McLuhan's writings were a "poetic" history, a new, human science complementing and supplementing hard science.

If McLuhan never made this claim directly, it was because — as he had told various correspondents and students — the density and complexity of his writing and his conversations, resulting in ambivalence and obscurity, were deliberate. From his study of Bacon and mnemonic alchemy, he had learned the power of crypsis, the secret power of parables and riddles. For McLuhan the coming of the digital age and the global cosmopolis were the return of the poetic — the quintessential characteristic of all modes of cultural production. To his credit and his integrity, he maintained consistently that his knowledge of the poets and artists and the history of poetics — the technological making of artifacts — were the keystone of his works. It is within this context that the main aspects of McLuhan's method must be examined and placed to avoid the confusion generated by ideologically theorizing McLuhan as primarily an Innisian, structuralist, postmodernist, or post-Marxist, rather than regarding him as a poet — pietistically Catholic and temperamentally anarchistic.

His method, characterized by this very schizoid streak, is exemplified by how he asserts that the Thomistic concept of the analogy of proportionality is central to his probes; yet in using analogies he is most interested, like the contemporary post-structuralists, in the exploitation of radical difference. Because for McLuhan each new medium is a new language, regardless of the precision or correctness of his analysis of technical details, its poetic overtones open up a series of illuminating synchronic and diachronic interpretations of it as a particular artefact. So in *Laws of Media* (McLuhan & McLuhan, 1988), he describes his tetrads as providing proportional poetic presentations that dramatize differences. This raises a second aspect of his method, for the tetrad is hermeneutic and rhetorical — a poetic, not a logical or dialectical, construct. This underlines the ambivalent play throughout his books of dyads, triads and quarternaries: the dyads, of contradiction and contrariety; Hegelian and Piercean triads; and Viconian-Joycean, mythopoetic quarternaries. In *The Gutenberg Galaxy* (McLuhan, 1962), he establishes both the dyad of speech and alphabetic writing and the dyad of script and print, each then being placed in a new relationship in the triad of language as gesture, which is then further assimilated into his conception of tactile space (i.e., the CNS as the *sensus communis*) with its implications for technologies as cyborgian extensions.

This strategy becomes even more complex when he supplements it with Joyce's multiplex verbal complexity and Lewis Carroll's logical play, characteristic of the grammarian, rhetorician and the counter-dialectician. Verbal play has a natural affinity with modernist poetry and modernist criticism, most particularly in Joyce, but also in Elizabethan and Neo-Augustan literature, and in nonsense language. McLuhan uses this play with language and logic as the foundation of a contemporary science of discovery—a mnemonic, Baconian, Viconian science and a way of "generating fluid concepts and creative analogies" (to borrow the title of Richard R. Hofstadter's, 1995, book on artificial intelligence). Going beyond McLuhan requires advancing his poetic method directed toward exploring the postliterate world of the hypersensory, the new technological artifactual cosmopolis where synaesthesia and coenesthesia produce a more inclusive, tactile space resulting from digitization, while exposing his inconsistencies and prejudices. His implicit pessimism, his apparent preference for the age of literacy, his nostalgia for the past, his near-reactionary political stance, are contradicted by his anti-dialectical hermeneutics and Joycean playfulness, by his adoption of the stance of a learned, yet anarchistic satirist of the contemporary "chaosmos," of his early willingness to see human communication as enmeshed in a dynamic system.

To genuinely move beyond McLuhan in the digital age it is necessary to respect his complexity as well as his unique analysis of the integration of arts, poetics, history, literature, technology, and science as the basis for developing a more sophisticated poetic history of technology. McLuhan's remarks about computers in his artifactual analysis (dating from the late 1970s) speak prophetically:

> It steps up the velocity of logical sequential calculations to the speed of light reducing numbers to body count by touch. . . . It brings back the Pythagorean occult embodied in the idea that "numbers are all"; and at the same time it dissolves hierarchy in favor of decentralization. When applied to new forms of electronic messaging such as teletext and videotext, it quickly converts sequential alphanumeric texts into multilevel signs and aphorisms, encouraging ideographic summation, like hieroglyphics [sic]. (McLuhan & Powers, 1989, p. 103)[1]

---

[1]This quotation is taken from the posthumously published *The Global Village: Transformations in World Life and Media in the 21st Century* (McLuhan & Powers, 1989). It was edited and rewritten from McLuhan's working notes, which had to date from the late 1970s, since he died in 1981.

Here, McLuhan's "hieroglyphs" more than anticipate Gibson's (1984) later remarks in *Neuromancer* about "iconics," and McLuhan's particular use of the hieroglyph, like that of mosaic, primarily derives from Joyce and Giambattista Vico. The concluding chapters of my books, *Beyond the Word* (Theall, 1995) and *James Joyce's Techno-Poetics* (Theall, 1997), provide a detailed analysis of Joyce and the modernists as a prehistory and futurological analysis of cyberspace. But Joyce's own work is the master exemplum of the socioecological role of the poetic in human communication. McLuhan's project begins from Joyce and the arts of radical modernism, and teaches how from future artists one can develop modes for understanding the increasing fluidity and metamorphosis of a world of synesthesia and the orchestration and convergence of all modes of artifactual production.

REFERENCES

Bateson, G. (1972). *Steps to an ecology of mind.* New York: Ballantine.
Baudrillard, J. (1995). *Symbolic exchange and death* (L. H. Grant, Trans.). Reprint London: Sage. (Original work published 1976)
Baudrillard, J. (1981). *For a critique of the political economy of the sign* (C. Levin, Trans.). St. Louis, MO: Telos Press.
Brand, S. (1987). *The media lab: Inventing the future at MIT.* New York: Viking.
Carpenter, E. (2000). Appendix B. In D. F. Theall, *The virtual McLuhan.* Montreal: McGill-Queens University Press.
de Kerckhove, D. (1995). *The skin of culture: Investigating the new electronic reality.* Toronto: Somerville.
Gordon, W. T. (1997). *Marshall McLuhan: Escape into understanding.* Toronto: Stoddart.
Hofstadter, R. (1995). *Fluid concepts and creative analogies.* New York: Basic Books.
Joyce, J. (1960). *Finnegans wake.* New York: Viking. (Original work published 1939)
Kroker, A. (1984). *Technology and the Canadian mind: Innis/McLuhan/Grant.* Montreal: New World Perspectives
Languirand, J. (1972). *De McLuhan a Pythagore.* Montreal: Ferron Editeur.
McLuhan, M. (1962). *The Gutenberg galaxy.* Toronto: University of Toronto Press
McLuhan, M., & McLuhan, E. (1988). *Laws of media: The new science.* Toronto: University of Toronto Press.
McLuhan, M., & Powers, B. R. (1989). *The global village: Transformations in world life and media in the 21st century.* New York: Oxford.
Ong, W. (1982). *Orality and literacy: The technologizing of the word.* London: Methuen.
Theall, D. F. (1995). *Beyond the word: Reconstructing sense in the Joyce era of technology, culture and communication.* Toronto: University of Toronto Press.
Theall, D. F. (1997). *James Joyce's techno-poetics.* Toronto: University of Toronto Press.

Theall, D. F. (2000). *The virtual marshall McLuhan*. Montreal: McGill-Queens University Press.

Wells, H.G. (1920). *The outline of history: Being a plain history of life and mankind*. London: Newnes.

Yates, F. A. (1974). *The art of memory*. Third reprint. Chicago: University of Chicago Press. (Orignal work published in 1966)

SECTION II

The Media on McLuhan

5 McLUHAN IN THE DIGITAL AGE

WHERE ARE YOU NOW THAT WE NEED YOU?

Neil Hickey

Columbia University,
Graduate School of Journalism

Somebody, and I don't know who, said that there's nothing as dangerous as an idea, especially if it's the only one you've got.

That was never McLuhan's problem. John Culkin, my friend of many years, and to whose memory I dedicate these few observations, once told me that McLuhan was never offended if somebody said to him, about one of his verbal filigrees—"That is a preposterous idea!"

McLuhan would simply respond: "You don't like that idea? OK. I've got another one."

That attitude is a version of the old theorem that a truly educated person is one who can hold two opposing ideas in mind and not lose the ability to act.

The word *idea* is thus doubly relevant here. There's a related term that's become a favorite in Cyberia recently, and that's the word *meme*. It doesn't appear in any dictionary I've consulted, but among the digeratti, it means "a contagious idea." Or an idea that spawns, or generates, or suggests other ideas—a kind of benevolent, productive virus that emerges from the seed of related conceptions. The memes always fly about like swarms of bats anytime close readers of McLuhan get together.

As a mere working journalist, I can't pretend to parse all of McLuhan's cerebrations, and indeed it's a perilous business for any but the most adventurous. Or the most reckless. I've written only one article (Hickey, 1989) about McLuhan, and that was on the occasion of the 25th anniversary of the publication of *Understanding Media* (McLuhan, 1964).

I have, however, covered television and telecommunications for longer than I care to say. The title I've attached to this chapter is "McLuhan in the Digital Age: Where Are You Now That We Need You," and I hope to convey just an inkling of why that's a useful question.

McLuhan died on the first day of 1980. So varied, so mind-stretching, so unpredicted are many of the ways this planet now communicates with itself that speculation inevitably arises about what in heaven's name McLuhan would have to say about it all.

We are moving from an analog to a digital world; from waves to bits; from relative paucity of electronic lines interconnecting us, to a superfluity; to an embarrassment of synapses in our collective brain, most of which we are not yet certain how to employ.

Let's just place ourselves momentarily in that first day of 1980, and take a look around at that world.

- Ronald Reagan was about to be inaugurated as president, the "evil empire" of the Soviet Union was intact, and eastern Europe was still in its thrall.

- Here at home, CNN was just being launched, to enormous incredulity about the need for news on television 24 hours a day.

- The three old-line television networks, ABC, CBS, and NBC were still in their original configurations, before being subsumed into Disney, Viacom, and General Electric.

- AT&T was still Ma Bell, before it gave birth to little Bells, the regional phone companies that handle our local telephone calls.

- Geostationary satellites were hanging in place 24,000 miles over the equator, but nobody yet had the tiny pizza-sized dish antennas that allow people to receive television pictures directly from satellites, right in their own living rooms.

- Warner Brothers was a movie and television company, Time Inc. was a magazine company, and nobody had yet heard of an outfit called America Online, nor knew what in God's name an Internet service provider was.

- And perhaps most significantly, the word *computer* to almost everybody meant a giant mainframe machine owned by large businesses, the government, and universities, and not a desktop gadget that you and I and millions of others could actually own and use right in our own homes.

A correlative of that seismic shift, the World Wide Web—more so than any other bit of gimcrackery in this whole arsenal of astonishing new tools—binds up this planet, this big blue marble, this third rock from the Sun, this Spaceship Earth, yes, this global village; binds it and ensnares it and allows it to think about itself more efficiently than ever before; helping to make the planet a cerebellum satellite that's verging toward full reflexiveness, thanks to this electric prosthesis, this extension of mind.

May I offer this brief quote from McLuhan:

> The total-field awareness engendered by electronic media is enabling us—indeed compelling us—to grope toward a consciousness of the unconscious, toward a realization that technology is an extension of our own bodies. We live in the first age when change occurs sufficiently rapidly to make such a pattern recognition possible for society at large. Until the present era, this awareness has always been reflected first by the artist, who has had the power—and courage—of the seer to read the language of the outer world and relate it to the inner world. (Sanderson & McDonald, 1989, p. 4)

Mark Twain pointed out that the human being is the only animal that blushes—or needs to. It's the only animal, too, that can imagine itself in its dilemmas and its potentialities, in the promise of its own evolution into something un-imaginable, as we crawl forward out of the penumbral darkness of this first 100,000 years of our consciousness—an almost unmeasurably short period in the 13 billion years since the primal explosion—and toward a version of consciousness, in another 100,000 or 1 million years, that is, at this moment, beyond the computational powers of what I call our shoulder-top computer—the one that really goes everywhere with us—more so than your palm-top or your lap-top or your desk-top.

I was enormously relieved recently, and I'm sure you were too, to learn that—contrary to earlier supposition—there is probably insufficient gravity in the universe to cause it, in 5 or 10 billion years, to reverse its outwardbound course and collapse inward upon itself, and disappear into the same fiery hole from which it emerged. I breathed a great sigh of relief. Until then, it appeared that the race would neither survive nor prevail, and there was nowhere one could go to escape.

And after all the trouble we went to create the Renaissance, the Pyramids, the rule of law, Beethoven's Ninth Symphony, the golden rule, frozen food, Disneyland.

But not to fear. There exists, it appears, an anti-gravity, a so-called repulsive force that will keep our universe expanding unto infinity. And expanding, too—I feel sure—our consciousness, in evolutionary time, until we realize at last we are not different from the godhead, and behave accordingly.

The macrocosm and the microcosm have their discrete charms, and are endlessly engrossing whether we look up or look down. We exist precariously between the two and have only the dimmest understanding of each.

Sometime in the 1960s, I interviewed Buckminster Fuller—with whom McLuhan was acquainted. Fuller fell to speculating about the nature of thought. He had a definition, and it has remained in my mind all these years. Thought, said Fuller, is "ultra, ultra high frequency electromagnetic wave propagation." In other words, mind is a hugely efficient radio transmitter; its output is thought, which, as he put it, is "beautifully conserved," so that every thought ever thought is still present in the ether and can be subtly retrieved—a version, perhaps, of Teilhard's noosphere.

Some of his best engineering and architecture ideas, Fuller said, came to him unbidden when he was walking alone on a beach at night, his mind empty and available to this collective consciousness, past and present. Mystics and sages would have pointed out to him that the humble act of listening, that innocent receptivity, is the purest form of prayer.

Fuller also had the notion that the portion of the electronic spectrum that carries television pictures is especially pervasive and long-lived in our universe, so that television signals created 50 years ago have had time to travel 50 light years, and may have reached intelligent beings elsewhere. And if so, those bemused creatures are lounging about watching Milton Berle, Ed Sullivan, *Gunsmoke*, and *Gilligans' Island*, and wondering what in God's name to make of them.

McLuhan did, in fact, flirt with the ideas of Pierre Teilhard de Chardin, as Philip Marchand (1989) points out in his biography. In the 1969 *Playboy* interview, McLuhan said that the computer:

> holds out the promise of a technology-engendered state of universal understanding and unity, a state of absorption in the Logos that could knit mankind into one family and create a perpetuity of harmony and peace. . . . Psychic communal integration, made possible at last by the electronic media, could create the universality of consciousness foreseen by Dante when he predicted that men would continue as no more than broken fragments until they were unified into an inclusive consciousness. In a Christian sense, this is merely a new interpretation of the mystical body of Christ.

On other occasions, McLuhan was known to say that "The Prince of this world is a very great electric engineer."

There's that word again—electricity. Nobody knows what electricity is. We know what it does, but not how or why. Isaac Bashevis Singer declared that one of the greatest imponderables for him was: "Why is a pin attracted to a magnet, and not to cottage cheese?"

I know of a professor who asked a student in physics class: "How does gravity work?" The student frowned, in deep thought, groped, stammered, stared about in desperation for help, and finally said: "Oh, I know the answer. I know it! But I've forgotten it." The professor said: "That is indeed unfortunate. Because in all of history only two persons have known how gravity works—God and yourself. And now one of you has forgotten."

A brief digression into the mundane: The effects of satellites on our lives are far greater now than in 1980. Still, McLuhan perceived their import in the 1970s, well before he died. Satellites, McLuhan said, "changed the planet totally, not into a global village, but a global theater" (Sanderson & McDonald, 1989, p. 4). In 1991, during the Gulf War, I found myself in Saudia Arabia as a journalist, living in Dhahrann near the Kuwaiti border. Every day, U.S. officials conducted two live televised press conferences— one from allied military headquarters in Riyadh, 200 miles to the rear, and one from the Pentagon in Washington, DC.

With the other journalists, I crowded around a television set twice a day to get the official news of the war's progress, as relayed by CNN. And we knew that Saddam Hussein in his bunker in Baghdad was doing exactly the same thing, watching right along with us. We knew also that what the generals in Riyadh and Washington were conveying in those press conferences was aimed at Saddam Hussein as much as it was to the public and ourselves. So the information needed to be decoded, if possible. How much of it was tactical propaganda and misinformation, and how much of it could be believed? CNN had become a player, a participant in the conflict as much as an observer. For the first time in the history of warfare, there existed a live, simultaneous information loop that was an aspect of the war.

On the day the Iraqis began evacuating Kuwait, I hitched a ride with a Saudi truck convoy and made it into Kuwait City as the Iraqis were beginning their hasty retreat north along the Basra road to Baghdad. Their sterno cans were still warm on the sandbagged trenches and earthwork defenses. Jubilation reigned among the Kuwaitis. George Bush was a national hero there. A Kuwaiti gentleman in a white robe and red-and-white checkered headdress, seeing I was an American, approached and told me an interesting fact.

When the Iraqis invaded Kuwait City, he said, their first move was to systematically destroy all the satellite receiver dishes they saw on the rooftops of Kuwaiti homes and apartment buildings. It was a calculated and successful effort to impose informational isolation on the Kuwaitis, to prevent them from watching CNN and the BBC, and thus knowing how the war was progressing; to defuse their hope of liberation; to demoralize them by strangling their supply of information.

I found that tactic fascinating, representing as it did a level of media sophistication I hadn't expected of a ragtag desert army. It was war in the

Information Age, with words and facts and news being weapons as much as bombs and bullets.

One media theorist once suggested that humans can live longer without food and water than without information. It's an idea worth analyzing.

Fifty years ago, Claude Shannon, a Bell Labs engineer, proposed the first modern definition of information. He called it a message that reduces uncertainty. And he added that the amount of information carried by any message can be quantified by studying the extent to which it reduces uncertainty. I like that.

So let us, by "a commodious vicus of recirculation," return to where we began. What would McLuhan have to say about the phenomenal advances in telecommunications in the years since 1980? We can only speculate. But I suspect his analysis would be hugely enlightening, useful, playful, outrageous, inconclusive, maddening, gnomic, percipient—and fun.

Here's a pithy probe from McLuhan that my eye fell on recently: "Discovery," he said, "comes from dialogue that starts with the sharing of ignorance" (Sanderson & McDonald, 1989, p. 4). I've shared lots of mine, and I trust that the days and years ahead will produce memes galore, and thus lead to discovery.

REFERENCES

Hickey, N. (1989, June 10). Marshall McLuhan: 'Televisionary' or crackpot. *TV Guide*, pp. 30–32.

McLuhan, M. (1964). *Understanding media: The extensions of man.* New York: McGraw Hill.

Marchand, P. (1989). *Marshall McLuhan: The medium and the messenger.* New York: Ticknor & Fields.

McLuhan, M. (1969, March). Playboy interview: Marshall McLuhan. *Playboy*, pp. 53-74, 158.

Sanderson, G., & McDonald, F. (Eds.). (1989). *Marshall McLuhan: The man and his message.* Golden, CO: Fulcrum.

6 HOLD THE 21st CENTURY! THE WORLD ISN'T READY

INTERNATIONAL RELATIONS AND THE BIAS OF TECHNOLOGY

Michael J. O'Neill

Author and former Editor
of The New York Daily News

As Pangloss would say, intellectuals enjoy the best of all possible worlds. They don't need any licenses or special credentials; they simply bestow the honor on themselves. And, most satisfying of all, they can be wildly wrong without doing the slightest damage to their careers. Norman Podhoretz jumps through hoops on the political left one decade and then switches to the right the next, and still claims an unbroken record of brilliance. Our most famous Kremlin watchers didn't have a clue to the imminent collapse of communism, but they never turned in their pundit cards. Although Francis Fukuyama's ideas about our exultant arrival at the end of history began unraveling as soon as he floated them, they made him a celebrity.

Daniel Bell (1976) called Marshall McLuhan's ideas "trivial . . . Turkish baths of the mind" (pp. 73, 107). But he himself failed to recognize the genetic role of technology in the new world he was supposedly defining in his 1973 classic, *The Coming of Post-Industrial Society*. During the very years when instant communications were remaking international relations and creating a new global economic system, the master statesman Henry Kissinger still clung to the 19th-century *realpolitik* of his hero Bismarck.

Today's world is McLuhan's witness. Time has validated insights he had more than three decades ago. For all his flights of fancy and the clouds of jargon that befogged some of his collaborative publications, he was unerring in identifying the core elements of an electronic revolution that would profoundly alter the contours of human experience. He foresaw the extraordinary contraction of time and space, the acceleration of change, and the global extension of consciousness. He anticipated the multiplication of human transactions and interactions that are now driving us into a new era we do not yet understand.

Thanks largely to new technology, our planet is now spinning too fast for rational management. Political and social institutions formed in the Industrial Age are running far behind the curve of change. Despite all the euphoria about the victory of market capitalism and liberal democracy, there are so many contradictory trends, so many social and economic upheavals that it is impossible to be sanguine about our passage into the 21st century. Samuel Huntington's (1998) apocalyptic *Clash of Civilizations* may not happen, but turmoil and conflict are certainly more likely than the New World Order that George Bush promised us.

One reason is that change is operating at different speeds in different layers of societies in different parts of the world, all at the same time. The context of life is out of synch with living, so there is a sheering effect between economic and technological forces on the one hand and social and political adjustment on the other. In China we see astonishing progress: huge increases in gross national product, more than 200 million people suddenly freed from poverty, the farm population reduced from 70% to 50% in less than two decades, per capita income doubled in just 9 years, a feat that took nearly half a century in the United States (Hughes, 1998, p. 67ff; Pei, 1998, p. 68ff; Yergin & Stanislaw, 1998, p. 376). Never before in history has there been such change on so large a scale and in so short a time.

Yet behind all the successes, Minxin Pei (1998) warns in *Foreign Affairs,* lie "massive socioeconomic dislocation, a rapid shift in values and beliefs, and mounting pressures on the political system . . ." (p. 74). In the interior of China, especially, people see on television how much worse off they are than their East Coast brethren and millions stream like a gold rush into already overcrowded cities where their unskilled labor is unwelcome and their sense of exclusion and frustration only deepens. Other millions of workers face layoffs as bloated state enterprises are shut down, sold, or simply founder, raising the specter of street protests and widespread unrest in the very heartland of an economic boom (Hughes, 1998).

The fact is that the joys of progress are unevenly distributed in China and, indeed, all along the frontiers of the global economic revolution. In many nations, there is no joy at all, only more misery, despair, and rising tides of anger against the advanced nations and multinational corporations they blame for their failure to share in the wonders of onrushing new technology. The same technology—the instant, visual, and incessant communication—now tells everyone on earth where he stands in the hierarchy of fortune and, in the process, contributes to a brooding sense of unfairness.

The problem of equity is one of the most dangerous issues confronting the new century, just as equitable distribution of wealth was a central feature of the ideological debates and wars of the last 100 years. "Inequality," says the French thinker Jacques Attali (1991), "will cleave the new world order as surely as the Berlin wall once divided East from West" (p. 12). The life-and-death question for civilization is whether that inequality can be constrained—whether the great disparities we already see can be narrowed and the human consequences made more tolerable—before mass discontents lead on to even more general violence and war. "For many," as Yergin and Stanislaw (1998) argue, "the market system will be evaluated not only by its economic success but by the way in which that success is distributed. How widely shared is the success? Is the system fair and just? Or does it disproportionately benefit the rich and the avaricious?" (p. 383).

Despite rising living standards in many areas of the world, the gap between winners and losers is ominously wide—not only between high-tech and developing nations, or between different regions and different cultures but also between the rich and poor, the educated and uneducated within even the most advanced societies. Although many factors are involved, I cite just two that relate to the theme of this chapter, specifically two biases—the bias of new technology, to paraphrase Harold Innis, and the bias of the global market economy that is itself a by-product of surging new technology.

To be sure, technology has always favored the skilled over the unskilled. But the present revolution has changed the whole axis of economic life so abruptly and so universally that the changes are more extreme and the social shocks more severely felt. Suddenly, it is knowledge rather than territory and natural resources that is the chief index of power. The value of labor is measured by education; the success of nations depends on technology and pools of highly trained talent.

These differences are exacerbated by a computer-driven global economy that is almost totally consumed with self-aggrandizing goals. The great transnational corporations roam the earth promoting consumerism, increased market shares and profits with little concern for the larger needs of any society. Governments, released from their Cold War duties, are all scrambling for national advantage in an economic free for all. Like a giant centrifuge, the whole international system concentrates wealth and power and separates out the poor and the weak. Because commerce outpaces education and cultural accommodation in many areas of the world, the globalization process is inherently divisive and destabilizing.

Compounding the problem is another product of the electronic revolution: the instant, pervasive, and worldwide movement of information, data, capital, industries, and jobs, as well as a corollary, unprecedented increase in people-to-people interactions and population mobility. The result is a traumatizing volatility that sends Asian economies soaring one year and plunging the next, roils international markets and destroys governments from Jakarta to Moscow. Adding to the turbulence and danger, as Paul Kennedy (1993) points out, is an ominous disjunction between prosperity and population growth: "[There is] a growing mismatch between where the world's riches, technology, good health, and other benefits are to be found," he says, "and where the world's fastest-growing new generations possessing few, if any of those benefits, live. A population explosion on one part of the globe and a technology explosion on the other is not a good recipe for a stable international order" (p. 331).

And when the technological explosion also produces spectacular shifts in both the kind and number of jobs that the global economy will support, millions of workers in traditional industries find themselves hopelessly unemployable but other millions race off to other cities or other nations in pursuit of new opportunities they quickly hear about. People are no longer as locked into their own separate cubbyholes of life as they once were before modern communications put them in daily contact with the rest of the world. When they see others improving theirs lives, they no longer accept suffering and want as their karma, a fate from which there is no escape; they demand better things for themselves and parity with the more favored few. So everywhere one looks around the globe societies are in incredible flux.

"With the populations of the industrial nations growing older and those of the developing world continuing to explode," says the Japanese economist and former bureaucrat, Sakaiya Taichi (1997), "we may see the start of major movements of peoples like those of the third through sixth centuries" (p. 10). Not the least of the dangers is that shrinking advanced societies will find themselves fighting to defend themselves against poor masses flooding across their borders in search of a better life. These new nomads of the modern age, as Attali (1991) puts it, will be looking for "oases of hope, emerald cities of plenty and high-tech magic" or, if unsuccessful, they will redefine hope in fundamentalist terms outside modernity: "This dynamic threatens true world war of a new type," he said, "of terrorism that can suddenly rip the vulnerable fabric of complex systems" (pp. 76–77). It is a vision that recalls Jean Raspail's (1973) hauntingly ironic novel, *The Camp of Saints*, in which liberal democratic ideals are quickly overcome by racial fears when 1 million Indians invade France in search of Western abundance. "'Their fate, indeed, is tragic. But our own, in turn, is no less so,' said the French president in ordering his troops to fire, if necessary, to block their advance" (p. 210).

All of these cross currents of change and contradiction seem eerily reminiscent of the social upheavals of the industrial revolution. Communism, fascism and nazism, as Zbigniew Brzezinski (1989) observes, "were all responses to the traumas of the industrial age, to the appearance of millions of rootless, first-generation industrial workers, to the inequities of capitalism, and to the newly acute sense of class hatred bred by these conditions" (p. 6). Even more directly, I add, it was the spectacular failure of the governing elites to deal effectively with these conditions that led on to calamity.

And that is the question again now, in the blinding glare of American triumphalism—whether the dismal "march of folly" (Tuchman, 1984) in the 1920s and 1930s will be repeated, whether the elites of today will show any more wisdom than their predecessors.

What makes the present challenge even more daunting than before is the unprecedented velocity and scale of change. The electronic acceleration of history means that troubling new trends must be caught at much earlier stages if there is to be any chance of altering their course and affecting outcomes. The politics of reaction and crisis management needs to give way to a new early warning system based on social detection and prevention: preventive politics, preventive diplomacy and even preventive journalism. A systematic effort to patrol ahead for early signs of stress in the deepest recesses of society, to search out root causes in hopes of taking timely action to prevent cataclysmic results. (O'Neill, 1993, 1996)

This is an alien idea. Although politicians, diplomats, and journalists pose as movers and shakers, they are mostly reactionaries. They do not create change; they only react when long-festering problems become full-blown crises on the evening news shows. The media, for example, do a superb job of covering disasters after they happen but rarely see them coming in time to help the public avoid them. Political leaders only act when they are forced to and, in any case, are too busy hustling money these days to think about public needs. And traditional diplomats still have not caught on to the fact that the real action in the information age is not in government ministries but on the front lines of peoples' lives, in neighborhood groups and village councils, in unemployment lines, in ethnic or religious or economic enclaves where the technological revolution is not an abstraction but a shattering daily personal experience. Local activism is a major political force, for example, in countries like China and Russia. Moscow's popular mayor Yuri Luzhkov was doomed to run for president simply because he was surprisingly successful in improving city services.

One message delivered by the medium McLuhan talked about so many years ago is that the rational management of human affairs has to begin at the grassroots where television now keeps people so quickly and so universally informed that they do not need leaders to tell them what is happening, or how to think or feel. Mass emotions, immediately expressed in polls, protests, migratory movements, or violence, increasingly drive decisions from the bottom up instead of from the top down. And the bottom is where new early warning techniques are needed and where prevention has to begin.

The idea of prevention as a new-age strategic principle only bobbed to the surface a few years ago when it attracted the attention of The Council on Foreign Relations, Carnegie Corporation, United States Institute of Peace, and other similar groups. They launched a series of prevention projects on the premise, as the scholar Michael Lund (1997) put it, that "pre-crisis and pre-violence interventions into conflicts are generally easier, cheaper, and save more lives than reactive responses" (p. 3).

In its first initiative, the Council sent a team to Kosovo under the leadership of a leading American journalist, Seymour Topping. He and his colleagues carried their cause all the way up to Yugoslav President Milosevic and won a number of concessions. But the subsequent massacre of ethnic Albanians was a bloody repudiation of progress. Failures in Somalia, Iraq, Bosnia, Indonesia, Afghanistan, Congo, and dozens of other world troublespots similarly dramatized the difficulty of preventing mindless violence in the absence of international conviction and a willingness to act.

One of the classic acts of preventive politics was the Marshall Plan which, together with other bold American initiatives, saved western Europe from economic collapse and a threatened communist takeover after World War II. However, not to take any shine off the extraordinary statesmen involved, Russia's seizure of eastern Europe provided a powerful incentive for action that even Congress could recognize. The issues were also grimly clear and mostly limited to Europe; the historic venue was much less complicated than it is now.

Our contemporary world is very different. The same glories of the electronic age that are creating so much progress also make it more difficult to deal with the economic and social consequences. An example was the inability of traditional institutions like the International Monetary Fund to cope with wildly gyrating world markets and crumbling national economies in the late 1990s. Although world leaders still pay lip service to lofty international goals and even the United Nations, they actually spend most of their time promoting their own country's narrow interests. Except perhaps for someone like Vaclav Havel, no one seems to be thinking imaginatively or forcefully about the larger needs of humanity. So no effective strategy is yet in place for dealing with the conflicting forces and inequities at work in the "totally new environment" that McLuhan predicted. Clearly, the international community—if there is such a community—is not ready yet for the 21st century. This is not a good omen.

"Rapid social change, pressing hard against the limits of what people can bear, seems certain to continue to afflict mankind" William H. McNeill (1979) observes. "The whole process may be conceived as a kind of race between the rational, disciplined, cooperative potentialities of mankind, and the urge to destroy, which also lurks in every human psyche" (p. 537).

REFERENCES

Attali, J. (1991). *Millennium*. New York: Times Books/Random House.

Bell, D. (1973). *The coming of post-industrial society*. New York: Basic Books.

Bell, D. (1976). *The cultural contradictions of capitalism*. New York: Basic Books.

Brzezinski, Z. (1989). *The grand failure*. New York: Charles Scribner's Sons.

Hughes, N. C. (1998, July/August). Smashing the iron rice bowl. *Foreign Affairs, 77*(1).

Huntington, S. (1998). *The clash of civilizations and the remaking of world order*. New York: Touchstone Books.

Kennedy, P. (1993). *Preparing for the twenty-first century*. New York: Random House.

Lund, M. S. (1997). *Encyclopedia of U.S. foreign relations* (draft paper). New York: Council on Foreign Relations.

McNeill, W. H. (1979). *A world history*. New York: Oxford University Press.

O'Neill, M. J. (1993). *Roar of the crowd: How television and people power are changing the world*. New York: Times Books/Random House.

O'Neill, M. J. (1996). Developing preventive journalism. In K. M. Cahill (Ed.), *Preventitive diplomacy, stopping wars before they start*. New York: Basic Books.

Pei, M. (1998, January/February). Is China democratizing? *Foreign Affairs, 77*(1).

Raspail, J. (1973). *The camp of saints*. Petoskey, MI: The Social Contract Press.

Taichi, S. (1997). Escaping the culture of bureaucratic leadership. *Japan Echo, 24*(2).

Yergin, D., & Stanislaw, J. (1998). *The commanding heights*. New York: Simon & Schuster.

7 | THE INVENTION OF LASAGNA
MADE THE PULLMAN CAR OBSOLETE

OR HOW I GOT MARSHALL Mc LUHAN'S MESSAGE

Marvin Kitman

The invention of Marshall McLuhan made obsolete the way we thought about Marshall McLuhan. Back in the days when I was starting as a TV critic (1967), everybody had to have a position on McLuhan. Thinking on McLuhan's ideas at the time was sharply divided. Some people thought he was right. Others thought he was wrong. The majority, however, were in another group that public opinion analysts sometimes referred to by the technical terms, "don't knows" or "don't cares."

The truth was that in the then 17th year of the McLuhan Age, when I first began my studies of the man who had revolutionized the thought processes of post-Gutenberg man, a lot of people were still afraid to have any opinion about the great Canadian philosopher. This was understandable. Tom Wolfe (1969) had explained that McLuhan was perhaps "the most important thinker since Newton, Darwin, Freud, Einstein and Pavlov" (p. 138). Many assumed that the kind of appraisal necessary to arrive at an opinion about whether McLuhan was right or wrong would take years of close study.

I had that same misconception. For years I had felt guilty about not coming to grips with the man's work. Having no opinion, I used to dread the subject when it was raised at cocktail parties. When a girl in deep cleavage asked me what I thought of a point like "schizophrenia may be a necessary consequence of literacy," I would answer: "I missed that one. Damn that Evelyn Woods course."

Thumbing through one of his books, I came across an interesting McLuhan theorem, "As people become more involved," he wrote, "the less they know."

He had a very good point there, I said to myself. Later, when I applied the theory to McLuhan's work, I found it really held up in practice, too. I became fully relaxed about McLuhan. The less I knew about him, the greater was my understanding. Since conquering my irrational fears and anxieties, nothing gave me greater pleasure than turning other people on to McLuhan.

One way to get his message, I used to explain, was by reading his books. There were three major works: *The Mechanical Bride* (McLuhan, 1951), *The Gutenberg Galaxy* (McLuhan, 1962), and *Understanding Media* (McLuhan, 1964). If this is the way you want to go, I would add, there were several things you should know.

Don't be put off by McLuhan because he was difficult to understand. There were only two things about his writing that made this so: the style and content.

Even intelligent men had found McLuhan a challenge. "The style is viscous fog, through which loom stumbling metaphors," wrote the Oxford fellow, Christopher Ricks. When Prof. McLuhan used big words, I would explain, this was more than compensated for by the organization of his material. "The man's work reads for pages," observed Prof. Benjamin DeMott of Amherst, "like a Marboro clearance ad."[1] This meant that you could start reading McLuhan on page 78 or 191 without losing the drift.

McLuhan's scholarship was vast. "He has looted all culture from cave painting to *Mad* Magazine," wrote critic Dwight McDonald, "for fragments to shore up against the ruin of his system." These multilayered references, I would explain, sometimes made things as clear as frosted glass. "It is perhaps typical of very creative minds," wrote Prof. Kenneth Boulding of Michigan, "that they hit very large nails not quite on the head." And, in a final note of despair, Prof. George P. Elliott of Syracuse confessed, "it is not possible to give a rational summary of McLuhan's ideas."

Early in my study of what many critics of the day were calling *McLuhancy*, I recognized why these men were having so much trouble with their basic McLuhan. They gave it their undivided attention. The secret of success with McLuhan was giving him your divided attention.

---

[1]Marboro was a leading clearance book sales emporium of the 1960s.

I always read him with the television set on, although I'm sure the radio or a hair dryer worked just as well. It was the mixing of media, McLuhan said, that makes children in this electronic age so smart.

Television hockey games, I discovered, were an especially useful tool for increasing one's understanding of McLuhan. What we had here is the same environmental principle one finds in action when one drinks a glass of tea while reading Tolstoi's *War & Peace*. McLuhan, as you know, was a Canadian. Hockey was the national sport of Canada. I didn't know whether McLuhan was a hockey fan or not (it was perhaps significant that hockey was one of the few subjects he didn't make reference to in his works). But many of his chapters read as if they had been written while *somebody* in McLuhan's house in suburban Toronto had the Maple Leafs games turned on the telly.

The primary offensive strategy in hockey is to shoot the puck into the opposition team's defensive zone. Then the attacking team rushes after the puck and sees what happens. On Madison Avenue this is called running an idea up the flagpole and seeing if anybody salutes. McLuhan calls his thought process "exploring."

"I am an investigator," he wrote in a brief introduction to Gerald Emanuel Stearn's (1967) important anthology, *McLuhan: Hot & Cool*. "I make probes. I have no point of view. I do not stay in one position." (Frank Mahavolich, the brilliant and eccentric center of the Toronto Maple Leafs, explained his style in essentially the same way, shortly before he had a nervous breakdown) . . . "I don't explain—I explore."

At any rate, I gained so much confidence by giving McLuhan's books my divided attention that by March 1967, I was able to consider accepting an assignment from the *New York Times Sunday Book Review* to review his newest book. If it had been any other philosopher's book, I would have bowed out immediately, pleading ignorance. But I felt that I understood McLuhan as much as any of the other critics.

When the editor mentioned the name of the book, "The Medium is the Massage" (McLuhan & Fiore, 1967), it reminded me of what Samuel Goldwyn once said: "If I want a massage, I go to Luxor Baths." But I agreed to look at the book anyway because I was curious about whether I had really gotten McLuhan's message.

The Medium is the Massage was a major publishing event in1967. "For the first time," explained Jerry Agel, the "coordinator" of the book, "Marshall puts his message in terms anyone can understand. He is a genius."

It was such a vital message, I also learned McLuhan and his associates broke with publishing tradition by publishing the paper edition before the hardcover. "We didn't have the time to wait a year," Agel explained, "to get Marshall's message into the hands of the ordinary people."

As was my way, I turned on the Stanley Cup hockey playoff game between the Montreal Canadians and the New York Rangers and began reading the paper version of *The Medium is the Massage*. It took 27 minutes. Next I read the hardcover edition, containing the same text and pictures, only one and three quarters larger and more than seven times expensive. It also took 27 minutes. When the media finished working me over completely, I found that I couldn't agree more with everything McLuhan had been saying all those years. We differed on one point. I naively thought the commercial was the message.

There was no longer any doubt in my mind that I was a McLuhanite. So I urged the people who read the *New York Times Book Review* on Sunday March 26, 1967 not to buy McLuhan's newest book, in either the paper medium or the cloth medium.

McLuhan argued forcefully in his work that the invention of television makes books obsolete. Anybody who purchased a McLuhan book, I explained, is playing into the hands of his enemies in the intellectual establishment. High sales figures could only discredit him as a prophet and thinker. Besides the invention of the Albert Schweitzer Chair (then a $100,000 seat in the humanities McLuhan had taken at Fordham University the previous fall) made the need to buy his books obsolete.

(If I was wrong about this theory—or any of the others I was advancing thus far in the review, I explained parenthetically to McLuhan, in case he was reading the old-fashioned media, please understand that I was only probing. By that I mean, I'm trying to think linearly. Before I fell under your influence, I reasoned circularly.)

Anyway, the proper way to study McLuhan's ideas was to watch them being presented on television.

Print, he said, is a "hot" medium; television is "cool." "Hot" was something that involved only one of the senses (visual, aural, etc.). These media included print, radio, topless waitresses. "Cool" was a medium involving all the senses at once (i.e., television). It was considered to be McLuhan's most nonsensical idea.

Back in the late 1960s the television industry was hot about McLuhan's theories, especially the part that said TV was the most important media in the electronic age. This was like telling an ugly woman she was beautiful.

As a result, a major commercial network (NBC) even gave McLuhan 1 hour on a Sunday afternoon in March 1967 to explain his message. The invention of Marshall McLuhan made obsolete the way we judge a man's ideas on television. It was no longer possible to use the outdated criteria to form one's opinions: It is not *what* he says that is important but *how* he says it. If the medium *is* the message, one must use such new criteria as (a) If a philosopher's eyes are closely set, he looks sneaky, and (b) Be suspicious of the man who doesn't look you in the eye while he talks to you.

McLuhan opened his discussion of McLuhanism that afternoon by looking at my refrigerator in the kitchen. He looked at my dog sleeping in the corner of the living room. He even noticed that my wife still hadn't made the beds upstairs at 4 p.m. In the 60 minutes of this otherwise cool show, he never once looked me in the eye.

This may explain why I finally found a few of McLuhan's concepts questionable. For instance, he argued that television is a superior educational tool than a book. If he was right, that meant every parent who yells at a child, "shut off that damn TV set and do your homework" was wrong. The modern with-it parent who wanted his or her kids to get into the best college will have to warn, "Junk food and books are bad for you. Watch more TV." Otherwise tomorrow's high school graduate will have trouble answering an important question on college entrance applications: "List several TV shows you have watched lately."

It was also hard to accept his idea that computers are modern man's enemy, in the sense that the "electrically computerized dossier bank" is a gossip column (i.e., like the average FBI file containing verified and unverified facts). This may be true for the person who has something to hide. But the fact that computers know all is not a total evil, at least for many lonely Americans. It proves that someone out there *cares.*

But there I went again falling into the old trap of discussing the message instead of the medium.

The third and most effective medium for getting McLuhan's message, I argued, was on the telephone.

If the wheel is an extension of the foot, as the professor correctly reported, and the book is an extension of the eye, then the telephone must be an extension of the ear. According to McLuhan, the spoken word is the most emotional form of communication. But to have a really meaningful communication experience it was necessary to establish a connection. When I raised this problem in my *Times* review, I solved it by including Marshall McLuhan's private telephone number at the University of Toronto (416 WA8-3328) along with a recommendation that readers ask him directly for the message.

Random House (the publisher) was charging $10 for McLuhan's message in its laughably 15th-century media (the hardcover book). Bantam Books was charging $1.45 for its pitifully dated media (the paperback). But the cutting-edge people at AT&T were charging only 80 cents for a long distance message (the station-to-station rate from New York City at the time). I advised serious students to call him after 6 p.m., taking advantage of evening rates. If anybody wanted to show the professor they really understood the workings of media, they might call "collect."

This would have been an absurd proposal in1964, when McLuhan published his definitive work *Understanding Media*. The message was still well hidden. By 1966, however, McLuhan had rendered all the fat out of it. He boiled the message down to 17 words. In 3 minutes or less on the phone,

McLuhan could have easily given a person the whole message and still have time left over to throw in a couple of his one-liners, like "casting my perils before swains."

It seemed like such a sound with-it way to get the message directly into the ears of the people that, in view of the urgency, I was surprised that McLuhan hadn't thought of it himself. When he had to leave his office, he could have left the message with his secretary. If he got bored with hands-on teaching, he could have used another wonder of the electronic-circuitry age, the recorded message. And if there was no answer in Toronto, the people could always call a medium and ask her for a message.

Later I learned that 327 *New York Times* readers followed my advice and called the professor concerning his message. Although this may sound impressive, more than 1 million people went out and bought the book. I never realized how widespread was the movement to destroy McLuhan.

I found out about these facts in a curious way. Several months after the review appeared, I received a mysterious phone call in my office in New Jersey. "Will you accept a call from a Mr. Marshall McLuhan?" the operator asked. She added that he was calling from San Francisco, and that it was collect.

"It depends on what he has to say, "I answered noncommittally. "I'm familiar with his work."

The operator said she couldn't find out what his message was in advance. I explained that I was a starving writer, but a phone call hardly would make a dent in McLuhan's stipend at Fordham. "Money is a metaphor," I said repeating one of the important McLuhan thoughts memorized earlier in my studies.

Mr. McLuhan answered over the operator's voice, "The medium is the message."

While I argued with the operator about how I didn't think the phone call sounded like it would be worth much, and that I definitely hadn't accepted the charges, McLuhan went right on talking. He announced what he claimed was good news: "You've been awarded the Electric Chair in Canadian Literature at Fordham."

This was confirmed by another voice. It sounded like Father John Culkin, S.J., director of the School of Communications at Fordham, but I couldn't swear to it. There was so much confusion with the four of us talking. As soon as the two other voices joined the discussion with the operator and myself, it became obvious that a collect conference call was in session. The phone company was going to get stuck with a big bill.

McLuhan monopolized the conversation, quoting liberally from the truths in his books. Occasionally, I tried to hold up my end of the conversation saying things like "The invention of eye glasses makes lasagna obsolete."

"What?" he asked.

A little less sure of myself I answered, "The invention of the Pullman car makes the draft lottery obsolete."

My intellectual hero said a lot of things, most of which were beneath the dignity of high office and my stature as a TV critic. I still don't know what he was so mad about.

Over the years, I continued being a leading McLuhanite TV critic. I was the first to realize that since the medium was the message, the way to view television was not from the old-fashioned vantage point (i.e., the front of the screen), but to turn the set around and review the back of the set, where all the action was taking place. Watching the oscillators and rectifiers humming in symphony with the orthicon tube was a thing of beauty, much more fascinating than *Captain and Tenille, Tony Orlando and Dawn,* and even *Supertrain.*

Jack Gould puzzled in his *New York Times* essay about the McLuhan phenomenon, "Has overexposure in the television age already cut short the McLuhan influence?" I thought not; it was just beginning.

Just that night I was explaining to my wife, "The invention of the home videotape-recorder rig makes Jack Gould obsolete."

"What?" she replied.

"I've got it, the invention of the camera makes conspicuous consumption obsolete."

"It's getting late," she said.

"The idea is that rich people need to impress poor people that they're superior. The rich distinguish themselves by their ability to be in contact with each other. For example, poor people can't see the rich people's art collections. But the invention of the camera, which takes pictures of the art for *Life* magazine exposes everybody to everything . . . "

"Turn off the lights, it's 3 a.m."

"What about this one? The invention of your father makes my getting a regular job obsolete."

"You finally have something," she conceded.

REFERENCES

McLuhan, M. (1951). *The mechanical bride: Folklore of industrial man.* New York: Vanguard.

McLuhan, M. (1962). *The Gutenberg galaxy: The making of typographic man.* Toronto: University of Toronto Press.

McLuhan, M. (1964). *Understanding media: The extensions of man.* New York: McGraw Hill.

McLuhan, M. & Fiore, Q. (1967). *The medium is the massage: An inventory of effects.* New York: Bantam.

Stearn, G. E. (Ed.). (1967). *McLuhan: Hot and cool*. New York: The Dial Press.
Wolfe, T. (1969). What if he is right? *The Pump House Gang* (pp. 133–170). New York: Bantam.

8 Mc LUHAN AND HOLEOPATHIC QUADROPHRENIA

THE MOUSE-THAT-ROARED SYNDROME

Bob Dobbs

The Marshall McLuhan Institute

much of III.3 (Book Three, Chapter Three-*ed.*) is telephone conversation. . . . As III.3 opens with a person named Yawn and III.4 displays the ingress of daylight upon the night of *Finnegans Wake*, the note on VI.B.5.29 is interesting:

> Yawn telegraph
>
> telephone
>
> Dawn wireless
>
> thought transference.

Roland McHugh (1976, p. 19)

Orion of the Orgiasts, Meereschal MacMuhun, the Ipse dadden, product of the extremes giving quotidients to our means, as might occur to anyone, your brutest layaman with the princest champion in our archdeaconry, or so yclept from Clio's clippings, which the chroncher of chivalries is sulpicious save he scan, for ancients link with presents as the human chain extends.

James Joyce (1939, p. 254)
(In McLuhan's private library in one of his copies of *Finnegans Wake* he has pencilled in the words "me" and "moon child" next to Joyce's "Meereschal MacMuhun.")

The ordinary desire of everybody to have everybody else think alike with himself has some explosive implications today.

The first sentence in the first article that McLuhan (1953a, December, p. 117) wrote for *Explorations*, "Culture Without Literacy"

Entertainment in the future may have quite different patterns and functions. You'll become a yogi, you'll do your self-entertainment in yoga style.

McLuhan (1967a, p. 40).

T. S. Eliot's famous account of 'the auditory imagination' has become an ordinary form of awareness; but Finnegans Wake, as a comprehensive study of the psychic and social dynamics of all media, remains to be brought into the *waking* life of our world.

McLuhan (1970a, p. 18)

At electric speeds the hieroglyphs of the page of Nature become readily intelligible and the Book of the World becomes a kind of Orphic hymn of revelation.

McLuhan, (1970b)

The future of government lies in the area of psychic ecology and can no longer be considered on a merely national or international basis.

McLuhan and Nevitt (1972, p. 227)

"And do you know," [Eric McLuhan] enthuses, "there are actually [four] *laws* governing media communications? At last we can prove to people that we aren't just theorists. This is a real science. . . . We know there is one more law," says Eric. "And we'll find it. Sooner or later." Ward (1980, p. D1).

Marshall McLuhan made two decisions in 1937: one was the spiritual strategy of becoming a Roman Catholic, and the other was the secular strategy, after intensive study at Cambridge, of translating James Joyce's Work-in-Progress (later given the title of *Finnegans Wake* in 1939) into an aesthetic anti-environment useful for countering and probing the cultural assumptions of a practicing Catholic. For the next 20 years, he refined his understanding of, first, the Thomist concept of analogical proportionality as the expression of the tactile interval, and second, its usefulness in perceiving the cultural effects of the new electric technologies, through an ongoing dialogue, analysis, and sensory meditation on the nature of metaphor and consciousness (including extrasensory perception) as an artifact. Because McLuhan (1954a, p. 70) defined *metaphor* as the act of looking at one situation through another, each situation constitutive of figure-ground interplay (a concept borrowed from Gestalt psychology), then a metaphor was an instance of mixed media, or two figure-grounds. And so was consciousness—because of its essential subjective experience as doubleness, which is doubled again as the objective effect of its autonomous interplay with other consciousnesses. Metaphor, for McLuhan, was "hylomorphic" (see Molinaro, McLuhan, & Toye, 1987, p. 460). In retrospect, the equation McLuhan was playing with could be flattened out as: metaphor=mixed media=doubleness=consciousness=tactile interplay=the Christian Holy Cross=figure/ground=analogical mirror=iconic fact=cliché/archetype=resonant field=hendiadys=menippean irony, each and all (except for *metaphor*) squared. However, after he made personal contact with Wyndham Lewis in 1943, their dialogue enhanced his appreciation of adopting Wyndham Lewis' social probing style as a political anti-environment to McLuhan's own commitment to the poetry of T. S. Eliot, Ezra Pound, W. B. Yeats, and James Joyce. Hence, his own studies simulated the doubleness he was observing technically. For the rest of his career, McLuhan juggled the artistic approaches of these five artists in miming the tactile qualities of the analogical drama of proper proportions—the drama of being and perception. For him, language was the drama of cognition and recognition, or consciousness.

McLuhan also meditated and formulated with the process pattern that there had been three Copernican Revolutions in the collective consciousness: the first, via Copernicus, had thrown man as an image to the edges of the universe; the second, via Kant, threw man into an inner landscape; and the third, via the 20th-century revolution of pattern recognition, threw man inside the machine. His growing understanding of the third revolution in collective perception allowed him to see that the managers of contemporary society operated by means of the principle that the technological unconscious (the "archetypes of the social unconscious," McLuhan & Parker, 1969, p. 31) is a massage in all facets of modern life. For example, Keynesian economics was the recognition, in the 1930s, that money would now be a technically managed medium, or a guaranteed environment. In all areas of decision making, this principle meant the use of the technique of the suspended judgment in parallel with a multilevelled application of the anthropological concept of "phatic communion" (McLuhan 1953/1969, p. 8).

McLuhan, however, revealed an aspect of this principle that included the concept of a collective extrasensory perception as an hylomorphic ("organic," see Molinaro et al., 1987, p. 460), dramatic quality and effect of any electric environment—an anticipation of the recent popular concept of the *meme*. Privately, he would refer to one facet of the complex extrasensory characteristics of this third Copernican revolution as the "'Prince of this World', . . . a great electric engineer, and a great master of the media'" (Molinaro et al., 1987, p. 387). McLuhan was anticipating what I would term *tetrad management*, the managerial "postures and impostures" (McLuhan & Nevitt, 1972, pp. 15, 26) resulting from an environment of *"participation mystique"* (McLuhan, 1966, p. 31) (effects merge with causes) and "anticipatory democracy" (cited in Ponte, 1972, pp. 34, 44; effects precede causes).

By June 1952, after television had become an environment in the United States, Harold Innis had died, and McLuhan had gotten tenure as a professor, he was ready to present his insights into the tentative maneuverings of tetrad management in a multidisciplinary format as an anti-environment to the new technical developments in society. Thus was born the *Explorations* experiment, which ran its course until 1957.

This project was obsolesced by Sputnik on October 4, 1957. During the following 20 years McLuhan studied the consequences of the post-tactile and post-television environments created by the new computer and satellite technologies (with an eye on the new laser inventions, also) that had cracked all the visual, acoustic, and tactile mirrors. The multimedia gestures that McLuhan made in this second 20-year phase were based on a post-tetradic sensibility of Menippean tactility, or Menippean phatic communion, that is from the perspective of the "pentad-manager" (Zingrone, 1991)—one who understands that the Present can only be an art form.

Returning to the first phase (1937-1957) we see, from McLuhan's perspective, he had enthusiastically performed as an agent and catalyst for a discriminating plenary awareness under electric conditions of the interplay between private and public awareness as an artifact. Miming the Logos (speech as an archetype, see McLuhan & Nevitt, 1974) this entailed retrieving the five parts of rhetoric (*inventio, dispositio, elocutio, memoria,* and *pronuntiatio*) and the four Aristotelian causes (formal, material, efficient, and final) in parallel with the four traditional levels of exegesis (literal, allegorical, moral, and eschatological) and applying them as a grammarian, rhetorician, dialectician, musician, mathematician, geometer, astronomer, psychologist, sociologist, anthropologist, scientist, psychic, doctor, and politician either simultaneously or separately in their traditional specialized contexts, depending on the medium and audience addressed. This method was McLuhan's conscious strategy of mirroring and testing the conventional "schizophrenic" (McLuhan & Watson, 1970, pp. 161-162) lives of the ordinary citizen: McLuhan as cyborg and floating, winking tetrad (see the four-level interplay of the SI/SC/HD/LD charts in McLuhan's *Report on Project in Understanding New Media*, 1960). In this regard, he explored meditative attention a great deal further and deeper than the popular and influential Menippean religionist, Jiddu Krishnamurti (1895-1986), or any of his imitators or successors. This phase of McLuhan's career inaugurated a new and enduring private and collective yoga inside an immanent "communication ecology" (McLuhan, 1967b).

Reviewing the second phase (1957-1977) we can observe, again from McLuhan's vantage-point, that he "acted" under and "mimed" the new and more challenging electronic (postelectric) conditions of the computer- and satellite-mandated programming of the whole planet. This meant that the technological environments, the "media," were retrieved as coordinated rhythmic modulations to replace the formerly retrieved formulaic "Logos" in his advocacy for, and training of, perception as a counter-program of "awareness" (see McLuhan, 1954b; McLuhan & Nevitt, 1972, pp. 11, 297) for now-fused whole populations in the global theater. This approach was McLuhan's conscious strategy of probing and mirroring the "quadrophrenic" (post-tetrad) lives of the cyborgian citizens and their "pets": McLuhan as Pollstergeist and multiclairvoyant pentad (Zingrone, 1991) probing the environment of electronic "autonomy" in the situation of the postfusion of Nature and Technology *via* satellite (see *Up the Orphic Anti* and *Silencing the Virtually Solar Theatre* at www.mcluhaninstitute.org in Baedeker section).

Granted, I have just uttered, and you have just eaten, a huge mouthful. But I am qualifying and supporting these themes, as you can see and taste, with selective quotations culled from my archives,[1] which includes the largest private collection of McLuhan's creative output—outside of Langley, Virginia. This meal will include as many of the appropriate citings that the law and space will allow. Above all, these are offered in the spirit of modeling the mosaic of psychic surgery that McLuhan had at his fingertips.

---

[1] I included 105 quotations from McLuhan's writings in the original version of this chapter to support its argument. They have not been included in the published version for space reasons, but those who are interested can contact me to review them.

It is the difference between matching and making, between spectator-
ship and total dramatic participation. Through the drama of the mouth,
we participate daily in the total re-creation of the world as a process.
(McLuhan cited in Molinaro et al., 1987, p. 347, letter dated December
15, 1967)

I now retrace what I have already said and define a few details and then
elaborate on them. The first key to my understanding of McLuhan is grasp-
ing the emphasis he placed on the drama of cognition as an artifact, in contrast to Freud's study of the dream as an artifact. This drama is based on the
doubleness of consciousness, the folding back on itself—the complementary process of "making" and "matching" that is necessary to create the resonance of coherent consciousness. An example of the "making" aspect of perception is the reversal of the rays of light that occurs in the retina as part of
the process of creating the experience of sight. Another example is the fact
that when food is ingested, what comes out at the other end is not the same
as what went in. This sensory alteration, or closure, occurs with all sensory
input. McLuhan used the transforming power of the movie camera and projector as a model of this drama of cognition. When the camera rolls up the
external world on a spool by rapid still shots, it uncannily resembles the
process of "making," or sensory closure. The movie projector unwinds this
spool as a kind of magic carpet that conveys the enchanted spectator anywhere in the world in an instant—a resemblance of the human's attempt to
externalize or utter the result of making sense in a natural effort to connect
or "match" with the external environment. The external environment
responds and the person is then forced to reply in kind and "make" again.
This systole–diastole interplay is McLuhan's "drama of cognition" and it is
parroted by the movie camera and projector. (Has it occurred to you yet of
what the live pick-up in the television camera is a parrot?) This drama is the
archetype for all creative activity produced by humanity, from ritual, myth,
and legend to art, science, and technology. McLuhan understood that James
Joyce was the first person to make explicit the fact that the cycle of Ritual,
Art, Science, and Technology imitates, is an extension of, the stages of apprehension. And this is possible because the extensions have to approximate our
faculties in order for us to pay attention to them.
     "So extraordinary is this unawareness that *it* is what needs to be
explained. The transforming power of media is easy to explain, but the
ignoring of this power is not at all easy to explain" (McLuhan, 1994, p. 304).
"Examination of the origin and development of the individual extensions of
man should be preceded by a look at some general aspects of the media, or
extensions of man, beginning with the never-explained numbness that each
extension brings about in the individual and society" (McLuhan, 1994, p.
6)—from *Understanding Media: The Extensions of Man.*

The second key to understanding McLuhan is guessing that he realized that the implicit discovery of the 19th century via Marx, Schopenhauer, and Hertz was the fact that the medium is the message: Life, Art, and Science imitate, are an extension of, the technologies they use. But the concomitant mystery and problem evoked by this second insight is the need to explain why human beings cannot recognize this cultural fact. McLuhan realized that the effects of television had been spelled out in *Finnegans Wake*, in that the structure of the television medium resulted in a vivid x-ray of whatever culture employed this medium. Thus, the traditional spell or numbness that hypnotized any culture, and created a subliminal bias in that culture, could be overcome through the comprehensive, plenary, perceptual bias of television. In addition, McLuhan, at first, pretended to believe that Joyce had come up with a plausible sensory and mental strategy to explain and counteract this natural "numbness," including the numbness induced by television (by virtue of the fact that *Finnegans Wake*, in the end, is a printed book), thanks to Joyce's training in the thought and perception of the "angelic doctor"(1953b), St. Thomas Aquinas. But later, adequate scientific experiment and study by Hans Selye proved and explained the physiological basis for the cultural numbing process. (Selye's results were published in the first issue of *Explorations* in December 1953.) McLuhan then saw with Archimedean delight that Joyce had manifested the truism that the effects of an artist's work precede the causes.

How did McLuhan create a sensibility that could perceive the nature of his time with such acumen? By means of a thorough study not only of poetry as presented in the Western canon but also of the mystical, esoteric, and Manichean traditions in the alchemical concerns of the grammarian. Such were the preoccupations and background of his doctoral thesis on Thomas Nashe. An essential program of these pagan doctrines has always been to use the senses as a laboratory. This sensory expertise, coupled with his Thomistic bias, was the knowledge that gave McLuhan the advantage over other students of Joyce, Lewis, Pound, Eliot, and Yeats.

> But, he [John Lindberg] argues, we now have the key to the creative process which brings all cultures into existence (namely the extension into social institutions of the central form and mystery of the human cognitive process). (McLuhan, 1954a, p. 174)

This advantage also enabled McLuhan to immediately exploit Harold Innis' studies, once he encountered them, to engage, as a post-man/machine merger, the 1950s in a prophetic challenge to the fused cluster of sex, death, and technology he saw all around him. He understood that the tactility ("the central form and mystery of the human cognitive process") of the television environment added the dimension of living thought, or the dancing drama of cognition, to that triad and loosened the grip of the mechanical Medusa. This was cause for a cautious and temporary celebration as any poet or scientist with a new vision will naturally express. However, the implied harmonies of this vision ended when Sputnik whirled around the planet.

> The mirror, like the mind, by taking in and feeding back the same image becomes a wheel, a cycle, able to retrieve all experience. (McLuhan & Watson, 1970, p. 163)

McLuhan took seriously Joyce's ambivalence toward radio and television as communication technologies that did not have the traditional characteristics of former arts that had held up an energizing mirror to their respective cultures. The reason, for McLuhan: if you have ever looked at yourself in the television monitor while the television camera is focused on yourself, you can observe that your electrified image is not reversed as it is in a flat mirror. In other words, there is no visual reflection in the television "mirror." The viewer falls into it. The viewer becomes the screen and is forced to start swimming. Now imagine a whole society dunked in such a manner. How does it get a perspective on itself? What serves as a mirror or anti-environment to the new mode of collective consciousness, if it can be considered a consciousness at all? Does the society really need a mirror anyway, when it is fused and splashing in the same pond?

The needs of the West, as articulated by Joyce and McLuhan, would certainly scream loudly in the affirmative. And the West quickly gave us one—the satellite, with a little help from the computer. These two great technological cloaks enabled the establishment of an integrated fulcrum from which to orchestrate the sensory mixes induced by older media for the intended harmony of all. Or such a potential, at least, McLuhan foresaw. Would others? Not likely, and certainly not enough to implement McLuhan's vision. As a result, the satellite and computer environments were built with a fragmented perspective and with increasingly fragmented consequences. And thus, the 1960s ushered in a decade of social turbulence on a worldwide scale as every culture had a thrombosis and embarked on a violent identity quest. And this also was an effect that Joyce included in the possible scenarios suggested in *Finnegans Wake*.

Now, after having reviewed this background, I examine the condition and nature of "quadrophrenia" (McLuhan, 1974). McLuhan's prolonged study of the qualities and functions of metaphor led him to see that the characteristics of the tetrad (enhancement, obsolescence, retrieval, and reversal) were intuited by Joyce and demonstrated in *Finnegans Wake* as the constituent properties of metaphor (The four parts of the Wake admit of the tetradic structure from the widest possible perspective: Book One handles enhancement, or the extensions; Book Two the obsolesced; Book Three the retrievals; and Book Four the reversal). Using the Wake as a guide, he turned his meditative double focus on television and observed that the contents of television (the evolutionary species and by-products of the interplay between culture and technology) would manifest in regular epicycles of tetradic action as long as no new environments were created.

> Everyone will be involved in role-playing, including those few elitists who interpret and/or manage large-scale data patterns and thus control the functions of a speed-of-light society. (McLuhan & Powers, 1981, p. 199)

But once they were, then the tetrad would be obsolete and Humpty Dumpty would fall off the wall and shatter again. However, this time it would be the after-image of a fall because humanity's technological evolution had ended with television as all "hardware" had flipped and fused into "software" and what remained was a complex collective ESP the patterns of which would be invoked by constant audience research, polling and surveillance. These new "weather" patterns, since they were multisensuous and abstract, McLuhan (1980) called "pollstergeists." These are what plagued the human citadel of consciousness as it stared from its cave at the newly retrieved quantum fluctuations of a still-born "astoneaged" (McLuhan & Nevitt, 1972, pp. 21, 36) society. The content of this situation, the human users and "media" themselves, imploded into a rapid, Sisyphean, and tetradic oscillation through the states of metaphor, metonymy, synechdoche, and irony that registered emotionally as states of paranoia, schizophrenia, hysteria, panic, and ecstasy. This is the condition I have designated as *quadrophrenia* in which the living metaphoric coherence of the collective consciousness appears to be usurped. Knowing it was unlikely "those few elitists" were going to take an active interest in his new discoveries, he retrieved Menippean satire as a hobby. Simulating the printed book's archetypal response to this dissolution of the tetrad-manager, McLuhan produced an after-image of the epyllion—the *Gutenberg Galaxy* and *Understanding Media*. And this is where the symptoms of quadrophrenia make their entrance. McLuhan knew that he had to mime discontinuously the splintering after-images of human/technological cognition to manifest an "impossible" (McLuhan & Nevitt, 1972, p. 142) anti-environment to the seduction effected by the pollstergeists. This is why an anticipated cursory inspection of McLuhan's books produced the intended effect that they were rampant with confusion—an early and persistent complaint by his critics, which proved the success of the technique ("You mean, my whole fallacy is wrong," the line created by McLuhan for his cameo in *Annie Hall*, and used on public occasions such as convocation addresses when heckled by audience members). One minute he seemed to be a utopian, the next a neo-

Luddite, then a Gnostic, still later an agent of the Vatican, or a Zen Buddhist, then a technological determinist, pseudo-scientist, Manhattan Project romantic, and on and on and back and forth. But the classifiers couldn't see the method in the actor's performance—the miming of the fate that the Pollstergeist needed "a rapid succession of innovations as ersatz anti-environments" (McLuhan & Parker, 1969b, p. 31) to disguise the fact it had long disappeared. His satiric retrieval of the mini-module of acoustic and tactile mirrors via the constituency of the homeopathic print mirror, in the genre of a "memory theatre," reflected the contemporary Medusan after-image of collective technological quadrophrenia, and its complementary human echo.

> Dante's Commedia was recognized as a "memory theatre" in its time and later, as were the Summas of the philosophers. Vico was the first to spot language itself as a memory theatre. *Finnegans Wake* is such a memory theatre for the entire contents of human consciousness and unconsciousness. (McLuhan, cited in Molinaro et al., 1987, p. 339, letter dated December 1, 1966)

But there remained two more surprises. First, the Pollstergeist would generate the means for its own metaphysical self-consciousness, its own doubleness, or folding back on itself—the instant replay. This technology would allow the Pollstergeist to wallow in and exploit its own "memory theatre," and, like an artist, create the effects beforehand, anticipating its first extension, of its own subsequent evolutionary leap—the hologram.

The stage for the second surprise was set by the implementation of the new digital chip as a technological environment in tandem with the established instant replay environment to usher in an unprecedented collective effect: the reincarnation of the Pollstergeist as the Android Meme. In short, the extensions of humanity had evolved to the point of actualizing their own drama of cognition. It thought like us, it intuited like us, and it anticipated like us. But we were "still" (McLuhan & Nevitt, 1972, p. 11) suspicious. It seemed to have no staying power. So humanity was left in the situation of having its ability to code and decode in "real time" (McLuhan & Powers, 1989, p. 178) frustrated and paralyzed. It could only come up with a rearview mirror term for the Android Meme's subtle collective actualization—*virtual reality*.

As the Android Meme, in its own "anthropomorphic theatre," began to extend and hypnotize itself, it enjoyed miming and simulating the natural human modes of cognition—paranoia, schizophrenia, hysteria, panic, ecstasy, individual sensation, collective hope or phobia, national myth-making and cultural norm-functioning. McLuhan did not live to see the Android Meme in action, but as an effective "empath" (cited in Callwood, 1974), he mimed the effects before the causes showed up. To accomplish this he intuited the "fifth element," what I call the *holeopathic cliché probe* (McLuhan & Watson, 1970, pp. 107, 165), by means of an understanding of the homeopathic effect (creating and maintaining memory in water), which is a process of "etherealization" (Toynbee) or "doing more with less" (Fuller) that is invisible and postfusion, and projecting that effect as the consequences of the hologram when it becomes an environment that starts to evolve.

If you mate "hologram" and "homeopathy," you might create the term *holeopathic*. I did. All evolution is the process of bashing and mating of clichés and archetypes. But when evolution can only be a nonlinear process of resonance and modulation, there are no archetypes and we are left with only cliché probes. And the human response is to stubbornly and cynically express quadrophrenia because we cannot avoid the four laws of the tetrad. But McLuhan playfully did this technically and artfully—the stance of the pentad manager, who knows the Present could only be a fragile art form. Most everyone else, unless they retrace the stages of apprehension I have just outlined, is forced to painfully and reluctantly be a tetrad manager—an unconscious response to the Internet and World Wide Web, the simulation of all electric and electronic technologies—from the telegraph to the satellite—for hoicking up an ersatz private identity. So, in conclusion, we see McLuhan made fun of those who live in the nineties, the mice who roar, by the traditional means of having perfect pitch when sung to by an inaudible environment of holeopathic quadrophrenia.

Anyway, this is what always occurs to me whenever I'm in the presence of Marshall McLuhan and contemplating how the world ignored his scientific discoveries. But still, there is one question we are all curious about: What would McLuhan say of the1990s if he were alive today? Well, I happened to ask him a couple of years ago. Through a trance medium, when I asked him this question, he confidently asserted that he certainly would create his own web page, but then he added: "and I would let James Joyce write the instructions on how to get to it."

Yup, the medium is the message . . . under electric conditions.

REFERENCES

Callwood, J. (1974, November 25). The informal Mr. McLuhan. *Toronto Globe and Mail*, p. 22.

Joyce, J. (1939). *Finnegans wake*. New York: Viking Press.

McHugh, R. (1976). *The sigla of Finnegans wake*. Austin: University of Texas Press.

McLuhan, M. (1953a, December). Culture without literacy. *Explorations Magazine, 1*, p. 117.

McLuhan, M. (1953b). Maritain on art. *Renascence, 6,* 44.

McLuhan, M. (1954a). *Catholic humanism and modern letters.* Christian Humanism in Letters: The McAuley Lectures, Series 2, p. 70.

McLuhan, M. (1954b, April 9). Sight, sound, and the fury. *Commonweal Magazine,* p. 11.

McLuhan, M. (1960, June) *Report on Project in Understanding New Media* (U.S. Office of Education Reports, 61-3619, Project 279). Urbana, IL: National Association of Educational Broadcasters.

McLuhan, M. (1966, Spring). The crack in the rear-view mirror. *McGill Journal of Education,* p. 31.

McLuhan, M. (1967a, March 15). Like yoga, not like the movies. *Forbes,* p. 40.

McLuhan, M. (1967b, September). Toronto is a happening. *Toronto Life Magazine,* pp. 23-29.

McLuhan, M. (1969). Joyce, Mallarmé, and the press. In E. McNamara (Ed.), *The interior landscape: The literary criticism of Marshall McLuhan, 1943-1962* (p. 8). New York: McGraw-Hill. (Original work published 1953)

McLuhan, M. (1970a, March). Letter to *Playboy Magazine,* p. 18.

McLuhan, M. (1970b, July 3). *Libraries: Past, present, future.* Address at Geneseo, New York.

McLuhan, M. (1974, May 10). McLuhan McLuhan McLuhan. *New York Times* (op-ed).

McLuhan, M. (1980, January 7). Living at the speed of light. *MacLean's Magazine,* p. 33.

McLuhan, M. (1994). *Understanding media: The extensions of man.* Cambridge, MA: The MIT Press. (Original work published 1964)

McLuhan, M., & Nevitt, B. (1972). *Take today: The executive as dropout.* Don Mills, ON: Longman Canada.

McLuhan M., & Nevitt, B. (1974, September 21). A media approach to inflation. *New York Times* (op-ed).

McLuhan, M., & Parker, H. (1969). *Counterblast.* New York: Harcourt, Brace & World.

McLuhan, M., Parker, H., & Thompson, G. (1969b). *Counterblast.* Toronto: McClelland and Stewart Limited.

McLuhan, M., & Powers, B. (1981, Summer). *Journal of Communication, Vol. 31*(3), 199.

McLuhan, M., & Powers, B. (1989). *The global village: Transformations in world life and media in the 21st century.* New York: Oxford University Press.

McLuhan M., & Watson, W. (1970). *From cliché to archetype.* New York: Viking Press.

Molinaro, M., McLuhan, C., & Toye, W. (Eds.). (1987). *Letters of Marshall McLuhan.* New York: Oxford University Press.

Ponte, L. (1972, February 25). Kandy kolored massage. *International Times,* pp. 34, 44.

Ward, O. (1980, March 30). Now! Son of Guru! *Toronto Star,* p. D1.

Zingrone, F. (1991). Laws of media: The pentad and technical syncretism. *McLuhan Studies, 1*(1), 109–115.

THE MECHANICAL BRIDEGROOM STRIPPED BARE

9

A CATECHISM OF McLUHANISM FOR UNBELIEVERS

Mark Dery

New York University

"The truth shall set you free," reads the inscription on Marshall McLuhan's gravestone, written in the *Future Shock* computer typeface popular in the 1960s. McLuhan died in 1980, but his truisms have indeed freed him, if only metaphorically. He lives on, through his axioms, in advertising taglines, the forecasts of corporate futurists, and the received truths of cyberculture.

"Much of what McLuhan had to say makes a good deal more sense in 1994 than it did in 1964," writes Lewis Lapham (1994), in his introduction to the MIT Press' 30th anniversary reissue of McLuhan's (1964/1994) seminal work, *Understanding Media: The Extensions of Man.* The tongue-in-chic nonsequiturs of the now-defunct cyberdelic lifestyle magazine *Mondo 2000* crossed McLuhan's aphorisms with *The Philosophy of Andy Warhol.* The *Mondo 2000 User's Guide to the New Edge* (Rucker, Sirius, & Mu, 1992) featured a full-page head shot of McLuhan, accompanied by a breathless eulogy: "This guy was *way* ahead of his time" (p. 166). *Wired, Mondo's* yuppie-with-a-ponytail successor, canonized McLuhan as its "Patron Saint." The magazine's 1993 premiere issue opened with a quote from McLuhan's collage book, *The Medium is the Massage* (so titled because "all media work us over completely"), scrolling over digitized images: "electric technology . . . is reshaping and restructuring patterns of social interdependence and every aspect of our personal life." *Wired's* worshipful invocations of McLuhan continued in its January 1995 issue, where the "mediologist"

95

Regis Debray took stock of McLuhan's intellectual legacy, and in its January 1996 issue, in which a writer "channeled" the communications theorist, posing questions that were then "answered" by McLuhan from beyond the grave, via selective quotes. Even the magazine's direct mail subscription campaign included a scriptural flourish from the switched-on Gospel of McLuhan.

As recently as 1988, a *New Republic* reviewer of the *Letters of Marshall McLuhan* sniffed, "It is hard to imagine that anyone still cares about McLuhan—or even remembers him" (Van Leer, 1988, p. 35). These days, he simply won't stay buried: he pops up in critical anthologies (*Forward Through the Rearview Mirror: Reflections on and by McLuhan*, edited by Paul Benedetti and Nancy Dehart, 1997), new biographies (W. Terrence Gordon's, 1997, *Marshall McLuhan: Escape Into Understanding*), and old biographies newly revised (Philip Marchand's, 1989, *Marshall McLuhan: The Medium and the Messenger*). HardWired, *Wired*'s brief-lived venture into book publishing, reprinted *War and Peace in the Global Village* and *The Medium is the Massage*; Michel A. Moos (1997), a critic of culture and technology, collected his obscure essays in *Media Research: Technology, Art, Communication*; and the CD-ROM publisher Voyager repackaged his ideas, in suitably nonlinear, postliterate form, for the age of multitasking and *Mortal Kombat* (*Understanding McLuhan*).

As McLuhan's unexpected resurrection makes clear, the cultural currency of the man Leslie Fiedler pronounced "two-thirds an absolutely fascinating analyst of society and culture and one-third mad" has yet to stabilize. Of course, it fluctuated wildly even in his heyday. In his widely read essay on McLuhan, "What If He Is Right?," Tom Wolfe (1967) ventured, "Suppose he *is* what he sounds like—the most important thinker since Newton, Darwin, Freud, Einstein and Pavlov?" (pp. 31-32). Abbie Hoffman, John Lennon, and Susan Sontag championed his ideas; others, many of them academic colleagues (McLuhan was a professor at the University of Toronto), were less favorably disposed toward the "Oracle of the Electric Age," as *Life* dubbed him. In *Marshall McLuhan: The Medium and the Messenger*, Philip Marchand (1989) notes that the "great majority of intellectuals and academics, it is safe to estimate, remained hostile to McLuhan," put off by his recondite prose style (remember, this was before French theory made impenetrability fashionable), his nonchalant attitude toward factual accuracy, and his seeming indifference to the political implications of his theories or to matters of social justice (McLuhan was more incensed by public littering than by the Vietnam War, see Marchand, 1989). Then, too, there was the ticklish business of his saturation exposure in the media and his often cozy relationship with Madison Avenue, an association perceived by many in the academy as evidence of his venality and superficiality (this was before William Burroughs shilled for Nike and Camille Paglia turned cultural criticism into a cross between Harold Bloom and *Headbanger's Ball*). McLuhan answered such charges with droll ripostes. "Some of my fellow academics are very hostile, but I sympathize with them," he told a *Maclean's* interviewer. "They've been asleep for 500 years, and they don't like anybody who comes along and stirs them up" (cited in Marchand, 1989, p. 182).

Renewed interest in McLuhan, catalyzed by the explosive growth of the Net, and the popularity of cyberzines such as *Wired*, has revived the debate over his ultimate significance. To some, he remains the preeminent theoretician of the Information Age, the first public intellectual to proclaim that electronic technologies—specifically, TV, whose effects were becoming manifest as the first TV generation came of age, and computers, whose influence was beginning to be felt in the corporate workplace and the automated plant—were transforming us into post-"Gutenbergian" beings, vertiginous selves eddying crazily around a "worldpool of information" (*The Medium is the Massage*). To others, he is one more worse-for-wear relic in the time capsule of the 1960s, a decade increasingly demonized by American conservatives as a breeding ground for Great Society social programs and "countercultural McGoverniks," to quote Newt Gingrich.

Before we consider his relevance to our historical moment, let's review his greatest hits. To discover McLuhan's fundamental insights, we must hack away his overgrown prose. His writing is a trackless thicket of jokes, Joycean puns, literary allusions, and cracker barrel anecdotes, at once digressive and maddeningly repetitive. It is this last quality that renders his basic theses unavoidable; formulated in the gnomic one-liners that have ensured him a postmodern half-life, they are driven home with drumbeat insistency in his best-known works—*The Gutenberg Galaxy: The Making of Typographic Man* (1962), *Understanding Media*, and *The Medium is the Massage* (McLuhan & Fiore, 1967), the million-selling, McLuhan-made-easy paperback that eroded his reputation among the intelligentsia even as it secured it among the masses.

Technological determinism is the keystone of McLuhan's theories. If Marx believed that class struggle was the engine of history, then McLuhan held that the *engine* was the engine of history: He saw technological change—specifically, new forms of communication—as the prime mover behind human history. "Societies have always been shaped more by the nature of the media by which men communicate than by the content of the communication," he wrote. In other words, the *medium* is the message (McLuhan & Fiore, 1967).

In *The Gutenberg Galaxy*, a rambling, encyclopedic rumination on the cultural shock waves caused by the introduction of the phonetic alphabet and the printing press, McLuhan juxtaposes preliterate, non-Western tribal man with Western "scribal man" (a product of pre-1500 "manuscript culture") and "typographic man" (an artifact of post-1500 "print culture").

Preliterate man, he argues, "lives in the implicit magical world of the resonant oral word"—a mythic dreamtime in which time and space are one, "an
acoustic, horizonless, boundless, olfactory space" utterly unlike the rectilin-
ear "visual space" configured by the Western, literate worldview (McLuhan,
1962, p. 28; also see McLuhan & Fiore, 1967).

A passionate convert to pre-Vatican II Roman Catholicism, McLuhan
limned human history as a fall from grace: The phonetic alphabet was the
forbidden fruit, condemning Western civilization to a postlapsarian world of
isolation, objectivity, and rationality. His rendering of this event, in a 1969
Playboy interview, sounds unmistakably like Biblical allegory. The alphabet,
he argues, "shattered the charmed circle and resonating magic of the tribal
world, exploding man into an agglomeration of specialized and psychically
impoverished individuals, or units, functioning in a world of linear time and
Euclidean space" (McLuhan, 1969, p. 59). The invention of moveable type
(the first assembly line, in McLuhan's way of thinking) and shortly thereafter the portable book (which brought solitary reading to the masses),
helped foster the worldview that structured Western consciousness from the
15th through the 20th centuries. It crystallizes in the Enlightenment and
attains its apotheosis in industrial modernity, where its insistence on linearity, compartmentalization, classification, detached observation, and a fixed
point of view are dramatically evidenced in the Fordist assembly line, the
"human engineering" of F.W. Taylor, and (pace Foucault) the panoptical
design of the Machine Age factory, office, and asylum.

In *Understanding Media*, McLuhan (1964/1994) announced that the
Information Age—ushered in, for his purposes, by the invention of the telegraph in 1844—reversed the course of history. "After three thousand years
of explosion, by means of fragmentary and mechanical technologies, the
Western world is imploding" (p. 3), he wrote. By this, he meant that the
hyperaccelerated, nonlinear nature of electronic media was "demesmeriz-
ing" Western culture, snapping it out of the "typographic trance" into which
the printing press had thrown it. Cybernetic culture, quoth McLuhan,
returns us to the preliterate worldview—mythic rather than rational, tactile
rather than visual, integrated rather than atomized. Electronic interconnectedness has transformed our wired world into a "global village" in which our
lives are inextricably intertwined with each other's and with the larger drama
of our culture, even our planet. "Ours is a brand-new world of allatonce-
ness," he wrote, in *The Medium is the Massage*. "'Time' has ceased, 'space'
has vanished. . . . We are back in acoustic space. We have begun again to
structure the primordial feeling, the tribal emotions from which a few centuries of literacy divorced us" (McLuhan & Fiore, 1967, p. 63).

The notion of a *global village*—the concept that, more than any of
McLuhan's ideas, was reflexively invoked throughout 1990s cyberculture—
offers a springboard for our critique of McLuhan. It is a commonplace that

the global village is upon us, made possible by computer networks, fax machines, satellite hookups, videoconferencing, and of course the telephone. But has telecommunications truly realized McLuhan's vision? Certainly, the instantaneousness of communications technologies has collapsed the distances between cultures, literally as well as figuratively. But what makes McLuhan's global village a village is not so much the interactivity enabled by its virtual commons as the sense of profound *involvement* that supposedly flows from our electronic interconnectedness. "In the electric age," he asserts in *Understanding Media* (1964/1994), "we necessarily participate, in depth, in the consequences of our every action . . . the electric implosion . . . compels commitment and participation" (pp. 4-5).

TV's role in galvanizing opposition to the Vietnam War or, more recently, in mobilizing humanitarian aid for starving Somalis or brutalized Bosnians would seem to bear this out. Then again, the curious inertia of an international community awash, nightly, in graphic images of butchery in Rwanda would seem to suggest that "commitment and participation" do not spring spontaneously from our electronic window on the world. Absent social consciousness and, more importantly, political will on the part of the global community, the wires that connect us are not ties that bind, merely plumbing for a deluge of images that initially jolts us, soon numbs us, and ultimately bores us. "Social service organizations and their donors complain about 'compassion fatigue,'" notes Randall K. Bush (1992). "Not only have we seen the starving children . . . before, but we have also donated to relief efforts after such events before. . . .We switch channels to something else" (p. 810). On an uglier note, the peace movement that sprang from the living room horrors of history's first TV war must be weighed against the troglodytic chest-thumping that greeted images of Iraqis barbecued alive on the Basra highway in history's first Nintendo war: Gulf War 1.0. The global village's epitaph is written on the Gulf War T-shirt that read, "Kick Their Ass, Take Their Gas." Of course, TV, we are told, is an outmoded, top–down, one-way medium; virtual communities, with their inherently democratic structure, are likelier candidates for McLuhan's global commons. Or are they? "'At first I thought this was Marshall McLuhan's global village coming to reality,' said Neil Harris, a manager at [a company] which sets up computer conferences and sells information to about 200,000 members around the world. 'But it's not that at all. It's a lot of people connecting in hundreds of small communities based around highly specific interests'" (cited in Markoff, 1991, p. 2). Jeff Salamon (1994), writing in *The Village Voice*, agrees: "Contrary to grand predictions that the Internet would open up our world, it has mostly offered people the opportunity to pack themselves into ever smaller worlds, where enthusiasms mutate into obsessions, and a reality check is a parallel dimension away" (p. 27).

"We *are* far more deeply enmeshed with each other as inhabitants of this planet than ever before, as a result of the media McLuhan was discussing," argues Howard Rheingold, author of *The Virtual Community*, in an e-mail interview.

> But . . . that doesn't mean the human condition has become rosier. We're all in on the action in Bosnia, but we can't do anything about it. The Internet, on the other hand, is important not so much for *any* of the truly remarkable uses it has been put to thus far, but for the way it redistributes the power to disseminate as well as absorb communication. I think you are correct to point at the atomization of interests as a disintegrative effect of the same technology that brings integration at other levels. We do connect across all kinds of boundaries. But we all pull the fabric apart in pursuit of our interests. It's a version of . . . the tragedy of the commons. Humans are social beings; modern citizens are individuals.

Ironically, the secession from the meatworld speaks partly to a widespread desire to reclaim the notion of community—a notion rendered increasingly obsolete by the racial, economic, and political tensions that are balkanizing American culture, and by the very electronic media McLuhan believed would knit us together. The social and psychic integration he contended would result from communications technologies is belied by the fragmentation of online society into atomic "special interests" and by the terminal anomie (pun intended) that results from lives lived, more and more in the electronic spaces of TV, videos, movies, computer games, BBSs (Bulletin Board Systems), MUDs (Multi-User Domains), and so forth. McLuhan's "complex and depth-structured" homo cyberneticus, "emotionally aware of his total interdependence with the rest of human society," can be found in the online Samaritans who leapt to the aid of the Cornell University student who posted an electronic suicide note, or in Rheingold's (1993, pp. 19-20) moving account of an online community's embrace of a member whose infant daughter was fighting a desperate battle with croup. But these are the exceptions that prove Ballard's Rule.

In his introduction to the French edition of his science fiction novel *Crash*, J.G. Ballard (1985) identified "the most terrifying casualty of the century: the death of affect," and linked the "demise of feeling and emotion" to "the preempting of any free or original imaginative response to experience by the television screen" (pp. 4-5). Those who see the virtual community (VC) as an electronic agora, restoring a sense of community and reviving public discourse in the age of the corporate media monopoly, will protest that VCs are not TV; duly noted. But the bright promise held forth by VCs must be considered in the context of the culture at large, where (in America, at least) the flight into cyberspace takes place at a time when urban public space, as Mike Davis (1990) documents at length in *City of Quartz*, is increasingly privatized and segregated in the name of "redevelopment"; when working-class urbanites fortify what Davis calls their "prison cell houses" with bars and grates while middle-class suburbanites retreat into privately policed gated communities; when the fear of crime and a chimerical drug war are used to justify the whittling away of civil liberties; and when Secretary of Labor Robert B. Reich (1991) warns of the "secession of the rich"—the abdication of social responsibility by an Information Age elite "linked by jet, modem, fax, satellite and fiber-optic cable to the great commercial and recreational centers of the world, but . . . not particularly connected to the rest of the nation" (p. 16). In such a context, virtual communitarianism that does not bear fruit in the meatworld in the form of community involvement, grassroots activism, and the like cedes the territory of the real to the powers that be and escapes to a kinder, gentler place by rolling itself up in the map. It is indistinguishable, in all the essentials, from TV escapism.

Thus, the global village has arrived, but it bears only a passing resemblance to McLuhan's Paradise Retribalized. He was wide of the mark in his contention that "electric technology has meant for Western man a considerable drop in the visual component in his experience" (*The Medium is the Massage*). Western culture in the late 20th century, when we spend more and more of our lives staring at video monitors or computer terminals, is utterly dominated by "the visual component." McLuhan was resoundingly wrong, as well, in his flabbergasting assertion that TV, universally regarded as a heat lamp for couch potatoes, "demands participation and involvement in depth of the whole being" and would therefore sound the death knell for "the consumer phase of American culture." Watching TV is a famously drool-inducing experience: a series of studies conducted in the mid-1970s found that "most viewing involves less concentration and alertness—and is experienced more passively—than just about any other daily activity" (Kubey, 1990, p. 27). Moreover, TV, as everyone but its giddiest celebrants concede, is consecrated to consumption; advertising is the medium's lifeblood, from 30-second spots to program-length infomercials to home-shopping channels to the nonstop flackery of movies and records that is the raison d'être of entertainment news shows, late-night talk, and, increasingly, local news. McLuhan's analysis was based on his pseudoscientific theory that the technical nature of the TV image, composed of innumerable dots, requires the viewer's "convulsive sensuous participation" to "'close' the spaces in the mesh," making the picture coherent (McLuhan, 1964/1994, p. 314). It was wrong in his day—there is nothing sensuous or participatory about an automatic, unconscious visual mechanism—and it is doubly wrong now, in the age of HDTV and DVDs when the quality of the image has improved many times over.

Finally, instead of McLuhan's "depth-structured" global citizens, we witness the rise of depthless individuals whose fundamental empathy, let alone their sense of social responsibility, has been seriously diminished. Obviously, this diminution is largely the product of social, economic, political, and sometimes psychological factors, but it is aided and abetted by the electronic media that disengage us from "the consequences of [our] every action." Again, the first Gulf War is a case in point. U.S. Marine Lieutenant Colonel Dick White, interviewed upon returning from a bombing run, enthused, "It was like turning on the kitchen light late at night and the cockroaches started scurrying . . . We finally got them out where we could find them and kill them" (cited in Fisk, 1991, p. 379). A god's-eye perspective, high over Iraq, and the unreality that sets in after long immersion in the screens of a high-tech cockpit, turned bombing runs into video games. And as the tagline in a Nintendo TV spot ran, "Once you start playing, nothing else matters."

The profanity of such images stands in stark contrast to McLuhan's (1969) sublime vision, in the *Playboy* interview, of a global village "in which the human tribe can become truly one family and man's consciousness can be freed from the shackles of mechanical culture and enabled to roam the cosmos" (p. 158). Nonetheless, as noted earlier, we are habitually told—often by advertisers and laissez-faire futurists—that we are living in a global village. And, in a sense that would have horrified McLuhan, we are: the viral infestation of international markets by McDonald's, Coca-Cola, Levi's, pop music, and Hollywood blockbusters is creating what *Fortune* has called a "one-world pop-tech civilization" (Huey, 1990, p. 50). The social critic Benjamin R. Barber calls it "McWorld," a Family of Man created not by the electronic interconnectedness McLuhan extolled but by MTV, Macintosh, McDonald's. As it approaches, McLuhan's "retribalized" world of "electronic interdependence" looks less like a Global Village than it does Planet Reebok or NikeTown.

But advertisers and futurists are not the only ones who celebrate the global village. Perhaps *because*, rather than in spite of, the disparity between our turbulent present and McLuhan's luminous future, his ideas cast a powerful spell on fringe computer culture, where they have acquired a New Age aura. By the late 1960s, McLuhan's concept of the global village had evolved into a techno-mystical vision of the "[p]sychic communal integration, made possible at last by the electronic media," (McLuhan, 1969, p. 72) of all humankind. A global computer network, he told *Playboy*, holds forth the promise of electric telepathy. "If a data feedback is possible through the computer," he mused, "why not a feed-*forward* of thought whereby a world consciousness links into a world computer? Via the computer, we could logically proceed from translating languages to bypassing them entirely in favor of an integral cosmic unconsciousness somewhat similar to the collective unconscious envisioned by Bergson. The computer thus holds out the promise of a technologically engendered state of universal understanding and unity, a state of absorption in the logos that could knit mankind into one family and create a perpetuity of collective harmony and peace" (McLuhan, 1969, p. 72; see also 1964/1994, p. 80). *Star Trek*'s Universal Translator meets the Harmonic Convergence.

In the early 1990s, ravers, zippies, and other members of cyberdelic culture overlaid these ideas with a New Age eschatology that saw the wiring of the world as "the final stage in the development of Gaia," as Douglas Rushkoff put it in *Cyberia: Life in the Trenches of Hyperspace*. Jody Radzik, identified in a *Rolling Stone* feature on smart drugs and rave culture as "one of the [rave] crowd's resident gurus," prophesied that " '[t]he planet is waking up . . . Humans are the brain cells. The axons of the nerve cells are the telephone lines'" (cited in Wolf, 1991, p. 60).

John Perry Barlow, an unavoidable presence in 1990s cyberdelic culture who referred to McLuhan in an e-mail interview with this author as "a metatouchstone for all of my thoughts on media, information, and mind," took this idea to the bank. A New Age neo-liberal whose sermons on the corporate lecture circuit reconcile hippie mysticism, laissez-faire capitalism, and breathless cyberhype, Barlow assured me, in that interview, that "we are engaged in a Great Work, the creation of the Collective Organism of Mind on a global scale . . . I believe that the Internet is creating a new neurosystem which will ultimately interpose itself continuously between every human synapse on the planet and every other. 'Thoughts' are already arising in this meta-organism which are dimly perceptible to us. They will become more perceptible even as our 'own' thoughts gradually disappear into the whole."

The retrofitting of McLuhan's theories, by Barlow and other true believers, does less violence to the media guru's ideas than might be thought, at first glance. On closer inspection, McLuhan's current fandom, and its selective appropriation of his ideas, illuminates the deeper meanings of his thought. "Thus you will know them by their fruits," quoth the Lord in Matthew 7:20, a scriptural allusion a devout Catholic like McLuhan would surely appreciate. McLuhan's (1992) quest to create an exact science of media criticism (his last, posthumous book was titled *Laws of Media: The New Science*) foundered on his confusingly counterintuitive terminology (TV is a "cool" medium, the book a "hot" one) and his corkscrew reasoning (he once described a nuclear explosion as "information," and asserted that the "German Jew [was] victimized by the Nazis because his old tribalism clashed with their new tribalism"). Even so, he wrapped himself in the mantle of the objective scientific observer, insisting in the *Playboy* interview that as "an investigator, I have no fixed point of view, no commitment to any theory—my own or anyone else's" (McLuhan, 1969, p. 54). Later in the same interview, however, the mantle slips: He views the "upheavals" caused by the electric age, he says, "with total personal dislike and dissatisfaction."

McLuhan's "retribalized" technoculture, it turns out, is the sort of quietly reactionary utopia that would have gladdened the heart of one of his major influences, the Catholic intellectual G.K. Chesterton: characterized by "little radical social change," it is "essentially conservative" (McLuhan, 1969, p. 70) in nature. "It's paradoxical that in the transition to a retribalized society, there is inevitably a great explosion of sexual energy and freedom," McLuhan (1969, p. 65) told *Playboy*. "But when that society is fully realized, moral values will be extremely tight. . . . We can see in our own time how, as we begin to react in depth to the challenges of the global village, we all become reactionaries" (p. 70).

In *Media and the American Mind: From Morse to McLuhan*, Daniel J. Czitrom (1982) contends that "McLuhan expressed a personal variant of the Tory, neo-Catholic, antimodern tradition flourishing on both sides of the Atlantic" (p. 167). Like T.S. Eliot and Chesterton, whose polemic *What's Wrong with the World* had a lifelong influence on him, McLuhan championed the traditions of Christian Europe against the moral corrosions of socialism *and* untrammeled capitalism. As early as 1934, in his article "Tomorrow and Tomorrow?," he inveighed against the corruption of the modern world and looked back longingly on the agrarian idyll of the Middle Ages, as romanticized by Carlyle, Ruskin, and William Morris. As late as 1969, he declared that "no one could be less enthusiastic" about the social changes brought about by electronic media than himself, and that he "would be most happy living in a secure preliterate environment" (McLuhan, 1969, p. 158). He found "most pop culture monstrous and sickening" (Marchand, 1989, p. 43). TV was a "vile drug that permeates the nervous system, especially in the young" (Marchand, 1989, p. 61). A confirmed gadget-loather, he once lamented, "I wish none of these technologies ever happened" (Marchand, 1989, p. 131). In "Tomorrow and Tomorrow," he expressed equivocal approval for fascism, guardedly embracing its Wagnerian visions of modern paladins embarked on a holy war against the "emasculating" industrial utopias of socialism and capitalism (as discussed in Marchand, 1989, p. 27). On which note, homosexuality appalled him, feminism galled him, and both were in league against the traditional social order of a happier time when men were men and Father Knew Best. In his 1944 essay "Dagwood's America," he inveighed against the purported emasculation of the modern male by a generation of domineering Blondies; in 1974, he informed an interviewer that "a woman can have all the influence she wants without ever leaving her armchair" (cited in (Marchand, 1989, p. 62).

Thus, in a supreme irony, the Oracle of the Electric Age turns out to be a tweedy brother of today's neocons. A closet Rousseauite and a recovering

Luddite, he is ill-suited to his office as the patron saint of *Wired*, a "future friendly" magazine that celebrates the "revolutionizing [of] the old order" through technological change (*Wired*, 1995).

McLuhan's unexpected resurrection, just in time for the 21st century, finds him in a strange new incarnation. He appears, in fringe computer culture, as the household deity of the switched-on noosphere—the first theologian of information, a postmodern heir to his intellectual mentor, St. Thomas Aquinas. (His theory of communications, insisted McLuhan, was "Thomistic to the core" [cited in Marchand, 1989, p. 255].) Among the secular, his lasting contribution to our understanding of the world remains the revelatory thunderbolt that our technological environment shapes our worldview—that the medium is the message. But for those who believe they are neurons in an emergent global meta-mind, he is the medium's messenger.

REFERENCES

Ballard, J.G. (1985). *Crash.* New York: Vintage Books.

Barlow, J.E. (1995). E-mail interview with the author.

Benedetti, P., & Hehart, N. (Eds.). (1997). *Forward through the rearview mirror: Reflections on and by McLuhan.* Cambridge, MA: MIT Press.

Bush, R.K. (1992, September 9-16). Not global villagers, but global voyeurs. *The Christian Century*, p. 810.

Czitrom, D.J. (1982). *Media and the American mind: From Morse to McLuhan.* Chapel Hill: University of North Carolina Press.

Davis, M. (1990). *City of quartz: Excavating the future in Los Angeles.* New York and London: Verso.

Fisk, R. (1991). Free to report what we're told. In M. L. Sifry & C. Cerf (Eds.), *The Gulf War reader: History, documents, opinions* (p. 379). New York: Times Books.

Gordon, W.T. (1997). *Marshall McLuhan: Escape into understanding.* New York: Basic Books.

Huey, J. (1990, December 31). America's hottest export: Pop culture. *Fortune*, p. 50.

Kubey, R. (1990, August 5). A body at rest tends to remain glued to the tube. *The New York Times*, Arts & Leisure section, p. 27.

Lapham, L.H. (1994). Introduction to the MIT Press edition: The eternal now. In M. McLuhan, *Understanding media: The extensions of man* (pp. ix-xxiii). Cambridge, MA: MIT Press.

Marchand, P. (1989). *Marshall McLuhan: The medium and the messenger.* New York: Ticknor & Fields.

Markoff, J. (1991, July 28). Locking the doors in the electronic global village. *The New York Times*, Week in Review section, p. 2.

McLuhan, E., & McLuhan, M. (1992). *Laws of media: The new science.* Toronto: University of Toronto Press.

McLuhan, M. (1962). *The gutenberg galaxy: The making of typographic man.* New York: Mentor.

McLuhan, M. (1969, March). *Playboy* interview: Marshall McLuhan. *Playboy*, p. 59.

McLuhan, M. (1994). *Understanding media: The extensions of man.* Cambridge, MA: MIT Press. (Original work published 1964)

McLuhan, M., & Fiore, Q. (1967). *The medium is the massage: An inventory of effects.* New York: Bantam Books.

Moos, M. (1997). *Media research: Technology, art, communication.* New York: Routledge.

Reich, R.B. (1991, January 20). Secession of the successful. *The New York Times*, p. 16.

Rheingold, H. (1993). *The virtual community: Homesteading on the electronic frontier.* Reading, MA: Addison-Wesley.

Rudy Rucker, R., Sirius, R.U., & Mu, Q. (Eds.). (1992). *Mondo 2000: A user's guide to the new edge.* New York: HarperPerennial.

Salamon, J. (1994, September 13). Revenge of the fanboys. *Village Voice*, p. 27.

Van Leer, D. (1988, July 18 & 25). Medium cool. *The New Republic*, p. 35.

Wired. (1995, January). The *Wired* scared shitlist. Archived online at http://www.Wired.com/Wired/archive/3.01/Shitlist.html.

Wolf, G. (1991, September 5). Don't get wasted, get smart. *Rolling Stone*, p. 60.

Wolfe, T. (1967). The new life out there. In G. Stearn (Ed.), *McLuhan: Hot & cool* (pp. 31-32). New York: Signet.

SECTION III

Art and Perception

10 THE INTERFACE BETWEEN WRITING AND ART

Denise Schmandt-Besserat

The University of Texas at Austin

One of Marshall McLuhan's greatest insights was to recognize that writing was not a passive conduit of information but that it changed the way we think (McLuhan, 1997). According to McLuhan (1997), for example, we owe to writing our inclination to organize information in a linear way. Nothing seems to illustrate this point better than ancient Near Eastern art.

PROTOLITERATE EGYPTIAN ART

Early in the 20th century, Egyptologists noted a drastic change in the composition of decorated palettes coinciding with the advent of writing in Egypt, about 3000 BC. Palettes are stone monuments of roughly oval shape, about 60 cm long, 40 cm wide and 2.5 cm thick, which are provided with a low circular depression or cup on the obverse (Figs. 10.1 and 10.2) It is generally assumed that the artifacts served to grind pigments in rituals of unknown significance. According to von Ranke (1924-1925), a first group of palettes, devoid of inscriptions, features motifs carved in bas-relief scattered over the entire surface. But, a second series bearing hieroglyphs, and therefore presumed later, displays figures neatly organized in a linear composition. A diagnostic example for each group is presented here.

A palette excavated at Hierakonpolis and now kept at the Oxford Ashmoleum Museum is typical of the first, preliterate set (Kemp, 1989, Fig. 12). The verso displays wild and fantastic beasts (Fig. 10.1). They include two lions, two gazelles, two panthers (one of which has an enormous neck), an oryx, a ram or mouflon; a dog with round ears similar to those framing the palette; a griffin with a feline body and the head and wings of a bird; a bull, a giraffe, an ibex and, finally, a fox playing the flute. The beasts are scattered in a joyous chaos seemingly with the only concern of covering the entire field. Nothing in the composition indicates that the animals are relating in any way to one another. The lions nor the griffin seem to attack the

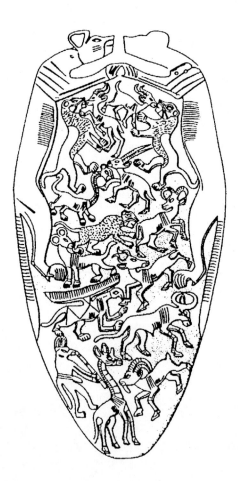

Figure 10.1   Oxford Palette from Hierakonpolis, Egypt, after Kemp
              (1989).

Figure 10.2   **Narmer Palette from Hierakonpolis, Egypt, after Kemp (1989).**

gazelles and antelopes. No one seems to mind the tune the fox plays on the flute. In particular, the jumbled composition does not distinguish which animal is more significant, more admired or feared. All the images are on the same scale. They are treated uniformly, using the same amount of details or depth of relief. We may assume that the depicted animals had a meaning. If so, as suggested by Malek (1986), the palette may have evoked the chaos of desert life.

The Narmer palette is a perfect example of the second, literate group (Fig. 10.2). The monument on display at the Cairo Museum is famous for being the earliest Egyptian monument to bear writing. Hieroglyphs identify the Pharaoh, the royal attendants (the sandal bearer and scribe placed respectively behind and in front of the king), as well as the fallen enemies. The images illustrate the political unification of Upper and Lower Egypt by king Narmer (Saleh & Sourouzian 1987). On the reverse, the pharaoh wearing the crown of Upper Egypt smites Lower Egypt, symbolized by a bearded enemy. On the obverse, the two united countries are symbolized by a pair of intertwining mythical creatures. Above, Narmer, now wearing the crown of Lower Egypt, inspects the carnage of the battlefield. The goddess Hathor, represented with the horns and ears of a cow, presides over both sides.

As von Ranke (1924-1925) recognized, the first appearance of writing in Egypt coincided with a radical change in art. The jumble of images typical of the preliterate monuments gave way to figures neatly ordered in a linear composition. Furthermore, the Narmer palette shows a concern for balanced spatial units. This is particularly evident on the second frieze of the obverse, where the Pharaoh and his retinue occupy a space equal to that of the procession of standard bearers and to the pile of decapitated enemies. The use of parallel registers to organize the figures resulted in a more clear and harmonious composition. But the significance of linearity was not esthetic alone. It was semantic. The linear structure increased the amount of information art could communicate.

In the Narmer Palette, registers were used to convey hierarchy. The deity is placed at the highest level, above royalty. In turn, the king is above the symbol of unification and, finally, the enemies, denied a ground line, seem to float helplessly at the lowest possible level. The linear composition further denotes relation, movement, rhythm, timing, direction and intention. For example, because they share the same register, it is evident that the pharaoh and his entourage march in step with a procession of standard bearers in the direction of the battlefield to be inspected. Linearity also facilitates indicating rank by size. The pharaoh is immediately identifiable by being double the size of his attendants, who in turn are twice as large as the standard bearers. Therefore, as a result of linearity, literate palettes, like that of Narmer, were *narrative*, whereas the preliterate examples were only *evocative*. But can the style change truly be attributed to writing? Mesopotamia, where writing was first invented ca. 3100 BC, provides a second opportunity to test Mcluhan's idea.

PRELITERATE MESOPOTAMIAN ART

Stamp seals, which enjoyed their greatest popularity about 3500–3300 BC, are as typical of protoliterate Mesopotamia as palettes are of predynastic Egypt. The hemispherical or animal shaped stone artifacts, a few centimeters across, played an important administrative role for controlling goods (Fig. 10.3). The motifs carved on their base in negative relief left a positive imprint when pressed on the clay securing jars, baskets, or bundles of merchandise. Among the most popular designs featured on stamp seals were animals formed by loosely connected drill holes (Figs. 10.3 and 10.4). Like the Hierakonpolis palette in Egypt, the guiding principle for their composition was "*horror vacui*" — the concern for completely covering the field. A varying number of animals were placed head to tail either spreading out or squeezed in, in order to fill the entire surface. Also like the prehistoric

Figure 10.3 (A) Hemispherical Stamp Seal, Uruk Period, ca. 3500 bc, from Ischali (A7233, Photograph P27221), Courtesy Oriental Institute, the University of Chicago.
(B) Stamp Seal, Uruk Period, ca. 3500 bc, from Nuzi (1931.162.6) Photo by Michael A. Nedzweski. Courtesy Fogg Museum, Harvard University.

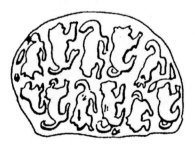

Figure 10.4 Stamp seal from Uruk, after Amiet (1980).

Egyptian palettes, the typical preliterate Mesopotamian seal composition ignored linearity and was governed only by symmetry or shape reversal. The animal motifs may well have had a particular significance that now escapes us. For example, it is conceivable that the small beast, shown singly or repeated, could have been the symbol of a particular deity.

LITERATE MESOPOTAMIAN ART

The Uruk vase, the earliest Sumerian monument to bear a glyph is the closest Mesopotamian parallel to the Narmer Palette (Heimpel, 1992). The one meter high vessel (Fig. 10.5), dated about 3100–3000 BC, is made of alabaster and carved with bas reliefs over its entire cylindrical body (Heinrich, 1936, pp. 15-17, pl. 2-3; Lindemeyer & Martin, 1993, p. 81, pl. 19-25). Because it was excavated in the temple precinct of Inanna, the patron goddess of Uruk, the piece is viewed as a ritual vessel (Amiet, 1980). The vase excavated in 15

fragments has been restored, except for one major break in the upper register. Part of a robe, which is still visible, identifies the missing figure as the ruler in his typical skirt made of a particular net-like fabric (Fig. 10.6). The elaborate pictorial narrative is generally interpreted as commemorating the New Year festival, the greatest fertility ritual of Uruk (Van Buren, 1939-1941). The upper frieze illustrates the moment immediately preceding the culmination of the event, the sacred marriage ceremony. The ruler appears in front of the goddess of Love at the temple gate, identified by the two reed poles. The bridegroom is followed by a long procession of nude men carrying gifts of products of the fields and orchards and by a flock of sacrificial animals. In return, two acolytes of the deity, mounted on rams, present the ruler with the written symbol *e n* (lordship)—the insignia of authority (Strommenger, 1964). The vase, featuring 14 anthropomorphic figures, 10 animals, 30(?) plants and 16 vessels

Figure 10.5   **Alabaster vessel from Uruk, Lindemeyer & Martin (1993). Courtesy German Archaeology Institute, Division Bagdad.**

Figure 10.6 Line drawing of the Uruk vessel carvings mapped onto a flat surface from Lindemeyer & Martin (1993). Courtesy German Archaeology Institute, Division Bagdad.

filled with offerings, constitutes the largest and most elaborate protoliterate composition.

The structure of the Uruk vase is remarkably clear and harmonious. It is linear. The story is divided into five parallel registers featuring alternatively water, plants, animals, humans and, on the uppermost level, the meeting of Inanna and the ruler at the temple gate. Linearity is emphasized by all possible means. First, the friezes are separated and highlighted by blank bands. Second, linearity is underscored by isochephaly—the depiction of all heads at the same height. Third, each of the four lower registers repeats a single motif, namely, wavy lines (water); ears of cereal alternating with palm shoots; pairs of rams and ewes, and men bringing offerings. On this fourth register, each individual is identical to the next. All are males of equal size, sharing similar squat proportions; they are shaven and sport the same hair-do; they walk in step, right foot forward, and perform the same gesture.

A glance at the tablet illustrated on Fig. 10.7 will suffice to realize that the composition of the Uruk vase replicates that of a Sumerian text (Schmandt-Besserat, 1992). The tablet, dated about 3100 BC, featured a list of goods. Namely, four large measures of grain represented by four circular signs, and four small measures of grain by four wedges. On the tablet as on the vase, the data are presented in parallel horizontal lines, each line is separated from the next by a blank band, and each line features a single sign repeated as many times as necessary.

Returning to the vase, the linear composition is exploited to convey hierarchy. Inanna and the ruler occupy the top register, above the common citizens. They, in turn, are placed above the animals, plants, and water. Note that the two main characters, Inanna and the ruler, occupy the center of the upper frieze. Note also that Inanna, the most important figure since she is a deity, is placed to the right and the ruler, her subordinate, is on the left. This matches the layout of a tablet. More precisely, Sumerian texts are structured as follows:

- Signs are placed in a hierarchical order. In Fig. 10.7, circular signs representing large units occupy the top line, followed by a line of wedges standing for lesser units of grain.
- Whenever possible, signs are displayed at the center of a tablet (Fig. 10.8).
- When, exceptionally, different signs are placed on a same line, the greatest unit is to the right and the lesser ones to the left. For example in Fig. 10.9, the large circular sign on the right stands for a larger amount of grain than the small circular signs on the left.

On the vase, the importance of the figures is indicated by their size. Plants and animals are of equal height; humans are twice as tall, and the goddess and the ruler, three times. Lastly, the deity is (presumably) slightly larger than the ruler, who in turn, is larger than his fellow citizens. This echoes the sequence of signs for grain metrology (Schmandt-Besserat, 1996, p. 81; see Fig. 10.10):

- Circular signs and wedges in different sizes stood for measures of grain. A large circular sign meant a larger quantity of grain than a small circular sign (Fig. 10.9). A large wedge represented

Figure 10. 7   Impressed tablet from Godin Tepe, Iran, ca. 3100 bc.
Courtesy T. Cuyler Young, Royal Ontario Museum,
Toronto, Canada.

Figure 10. 8   Impressed tablet from Godin Tepe, Iran, ca. 3100 bc.
Courtesy T. Cuyler Young, Royal Ontario Museum,
Toronto, Canada.

Figure 10. 9   Impressed tablet from Susa, Iran, ca. 3100 bc. Courtesy
Musée du Louvre, Département des Antiquités
Orientales, Paris.

CEREALS

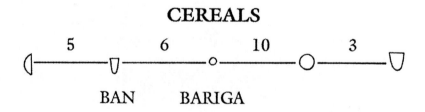

Figure 10.10   Sumerian signs for grain measures, after Schmandt-
Besserat, D. (1992).

a greater measure of grain than a small wedge. (Fig. 10. 9 displays large wedges and Fig. 10.7, small ones).

Finally, the vase used direction to string all the images of the various registers into a single narrative. Note how the animals walk toward the right, the offering bearers toward the left, and the ruler, again, toward the right. The alternating direction creates the illusion that the worshippers and sacrificial animals follow the ruler in a long procession winding around the vase. This mimics the way scribes wrote:

• Signs of a same kind were entered from right to left, but when space ran out, the line was continued boustrophedon, that is to say, reversing the direction from left to right (Fig. 10.11).

Figure 10.11   Impressed tablet from Godin Tepe, Iran, ca. 3100 bc.
Courtesy T. Cuyler Young, Royal Ontario Museum,
Toronto, Canada.

The story of the New Year festival can be read on the vase either upward or downward. Starting at the bottom the narration follows the solemn procession bringing the offerings to the goddess. From the top, the story starts at the temple filled with victuals proceeding downward toward the water that brings prosperity to the land. The same is true for the lists of goods featured on the tablets:

- The signs can be read from top to bottom and from bottom to top without loss of meaning.

In summary, in Mesopotamia, where the earliest phases of writing are well documented, it becomes evident that art borrowed far more than linearity from writing. The carved frieze used the syntactical strategies of a text to convey information. These strategies included the location, position, direction, and the relative size of the images. As a result, instead of being limited to simply evoke, art achieved the ability to communicate more complex and specific information. Like the Narmer palette, the Uruk vase was able to narrate the sequential development of an important event, as well as the interaction between the major participants.

CONCLUSION

The Mesopotamian and Egyptian civilizations that created pristine scripts, offer a unique insight on the impact of writing on cognition. The veering from a spread of images to a linear art structure, following the invention of writing, suggests that preliterate cultures apprehended images globally, but literate societies approached a composition analytically. That is to say, figures were analyzed in succession, like the signs of a text, according to their relative size and position. But how could the change be so immediate and radical? Recent clinical studies highlight that literates and illiterates process information in different areas of the brain (Gibson, 1998; Lecours, 1995). The irreversible physiological alteration caused by literacy explains the shift in organizing information. Ancient art lends support and physiology verifies McLuhan's intuition that writing changed thought processes.

REFERENCES

Amiet, P. (1980). *Art of the ancient Near East*. New York: Harry N. Abrams.
Gibson, K. R. (1998). Review of the book *The origins and evolution of writing*. *American Anthropologist, 100*(1), 213-214.

Heimpel, W. (1992). Herrentum und Königtum im vor-und frühgeschichtlichen alten orient. *Zeitschrift für Assyriologie und Vorderasiatische Archaeologie, 82*(1).

Heinrich, E. (1936). *Ausgrabungen der Deutschen Forschungsgemeinschaft in Uruk-Warka* [Excavations of the German Research Society. Vol. 1. The small objects of the archaic temples level at Uruk, German Research Society, Otto Harrassowitz Publishers] (Vol. 1). Berlin: Kleinfunde aus den Archaischen Tempelschichten in Uruk, Deutsche Forschungsgemeinschaft, Komissionsverlag Otto Harrassowitz.

Kemp, B. J. (1989). *Ancient Egypt: Anatomy of a civilization.* London: Routledge.

Lecours, A. R. (1995). The origins and evolution of writing. In J.P. Changeux & J. Chavaillon (Eds.), *Origins of the human brain* (pp. 213-235). Oxford, UK: Oxford University Press.

Lindemeyer, E., & Martin, L. (1993). *Uruk, Kleinfunde III* [Uruk, small objects, Vol. III]. Mainz am Rhein: Philipp von Zabern.

Malek, J. (1986). *In the shadow of the pyramids.* Norman: University of Oklahoma Press.

McLuhan, M. (1997). *Media research.* Amsterdam: Overseas Publishers Association.

von Ranke, L. (1924-1925). Sitzungsberichte der Heidelberger Akademie der wissenschaften [Reports of the sessions of the Heidelberg Academy of Sciences — class of philosophy and history]. *Philologische Historische Klasse, 5*, 3-12.

Saleh, M., & Sourouzian, H. (1987). *The Egyptian museum, Cairo.* München: Prestel-Verlag.

Schmandt-Besserat, D. (1992). *Before writing.* Austin: University of Texas Press.

Schmandt-Besserat, D. (1996). *How writing came about.* Austin: University of Texas Press.

Strommenger, E. (1964). *5000 years of the art of Mesopotamia.* New York: Harry N. Abrams.

Van Buren, E. D. (1939-1941). Religious rites and ritual in the time of Uruk IV-III. *Archiv für Orientforschung 13.*

11 DID PICASSO AND DA VINCI, NEWTON AND EINSTEIN, THE BUSHMAN AND THE ENGLISHMAN SEE THE SAME THING WHEN THEY FACED THE EAST AT DAWN?

OR, SOME LESSONS I LEARNED FROM MARSHALL McLUHAN ABOUT PERCEPTION, TIME, SPACE, AND THE ORDER OF THE WORLD

Edward Wachtel

Fordham University

Perhaps I should begin with the second half of my lengthy title. From Marshall McLuhan, I learned three things about perception, space/time, and the order of the world. First, he taught me that technological environments can influence our perceptual approach to the world. Second, I learned that when our perceptual approaches vary, the forms of space and time that we "see" also vary. Third, McLuhan taught me that every culture encodes its own view of space/time in its paintings and drawings. From these lessons, I was able to conclude that Picasso and da Vinci, Newton and Einstein, the Bushman and the Englishman had different conceptions of time and space. So, when they faced the East at dawn, they each saw very different things.

For the purposes of this chapter, I limit myself to a brief exploration of two space conceptions separated by 15,000 years. The first is evidenced by the painted caves of Paleolithic Europe. The second space conception was made visible on the walls and canvases of Renaissance Europe. If you permit me a slight modification of my title, I will change it to: "Did the People of the Paleolithic and the Residents of the Renaissance See the Same Thing When They Faced the East at Dawn?"

THE NATURE OF SPACE/TIME

Albert Einstein once said that "the normal adult never bothers his head about space-time problems" (Seelig, 1954, p. 71). Nonetheless, to develop my thesis, I must ask you to so inconvenience yourselves. As adults raised in Western cultures, we generally think and speak as if we could "see" space and "feel" time. Along with Isaac Newton, we think of space as a kind of empty container in which we can put things. We may speak of a room containing a certain number of cubic feet of space, and in turn we think of ourselves as "occupying" the space in that room.

We think of time as a linear flow that we can feel, and that carries the room from the past, through an instant we call the present, into the future. For example, if you are bored, you may look at your watch and wonder why time *feels* like it's going so slowly. We also think of space and time as having a fixed existence in the world outside ourselves. We are wrong on all three counts.

As Emmanuel Kant (1781/1965) demonstrated in 1781, time and space are only categories of the mind. In 1916, Albert Einstein concurred. He said, "space-time does not claim existence on its own, but only as a structural quality of the field" (Einstein, 1916/1961, p. 155).

I might summarize these points by saying that space/time is a conceptual framework that we impose on the world to structure it.

DEVELOPMENT OF SPACE/TIME CONCEPTION

How do we learn or develop a space/time conception? Jean Piaget described the long journey from the blooming confusion of infancy to a mature, visual world of stable spatiotemporal relations. Surprisingly, this development may take more than 14 years. Piaget emphasized that we build our conceptions through the interplay of sensory and motor apparati (Piaget & Inhelder, 1948/1967). In other words, we learn the world by seeing and touching; by seeing and moving; not by visual perception alone.

Although Piaget stressed the necessity for environmental interaction in the development of space/time conception, he never asked whether different environments might generate different conceptions over time or across cultures. However, Marshall McLuhan did. He decided that different technological environments led to distinct conceptions of space/time which he referred to as *visual, acoustic,* and *tactile-muscular* spaces (McLuhan, 1962; McLuhan & Parker, 1968).

The final lesson I learned from McLuhan was how to read space/time conceptions from styles of representation. This lesson was supplemented by the works of S. Giedion (1960, 1962, 1971), Ernst Gombrich (1960), Erwin Panofsky (1927/1991), and John White (1967). My own contribution is limited to a new focus on the temporal dimension in the representation of time and space (Wachtel, 1985, 1995).

TIME AND MOTION IN PAINTING

From Paleolithic times to the present, all painters have been challenged by a fundamental problem: how to express the four dimensions of experience on a two-dimensional surface. Most of us have considered this problem with regard to the third dimension—depth. Less often, do we attend to the struggle to represent the fourth dimension—time. All human experience involves a temporal dimension. The things we experience change and move. They have duration. We change and move: we shift focus, we walk around objects, we rotate them. In short, we experience the world *in time*.

Painters have dealt with time, motion, and change in a number of ways. In any painting, we can see the perceptual stance that the painter took and that the viewer must take. By analyzing the perceptual approach, we can describe how the artist has integrated time and space. And by extension, we can see the space/time conception of their cultures. Figure 11.1 is an example of how to see a perceptual stance and its implications for time and space.

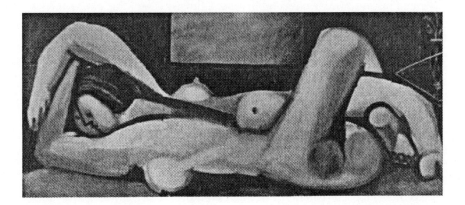

Figure 11.1   Pablo Piccasso, sketch of reclining nude.
Provence Unknown.

Please note the interesting spatiotemporal arrangements in this figure. Picasso has painted his model with one breast facing upwards and one down toward the bed. Her face is "split" in a way reminiscent of Picasso's earlier, Cubist works. We are shown much of her torso in a side view, yet her buttocks are displayed frontally.

How are we to understand these features as a perceptual approach or stance? When Picasso looked at his model, either he moved around her to see these features at different times, or she moved to display herself from different angles. The time that is represented is the time it takes for the model to move or for the viewer to move and see. There are obvious spatial implications: three dimensionality is reduced or entirely flattened and our ability to fix objects in a spatial relationship to each other is lost. I would characterize this space conception as one which has some integration of space and time.

More than 1,000 generations ago, in Paleolithic France and Spain, cave painters used other methods to represent space and time. It is time to turn to these methods.

I must point out that because of electric lights and still photography, cave paintings have been misrepresented for the past century. I must continue this misrepresentation, because I have only still photographs to illustrate my points. Nevertheless, I show some images, point out certain characteristics and try to indicate how they were viewed 20,000 years ago, and how they should be seen today.

In Fig. 11.2, the image of a bull with a deer superimposed over it from Lascaux, you may note a common type of transparency found in many caves: an overlapping of images that we might expect to be represented in separate spaces, with outlines more distinct. I refer to this form of overlap as a *figure* transparency.

In addition to superimposing distinct animals, Paleolithic cave painters regularly engraved curled and straight lines over their creatures. This type of transparency is visible in Figs. 11.3a and b, from the cave at Peche-Merle. It represents a stag "hidden" by incised lines. In this case, the figure—the stag—is superimposed with lines that seem to serve only as a ground for the figure. I refer to this form of superimposition as a *figure/ground* transparency. (The sketch should help to clarify the image).

In a number of caves, there are pictures of creatures with "extra" body parts. In Les Combarelles there is an image of a mammoth with multiple trunks. In other caves there are animals with extra legs. In Fig. 11.4a and b, from the cave at Pair-non-pair, you will see an animal—probably an ibex—with two heads.

To these characteristics, I must add two more: A lack of vertical or horizontal orientation and a tendency for creatures to be incompletely represented (only heads, antlers, etc.). How are we to make sense of these unique characteristics?

To understand them, we must imagine that we are moving, that the only light source is a flickering lamp or candle and that the images are painted on unpredictable rock surfaces. If your imaginations are sufficient, you will not see fixed, still images with the characteristics I have indicated but rather, moving, changing imagery. In Fig. 11.2, you will witness a bull disappear and a deer take its place (and vice versa). In Fig. 11.3, you will see a stag appear suddenly, as if a small movement of its head or body gives over its outline from the camouflage of woods or tall grass. Compare Fig. 11.3 with the photograph of a deer standing in tall grass, (Fig. 11.5). In Fig. 11.4, you will not see an ibex with two heads, but the narrative movement of an ibex lifting its head from a grazing position to a vigilant stance.

The ancient artists who made these images had the tools of a painter, but the eyes of a cinematographer. They made movies by utilizing the irregular surfaces of the caves (Fig. 11.6), a light source that moves and flickers (Fig. 11.7), and a moving eye. The images are painted and etched under these circumstances so that they are visible from some viewpoints and not from others. (See Wachtel, 1993, for a more detailed discussion of the cinematic aspects of cave painting.)

Figure 11.2   Lascaux, Axial Gallery, Magdalenian bull with superimposed deer.
Giedion, S., *The Eternal Present*. Copyright ©1962, renewed, 1990 by Princeton University Press. Reprinted by permission of Princeton University Press.

Figure 11.3a   Peche Merle, Clay drawing of a Stag "hidden" under lines.
Giedion, S., *The Eternal Present*. Copyright ©1962, renewed, 1990 by Princeton University Press. Reprinted by permission of Princeton University Press.

Figure 11.3b   Sketch of Peche Merle stag.
Sketch by Nancy Ventura.

Figure 11.4a   Pair-non-Pair, An ibex with two heads. In flickering
               lamplight, the ibex will appear to shift from a grazing
               position (head down), to a vigilant stance (head up).
               Giedion, S., *The Eternal Present.* Copyright ©1962, renewed, 1990 by
               Princeton University Press. Reprinted by permission of Princeton
               University Press.

Figure 11.4b   Sketch of Pair-non-Pair ibex.
               Sketch by Nancy Ventura.

Figure 11.5   Deer hidden
in tall grass. Compare
with Figure 11.3. A move-
ment of its ear or tail
would betray the deer's
presence to a hunter.
Photograph by the author.

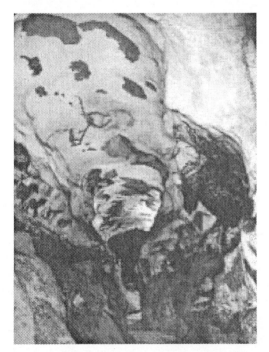

Figure 11.6   Lascaux, The
Axial Gallery. The caves
are not architecture. Even
unpainted surfaces seem
to change and move in a
flickering lamp light.
Fernand Windels, *The Lascaux
Cave Paintings*. London: Faber
and Faber, 1949. Every effort has
been made to trace the copyright
holders.

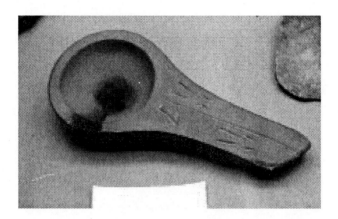

**Figure 11.7   Reproduction of a lamp used at Lascaux. The "projection
bulb" of prehistory. The concave end was filled with
animal fat. Either moss or fur was used as a wick.**
Le Musée National de la Prehistoire des Eyzies. Photograph by author.

In the Picasso sketch we viewed earlier, time is *represented* by the technique of multiple viewpoints. In cave painting, time is *included* in the viewing experience in a way that approximates the cinema.

In the 15th century, a radically different way of seeing is re-invented in
Italy. In painting, the technique is called perspective. In a perspective picture, time is reduced to a theoretical instant. That is to say, time is separated
from space and excluded from vision.

Figure 11.8 is an example of perspective construction.

In Raphael's *The Marriage of the Virgin*, the parallel lines of the plaza all
meet at the vanishing point. Raphael was kind enough to paint an open door-
way in the dome so we can see the horizon where they meet. You should be
able to feel how this construction forces you to view the image from one
fixed place. (If not, try any Renaissance picture with strong perspective lines
in an art book, or better, in a museum). Further, "correct" viewing demands
that only a single eye be used. By fixing the viewing conditions in this way,
perspective representation freezes all movement between the beholder and
the subject. Time is reduced to a theoretical instant, and the remaining three
dimensions of existence are envisioned as a rigid box of space.

The technology most responsible for the development of perspective is
the transparent glass window. Because of time limitations I can only assert
that transparent glass was invented in Rome, lost for a millennium and rein-
vented by the Venetians, probably in the 13th century. Perspective in painting also appears twice: following the discovery and rediscovery of clear

**Figure 11.8   Detail from Raphael Santi, Marriage of the Virgin
(ca. 1505).** Brera, Milan.

glass. (See Wachtel, 1978, 1995, for more on the history of glass and the development of perspective.) The logic of the relationship was well-understood by Renaissance painters. For example, early in the 16th century, Albrecht Dürer made this print to demonstrate how to construct the world using perspective.

This print (Fig. 11.9) demonstrates all the elements of perspective seeing. The single, fixed viewing eye, the equally fixed subject, and the transparent picture plane that locks them together. The best way to grasp these relationships is to try it yourself. If you trace the scene outside your window

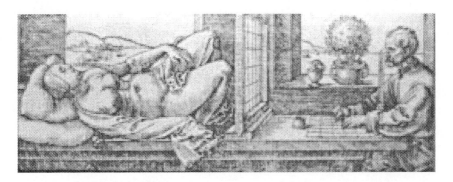

**Figure 11.9   Albrecht Dürer, Draughtsman Drawing a Reclining
Nude. Woodcut (ca. 1527).**

onto the window, you will make a perfect perspective representation. You will also discover that, to keep the correspondence of traced lines to the outside reality, you will be forced to use one eye in a fixed position.

SPACE CONCEPTION AND COMMON SENSE

The space conception that results from perspective has implications that go far beyond the realm of art. I suggest that the window, and the picture of space and time it presents, may also have influenced the sciences.

In 1686, Sir Isaac Newton published the *Principia*, his mathematical system of the physical world. His system explained the motion of bodies in space, and used a mathematics of time, called the fluxions or calculus. From the viewpoint of 20th-century hindsight, we know that his system was flawed. The fundamental flaw was not essentially mathematical, but conceptual. Newton's bodies moved in a space that was three-dimensional and absolute. His calculus described a time that was linear, separate from space, unchangeable and sliceable into theoretical instants. In short, Newton did not describe reality, but a particular, and it so happens, incorrect picture of reality. Where did this picture come from? I submit that the complete separation of space and time that provided the foundation of the mechanical world view had been painted on canvases and cathedrals since the 15th century. By Newton's time, this view of existence had penetrated to the deepest levels of Western consciousness. That is to say, it had become common sense.

In 1962, Marshall McLuhan called Newtonian visual space an "absurdity, . . . a mere abstract illusion severed from the sense of touch" (p. 26). He was joined in this criticism by Rene Magritte, who made the point visually.

Observe how, in Fig. 11.10, Magritte establishes the identity of the window view and the canvas by having them melt into one another. Next, he makes fun of the space that results from this mode of perception. He called the picture "The Promenades of Euclid." Note the plural. He is telling us that the space created by this way of seeing is a fiction and an absurdity. It is a space so preposterous that the upright spire in the foreground has the same form as the road that leads us back to the vanishing point. Both the spire and the road are the promenades of Euclid. The space and time they inhabit are the space and time the West has inhabited since the invention of the window.

If the art of the 20th century was predictive, as McLuhan believed, our common sense may be changing once again; to a sense that time and space are integrated, to a belief that causes and effects are not distinct, to a history that is less linear and more mythic. Perhaps toward a common sense that has more in common with Paleolithic times than with the past 500 years.

Figure 11.10   René Magritte, The Promenades of Euclid (1955).
Minneapolis Institute of Art. The William Hood Dunwoody Fund.

REFERENCES

Einstein, A. (1961). *Relativity: The special and general theory* (R. Lawson, Trans.). New York: Crown Publishers. (Original work published 1916)

Giedion, S. (1960). Space conception in prehistoric art. In E. Carpenter & M. McLuhan (Eds.), *Explorations in communication* (pp. 71-89). Boston, MA: Beacon Press.

Giedion, S. (1962). *The eternal present: The beginnings of art*. New York: Bollingen Foundation/Pantheon Books.

Giedion, S. (1971). *Architecture and the phenomenon of transition: The three space conceptions in architecture*. Cambridge, MA: Harvard University Press

Gombrich, E. (1960). *Art and illusion*. New York: Pantheon Books.

Kant, I. (1965). *Critique of pure reason* (N. Smith, Trans.). New York: St. Martin's Press. (Original work published 1781)

McLuhan, M. (1962). *The Gutenberg galaxy: The making of typographic man*. Toronto: University of Toronto Press.

McLuhan, M., & Parker, H. (1968). *Through the vanishing point: Space in poetry and painting*. New York: Harper & Row.

Panofsky, E. (1991). *Perspective as symbolic form* (C. S. Wood, Trans.). New York: Zone Books. (Original work published 1927)

Piaget, J., & Inhelder, B. (1967). *The child's conception of space* (F. Langdon & J. Lunzer, Trans.). New York: W.W. Norton. (Original work published 1948)

Seelig, K. (1954). *Albert Einstein*. Zurich, Switzerland: Europa Verlag.

Wachtel, E. (1978). The influence of the window on Western art and vision. *The Structurist, 17/18*, 4-11.

Wachtel, E. (1985). The impact of television on space conception. In S. Thomas (Ed.), *Studies in mass communication and technology* (pp. 168-174). Norwood, NJ: Ablex.

Wachtel, E. (1993). The first picture show: Cinematic aspects of cave art. *Leonardo, Journal of the International Society for the Arts, Sciences and Technology, 26*(2), 135-140.

Wachtel, E. (1995). To an eye in a fixed position: Glass, art and vision. In J. Pitt (Ed.), *New directions in the philosophy of technology* (pp. 41-61). Dordrecht, Netherlands: Kluwer Academic.

White, J. (1967). *The birth and rebirth of pictorial space*. Boston: Boston Book and Art Shop.

12 McLUHAN AND EARTHSCORE

Paul Ryan
New School,
New York, NY

In the summer of 1965 I was living in a garret on the Lower East Side of New York City pounding a typewriter. I defined myself as a writer. Midway through the summer, I tuned in WBAI's radio coverage of the International Writer Conference. The first thing I heard was this guy saying "Of course, in this age of radio, television, computers and satellites, the writer can no longer be someone sitting in his garret pounding a typewriter." It was McLuhan. His talk brought my linear sequential writing to a dead stop. For the next 3 months I could hardly read or write. Then I read *Understanding Media* (McLuhan, 1964), *Gutenberg Galaxy* (McLuhan, 1962), and all of McLuhan's source material I could track down. I found my way to Fordham. John Culkin hired me as part of the team that worked with McLuhan at Fordham. With Culkin's support, this position fulfilled my obligation to do alternate service as a conscientious objector during the Vietnam War. When McLuhan returned to Canada, I stayed on at Fordham through the good offices of John Culkin and began experimenting with portable video equipment. Subsequently, I defined myself as a video artist and developed a formal approach to using video for the interpretation of ecological systems. I called this formal approach Earthscore. Since its development in video, Earthscore has had many nonvideo iterations in education, worker training and on the Internet. All of these iterations are efforts to bring human behavior into compliance with the ways of the Earth (see Earthscore.org). Given that Earthscore originated out of explorations with the video medium following McLuhan's insights, in this chapter I emphasize the video version of Earthscore.

Earthscore is a notational system analogous to classical music with its staff, bars, and notes. Just as with classical music notation, we can orchestrate different musical instruments into a symphony, so with Earthscore we can orchestrate different electronic media into "symphonies of knowledge" that support living on earth in a sustainable way. In a nutshell, the relationship between McLuhan and Earthscore can be put as follows: McLuhan offered us the insight that satellites make it possible to approach living on earth as a work of art (McLuhan, 1995). Earthscore encodes a notational system for realizing life on earth as a work of art.

According to McLuhan (1988), nature ended when the Russians launched the Sputnik satellite. In other words, "nature" had been the "ground" for human life on earth. Human ways of living constituted different "figures" set against the "ground" of nature. Now with satellite technology providing a new "ground" for perceiving the earth, we begin to see earth itself as a "figure." The figure of earth includes both nature and the human. Grounded in the new perception provided by satellites, we can approach the relationship between humans and nature as an interaction that humans could shape into a process work of art. Earthscore is a formal approach to guiding that process (Ryan, 1993).

Against the background of McLuhan's insight about satellites, characterizing Earthscore as a notational system for a process of art relating nature and culture works well enough as a brief description. But to understand, in depth, the relation between McLuhan and Earthscore we must move from this nutshell description to the tree that nurtured the nutshell. That tree is Christianity. As scholar Walter Burkert (1996) argues, mediation between nature and human culture is a function of religion. To appreciate the critical differences between McLuhan and Earthscore, we must discuss religion.

Biographer Terrence Gordon (1997) makes clear that Marshall McLuhan grounded the singularity of his insights in the systemic of the Catholic religion. The "figure" of "McLuhan" was "grounded" in the practices of Catholicism. He was a convert, a daily communicant and a reader of Scripture.[1] McLuhan's critique of electronic man as "discarnate" man, was grounded in the doctrine of the Incarnation of Christ (Gordon, 1997).

---

[1] When I asked the liberal critic Conor Cruise O'Brien about McLuhan, O'Brien wanted to know when McLuhan converted to Catholicism. As an Irishman, O'Brien himself had struggled with Catholicism (see O'Brien, 1963). When I told him McLuhan converted in 1937, O'Brien said "Spanish Civil War. Not a good year to convert. What did Yeats say,

> "I never bade you go
> To Moscow or to Rome,
> Call the Druids home."

Although Catholicism helped ground Marshall McLuhan's critique of the electronic culture, Catholicism does not offer an operating system for living in electronic culture. The reason is that Catholicism teaches a central Christian doctrine of incarnation which balances transcendence and immanence. An immanent understanding of mind makes sense in a world connected by circuits, but Christian transcendence and electronic circuitry go together like oil and water. Christianity's understanding of God as transcendent came from the Old Testament. In that Testament, there were two distinct tiers. The immanent seeable physical plane populated by humans and the transcendent unseeable plane occupied by God. God was apart, separate and He could be completely indifferent to the human plane (Scarry, 1985). Humans knew the transcendent tier only by words spoken through holy men who offered the "Word" of God. Then, in the New Testament story of Christ, the Word that was God became flesh and dwelt among us. The transcendent and the immanent were fused in the person of Christ.

As a sophisticated convert influenced at Cambridge by G.K. Chesterton, McLuhan's relationship to Catholicism was complex in a way that I do not think any commentator has yet made entirely clear. Although the conservative McLuhan did not respond politically to the Spanish Civil War, he did keep a rendering of Picasso's Guernica on the wall in his Toronto home (T. McLuhan, personal communication, 1998) For a current articulation of the relationship between orality and liturgy in the radical orthodoxy of Christianity that I associate with McLuhan, see Pickstock (1998), a current teacher at McLuhan's Cambridge. This extraordinary book deals with Plato, Derrida, Scotus, Ramus, Descartes and the Roman Eucharistic Ritual (see also McLuhan, 1999).

Regarding McLuhan's radical orthodoxy consider the following remark:

> Let me make a little note here about the church and literacy. Alphabetic man is the only one who every tried to transform other cultures into his own. Oral societies never tried to convert anybody. The early church began with a liaison with the Graeco-Roman and the alphabetic. Ever since, the church has made inseparable the propagation of the faith and Graeco-Roman culture. Thus ensuring that only a tiny segment of mankind would ever be Christian. Would it appear to you, now that literacy is technologically expendable, that the church can also dispense with Graeco-Roman forms of literacy and hierarchy? I have been able to find no ecclesiastic or theologian for whom this is a meaningful question. (cited in Gordon, 1997, p. 224)

In response to a query whether McLuhan was grounded in the Scripture, McLuhan suggested that his ground was not Scripture but that he had been pursuing phenomenology for years in a nontechnical manner (Gordon, 1997, pp. 312-313).

In contrast to O'Brien's response, when I asked George Steiner about McLuhan, he called him a genius, urged me to go study with him and offered to take a personal letter from me to McLuhan on his trip to Toronto.

Chri anity's balancing of transcendence and immanence on the back of this God/Man worked well enough in Western Culture as long as language (i.e., "the Word") dominated consciousness. But this balance has been upset by electronic technology. The flood of events streaming into our nervous systems via electricity, from music to televised funerals, cannot be adequately processed in the syntax of a language sourced in transcendence.[2]

Electronic technology is all built from circuitry. Based on the formal study of circuits known as *cybernetic theory*, Gregory Bateson (1972/2000), a member of the original cybernetic group, concludes that "We now know, with considerable certainty, that the ancient problem of whether the mind is immanent or transcendent can be answered in favor of immanence" (p. 315, see also pp. 467-473). Bateson argues that the basic unit of mind is a circuit of differences that make differences immanent in the processes of life. Take the example of a blind man walking with a cane. Cybernetically, the blind man walking with a cane is understood as a self-correcting process. Differences in the ground make differences in the cane. Differences in the cane make differences in his arm, which, in turn, make differences in his body in where he steps next and differences in where he puts the cane next. Differences in where he puts the cane next record differences in the ground and so on round the circuit. Any break in the route of reference around the circuit jeopardizes the operational effectiveness of the circuit. If you take away the blind man's cane, he will have difficulty walking.

Our understanding of transcendence relies on metaphors, not circuits. Metaphor depends on the possibility of breaking the circuit of reference in order to set up understanding by analogy. This is a critical difference. Metaphors are figures of speech that express something by analogy with something else. By analogy, the blind man can be taken to mean a person who is not living in the state of grace. The song "Amazing Grace" uses this metaphor in the line "Was blind, but now, I see." The difference between unsighted and sighted corresponds to the difference between ungraced and graced. The objective of metaphoric thinking is to understand the state of grace by looking at blindness. The objective of cybernetic thinking is to keep the blind man walking. Cybernetic thinking is best conveyed in diagrams. Metaphoric thinking is best conveyed in language. Diagrams are not suited to convey metaphors. Language is not especially suited to convey cybernetic thinking. In using language to discuss circuits, it is possible however, using metaphor, to invite someone to think cybernetically.

---

[2]In this chapter, my use of the word *transcendent* is specific to Christian theology and not meant to include the range of authentic human experience beyond ordinary limits that many people testify to in their own lives, even if that experience is explained by the participants in terms provided by Christian theology.

Given this difference between immanent circuit and transcending metaphor, we can begin to see why a Christianity that has held immanence and transcendence in creative tension for so long cannot effectively mediate between nature and culture in the electronic age. Ongoing self-correction of the balance between nature and culture requires an operative understanding of the circuitry immanent in both nature and culture as well as an understanding of the pattern of circuitry that connects nature and culture. Transcendent metaphoric religious thinking cannot provide this understanding because it locates the pattern that connects on a separate tier, in an all knowing entity. I will return to this issue of transcendence and immanence.

EARTHSCORE AND ECOLOGY

The biologist C.H. Waddington (1970) reasoned as follows. As a species, we humans transmit information over generations in two ways. One is biologically through genetics. The other is through speech and writing. Speech and writing inevitably involve authority structures. Someone telling someone else what to do. "Look at me when I talk to you." "Do as I tell you." The developing integrity of a child's perceptual system is stunted and brought under the language commands of others. Inspired by the example of painters who had sweated blood to see nature without language, such as Cezanne and Monet, Waddington argued that it may be possible to institutionalize this effort and develop an information transmission system married to environmental realities, not to speech and writing. Inspired by McLuhan, I undertook an extensive exploration of video perception as an artist. Based on this exploration, I was able to codify a formal notational system for realizing an information transmission system based on shared perception of environmental realities along the lines posited by Waddington. Using this notation I was able to design a television channel dedicated to monitoring the ecology of a bioregion and, based on that shared perception, to develop a consensus about sustainable policies and practices (Ryan, 1993).

This notation system has five components:

1. Three comprehensive categories of knowledge.
2. A relational circuit to organize these categories.
3. A relational practice called *Threeing.*
4. A family of models for understanding the patterns of nature.
5. A way of interpreting these patterns for any community in terms of sustainability.

I now compare each of these five components of Earthscore with McLuhan's work. This is a delicate maneuver, so let me be clear that the concerns behind Earthscore and the concerns that motivated McLuhan are, I believe, part and parcel with each other. The concerns have to do with generating viable electronic cultures. McLuhan approached these concerns by using the rhetorical devices of oral culture to probe electronic culture. By contrast, Earthscore grows directly out of 25 years of experimentation with the video medium. The medium being the message, it is not surprising that working with different media would result in different structures of thought. Hopefully, this comparison will illuminate both structures of thought and advance the shared concern.

The first comparison is in terms of comprehensive categories. McLuhan's probing of everything is based on acoustic space and Thomistic philosophy. Earthscore's theory of everything is based on the phenomenology of philosopher, Charles Peirce.

McLuhan's approach to everything built out from a sphere of understanding created by acoustic space. He understood acoustic space as total, inclusive and involving. His own mind could be understood as a rich resonant chamber of commonplaces.[3] As a video artist, I approached whatever I was recording without script. When you go out with a video camera without a script, you are confronted with everything. To make sense out of everything, you need a theory of everything. After more than 20 years of working with video, I realized that an appropriate theory of everything could be found in the three comprehensive phenomenological categories of the American philosopher Charles Peirce (Apel, 1981). Technically, these categories are called *firstness, secondness,* and *thirdness.* In nontechnical terms, they refer to *quality, fact,* and *pattern.* Peirce argued that all phenomena present themselves in these three irreducible categories. In Earthscore, these three categories are the basis for the nonverbal perception of the environment.

Philosophically speaking, McLuhan was a self-proclaimed Aristotelian Thomist (Gordon, 1997). Thomism sees everything in terms of form and

---

[3]McLuhan was not afraid to consider anything and offered an approach to everything. I can remember at lunch him writing down a Thai word for "moving like a snake" mentioned by a former Peace Corp volunteer and telling everybody to write down anything that struck them. While at Fordham, when I wanted to know what McLuhan thought of something, I would ask a question. Sometimes the answer I got on the spot was an answer to a question asked by somebody else 2 weeks before. So I would listen for my answer to arise during a lecture on a 2-week delay. Usually, I would hear a brilliant relevant insight. He could connect anything with anything. However, I had to wait until it was processed through the richness of his chamber of commonplaces.

matter. Form and matter were meat and potatoes for McLuhan. For Peirce, the dyad of form and matter were not enough. This dyad was linked to an Aristotelian logic of classification that the West had exhausted. Peirce went after a logic of relationships, not of classes. He saw a logic of relationships as inherently triadic. McLuhan saw form and matter and the gap between as a gap that invited metaphor. Peirce saw the gap as filled by the "thisness" of Duns Scotus. Instead of the form–matter dyad, Peirce saw a threefold continuum of possibility, actuality, and formality. This continuum invites relational thinking without words. Where McLuhan would codify his percepts in language, Peirce's system allows for codifying percepts without language.

The second comparison is between what I call McLuhan's "metaphor that is meant" and the nonmetaphoric relational circuit. The "medium is the message" is a dictum that denies differences in a way that generates transcendence. The relational circuit is a sign of itself that organizes differences in a way that cultivates immanence.

The codification of McLuhan's famous teaching, "the medium is the message" is identical in structure to the way the Catholic Church codifies its teaching that the consecrated bread *is* the body of Christ and the consecrated wine *is* the blood of Christ. This isomorphic codification, this parallel in the structure of assertion without qualification, invites comparison. In the sacramental system that grounded McLuhan, this is a serious doctrine. For a Catholic, the Eucharist is where, colloquially speaking, "the rubber meets the road." The word of the priest makes the bread into the body of Christ. This is not symbolic, this is real. This is the critical point where Catholicism fuses a metaphoric understanding of a transcendence God with the immanent reality of a piece of bread. The fusion requires faith, belief without evidence. This is the metaphor that is meant. The metaphor short circuits perception. The authority of the word is blatantly asserted over the perceptual system. You cannot see the body of Christ, you see bread. Yet you must suppress your perceptions. You must believe the bread is the body of Christ. You must believe that there has been a "transubstantiation" which you cannot see. Once you believe what you cannot see, multiple meanings are unfolded in a sacramental context. This host of bread is the bread of angels. Christ so loved us that he gave himself to us as food and so on.

Within the peculiar alchemy of McLuhan's unconscious genius, within the "smythe of his soul," I think it is possible to see the "the medium is the message": and the multiple meanings he gave to this dictum (i.e., "massage," "mess-age") as a transformation of this sacramental coding process into a code of playful secular probes. The probes were unseriously serious. Just as the sacramental coding process suppresses the testimony of the senses to highlight the authority of the word, just so McLuhan himself tells us "the medium is the message" suppresses content in order to highlight the effects of technologies (Gordon, 1997).

When you suppress perception and highlight the word, you privilege language. As linguist Derek Bickerton (1990) argues, language is inherently hierarchic. Hierarchies built on the authority of language engender transcendent thinking as a way of offsetting the suppression of perceptions required by language itself. The Christians who came to North America interpreted what they saw as the land promised in Holy Scripture and failed to perceive the actual ways in which the land worked. Only now are we moving away from a kind of transcendental Christian tourism destructive to this continent and learning to live in terms of the actual ecological systems that support our lives here.

By contrast, the relational circuit does not work hierarchically. Let me offer a mundane schoolyard example to explain how the relational circuit organizes relationships without hierarchy. In a hierarchy, the biggest boy pushes the next biggest boy. The next biggest boy pushes the littlest boy. The littlest boy dare not come around and shove the biggest boy. He cannot loop back and complete the circuit of relationships. Rather, he might go out and kick a rock or scribble curses on the school building. By contrast take the child's game paper-rock-scissors. Three children, regardless of size, throw out a hand that indicates paper, (flat) rock (fist) or scissors (two spread fingers). The three children then playfully slap each other wrists according to the formula: paper covers rock, rock breaks scissors, scissors cuts paper. This organization of differences is immanent in the circuit of relationships among the children and does not engender transcendence but an immanent use of the mind. Without going into details, the relational circuit works in a similar way.[4] Just as the game of paper-rock-scissors references only itself, so the relational circuit is a sign of itself (Ryan, 1993). As a sign of itself, the relational circuit can be explained without reference outside itself, without reference to a transcendent, nonperceptible entity. The relational circuit is an immanent unit of mind.

The third term of comparison deals with what McLuhan called "primitive emotions." In the face of retribalization by electronic technology, McLuhan saw the need to "restructure the primitive emotions." Earthscore restructures the primitive emotions through a relational practice called Threeing.

The phrase "restructure the primitive emotions" (McLuhan, 1968) can be taken in two different ways. It can mean restoring primitive emotions the way they once were before literacy, or it can mean taking our primitive emo-

---

[4]In the child's game, the children have no choice. They must act according to the formula paper covers rock, rock breaks scissors, scissors cuts paper. In the relational circuit there is no fixed formula. Rather it is like a Cezanne composing a painting using *his little blues, his little browns and his little whites.* He works without hierarchy or formula, he composes art. Threeing is an art of behavior.

tions and creating structures for them appropriate to electronic cultures. Earthscore interprets this phrase in the latter sense.

In keeping with McLuhan's understanding of the primitive, I think it fair to approach primitive emotions as they once were through the work of Rene Girard (1977), particularly as articulated in his book *Violence and the Sacred*. Recall that Girard describes how relational ambiguities within a group are resolved. Under the authority of a priest figure, the ambiguities of intratribal interaction are heaped on the head of the sacrificial victim. In the Old Testament, this scapegoat is cast out into the desert to die and the ambiguities of group identity are temporarily resolved. In the New Testament, the sacrificial victim is crucified and Christian Churches coalesce around ritually reenacting the sacrificial crucifixion.

Threeing is a relational practice that works for three people the way the practice of yoga works for an individual. Just as yoga stabilizes well being for a practitioner, so Threeing can stabilize relationships among three or more people. Threeing resolves the ambiguities of small group human interaction without recourse to a sacrificial victim. How? Normally when three people get together, two combine and exclude the third party. As bilateral symmetric humans, this pattern is normal. We cannot look in four eyes at once. To look at Jack, I must choose not to look at Jill. To relate to you, I must choose not to relate to someone else. Within a tribal group this experience of excluding and being excluded repeats itself over and again. When this repetition of events of exclusion within the group accumulates in such a way as to threatens the cohesion of the whole group, a scapegoat is identified so that everybody else, everybody not a scapegoat, can reinstate themselves as members of the group, members of the nonexcluded "in" crowd. Everybody takes on the guilt of excluding. The experience of suffering exclusion, of being left out, is temporarily healed.

Threeing is a pattern of interaction that neutralized the effect of choice on relationships. A participant never is forced to choose between Jack and Jill. Choices are made in terms of positions in an unambiguous figure outlined on the floor. The figure is the relational circuit. Threeing is a nonverbal interaction that uses the relational circuit to restructure the primitive emotions (Ryan, 1993). As we know from Walter Benjamin, ritual allows people to experience emotions in a crisis proof setting. Ritualized Threeing provides us with the opportunity to restructure the primitive emotions in nonexcluding patterns that do not require a sacrificial victim. Using the relational circuit, it is possible to organize differences among people in terms of the relationships themselves. Such ordering of differences would not be a unity arrived at by common reference to an excluded sacrificial victim encoded in a sacramental system. Rather, the reciprocal relationships among people can themselves become sacred (Ryan, 1998).

The fourth comparison has to do with understanding of natural patterns. McLuhan understood natural patterns by analogy. Earthscore understands natural patterns as "chreods."

In my work with video recording and playback, using time lapse and slow motion, I came to understand natural patterns in a nonverbal way. Think of time-lapse studies of budding flowers and slow-motion studies of insects. Watching these moving images, it is possible to understand the pattern presented in a single gestalt without rational inference using language. The moving image allows the natural event to occur in the mind like a fist in the hand. It is a wordless event. There is a spontaneous, intuitive appreciation of a pattern in nature. Peirce would call this "the firstness of thirdness." This intuitive appreciation of natural patterns through perception is the fourth component of the Earthscore Notational System. In Goethe's terms, it is an exercise of "exact imaginative sympathy."

As a formal codification for the intuition of pattern—the firstness of thirdness—Earthscore uses the family of qualitative models developed by topologist Rene Thom (1975) know as catastrophe theory. These models are called *chreods*, from the Greek. *Chre* meaning necessary and *ode* meaning path. Nature is understood as an ensemble of recurring events such as the falling of leaves, the migration of geese, the ebb and flow of the tides. These recurring events have a necessary structure that can be modeled by chreods. By careful observation using video we can gather an understanding of these event patterns, come to understand how they connect with each other and how we might relate to them on a sustainable basis.

The route of reference between chreods and McLuhan is by way of Gerard Manley Hopkins and his doctrine of inscape. I have often used inscape to explain chreods (Ryan 1993), but here I must distinguish between chreods embedded in video as a nonverbal event and inscape as Hopkins used that doctrine in his poetry. This distinction, *mutatis mutandi,* also serves to differentiate between McLuhan's use of analogy and Earthscore's use of chreods.

In his reading of the Hopkins poem, "Windhover," McLuhan (1945) explicates how Hopkins works with analogical mirrors on three levels. Nature is mirrored in Christ and Christ mirrors the glory of God. Nature has "forged features" such as veins of a violet or the "roped" sides of a mountain. These are the features that can be observed with a video camera, embedded on tape and modeled using the chreods provided by catastrophe theory. As McLuhan says, Hopkins lays no claim to any perception of natural facts hidden from ordinary men. But in his sacramental view of the world Hopkins finds in nature an analogical mirror of Christ. Hopkins then works his way through the poem to a theme of imitating Christ in humble obedience to God, which gives beauty back to God through the mirror of man's moral life.

Earthscore does not move into this sacramental realm. Rather the chreod is embedded in the relational circuit, the topology of which is generated from a looped length of paper with a half twist called a moebius strip and not a mirror. This is a somewhat technical point, but an important one. When you attempt to shake hands with yourself in a mirror, it will not work. The mirror returns a left hand for your right hand. If you set up a video camera atop a monitor and attempt to shake hands with yourself it will work. The monitor returns a right hand for your right hand. Video feedback operates along the continuum of a moebius strip and not in terms of discontinuous mirror reverses. The relational circuit is a transformation of the moebius strip into a six part continuous figure (Ryan, 1993). This figure, as I have argued, is an immanent relational circuit. This circuit organizes the Earthscore Notational System. Gathering and organizing chreods within the relational circuit makes it possible to interpret the patterns of nature without resorting to mirrors, analogy or transcendence.

For Earthscore, Thom's models are to electronics what Euclid's models were to paper. Electronics has to do with events. The ecology is seen as an ensemble of events and these events can be electronically monitored, modeled and understood using catastrophe theory.[5]

The fifth comparison has to do with how Nature is interpreted by and for different communities. McLuhan used the semiotics of Saussure. Earthscore uses the semiotics of Peirce.

Semiotics is the study of signs. Saussure gave us a dyadic semiotics based on language. As Terrence Gordon (1997) explains, this semiotics was very congenial for McLuhan and toward the end of his life McLuhan studied Saussure and made use of his insights. Although there is record of some familiarity with Peirce's more generic semiotics, there is no evidence that McLuhan took to Peirce's semiotics the way he took to Saussure. Peirce's triadic semiotics grows from his phenomenological categories and embraces both the verbal and the nonverbal in one system. The power of this system

---

[5]By way of connection to McLuhan let me report on a meeting I had with Rene Thom. Thom and I had a brief correspondence about an early version of the relational circuit and he invited me to a talk he was giving at Columbia University in 1970. During the course of our conversation, without knowing I had anything to do with McLuhan, he suddenly said "You know, I think McLuhan was right." It was as if his own mathematical musing about the patterns of nature made it possible for him to see each technology McLuhan talked about as having a different morphology, like different plants. The effects of each technology could be understood by reference to its unique "chreod" or necessary pattern. This suggests to me that maybe, just maybe, McLuhan's approach to media could be formalized beyond the laws of media by using the models developed by Thom. In the *Laws of Media* this approach becomes the reverse parallelism of thinking we call chiasmus (reprinted in McLuhan, 1995).

can be seen in Gilles Deleuze (1989-1989) successful effort to classify the whole of cinema according to Peirce's semiotics. This is the same semiotics proper to Earthscore, the semiotics I was able to employ in designing an environmental television channel (Ryan, 1993). Using this system it is possible to represent the earth for humans living on the earth so that they can understand how not to destroy the earth. Because it is grounded in perception, this representational process can, in principle, include any language family and be used to monitor any cultural effort to comply with the ways of the earth. The Earth and the human can become part of the same circuitry of sustainability. More than that, we could learn to interact with the natural world as if our life on earth were a sacred work of art.

REFERENCES

Apel, K.O. (1981). *Charles S. Peirce, from pragmatism to pragmaticism.* Amherst: University of Massachusetts.

Bateson, G. (2000). *Steps to an ecology of mind.* Chicago: University of Chicago Press. (Original work published 1972)

Bickerton, D. (1990). *Language and species.* Chicago: University of Chicago Press.

Burkert, W. (1996). *Creation of the sacred.* Cambridge, MA: Harvard University Press.

Deleuze, G. (1986-1989). *Cinema* (Vols. 1 & 2). Minneapolis: University of Minnesota Press.

Girard, R. (1977). *Violence and the sacred.* Baltimore, MD: Johns Hopkins University Press.

Gordon, T. (1997). *Marshall McLuhan, escape into understanding.* New York: Basic Books.

McLuhan, M. (1945). The analogical mirrors. In E. McNamara (Ed.), *The interior landscape: The literary criticism of Marshall McLuhan, 1943-62* (pp. 63-73). New York: McGraw Hill.

McLuhan, M. (1962). *Gutenberg galaxy.* Toronto: University of Toronto.

McLuhan, M. (1964). *Understanding media.* New York: McGraw Hill.

McLuhan, M. (1968). McLuhan Lectures, Fordham University, unpublished. (Quoted from memory, Paul Ryan).

McLuhan, M. (1988, Summer-Autumn). At the moment of Sputnik the planet became a global theatre in which there are no spectators but only actors. *The Antigonish Review, 74-75,* 78-81.

McLuhan, M. (1995). *Essential McLuhan* (E. McLuhan & F. Zingrone, Eds.). New York: Basic Books.

McLuhan, M. (1999). *The medium and the light: Reflections of religion* (E. McLuhan & J. Szklarek, Eds.). Toronto: Stoddart.

O'Brien, C. (1963). *Maria Cross.* Fresno, CA: Academy Guild Press.

Peirce, C.S. (1931-1935). *Collected papers* (Vols. I-VI; C. Harthshorne & P. Weiss, Eds.). Cambridge, MA: Harvard University Press.

Pickstock, C. (1998). *After writing.* Cambridge: Cambridge University Press.

Ryan, P. (1993). *Video mind, earth mind.* New York: Peter Lang.

Ryan, P. (1998). *Face-to-face in a wired world.* The Bateson Lecture, New School University, New York.

Scarry, E. (1985). *The body in pain.* New York: Oxford University Press.

Thom, R. (1975). *Structural stability and morphogenesis.* Reading, MA: Benjamin.

Waddington, C.H. (1970). *Behind appearances.* Cambridge: MA: MIT Press.

Willmott, G. (1996). *McLuhan, or modernism in reverse.* Toronto: University of Toronto Press.

SECTION IV

Letters and Laws

13 "INTEGRAL AWARENESS"

MARSHALL McLUHAN AS A MAN OF LETTERS

Elena Lamberti

University of Bologna

Knowledge is ultimately not a fractionating but a unifying phenomenon, a striving for harmony. Without harmony, an interior condition, the psyche is in bad health.

Walter J. Ong (1982, p. 72)

Not too long ago, strolling around the campus of the University of Toronto, it was possible to admire elegant blue banners displaying the faces of the "Great Minds for a Great University," namely, the celebrities who, at one time, had been either students or scholars of that Athenaeum. It is not surprising that Marshall McLuhan was among them. His image was accompanied by a caption: "Marshall McLuhan. Media Prophet and Faculty." My focus in this chapter is to underline, instead, that Marshall McLuhan's true legacy is in his writing, in his "oral literature." I take both his books and articles, as well as his work as editor of *Explorations* and *A Dew-Line* as fundamental staples toward the definition of a new "grammar" capable of uttering, and so give shape to, our own environment.

The "myth" of Marshall McLuhan has been built on the amplification of a single aspect, a central one in the 1960s. McLuhan has been considered the "pop-philosopher," the defender of the new electric media. Because he spoke of the end of printing, he was thought to be an adversary of the "Gutenberg Galaxy." Needless to say, such an oversimplification interferes with a more articulated approach to McLuhan's works, which are themselves established on a more complex ground: A complexity that is immediately admitted and recognized only by those readers who acknowledge first that McLuhan was well learned in the literary domain, and that he was first of all a professor of English. He was a professor who had deeply investigated the classics, the Thomistic tradition, as well as the Romantic and the Symbolist achievements; a professor who was so well aware of the later Modernist's formal experiments that, from time to time, he used such experiments to give shape to his own "formal frame" in a unique way at once combining, in sharp aphorisms, an ancient oral tradition and a modern artistic search.

An anthology of poetry for high schools (McLuhan & Schoeck, 1964/1965), "The Role of Thomas Nashe in the Learning of His Time" (McLuhan, 1943), "Preface" to H. Kenner's *Paradox in Chesterton* (McLuhan, 1948), "Pound, Eliot and the Rhetoric of *The Waste Land*" (McLuhan, 1978/1979), "Maritain on Art" (McLuhan, 1953b), "Poetic vs. Rhetorical Exegesis" (McLuhan, 1944c), "From Eliot to Seneca" (McLuhan, 1953a), "Kipling and Forster" (McLuhan, 1944b), "Edgar Poe's Tradition" (McLuhan, 1944a) are but a few titles of a long list of books and articles written by McLuhan, the professor of English; a list in itself proving, as Eugene McNamara (1969) wrote, that "literature has mattered to professor McLuhan. . . . Despite the wider range of awareness implicit in his probes of the impact of new media on our mode of perceptions, the angle of vision, the interior landscape, remains the same. It is basically humanistic . . . " (p. vi). Yet, even today, for the general public and for many academic scholars, mentioning McLuhan immediately triggers stereotyped images: the "high-priest of pop-cult," "the global village," and, of course, "the medium is the message," this last often used and abused as an all-fitting formula.

Actually, each of these images sounds more like a parched label than a vital icon, or a real image. As Pound (1959), put it, "an image is that which presents an intellectual and an emotional complex in an instant of time" (p. 4). On the contrary, they all look more and more like mere formulas stating a common law, a given truth that no one bothers (nor dares) to question. They seem to form a commonly shared heritage: In a word, they somehow have turned into commonplaces. Or, in "nonsensical mcluhanese," they have turned into figures without a ground. The problem is that these commonplaces have created a persisting, negative bias against McLuhan since the 1960s, especially in Europe, where the slogans often arrived before the original books were available in translated editions. These stereotypes have more and more been taken, not as a limit in approaching his ideas, but as a point of departure for all discussions about them. More than the direct reading of McLuhan's books, it was important to either subscribe to or reject those formulas, or, even worse, modify them in order to prove something different from what was originally intended. It sounds like an old story: from archetype to cliché, a sort of "one-way road" leading from original statements to empty commonplaces.

Moving from archetype to cliché is a common pattern of the postmodern electric age. Reducing something too complex into something more accessible and universally recognizable reassures us. It has always been like that. Not that this is a bad habit in itself; actually, sometimes it is a necessity. Reading what is still unknown, whether an object or a more abstract experience or a feeling, through something that is well known by means of language is a process enabling us to accomplish a fundamental *mimesis* which, as both Havelock (1963) and Ong (1982) argued, also performs a cohesive social function. Furthermore, many artists, either following or revising the teachings of Aristotle, have explored mimesis' heuristic potentialities. Nevertheless, if we are not well equipped for such a reading, our critical attitude can easily be turned into (or deceived by) commonly accepted ideas. This is how commonplaces—clichés—are born.

It is something that never occurred to McLuhan who, on the contrary, took much pleasure in challenging almost everything that was commonly and too easily accepted, or even "proven." He inverted the direction and constantly moved from cliché to archetype, carefully investigating linguistic patterns, so much so that his so-called slogans are, in fact, polysemantic aphorisms built on a precise and not a casual combination of words. He was a man of letters, or, more precisely, he was a grammarian,[1] well learned according to the ancient precepts of the trivium, and he intentionally used his knowledge as a probe for exploring a modern, fast-moving world. Yet, from the point of view of many of the specialists who were looking at the same world, but who shared a different knowledge, or more accurately, a different attitude toward knowledge, McLuhan made an explicit and unforgivable mistake: He crossed the borders of different domains without

---

[1]In his doctoral thesis, *The Place of Thomas Nashe in the Learning of His Time* (1943), McLuhan carries out a deep analysis of the development of the liberal arts of the trivium, from their origins up to the English Renaissance. In particular, he reevaluates the role and study of "grammar." He develops Marrou's (1938) idea according to which *"la culture chrétienne augustinienne, emprunte moins à la technique du rhéteur qu'è celle du grammairíen"* (p. 1). He clearly states that his "exposition of the history of the trivium is being made from a grammatical point of view," as "exposition and interpretation of stated doctrines are grammatical problems; and derivative philosophy and almost all histories of philosophy are the products of grammarians" (McLuhan, 1943, p. 49).

exhibiting the right passport. He turned upside-down what had been effectively established by centuries of serious schooling, suggesting new ways of
explorations based on the shocking association of apparently distant ideas
and topics. And, what was even worse, he seemed to enjoy it.

As the new electronic technologies were deeply modifying our man-
made environment, McLuhan intuited that it was time to change our perspective and our methods of observing the environment itself:

> When Sputnik went around the planet, nature disappeared, nature was
> hijacked right off the planet, nature was enclosed in a man-made envi-
> ronment and art took the place of nature. Planet became art form.
> (McLuhan & Wolfe, 1996)

Since his first book, *The Mechanical Bride. Folklore of the Industrial
Man,* McLuhan (1951) adopted the "method of art analysis to the critical
evaluation of society" (p. v). This was the strategy that he followed in order
to counterbalance the numbing process implicitly supported by some of
"the best-trained individual minds" of the present age (p. v). If it is true that
the "numbing process" is itself an unavoidable and, somehow, a natural side
effect of the sudden impact of a new medium in a previously established
environment, it is also true that "the mechanical agencies of the press, radio,
movies and advertising" use such a process to "manipulate, exploit, control"
their audience (McLuhan, 1951, p. v). Therefore, following the example of
Poe's mariner in the short story "A Descent into the Maelstrom" who
escapes death because he stops to observe the way the vortex works,
McLuhan probed for new strategies of observation and exploration capable
of revealing the side effects of new media. He started his explorations, constantly looking for the hidden "formal cause" behind the more evident
effects that, as he used to repeat, always precede the cause. He ventured into
a new territory passing the new electric frontier with an artist-like attitude,
exploring for objective correlatives to express the new experiences. He realized that, for most of his contemporaries, this meant that he would be perceived as "an outlaw, a shaman, a scapegoat." In fact, he behaved as an artist
challenging the given rules:

> The artist—he wrote—cannot be the prudent and decorous Ulysses, but
> appears as a sham. As sham and mime he undertakes not the ethical
> quest but the quest of the great fool. He must become all things in order
> to reveal all. And to be all things he must empty himself. (McLuhan,
> 1969, pp. 31-32)

Hence his all-embracing attitude toward his own environment, as well
as his attitude toward playful experimentation. Why? Because, as he point-

ed out, "at play man uses all his faculties; at work he specializes" (Nevitt & McLuhan, 1994, p. 34). As if saying that intuition, St. Thomas' *simplex apprehensio*, the first, pure, original and even irrational perception of a new idea, comes easier if we clear our minds from too specialist, *a priori* biases. Only afterward, men can start to reflect on this intuition through thought and reasoning, and thus move to the *reflexio ad phantasmata* phase. The final *giudizio*, the final conception, statement, or truth, is in fact shaped through this careful process of probing and testing of the first intuition by means of *fantasie*, hypotheses, and connected ideas expressed through words.

"Crossing of the boundaries" and "playfulness" are features that do not exactly belong to the serious scholar, to the serious specialist. The specialist him or herself is someone who, according to Marshall McLuhan, no longer has a place in the electric age. As he started to probe the new electric media, McLuhan realized that the new electronically configured environment can no longer be mastered by old mechanical ways of classification. The new acoustic space is "organic and integral, perceived through the simultaneous interplay of all the senses" and, therefore, must be approached simultaneously, "because the ear, unlike the eye, cannot be focused and is synaesthetic rather than analytical and linear" (McLuhan, 1969, p. 59). Gutenberg's fragmented man must be recomposed into a whole, because an integral approach to knowledge is required to face the new environment. The fact that both the sciences and the humanities were still reinforcing boundaries and subdivisions, simply demonstrated that people were still looking at their own environment through a rearview mirror. Again, something known and reassuring (the old environment) was being used in order to filter, if not to control, something that was still in progress (the new environment) and emerging.

McLuhan did not look at his own world through a rearview mirror. Being a grammarian, he was well equipped to read his own time and, being artistically inclined, he overtly took the risk of exploring new forms of reading. He had forged his antennas at the school of two other great grammarians, Francis Bacon and Giambattista Vico, and had sharpened them through the teachings of Joyce, Eliot, and Pound. "Practical criticism" at Cambridge had taught him how to relate text and context through a careful investigation of language. All this led him to develop an all-embracing way of looking at his time, which enabled him to clearly perceive the ongoing reversal of that process that, starting from the Middle Ages, had brought writing first, and then printing to control and even determine language and, inevitably, thought, as words are metaphors outering our inner world. He perceived the quick reversal of literacy into postliteracy, the new orality brought about by the electric media. It took several centuries to move from orality to literacy, but less than a century to shift into the age of instantaneous information. Hence, the difficulty many people have in facing, or acknowledging such a change because the general attitude is that of approaching the new acoustic world with a still deeply visual orientation. To counterbalance the shocking, numbing effects on the human psyche due to such a sudden change, McLuhan suggested the making of a counterenvironment based on art and higher education, where "higher education" means not a snobbish, classlike system of education, but a true "classic" one. In other words, he proposed to resurrect the Ancients to counterbalance the Moderns.

He did even more: He was bold enough to appoint the artist as the sole individual capable of alerting the audience because of his or her own multisensorial (neither visual, nor fragmented) way of approaching reality.

> The artist is the man in any field, scientific or humanistic, who grasps the implications of his actions and of new knowledge in his own time. He is the man of integral awareness. (McLuhan, 1964, p. 71)

In this very passage, McLuhan clearly proposes how to overcome at once the traditional dichotomy of C.P. Snow's two cultures, the sciences and the humanities: "integral awareness." Here, embedded in the artist image, is suggested an attitude profitable for all scholars, for men (and women), in any field. "Integral," that is, unifying *forma* and *substancia*, ground and figure, at once connecting all things and being all things, but also, at a deeper level, untouched, pure, entire, intact, as to suggest an unbiased, childlike attitude of approaching knowledge, displaying both curiosity and playfulness. "Awareness," that is, an alert condition common to everyone engaged in any form of investigation. Finally, the artist image, itself the symbol of a new *forma mentis*, based also on the use of imagination as a *pass-par-tout* attitude opening all doors leading to the discovery of the new dynamic environment. And, to paraphrase Blake, if the doors of perception were cleansed every thing would appear to man as it is, infinite.

Sir Peter B. Medawar (1972), a biologist who won the Nobel Prize for Medicine in 1960, wrote:

> Imagination is the energizing force of science as well as of poetry. . . . To adopt a conciliatory attitude, let us say that science is that form of poetry (going back now to its classical and more general sense) in which reason and imagination act together synergistically. This simple formal property . . . represents the most important methodological discovery of modern thought. (p. 25)

Here, Sir Peter Medawar himself retrieves the idea of a common ground for the sciences and humanities, based on the fact that reason and imagination forge both the poetical and the scientific perception. It is in the process of identification that the two fields seem to diverge. "We all tell stories," continues Medawar (1972), "but the stories differ in the purposes we expect them to fulfill and in the kinds of evaluations to which they are exposed" (p. 31). I. A. Richards (1970) spoke of "scientific truth or statement" and "poetical truth or pseudo-statement," asserting that the former needs always to be proved, whereas the latter is simply accepted for what it is. Yet, the mere use of the expression "statement" seems to suggest that there is a deeper and fundamental level at which reason and imagination, sciences and humanities, scientific truth and poetical truth meet: that is language ("We all tell stories," admits Sir Peter Medawar). Words are the most peculiar among the man-made artifacts, and language acts as the unifying factor, as the cognitive agent, the medium embracing all other media, themselves man-made artifacts:

> Words are complex systems of metaphors and symbols that translates experience into our uttered or outered senses. They are a technology of explicitness. By means of translation of immediate sense experience into vocal symbols, the entire world can be evoked and retrieved at any instant. (McLuhan, 1964, p. 64)

It's an idea McLuhan, the grammarian, retrieved from the ancient doctrine of the Logos, also known as the Doctrine of Names, which once provided the language for both physics and metaphysics, and that he, together with his son Eric, elaborated into a "New Science." In the McLuhans' "Summa Grammatica," or *Laws of Media: the New Science* (1988), their notion of the "tetrad" is deeply based on the Logos: In it and through it, the ancient whole is recomposed and the two souls, speech and reason are once more combined and allowed to retrieve their primordial gnoseological function.

The tetrad is presented as a linguistic "heuristic device" built on four questions: What does each medium, each human artifact enhance? What does it displace? What does it retrieve? Into what does it reverse if pushed to an extreme? Just like the metaphor, the tetrad provides the tool to approach and perceive the essence of our new, man-made environment; it works like an all-embracing, unifying verbal equation for reading and revealing the new art-form landscape.

> It makes no difference whatever whether one considers as artifacts or as media things of tangible "hardware" nature . . . or things of a "software" nature. . . . All are equally artifacts, all equally human, all equally susceptible to analysis, all equally verbal in structure. Laws of Media provides both the etymology and exegesis of these words: it may well turn out that the language they comprise has no syntax. So the accustomed

distinctions between arts and sciences and between things and ideas, between physics and metaphysics, are dissolved. (McLuhan & McLuhan, 1988, p. 3)

Language is the cognitive factor, it is the *arché* to which everything returns. That's why the so-called "nonsensical mcluhanese" is all but "nonsensical." The puns, the aphorisms, the paradoxes are acoustic, all-embracing warning alarms. As said earlier, they form a poetical prose built on a serious combination of different "liberal arts," because McLuhan was a grammarian, and was a man of letters. His *verbo-voco-visual* words attack us, warn and alert us, forcing us to respond, to counteract or, in other words, to be awake. Just like Joyce's language, McLuhan's language constantly plays with us and, unexpectedly, ends up troubling us. That's why we need it, and that's why I consider McLuhan's writing to be his greatest legacy, a sort of "memorabilia" for our electric age. It is through the Logos that we can learn to play with McLuhan. Truly.

ACKNOWLEDGMENT

I wish to thank David Sobelman who discussed with me many of the ideas here presented, providing a significant contribution to their development. I also wish to thank Professor Robert K. Logan for his enthusiasm and help in editing this chapter. *Noblesse oblige*: a special thanks is to be extended to Professor Eric McLuhan who has supported and helped me in my research on Marshall McLuhan and for patiently revising with me many of the ideas in this chapter.

REFERENCES

Havelock, E. A. (1963). *Preface to Plato.* Cambridge, MA: Harvard University Press.
Marrou, M. (1938). *Saint Augustine et la fin de la culture antique.* Paris: Editions E. de Boccard.
McLuhan, M. (1943). *The place of Thomas Nashe in the learning of his time.* Unpublished doctoral dissertation. Cambridge, MA: Harvard University.
McLuhan, M. (1944a, January). Edgar Poe's tradition. *Sewanee Review,* 24-33.
McLuhan, M. (1944b). Kipling and Forster. *Sewanee Review,* 52, 322-343.
McLuhan, M. (1944c). Poetic vs. rhetorical exegesis. *Sewanee Review,* 52, 266-276.
McLuhan, M. (1948). Introduction. In H. Kenner, *Paradox in Chesterton* (pp. xi-xxii). London: Sheet & Ward.
McLuhan, M. (1951). *The mechanical bride. Folklore of industrial man.* New York: Vanguard.

McLuhan, M. (1953a, January). From Eliot to Seneca. *University of Toronto Quarterly*, 199-202.

McLuhan, M. (1953b). Maritain on art. [Review of the book *Creative intuition in art and poetry*]. *Renascence, 6*(1), 40-44.

McLuhan, M. (1964). *Understanding media: The extensions of man*. New York: McGraw-Hill.

McLuhan, M. (1969). James Joyce: Trivial and quadrivial In E. McNamara (Ed.), *The interior landscape. The literary criticism of Marshall McLuhan, 1943-1962*. New York: McGraw-Hill.

McLuhan, M. (1969, March). Playboy interview: Marshall McLuhan. *Playboy*, pp. 53-74, 158.

McLuhan, M. (1978/1979). Pound, Eliot and the rhetoric of *The Waste Land*. *New Literary History: A Journal of Theory and Interpretation, X*, 557-580.

McLuhan, M., & McLuhan, E. (1988). *Laws of media: The new science*. Toronto: University of Toronto Press.

McLuhan, M., & Schoeck, R.J. (Eds.). (1964/1965). *Voices of literature* (Vols. 1-2). New York: Rinehart & Winston.

McLuhan, S. (Producer), & Wolfe, T. (Writer). (1996). *The video McLuhan* [Video]. (Available from Video McLuhan Inc., 73 Sighthill Avenue, Toronto, Ontario M4T 2H1 Canada)

McNamara, E. (Ed.). (1969). *The interior landscape. The literary criticism of Marshall McLuhan, 1943-1962*. New York: McGraw-Hill.

Medawar, P.B. (1972). *The hope of progress*. London: Methuen.

Nevitt, B., & McLuhan, M. (Eds.). (1994). *Who was Marshall McLuhan: Exploring a mosaic of impressions*. Toronto: Stoddart.

Ong, W.J. (1982). *Orality and literacy*. London: Methuen.

Pound, E. (1959). A few don'ts by an imagiste. In T.S. Eliot (Ed.), *Literary essays*. London: Faber.

Richards, I. A. (1970). *Poetries and sciences. A reissue of Science and Poetry (1926-1933)*. London: Routledge.

14 WHY WORLD HISTORY NEEDS McLUHAN

James M. Curtis

University of Missouri

I first read McLuhan's (1964) *Understanding Media* in 1968, and that experience permanently changed my life. McLuhan showed me how to make sense of the world as no writer ever had before, and as no writer ever has since. As people who knew me in the early 1970s can attest, I had little interest in talking about anything except McLuhan's ideas. Although I did not manage to meet McLuhan himself, I did meet his close friend, Walter Ong, S. J., who remains an ideal of informed humane scholarship.

Ever since 1968, I have believed that if we take McLuhan seriously, he can transform our understanding of the world for the better. In 1978, therefore, I published *Culture as Polyphony* (Curtis, 1978), the first full explication and application of McLuhan's work. Having set forth the theory, in 1987 I wrote *Rock Eras: Interpretations of Music and Society*, the first application of McLuhan's ideas to rock 'n' roll.

Thirty years later, I still believe in the exceptional importance of McLuhan's work, although I believe in a revised version of it. Moreover, the extraordinary resistance to McLuhan's work that I have encountered in my own field of Russian Studies, and among academics generally, has helped me to clarify my concept of knowledge itself. This resistance, for which the code word is "skepticism," has persuaded me that *Understanding Media* challenges the predominant cognitive paradigms of the Western world. By doing so, it makes explicit the premises of those paradigms, and thus performs a very useful service.

With the exception of McLuhan's term, the *global village*, which has now passed into common usage, most people still express skepticism about the validity of his work. In my experience, such people are skeptical of everything except their own skepticism, which they have little apparent interest in examining. Mindful of the principle that the unexamined life is not worth living, I have taken it upon myself to examine this skepticism for them. When people say they are skeptical about McLuhan's work, what they mean is that they are skeptical about the academic validity of simplicity. Again and again in *Understanding Media*, McLuhan (1964) flaunts the simplicity of such breezy formulations as, "After three thousand years of explosion, the Western world is imploding" (p. 3). In response to this and other such statements, Donald F. Theall (1971) once wrote that he objected to "McLuhan's whole assumption that media affect all human beings in the same way" (p. 210). Of course Theall objects; if one were to admit the possibility that media affect all human beings in the same way, that would make it possible to simplify media study.

Whether you believe that McLuhan's statement about implosion is—or ever can be—true depends, not on issues of media as such, but on an epistemological issue: What is the relationship between simplicity and complexity in cognition? People like Theall who express skepticism about this or that aspect of McLuhan's work usually have a passionate commitment to complexity as an inherent part of all knowledge. They often reveal this commitment by using such phrases as "The irreducible complexity of human experience."

McLuhan's work, however, is consistent with that of Fr. Teilhard de Chardin, which posits a dialectical relationship between complexity and simplicity (see Teilhard de Chardin, 1965). Teilhard believed that natural phenomena do not endlessly become ever more complex; he believed, rather, that natural phenomena become ever more complex only until they reach a certain point, at which they reverse this trend, and simplify themselves.

This matter of simplicity also has relevance to McLuhan's, Ong's, and Teilhard's Catholicism. McLuhan (1964), in *Understanding Media*, said "There is a deep faith to be found in this new attitude—a faith that concerns the ultimate harmony of all being. Such is the faith in which this book has been written" (p. 5). Faith in "the ultimate harmony of all being" implies an ultimate simplicity that conflicts with the faith in complexity that derives from the generally secular quality of academic life. However, although religious belief is consistent with belief in the validity of simplicity, it is not a necessary precondition for it.

After arguing for the validity of simplicity for 30 years, I have become convinced that no arguments, no forms of persuasion, no evidence of any kind has, or ever can have, any effect on people who have a deep-seated, unconscious, and quasi-religious commitment to complexity as an inherent feature of knowledge. This commitment to complexity imposes distinct limits on all forms of disputation—especially disputation in academic life, where emotional and professional commitments fuse.

In keeping with my belief in simplicity, which derives from the work of McLuhan, Ong, and Teilhard, I wish to propose a simplification of McLuhan—an attenuation of his controversial difference between hot and cool media. For the purpose of understanding world history, we may say that both hot and cool media often have similar effects. Thus, the intriguing lament by a Tunisian villager from the early 1970s: "The radio has destroyed everything" (cited in Berger et al., 1973, p. 141; see also Keeler & Steiner, 1998).[1] Those who believe that what matters about media is their content may note that this man did not say that the content of this or that program fragmented his society. What he said was that "radio" as a medium did it. His lament expressed his sense that radio had fragmented the oral culture of his village—the classification of radio as hot or cool was, and is, irrelevant.

This matter of simplification also has great relevance to world history, a nascent discipline that urgently needs both greater simplification and greater methodological sophistication. The need for greater simplification derives from the sheer quantity of material relevant to the study of 20th-century history. Even someone who knew 15 or 20 languages could never manage to read a tiny fraction of it. Clearly, something radical must be done, and I propose to make the radical move of excluding three countries—the United States, Canada, and Australia—from this discussion. I wish to do so because these countries have unique histories: They were all founded by literate people who left Europe for various reasons. McLuhan noted the results of several generations of literacy, and incidentally explained the Tunisian villager's lament in this way:

> Highly literate societies, that have long subordinated family life in individualist stress in business or politics, have managed to absorb and to neutralized the radio implosion without revolution. Not so, those communities hat have had only brief or superficial experience of literacy. For them, radio is utterly explosive. (McLuhan, 1964, p. 300)

Indeed, if we examine the experience of the 20th century in the remaining major countries of the world, here is what we find: war, civil war, revolution, widespread use of torture, mass deportation of minorities, and mass starvation. As Alexander Solzhenitsyn (1972) said in his Nobel Prize address, "Our twentieth century has turned out to be more cruel than the

---

[1] I wish to thank Ray Gozzi for drawing my attention to this article.

previous ones" (p. 56). The extraordinary, and ongoing, cruelty of the 20th century is what world history most of all needs to explain. No matter what injustices have occurred in the United States, Australia, and Canada, they pale in comparison to those committed in the rest of the world.

When we speak of the cruelty of the 20th century, most people quite understandably think of Hitler and the Holocaust. Yet as a mass murderer, Hitler ranks a distant third behind Stalin and Mao Ze Dong. Hitler held power for only 12 years—a far shorter time than Stalin or Mao. Moreover, historians of the Holocaust have made a persuasive case for the uniqueness of the Holocaust as an operation planned to eliminate an entire people. If the Holocaust was unique, then that uniqueness limits its relevance as a model for a world history that seeks valid generalizations.

As an initial study of the horrors of the 20th century that excludes both the Holocaust and the histories of the United States, Canada, and Australia, I propose to apply McLuhan's media theories to the careers of the following leaders in the following countries: Joseph Stalin in the Soviet Union; Mao Ze Dong in the Chinese People's Republic; Idi Amin in Uganda; Pol Pot in Cambodia; and Saddam Hussein in Iraq. I have matched these leaders with their countries because historians have often followed Ralph Waldo Emerson's principle that "An institution is the lengthened shadow of one man," and studied such major figures in isolation. They have chosen not to ask a key question: "How did these leaders manage to retain power despite their extraordinary cruelty?" (A potential model for answering this question is Erikson, 1962). This chapter proposes to address that question.

Paul Theroux's (1995) travel book *The Pillars of Hercules* contains a seemingly baffling anecdote whose thread will lead us into our century's heart of darkness. Fortunately, for my purposes, it takes place in Albania, the country celebrated in the movie *Wag the Dog* as the most insignificant country on earth. In Albania, Theroux met some young men who passed for intellectuals, and here is what one of them told him about the effect of the propaganda disseminated by Albanian leader Enver Hoxha:

> Hoxha made us believe that we were the best people in the world. There was crime and violence and poverty in every country except ours. We believed everything we were told. We did not question anything. We did not ask why we had water shortages in summer and power shortages in the winter. We had no taxes. We believed we were the greatest country in the world, better than China which we had rejected, better than the Soviet Union, much better than the West. (Theroux, 1995, p. 272)

Although we do not know, and probably never will know, how many Albanians shared this attitude, quantification is irrelevant to the larger issue. It is the startling contrast between our perception of Albania as insignificant and the Albanians' perception of themselves as living in "the greatest country in the world" that needs explanation here. In order to explain this contrast, we begin by assuming that these people were not mentally deranged, but rather that they were interacting with the Hoxha regime in such a way as to produce their belief about themselves. I wish to argue that is such interactions that constitute the stuff of history.

Believing as I do in the validity of simplicity, I interpret the Albanians' belief about themselves as the culmination of a core narrative that has been repeated time and again in this cruel century. It is possible to formulate such a narrative if and only if one assumes the validity of the principle that "the medium is the message." That is, to say, it will not be possible to understand the similarities among the various destructive social processes of the twentieth century as long as one takes into consideration the overtly stated ideology of the leaders and their regimes. Clearly, Idi Amin and Pol Pot—to take only two examples—believed in different things and justified their regimes in different ways. (But note that even this statement begs the crucial question of how anyone would ever determine what a pathological narcissist believes; since political scientists cannot answer this question, they have ignored it.) However, in McLuhan's terms, to believe in the overtly stated ideology of the regime is to believe in content, and thus to deny that the medium is the message.

Having stated all this, I can now present what I construe to be the core narrative of oppression in the twentieth century.

A media complex usually consisting of literacy, radio, and railroads (among others) appears in a primarily oral society. This media complex creates an unstable dual process of both implosion and explosion. The explosion (or fragmentation, as McLuhan calls it) produces intense individualism among a few men (they are always men). Because this individualism appears in a society that lacks the literate infrastructure that accompanies individualism in the West, it takes on a strongly narcissistic quality. This narcissistic quality is accentuated by the experience of abuse in boyhood. These men subsequently become leaders of a movement whose slogans evoke the group identity of the impacted oral culture. Once this movement takes power, however, the group identity inhibits the leader's narcissism, and he attacks it. (For a discusion of the two-phase development of such regimes, see Curtis, 1978.) Media, which connect the society to the outside world, pose a threat to both the leader's narcissism and to the society's creation mythology. The leader then moves to close the society. Closing the society has two effects, which soon become indistinguishable: (a) It restores the uniqueness and therefore the validity of the creation mythology, because it removes all alternatives to that mythology; (b) it therefore increases both people's self-esteem and their dependence on the leader; and (c) it facilitates the reign of terror that the leader's narcissism requires.

Obviously, local differences deriving from geography, time period, and other factors, have occurred. These differences do not, however, invalidate the core narrative itself, which has great consistency not only with McLuhan's theories, but also with recent work in psychology and history. Although substantial evidence exists for the core narrative, not all of it is readily available, and in any case presenting it would require much more space than I have at my disposal in the present volume. I therefore cite only the most reliable evidence that bears directly on individual issues.

To show the validity and coherence of the constituent elements of this narrative, we may begin with its most discussed element, the personality of the leader. Clearly, men such as these, who have an ongoing need to order and/or supervise widespread torture and murder have no feelings of sympathy or compassion for their fellow human beings. A statement by Zhisui Li, who served as Mao's personal physician for many years, describes the other four leaders as well: "So far as I could tell, despite his initial friendliness at first meetings, Mao was devoid of human feeling, incapable of love, friendship, or warmth" (Li, 1994, p. 121). Psychologists have a term for people like Mao who are "devoid of human feeling"—they call them *narcissistic*. As it happens, we have a good deal of research on narcissism, especially on what is called *malignant* or *pathological* narcissism, and it has great relevance here.

Manfred Kets De Vries and Danny Miller (1985) state in their article, "Narcissism and Leadership: An Object Relations Perspective," that "We shall attempt in this paper to show that leadership effectiveness and dysfunction can often be explained by the narcissistic dispositions of the leader" (p. 548). In fact, there exists ample reason to believe that political leaders, especially in the 20th century, are intensely narcissistic (see, i.e., Volkan, 1980).

And what conditions produced their narcissism? Relying on the work of such influential psychologists as Heinz Kohut (1978), psychologists emphasize the experience of childhood. Thus, Jerrold M. Post (1997) states, "If the child is traumatized during this critical period of development, his emerging self-concept is damaged, leading to the formation of what Kohut calls 'the injured self'" (p. 678). This generalization applies both to Stalin— it is well-known that he was abused as a child—and to Stalin's latter-day admirer, Saddam Hussein. A recent biography describes the punishment that Hussein's sadistic step-father used to inflict on him: "His common punishment was to beat the boy with an asphalt-covered stick, forcing him to dance around to dodge the blows" (Karsh & Rautsi, 1991, p. 10). Psychologists surmise that when a boy experiences such abuse, a splitting off of the self from the abusive situation occurs; the result may be a man like Mao, who was "devoid of human feeling."

The presence of narcissistic personality traits in political leaders has particular importance because of these traits' broader implications for the personality as a whole. Psychiatrists David Garfield and Leston Havens (1991) noted the association between pathological narcissism (such as that in the five leaders mentioned here) and paranoia. They comment, "A central issue is trust versus mistrust" (p. 160). Because pathological narcissists distrust everyone, no one's praise ever assuages their anxiety, and thus their need to receive praise and inflict pain continues in an endless cycle until they die.

So far, this discussion has taken psychologists and psychiatrists at their word and used their own evidence. Not surprisingly, they restrict their evidence to psychological factors abstracted from cultural environments, and certainly from the media situation in the countries in question. However, if we turn to McLuhan (1964), who insisted that, "Environments are not passive wrappings but active processes" (p. vi), we can integrate psychological and media experience. McLuhan has this to say about narcissism:

> The Greek myth of narcissus is directly concerned with a fact of human experience, as the word Narcissus indicates. It is from the Greek word narcosis, or numbness. The youth Narcissus mistook his own reflection in the water for another person. This extension of himself by mirror numbed his perceptions until he became the servomechanism of his own extended or repeated image. (p. 41)

And what about the extensions of Stalin, Mao, and the others? That is to say, what media process was occurring in the countries that they ruled and terrorized? I have shown in *Culture as Polyphony* that literacy was rising rapidly in Russia before the 1917 revolution, and continued to rise rapidly afterward (Curtis, 1978). In Cambodia, "The number of high schools rose from 8 in 1953 to 200 by 1967, with 150,000 students" (Kiernan, 1996, p. 6). The situation in Russia and Cambodia forms part of a larger pattern, of course, since literacy has increased dramatically virtually everywhere in the world during the 20th century. Thus, detailed investigation for each of the other countries discussed here would probably show a comparable increase in literacy during the period just before the leader's takeover.

Thus, it seems reasonable to suppose that individual abuse occurring during a rapid, widespread increase in literacy produced a narcissistic personality. But none of these men possessed what anyone would call a literate sensibility; Saddam Hussein still could not spell his own name by the age of 10 (Karsh & Rautsi, 1991). To take a more extreme example, Amin was never more than semi-literate. Writing while Amin was still alive, David Gwyn (1967) reported that he "Has an exaggerated reaction to the written word. Put something in writing and you give it a kind of witchcraft quality" (p. 21). Like Amin, the other leaders discussed here retained the oral sensibility of their compatriots. Zhisui Li (1994) comments with amazement that, "In all the years I worked for him, I was never able to educate Mao in medicine. His thinking remained pre-scientific" (p. 105). And, more emphatically,

"Mao never used the word modernization with me. He was not a modern man" (p. 124).

One does not have to be a "modern man" to become a celebrity, and discussions of ideology and political structures have usually ignored the fact that the twentieth century has produced so many narcissistic political leaders because this is the age of the celebrity. It has become a commonplace in America to say that politicians are celebrities, but in America they have to compete with other celebrities in sports and entertainment for the attention of the public. Like true narcissists, each of our leaders found it immensely gratifying to be the only celebrity, the only individualist, in his country. As Dr. Li (1994) says, "To assert one's individuality in Mao's imperial court would have been an invitation to disaster" (p. 86). It would have been an invitation to disaster in the imperial courts of the other leaders discussed here as well.

These men commanded the apparatus of celebrity to satisfy their narcissistic needs by plastering the walls of buildings with flattering portraits, glorifying their lives in film, and so forth. De Vries and Miller (1985) resort to academic understatement when they say that in such situations, "Rituals of adulation can supplant task-related activity" (p. 586). Actually, rituals of adulation often became the primary function of the government as a whole. A narrative comment in Solzhenitsyn's (1968) novel *The First Circle* gives us the specifics of the "rituals of adulation" that Stalin ordered:

> On the ottoman reclined the man whose likeness had been sculpted in stone, painted in oil, water colors, gouache, sepia; drawn in charcoal and chalk; formed out of wayside pebbles, sea shells, glazed tiles, grains of wheat, and soy beans; carved from ivory, grown in grass, woven into rugs, pictured in the sky by squadrons of planes flown in formation, and photographed on motion picture film . . . like no other likeness during the three billion years of the earth's crust. (p. 86)

The apparatus of celebrity (which political scientists have usually confused with propaganda) had its desired effect. People in the West tended to believe that Stalin's purge trials of generals and Old Bolsheviks were just and fair, and Mao became a cult figure in the 1960s—thanks in part to that superb manipulator of fashion, Andy Warhol. In his book *Fame in the Twentieth Century*, Clive James (1993) makes an astute remark about Idi Amin in this regard. He notes that although Amin was a psychopath, the lengthy displays of ego that he called speeches seemed like entertainment to people outside of Uganda; after all, their lives were not at stake. As James puts it, "What the world saw [in Amin] was a brilliantly successful comedian" (p. 217).

To bring all these factors together, we may say that the five leaders under discussion grew up in a primarily oral society that was undergoing a rapid increase in literacy. We know that some of them were abused as boys, and we may reasonably surmise that all of them underwent some kind of trauma that produced a splitting off of part of the personality. Their experience of both abuse and literacy gave them the lethal combination of narcissism and paranoia.

Yet they did not live in a literate society; the only partial exception was Pol Pot, who lived in Paris for 3 years while he was a student. Literacy remained a remote, socially isolated phenomenon for them, as they themselves remained psychologically isolated. A literate consciousness never developed in their countries; it did not have time to produce the uniform, mass-produced environment with the pervasive infrastructure of literacy that the United States has long possessed. To understand why the absence of a literate environment matters, we must turn to the relationship between the narcissistic leader and the people of his country, on whom he visited so much suffering.

Surely it is readily apparent that these leaders could not have killed as many people as they did without the active, enthusiastic collaboration of many people. To understand how this collaboration occurred, we need to understand the nature of the symbolic interactions between the leader and the country. To do so, we may distinguish between the population as a whole and the relatively small group that has had various names in various countries, but which we may call "security forces."

The relationship between the leader and the security forces, who do the killing and torturing that he needs to have done, involves a seemingly paradoxical exchange of celebrity and empowerment. The security forces ensure that the leader retains his celebrity, and in return the leader empowers the security forces (who often consist of young men from the countryside) to do whatever they want to the population at large. Solzhenitsyn (1973) was the first to sense the significance of this empowerment, which often produced a situation that bordered on anarchy. In *The Gulag Archipelago*, here is how he addresses the members of the security forces, who wore blue caps in the Soviet Union:

> You have power over all the people of this military unit, or this factory, of this region that goes incomparably deeper than that of the commander, the director, or the secretary of the region. They are in charge of their work, their salaries, and their good name, but you are in charge of their freedom . . .

> Any object you've seen is yours! Any apartment you've noticed is yours! Any woman is yours! You move any enemy out of the way! The earth beneath your foot is yours! The sky above you is yours—it's blue!! (p. 160)

Similarly, one of the few men ever released from Idi Amin's Katabi barracks at Entebbe reported of the security forces that, "They would take them [the prisoners] out a few at a time and torture and kill them. This was now their amusement. It was for them like television for children" (Gwyn 1967, p. 21). This ultimate empowerment—the power of life and death, the power to inflict unbearable pain on anyone in their custody—must have made them "giddy with success," in Stalin's ominous phrase.

However, this empowerment represented only one part of the exchange; they received this empowerment in return for total subservience to the leader's celebrity. Because the leader's unstable psyche was incapable of receiving appropriate feedback from the world, he suspected everyone. Thus, members of the security forces often found themselves in cells with people whom they had recently tortured. The leader was always able to find new recruits for the security forces because he could entice them with promises of ultimate empowerment.

The more general problem, however, involves the leader's relationship to the population at large. Each of these narcissistic leaders was able to evoke genuine enthusiasm in his country. In World War II, thousands of Soviet soldiers died at Stalingrad and elsewhere with the phrase "For the Motherland! For Stalin!" on their lips. As for China, Dr. Li (1994) states what many Chinese people believed, and no doubt still believe, when he writes that, "To this day, ruthless though he was, I believe Mao launched the Great Leap Forward to bring good to China" (p. 356). How do we explain such continuing trust in these leaders despite overwhelming evidence of betrayal?

Jerrold M. Post (1986) made an exciting beginning by assuming that there occurs a fit, an emotional meshing, between the needs of the leader and the needs of the people. He refers to narcissistic leaders such as Mao as "mirror-hungry": "To nourish their famished self, they are compelled to display themselves in order to evoke the attention of others. No matter how positive the response, they cannot be satisfied, but continue seeking new audiences from whom to elicit the attention and recognition they crave" (p. 679). The fit occurs when such a leader meets an "ideal-hungry" population: "At moments of societal crisis, otherwise mature and psychologically healthy individuals may temporarily come to feel overwhelmed and in need of a strong and self-assured leader" (p. 683). Post seems to be referring here to what is sometimes called the "man on a white horse" syndrome.

Yet once again we find that psychologists deal only with psychological issues. Post does not address the issue of what constitutes a "societal crisis." In fact, the leaders under discussion did not necessarily come to power because of, or even during, a societal crisis. Stalin played only an insignificant role in the revolution of 1917; Amin and Pol Pot seized power in coups; Hussein in effect forced his predecessor, President Bakr, out of office, and so forth. Once in power, however, these leaders proceeded to create one crisis after another.

McLuhan's theories make it possible to explain the origin of the deeper societal crisis that kept the leaders in power. We begin such an explanation by recalling that oral societies have mythological, rather than legalistic, self-definitions. As Mircea Eliade (1954) explains in *The Myth of the Eternal Return*, "Every temple or palace—and, by extension, every sacred city or royal residence—is a Sacred Mountain, thus becoming a Center" (p. 121). Such a sacred site is not just any Center—it is the Center of the World, which connects heaven and earth. As such, it ennobles people and gives them a sense of their direct connection with the sacred, however the sacred is defined in that culture.

But when 20th-century media appear, the center cannot hold, in Yeats' telling phrase. And then people have the sense that another great poet, John Donne, expressed as "all coherence gone." When modern media, whether hot or cool, appear in a society that imagines itself as a Center, they have a profoundly de-centering effect. Media make people aware, not just that the world is much bigger than they thought it was; they make them aware that people in other parts of the world also think of themselves as living in centers. What they unconsciously considered the only center turns out to be just one of many centers. As a result, the very idea of a center—their center—becomes de-valued; their connection to the sacred is severed, and their social identity (the only identity that people in an oral society have) begins to disintegrate. Moreover, people who have come from a more literate society into a primarily oral society have often had more resources and more firepower at their disposal. As a result, they have managed to dominate oral societies in devastating ways. The Spanish Conquistadors in South America provide a classic example of this process at work.

Our five leaders, however, lived in a different time. They had a ready response to the de-centering process of media, a response that served both the needs of the population and their own needs: They closed the society. When they closed the society, they thereby re-centered it, because people were no longer reminded of the presence of other centers. Naturally, this gave a tremendous boost to people's self-esteem. Stalin justified closing the Soviet Union by calling for "Socialism in One Country." No matter what the justification, however, the result—a combination of greater self-esteem and greater technological backwardness—has remained the same.

Thus, we have returned to the situation of the Albanians who believed that, thanks to Enver Hoxha, they lived in the greatest country on earth. Hoxha and the Albanians offer an especially clear example of the fit between a "mirror-hungry" (i.e., narcissistic) leader and an "ideal-hungry" (i.e., a de-centered, population). Precisely because Albania is such a small country, the exchange between the leader and the population has particular clarity.

However, the process that occurred in huge countries like the Soviet Union and the People's Republic of China was essentially the same.

Can such a typology, in which a single core narrative purports to explain momentous events in different countries distributed around the globe, evoke anything but skepticism among historians and political scientists? If they have a commitment to complexity as an inherent feature of knowledge, probably not. However, at the beginning of a new millennium, perhaps a new era of interdisciplinary studies is beginning as well. If so, this essay has demonstrated the possibility of combining McLuhan's work with sober scholarship in order to address one of the great problems of our terrifying age.

REFERENCES

Berger, P., Bergen, B., & Kellerman, H. (1973). *The homeless mind. Modernization and consciousness.* New York: Random House.

Curtis, J. M. (1978). *Culture as polyphony. An essay on the nature of paradigms.* Columbia: University of Missouri Press.

Curtis, J. M. (1987). *Rock eras. Interpretations of music and society, 1954-1984.* Bowling Green, OH: Popular Press.

DeVries, M. K., & Miller, D. (1985). Narcissism and leadership: An objects relations perspective. *Human Relations, 38*(6), 583-601.

Eliade, M. (1954). *The myth of the eternal return.* New York: Pantheon Books.

Erikson, E. (1962). *Young man Luther.* New York: Norton.

Garfield, D., & Havens, L. (1991). Paranoid phenomena and pathological narcissism. *American Journal of Psychotherapy, 45*(2), 160-172.

Gwyn, D. (1967). *Idi Amin, Death-light of Africa.* Boston & Toronto: Little, Brown.

James, C. (1993). *Fame in the 20th century.* London: BBC Books.

Karsh, E., & Rautsi, I. (1991). *Saddam Hussein: A political biography.* New York: The Free Press.

Kiernan, B. (1996). *The Pol Pot regime. Race, power, and genocide in Cambodia under the Khmer Rouge 1975-79.* New Haven, CT & London: Yale University Press.

Kohut, H. (1978). *The search for the self: Selected writings of Heinz Kohut.* New York: International Universities Press.

Keeler, C. L., & Steener, H. L. (1998). The role of radio in the Rwandan genocide. *Journal of Communication, 48*(3), 107-128.

Li, Z. (1994). *The private life of Chairman Mao: The inside story of the man who made modern China* (T. Hung-Caho, Trans.). London: Chatto & Windus.

McLuhan, M. (1964). *Understanding media. The extensions of man.* New York: McGraw-Hill.

Post, J. M. (1986). Narcissism and the charismatic leader-follower relationship. *Political Psychology, 7*(4), 195-232.

Solzhenitsyn, A. (1968). *The first circle* (T. P. Whitney, Trans.). New York & Evanston, IL: Harper & Row.

Solzhenitsyn, A. (1972). *Nobel lecture*. New York: Farrar Straus Giroux.

Solzhenitsyn, A. (1973). *Arkhipelarg gulag*. Paris: YMCA Press.

Teilhard de Chardin, P. (1965). *The phenomenon of man*. New York & Evanston, IL: Harper & Row.

Theall, D. F. (1971). *The medium is the rearview mirror*. London: McGill-Queen's University.

Theroux, P. (1995). *The Pillars of Hercules. A grand tour of the Mediterranean*. New York: Fawcett Columbine.

Volkan, V. D. (1980). Narcissistic personality organization and "reparative" leadership. *The International Journal of Group Psychotherapy, 30*(2), 131-152.

15 HOW COOL IT WAS

THE USURIOUS ARTISAN AND THE MEDIEVAL ECONOMY

Neil Kleinman

The University of the Arts

There is economic greed, and there is industry. And sometimes it is difficult to tell them apart. In fact, what passes for greed today often turns into "respectable industry" tomorrow, and, similarly, today's industry begins to look a lot like greed.

These shifts in judgment are not merely the result of shifts in historical fashion. Something else is going on: When the new overwhelms the old, those being displaced do not go quietly. The losers are both passionate and vocal, and they lose no time explaining why the new money and the new marketplace are suspect. It's natural that they should defend their "tradition" with religious fervor. It is equally natural that they should see their adversaries as being both corrupt and demonic.

> Not even amendable to the restraints of corporation law, [the Standard Oil] "trusts" may realize the Satanic ambition—infinite and irresponsible power free of check or conscience. (Frederic Stimson, cited in Gellhorn & Kovacic, 1994, p. 17)

> [Microsoft's] monopolistic impulses unfairly crush competition and . . . if unchecked the company's relentless ambition will lead it to an unprecedented position of economic power . . . an evil empire greedily collecting tools at the nexus of the information revolution. (Levy, 1998, p. 38)

Such passion is not surprising. After all, the barbarians are coming down the hill and sweeping all before their advancing line. If we listen carefully to the economic pieties of the time, we can hear the clash of battle and witness rhetorical exchanges that tell us that something is happening, even if we're not sure what it is.

The merchant, who is to prosper in a new world driven by a cash-and-carry economy, threatens his neighbor the agrarian, who depends on a barter economy (Lopez, 1976). What can the farmer do but describe his new adversary as creating an arid world, devoid of community and human relationships?

The merchant, who sells only the products he makes, wakes up to find that he must compete with the international trader (Braudel, 1982). What should he say except that this competition threatens his local culture and local crafts?

The multistate retailer, who sells tangible goods on the roadways that were designed for cars and trains, discovers that those roads will get him nowhere. The Internet creates a different roadway and a different marketplace, which he's not prepared to deal with (Siwolop, 1998). What is he to say? The Internet is an evil empire, controlled by greedy monopolistic forces (Levy, 1998). The Internet is a chaotic and uncontrolled wilderness in which the values of civility, honesty, and industry will soon be lost (Corcoran, 1996; Denniston, 1996; Fisher, 1998; McGrath, 1996; Moylan, 1996). Customers will always want the human touch, he rationalizes, as the new marketplace pushes his business off to the side.

The purpose of this chapter is to begin, in a very preliminary way, to look at two slippery terms—*industry* and *greed*—in order to understand how economic practice weaves together attitudes towards money and morals.

This is not new ground, I should say at the outset. Jacques Le Goff (1990), in his provocative book *Your Money or Your Life*, connects money and morals in a study of usury in the 13th century, but as his title makes clear, he presents the connection as a choice between money and morals, that is, a choice between money *or* morals. I'm inclined to see it differently, or at least I want to emphasize a different point: that our idea of money and morals is joined—money *and* life, money *and* morals—because these two concepts are often merely different ways of saying the same thing. Clearly, this is not to be a linguistic or psychological analysis. It is part of an economic analysis: how we justify economic systems, especially when they are struggling to retain their economic integrity in the face of a new political and economic system.

What makes the 13th-century version of the tug between money and morals particularly interesting is that it represents, I think, an economic environment quite similar to the one we are now in. So many of the questions we now face—questions about property and ownership, collaborative and adversarial relationships, fair returns and predatory pricing, work and exploitation—are questions that were being actively addressed by the late Middle Ages. Fueling the debate was a range of technological innovation, which as in our time, forced people to reconsider what they did and what was worth doing (Crosby, 1993; Kleinman, 2000).

To frame these two concepts—industry and greed—it is best to begin with a few simple ideas:

1. An agrarian, communal society like that represented by the early Middle Ages places a premium on work that produces tangible objects and on work that requires direct personal interaction and involvement.
2. A commercial society like that represented by the late Middle Ages and early Renaissance places its money on work that produces intangible goods and on work that promotes exchanges at a distance.
3. An economy based on tangible objects (like the early Middle Ages) is likely to be one based on a service economy in which social and human relationships are important.
4. An economy based on intangible goods (abstractions like credit) is likely to be one based on a commercial economy in which service and human relationships are less important.

To show how these concepts work and how the opposing points of view confront each other, I focus on one big idea—the idea of *usury*. Like Le Goff, I think it is a pivotal notion. It symbolizes the debate between an old and new economy and draws a line between them.

If these four precepts are true, they can help us understand the meaning of the digital (or network) economy in which we have just begun to participate (Kelly, 1997). Understanding them may also help clear away some of the rhetoric and religious fervor that characterizes much of the debate about "the great fortunes" that are being made in cyberspace.

What is curious about our new economy is that it appears to share features of both an agrarian *and* commercial society: The production of intangible goods is paramount. (What is more intangible than information?) And there is increasing evidence that the digital economy is based on service relationships (Hagel & Armstrong, 1997). (What is more service-based than e-mail?)

What seems true is that our new economy is marked by a mix of "feudal" relationships—service-based, niche-driven (tribal) communities—and that it shares much with the past. Even as we become more technological, we may become more "agrarian" and communal. At the same time, we are not willing to let go of the constructs developed over the last 600 years. Even as we move into a postcapitalist culture, we continue to use the language of capitalism to describe ourselves (Drucker, 1993). That should not be surprising because the new economics of the 15th and 16th centuries also found it difficult to let go of medieval constructs like materiality and tangibility, which the society inherited from the feudal economy. We move forward but carry the past buried inside of ourselves.

To put this in perspective, let's start with the medieval debate, the debate between those in the older agrarian economy and those in the newer capitalist marketplace. Those who "proposed" usury (or took advantage of it) appreciated the fact that money could be made "where there is no production or physical transformation of tangible goods" (Le Goff, 1990, p. 18). On the reverse side, those who attacked usury understood—even if only vaguely—that an economic system based on intangible goods would destroy the trading and agrarian economic of the feudal society.

WHAT'S SO COOL ABOUT THE MIDDLE AGES?

Marshall McLuhan (1964) can help us understand the Middle Ages. He recognized that the feudal society was tribal, a culture in which people defined themselves in relationship to each other. What does it mean to be a lord? It means that one has duties and responsibilities to those above and below one in the social order. Property was not, as one historian explained, "income, but service" (Tawney, cited in Tigar, 1977, pp. 196-197). A set of responsibilities based on service—interactions that never grow static—is what defines the medieval culture, what makes it so "cool." Participate or become invisible. In that light, the Middle Ages was as cool a society as one might hope to find.

In contrasting hot and cool media, McLuhan used as his litmus the amount of participation required by each medium. Print was hot because the reader had only a secondary role. First came the author and the text, then came the reader who could look at the completed work but could not change it—except perhaps in his mind. The printed book, wrote one analyst,

> carries man away from intimate, complex relationships . . . from tribalism into nationhood, from feudalism into capitalism, from craftsmanship into mass production, from lore into science. It builds large-scale organizations because it develops abstract and simple human relationships, and permits the almost endless multiplication of messages and patterns. By contrast, speech is a cool medium, developing dialogue, response, feedback, complex and intricate patterns of personal relationships, family-centered societies, a familistic ethic, tribalism, and superstition. (Boulding, 1969, p. 71)

The Middle Ages were cool because its social compact was still communal (Le Goff, 1990) and used the cool medium of speech and interactive rituals.

Its institutions were shaped by personal relationships and family-centered alliances (Johnson, 1981). Its economy was based on face-to-face bargaining and barter between the artisan and the farmer, between the laborer and the priest (Braudel, 1977). The principles of property and ownership also spring from notions about community. Both in the commons and on Church and feudal lands, it was often hard to determine where the property line ended and ownership began. The rights of ownership were murky (Reynolds, 1994), and ownership itself was not as important as we might imagine. In fact, the economic value of ownership was suspect. As one historian observes,

> He who exploits his property with a single eye to its economic possibilities at once perverts its very essence and destroys his own moral title, for he has "every man's living and does no man's duty." (Tawney, cited in Tigar, 1977, p. 197)

If ownership was not of the greatest importance, the relationship between parties was, and even business deals were structured to develop or enhance such relationships.

To modern eyes, this emphasis created some bizarre behavior. Often there was no "profit" in economic transactions that appeared to be business dealings but were only exchanges of equally valued objects. Karl Polanyi describes transactions in which the giver and the getter were expected to find ways of exchanging "economically equivalent" objects. What was the profit in that? As Polanyi explains, "[t]he sole purpose of the exchange [was] to draw relationships closer by strengthening the ties of reciprocity" (cited in Le Goff, 1990, p. 19).

Such was the society and polity of the Middle Ages. Diplomacy, Church and State relations, local feuds and truces and, certainly, the chivalric traditions can best be appreciated if one sees them as a form of dance in which the players are trying to achieve a clarity about who they are—not a victory intended to destroy the opposing side.

WHAT'S SO HOT ABOUT USURY?

Usury prepared the way for modern capitalism because capitalism needed to stretch the limits of tangible property (Le Goff, 1990). The international trader, the banker, even the explorer could not long exist in a world limited by the simple, local exchange of products passed between those who made and those who consumed (Braudel, 1982).

1. If one wanted to trade at a distance, one needed a system of money and credit for which there would be a return consistent with the risk involved in lending money. Usury—the rent charged for lending money—provided such an incentive for lending money in risky circumstances (Braudel, 1982, p. 562).
2. If one wanted a fluid economy in which things not physically present could be bought and sold, one needed a system of credit in which one could add and subtract values without having the tangible property in hand. Usury made such a system of debit and credit possible by making money itself real—a form of property that was intended to increase in value as it was exchanged (Crosby, 1993).

Because usury produces a profit beyond the value of the thing being lent (the value of land *plus* interest or the amount of money being borrowed *plus* interest), usury is a necessary, almost inevitable, incentive for investment and a critical condition for the capitalization required of new enterprises.

As one might imagine, the freedom and incentive to lend money changed a number of relationships and roles (Reynolds, 1994). Perhaps the most obvious change, and the one on which all others depend, was the change from sets of static relationships to more dynamic ones. A lending economy is, above all else, a dynamic and fluid economy in which relationships are equally fluid: Strangers can buy from strangers with some ease; property can be exchanged for credit without a direct relationship between the buyer and the seller, and debt can be structured so that the principal is repaid over time, long after the property has been used or consumed. From these, other changes in relationships followed easily.

The original owner (say, a local noble) could sell his property—regardless of its size, value, family history, or feudal obligations.

> [Property's] raison d'etre [in the feudal system] is not only income, but service. It is to secure its owner such means, and no more than such means, as may enable him to perform those duties whether labor on the land, or labor in government, which are involved in particular status which he holds in the system. (Tawney cited in Tigar, 1977, pp. 196-197)

In fact, the value of property changed. With a sale, the original owner severed his feudal relationship to the land, to the prince he has been bound to through the land, and to the peasants who worked the land and whom he has been obliged to protect. Property was no longer to be valued by adding the revenue from the things produced and the potential value of the service required of those bound to the land. Instead the value of property became a matter of simple marketplace economics—the value of the things produced added to the relative value of potential rents compared to the return on the monies invested.

The new owner (say, a merchant who has done well and now wishes to buy an estate) took on the land but often did not take on the responsibilities that came with the land. Becoming a man of property no longer meant that the new owner was subject to the duties owed his sovereign nor those owed the peasants who used the land.

> Human society is dissolved into isolated individuals, and the world of goods split up into discrete items. One can no longer speak of a duty to use property or behave towards others in a certain way: all such duties as may be imposed by law are prima facie derogations from the fundamental "right of property." (Tigar, 1977, p. 197)

The banker or *lender* (which might be the Church, an individual, or a financial syndicate) had only an indirect relationship to the land. He might claim the land if the debt was not paid, but he expected nothing from the land except the economic return on his investment. He had no interest in the land or in what the land produced since the land was only a symbol for the value he was to receive.

> Of all merchants, the most accursed is the usurer, for (in contrast to the merchant) he sells something . . . [and then], after usury, he takes the thing back, along with the other person's property, which the merchant does not do. [The editor of the Church's Code of Canon Law (circa 1160) then explains why one may collect rent on a farm field or on a house but not on money.] . . . [T]he field [he says] is gradually exhausted by use, and the house is damaged by use, while money that has been lent neither diminishes nor grows old. (Code of Canon Law cited in Le Goff, 1990, pp. 28-29)

The intensity of the attack against usury tells us something about the vulnerability of those in charge of public and church business. In place of fealty, loyalty, and carefully defined relationships, the new age embraced profit, property, buying and selling, ownership, and production, and few in the establishment felt comforted by what they saw. What could they do except label it a sin? Said one monk: "The usurer wants to make a profit without doing any work, even while he is sleeping, which goes against the precepts of the Lord, who said, 'By the sweat of your face shall you get bread to eat'" (Thomas of Chobham cited in Le Goff, 1990, p. 42).

SO WHAT'S SO DESTRUCTIVE ABOUT USURY?

Usury destroys community by making relationship to property indirect, and that was what the Church fathers feared most. By encouraging the alienation of property, the dissolution of feudal bonds, and a redefinition of social and public roles, usury seemed to the Church to destroy the "complex and intricate patterns of personal relationship; [the] family-centered societ[y], [and the] familistic ethic" (Boulding, 1969, p. 71), which characterized the cool medieval culture, described by McLuhan. They quoted and then requoted passages from the scriptures to make the point.

From *Exodus* (22:24):

> If you lend money to one of your poor neighbors among my people, you shall not act like an extortioner to him by demanding interest from him.

From *Leviticus* (25:36-37):

> Do not exact interest from your countrymen either in money or in kind, but out of fear of God let him live with you.

From *Deuteronomy* (23:20-21):

> You shall not demand interest from your countrymen on a loan of money or of food or of anything else on which interest is usually demanded. You may demand interest from a foreigner, but not from your countrymen.

These passages evoked the kind of passion they did because they spoke to the anxiety people felt as they saw the fabric of their communities unravel. These scriptural lessons were intended to remind men of the duties they owed their community and to warn them of the curse that would visit them if they destroyed that community and the relationships that directly connected them to each other.

Usury would destroy communities and social compacts because it established new standards of behavior. It suggested that one could get wealthy without work, without labor, and without sweat. ("Every other sin has its periods of intermission; usury never rests from sin. Though its master be asleep, it never sleeps, but always grows and climbs," Caesarius of Hesiterbach, circa 1220, cited in Le Goff, 1990, p. 30.)

It set up walls between neighbors and weakened the impulse to collaborate and share. ("[If] all usurers, all rebels and all plunders would disappear, we would be able to give alms and provide for the churches, and everything would return to its original state," Cardinal Robert of Courcon, circa 1213, cited in Le Goff, 1990, p. 25.)

It subverted the order of State and Nature. It weakened the established order, made sloth a virtue, fractured communities, drove families from their land, found value only in what could be sold, and blunted the workman's craft and skill (Le Goff, 1990).

The idea of usury created a fundamental crack in the culture. It set the wrong image before men, an image of Nature that was abhorrent to the medieval mind. At best only an inanimate object with no spirit and no soul, in the usurer's hands, money became an end in its own right. Money is, after all, an abstraction—nothing more than paper or coin or some other financial abstraction, yet the usurer treated it as though it were fertile seed. As Thomas Aquinas wrote with obvious exasperation, "Money does not reproduce itself" (Le Goff, 1990, p. 29). How could something infertile become central to society, the priests wondered? Worse, how could something infertile become "productive" and reproduce? That did seem unholy.

In short, usury was, as the theologians wrote, *Contra Naturum*, against Nature and against God (Le Goff, 1990). The conclusion was simple, "Usurious profit," exclaimed Pope Leo I, "is the death of the soul" (Le Goff, 1990, p. 32).

MOVING FROM THE COLD TO THE HOT

When we move from one zone to the next, we don't change as much as we imagine. We still wear the clothes we started out with as much from habit as for protection. That is what happened with the concept of *tangibility*, which was so much a part of the theology that surrounded usury. The construct of *the tangible* was too useful to drop so it lingered on and was incorporated into the fabric of the new economics of the Renaissance even as the society embraced more abstract systems.

The medieval theologians had argued that usury was a sin because there was no production or physical transformation of tangible goods. With this they emphasized the requirement of materiality and, as a result, sanctified work. One cannot shape an object unless one works on it—labors over it. It is this principle of "work" that is at the center of all the criticism directed at usury with its apparently excessive generation of profits without little or no sweat. Remember: "By the sweat of your face shall you get bread to eat" (*Gen.* 3:19).

Work without labor, it was thought, devalued man because it deprived him of the chance to redeem himself—to save himself—from the burden of "original sin." Even more, usury falsely exalted Man, promised him a position higher than his Creator. God, after all, worked 6 days and rested on the seventh. The usurer and his infernal money machine seemed to make all days into holidays (Le Goff, 1990).

> It was during the thirteenth century that thinkers turned work into the basis of wealth and salvation, both on the eschatological level and on what we might call the economic level. "Let each person eat the bread he has earned by his effort, let dabblers and idlers be banished," exclaimed Robert of Courcon to the usurers. And, in our day, Gabriel Le Bras observes pertinently: "The major argument against usury is that labor constitute the true source of wealth. . . . The only source of wealth is mental or physical labor for there is no justification for gain other than human activity." (Le Goff, 1990, pp. 42-43)

The celebration of human activity, work, and labor made good economic sense to the Medieval Church. Its congregations consisted, for the most part, of those who worked on the land and with their hands, receiving little for their labors except the promise of a life in the hereafter blessed because they had done God's work.

Those who understand the practical value of usury were not without ingenuity. They found ways to change the intangible into something tangible—whether that is in the form of paper money, a bank account that can be drawn on and invested, real estate that can be conveyed out of the family, or a "piece" of intellectual property that can be marketed and sold. In such ways, they were able to appear to be "working" and "laboring" even when only their money was "at work."

The ability to make the abstract into tangible products ran through almost every aspect of the culture of the late Middle Ages. Men developed schemes, instruments, and methods to make visible and tangible what had heretofore been invisible (Crosby, 1993; Kleinman, 2000). Inventors and explorers found that they could "see" the invisible lines of the earth's magnetic declination by using magnetic compasses (Sarton, 1957). Scientists, reworking the principles of optics, found that they could "see" light, color, and reflection, as well as create perspectival drawing (Crosby, 1993; Sarton, 1957). Time itself became tangible. Where before there had only been the shadowy substance of time on a sundial, there were now clocks and watches that made it possible to measure, count and even carry time (Burke, 1978; Crosby, 1993).

Added to these transformations of intangible things to "tangible goods" was the fabrication of modern principles of credit, debit, and double-entry accounting. The ebb and flow of money became tangible. The values expressed in the ledger could be treated as though they were as real as coins in a bag of gold.

> When even the value of the genois and florin and ducat wavered, or when a transaction could not be closed because the number of coins offered in one currency was worth a fraction too much or too little of a whole number of the coins in the currency in which the price was expressed, or when currencies flew up and down in value so fast no one was confident of knowing their relative values—when all was in flux and yet bills had to be proffered and paid, Westerners took another giant step into abstract. They extended as never before the useful fiction of "money of account," an idealized scale consisting of what after a while was the arbitrarily fixed ratios of the values of prestigious coins. (Crosby, 1993, p. 72)

The transformation of intangible things to tangible goods was incorporated into the attitudes and then finally into the laws developed to create intellectual property (Kleinman, 2003). In modern copyright law, we see these tracings. "Copyright protection subsists," the law states, "in original works of authorship fixed in any tangible medium of expression" (Copyright Act of 1976, as amended, 17 U.S.C. Sec 102a).

The mind of the late Middle Ages understood that it must pretend to incorporate the values of an earlier time, when work and tangible forms were important, even as they developed an economy that pushed against the limits created by tangible objects.

BUT WHAT IF MONEY DID GROW ON TREES?

I want to underscore the notion that the value of work changes with the economic context: what we take to be industrious and productive in one age can appear to be merely greedy, perhaps even immoral and corrupt, in another. Thus, a man may be usurious in one age and industrious in another. As Braudel (1982) reminds us, we are practical, often before we are pious.

> In fact, in an age [the late 13th century] when economic life was beginning to take off once more, to forbid money from multiplying was attempting the impossible. Agriculture had taken more land into cultivation in this short period than it had in all the centuries since neolithic times. The towns were growing as never before. Trade was increasing in volume and vitality. How could credit have failed to spread across the thriving regions of Europe[?] . . .

The truth was that usury was practised by the whole of society: princes, the rich, merchants, the humble, and even the Church—by a society that tried to conceal the forbidden practice, frowned on it but resorted to it, disapproved of those who handled it, but tolerated them. "One went as furtively to visit the moneylender as one went to visit a whore"—but one went all the same. . . .

[B]y . . . the latter half of the eighteenth century, the quarrel was really over. Some latter-day theologians might still fulminate. But on the whole a distinction was made between usury and the regular price of borrowed money. . . ." Interest on money is useful and necessary to all" [wrote the 18th Century Portuguese financier Isaac de Pinto]; "usury is destructive and blameworthy. To confuse the two is like condemning the useful purposes of fire because it burns and consumes those who venture too near it." (pp. 562-566)

So it is when "cool" economic theories are applied in "hot" cultures. Neither good nor bad, perhaps the medieval usurer (a purveyor of the soon to be "hot" economics" of the Renaissance) looked the way he did because he was being judged by the "cool" theologians of the Middle Ages. By the 15th and 16th centuries, the concept of *usury* was little more than an artifice. The "cool" theologians had died or had embraced the new economy. The ability to make money by lending money and charging for it had been incorporated into the daily financial life of the times, and bankers and moneylenders did not need to hide their craft.

By the 15th and 16th centuries, the "sin" of usury was sin no more. It was almost as if the very form of usury had become the model for the new economics. When the Medieval Church condemned usury because it continued to make profits while all men slept, the Renaissance men of science found this to be the perfect model for their invention. From Da Vinci and Gutenberg on, the enterprise was to find systems that could, with little human labor, "mass produce" products while we—manager and worker alike—watched and rested (Kleinman, 2000). At the same time, scientific, legal, and economic practice was devoted to finding ways to make the intangible and ephemeral—whether intellectual property, credit, money, time, or space itself—into concrete and tangible objects that could be counted, traded, and sold (Crosby, 1993).

Usury was the necessary harbinger of things to come. "The great controversy surrounding usury," Le Goff (1990) accurately observed, "constitutes what might be called the 'labor pains' of capitalism" (p. 9). Without credit and liquid capital, there could be no investment in the new technology being developed, in the sailing ships that were to explore the new world, and in the bureaucracies of State that the new nation-states required. If a knight could not sell his land, invest his money in new ventures, he and his family would have continued to be locked into a social structure that allowed for no change.

Usury made ownership important and helped to straighten out property lines. It changed the economy from an exchange economy to one based on transactions, and each transaction—legal or business—had a winner or loser. Instead of being participatory, the economy, now driven by usury and the principles of credit and investment, became "adversarial," founded on the idea of a "zero sum gain."

The opposition to usury reflected an opposition to these changes. As the society hotted up—and usury, interest, and credit were the fuel that provided that heat—those in power found these economic tools and the changes they wrought intolerable and tried to find ways to take the wood off the flames. Of course, they could not succeed.

SO WHAT'S NEXT?

To those involved in the current debates about software, monopolies, and intellectual property rights, the arguments may sound familiar (Kleinman, 2003). The money lender of the 12th and 13th centuries and the creator of software and electronic information both trade in similar products—intangible things that are neither diminished nor exhausted by being used, things that may be given and then taken back "along with the other person's property" (Code of Canon Law, cited in Le Goff, 1990, p. 29). This is what McLuhan might call "hot economics."

Curiously, much of the recent discussion of the economics of the electronic networks repeats the language of the medieval Church fathers. Thus, Kevin Kelly (1997) sounds like an electronically bred Thomas Aquinas:

> The distinguishing characteristic of networks is that they have no clear center and no clear outer boundaries. The vital distinction between the self (us) and the nonself (them)—once exemplified by the allegiance of the industrial era organization man—becomes less meaningful in a Network Economy. The only "inside" now is whether you are on the network or off. Individual allegiance moves away from organizations and toward networks and network platforms. . . .
>
> A network is like a country. In both, the surest route to raising one's own prosperity is raising the system's prosperity. (pp. 190, 192)

How like the language of the cool medieval culture this sounds. It reminds us that as we move towards a cool digital economy, one that's more tribal

than industrial, we shall embrace personal relationships, family-centered
societies, a new form of tribalism, and content shaped by response and
feedback.

Thus, we revisit our past and reclaim values we thought outmoded, but,
as we reverse direction, there will be those who will not be silent. They
understand that these "cool" values undermine what they have made. We
have seen how the medieval usurer (a purveyor of "hot" economics") looked
to the "cool" theologians of the Middle Ages: he was disruptive of the social
order and was demonized for it. Why would we expect things to be different now? The priests of the "hot" culture—the industrial capitalists of the
last half millennium—finding themselves threatened by the barbarians of a
digital economy, demonize their enemy, as they themselves had been demonized. After all, what the new economy entrepreneurs promote is a society
that is less structured, less tidy, less bounded by defined lines of property
and ownership.

The economic wars of the 1990s and of the first decade of the 21st century might be seen as wars between the two visions represented by two cultures—one that is cool, interactive, and collaborative, and the other that is
hot, individualistic, detached, and competitive.

The tale is exhilarating, if not frightening. At its top on March 10, 2000,
the NASDAQ averages had increased a breathtaking 110% in 15 months
(Sloan, 2000). In the next three years, March 10, 2000 to March 10, 2003,
NASDAQ dropped by 75% (Tanaka, 2003). Although I don't wish to dis-
miss the economic exaggerations and distortions of what many call the "economic bubble" of the nineties, the stock market is as much a creature of
expectations and emotions as it is a place of realistic accounting and analysis, and the outcome is still unclear.

What may be clear, though, is that economies do not change quickly and
that we need to learn how to absorb new values carefully before we can
count on them to provide stability. One thing is clear, nevertheless: the
Network Economy has some persuasive truths that we can use to redefine
how we do business, and that among these, the most important is "service"—the way in which a producer creates a relationship with his customers,
as well as with his competitors. This is an idea that would have been easily
understood by the medieval landlord as he fulfilled his obligations both to
his lord and his tenants.

The importance of "service" is an economic principle that has not been
lost on those who propose business models meant to take advantage of network relationships.

> Virtual communities give people with similar experiences the opportu-
> nity to come together—freed from the constraints of time and space—
> and form meaningful personal relationships. . . . "We are only beginning

to imagine the people with whom we can collaborate." . . . "The most important aspect [of a network community] is that the members are the producers. They are the creators. They are the talent. We're just stringing it together." (Hagel & Armstrong, 1997, pp. 19-20)

The real commercial potential of virtual communities . . . will begin to emerge only as they aggregate a critical mass of members and develop rich transaction capabilities. . . . Virtual communities have the potential to drive a major shift in power from vendor to customer and, in the process, to shift the capture of surplus economic value from vendors to customers. (Hagel & Armstrong, 1997, p. 24)

A key assumption driving the formation of virtual communities is that members will over time derive greater value from member-generated content than from more conventional forms of "published" content. (Hagel & Armstrong, 1997, p. 29)

. . . [T]he virtual community organizer would argue that the distinctive value of online environments is their ability to capture and accumulate member-generated content (for example, member reviews of vendor offerings, member "tips," member experiences). If this is true, it follows that the real focus of interactivity is interactivity between the community members themselves, and that interactivity with vendors and publishers serves only to enhance the value of interaction among members. This perspective leads to the view that value over time will concentrate in "shared" community spaces (bulletin boards, chat areas, and the like) and that this value will be largely captured by the members themselves and the organizers of these shared spaces. (Hagel & Armstrong, 1997, pp. 37-38)

In all this, we are asked to accept a vision of an economy based on the idea that a community can be created that does the work and creates the value—one in which the individual is less important than the collective.

To succeed in these precepts, we shall have to rethink our commitments to rugged individualism and enlightened self-interest. This economy and its underlying value system will require that we are able to move beyond the notion of the "zero sum gain" and that we learn to redefine our relationships—both with those we traditionally treat as our customers and those we treat as our competitors. In short, this economy will require that we are willing to embrace McLuhan's idea of tribal economy: one based on response, feedback, complex and intricate patterns of personal relationships, family-center societies, and (yes) superstition (Boulding, 1969). It's a promising thought, but one that is subversive of our secular humanism and, therefore, as subversive today as was the idea of usury in its day.

As McLuhan appreciated some 35 years ago, we are where we were in the early 15th-century, about to cross the divide between the cool and the hot, only this time, we are going in the opposite direction.

The nice thing about being at the top of the Great Divide is that the view is wonderful. But as the current economic and political upheavals of the first years of the 21st century remind us, the difficulty lies in getting down.

REFERENCES

Boulding K. (1969). The medium and the message. In G. Stearn (Ed.), *McLuhan: Hot & cool* (pp. 68-75). New York: Signet.

Braudel, F. (1977). *Afterthoughts on material civilization and capitalism* (P. Ranum, Trans.). Baltimore, MD: Johns Hopkins University Press.

Braudel, F. (1982). *The wheels of commerce* (S. Reynolds, Trans.). New York: Harper & Row.

Burke, J. (1978). *Connections.* Boston, MA: Little Brown

Corcoran, E. (1996, August 4). Going for the cold. *Washington Post,* p. H1+.

Crosby, A. (1993). *The measure of reality.* New York: Cambridge University Press.

Denniston, L. (1996, June 13). Internet "indecency" ban upset. *Baltimore Sun,* p. 1A.

Drucker, P. (1993). *Post-capitalist society.* New York: HarperCollins.

Fisher, L. (1998, May 19). No sympathy for Gates. . . . *New York Times,* p. D4.

Gellhorn, E., & Kovacic, W. (1994). *Antitrust law and economics.* St. Paul, MN: West Publishing.

Hagel, J., III, & Armstrong, A.G. (1997). *NetGain.* Boston, MA: Harvard Business School Press.

Johnson, M. (1981). *The Borgias.* New York: Holt, Rinehart & Winston.

Kelly, K. (1997, September). New rules for the new economy. *Wired,* pp. 140–44+.

Kleinman, N. (1996). Don't fence me in: Copyright, property and technology. In L. Strate, R. Jacobson, & S. Gibson (Eds.), *Communication and cyberspace: Social interaction in an electronic environment* (pp. 59-82). Cresskill, NJ: Hampton Press.

Kleinman, N. (2000). The Gutenberg promise: Stones, mirrors or a printing press. In S. Gibson & O. Oviedo (Eds.), *The emerging cyberculture* (pp. 61-96). Cresskill, NJ: Hampton Press.

Le Goff, J. (1990). *Your money or your life.* (P. Ranum, Trans.). New York: Zone Books.

Levy, S. (1998, March 9). Microsoft vs. the world. *Newsweek,* pp. 36-38+.

Lopez, R. (1976). *The commercial revolution of the Middle Ages,* pp. 950-1350. New York: Cambridge University Press.

McLuhan, M. (1964). *Understanding media: The extensions of man.* New York: McGraw-Hill.

McGrath, C. (1996). The Internet's arrested development. *New York Times Magazine,* pp. 80-85.

Moylan, M. (1996, July 18). Is technology friend or foe of workers? *The Philadelphia Inquire,* p. F6+.

Reynolds, S. (1994). *Fiefs and vassals.* New York: Oxford University Press.

Sarton, G. (1957). *Six wings: Men of science in the renaissance.* Bloomington: Indiana University Press.

Siwolop, S. (1998, August 23). Books did for Amazon, but what's next? *New York Times,* p. 5.

Sloan, A. (2000, April 24). The $2.1 trillion market tumble. *Time,* pp. 22-26.

Tanaka, W. (2003, March 11, 2003). Gauging Net stocks' future. *Philadelphia Inquirer.* p. D1+.

Tigar, M. (1977). *Law and the rise of capitalism.* New York: Monthly Review Press.

16 TURNING THE MACHINE OFF—VIOLENCE IN A TECHNOLOGICAL SOCIETY OR McLUHAN IN THE AGE OF THE SMART BOMB

Stephanie B. Gibson
University of Baltimore

I have been fixed on a quote from *Understanding Media* (McLuhan, 1964) that has been tacked up on my bulletin board for several years: "The spectacle of brutality used as a deterrent can brutalize." But when I went back to the text to find exactly where it was, I found that I had neither the time nor the patience to wade back through the book looking for a specific sentence that for some reason I had left unmarked. I spent inordinately long periods of time staring wistfully at my book wishing that I could do an electronic search, trying to will the dead print into electronic form. This is how accustomed to smart technology we have become. And it is also an example of how deeply technology has invaded our psyches.

This invasion, taken for granted under most circumstances, has had a wide range of effects. Our banking is easier (according to the banks), our television choices are broader (according to the cable companies), and our general access to information is increased (according to the World Wide Web). Along with these technological developments come many effects we think little about and which are not so beneficial, as Edward Tenner (1996) illuminated in *Why Things Bite Back*, and which have questionable impact on our psyches as Sherry Turkle (1995) explored in *Life on the Screen*. But few have examined the violence contained in the technology itself. I am not speaking of technology intended to inflict violence such as weapons systems, missiles, or armament. Rather, I am thinking of technology that we use every day and how it worms its way under our skin and convinces us to think, Orwellianly, that violence is not violence. As technology becomes more and more invasive our concepts of violence also change and one result is that cultures begin to invent technologies designed to inflict increasing brutality that looks less and less violent.

McLuhan spoke of the violence of the media (in an article so titled) saying:

> The violence that all electric media inflict on their users is that they are instantly invaded and deprived of their physical bodies and are merged in a network of extensions of their own nervous systems. . . . The loss of individual and personal meaning via the electronic media ensures a corresponding and reciprocal violence from those so deprived of their identities; for violence, whether spiritual or physical, is a quest for identity and the meaningful. The less identity, the more violence. (Sanderson & Macdonald, 1989, p. 92)

Clearly, our own nervous systems have been so far extended and invaded by the electronic media with which we live intimately that it no longer appears to be invasion of any sort. We invite technologies into our workplaces, into our homes and into our lives. We say we can't live without them. We make them an inextricable strand of our everyday life. When the computer goes down, the business of life ceases. The interface we have attained with one another and with the world is total, whether we admit to it or not.

PASSIVE VIOLENCE IS STILL VIOLENCE

Contemporary, more invasive, technologies alter violence from physical to psychic, emotional, and spiritual. Resultingly, our conscious perceptions of violence are also altered. But our unconscious perceptions, our feelings of having been violated—sometimes brutally—at a fundamental level, remain. In industrial cultures you were able to see when a person had been assaulted by a technology—she was missing a hand or an eye, or had a spike driven through his head as Phineas Gage did in the first, albeit accidental, lobotomy. But it is often impossible to see when someone has suffered from the violence of digital technology. We cannot see his fragile emotional condition, her tenuous grip on pieces of her identity, her loss of faith. This nonphysical violence is difficult to conceptualize because it has none of the hallmarks we associate with traditional violence—blood, bruises, eviscerated flesh, shattered bones. We may not yet as a culture believe that it is actual violence. Contemporary technology is clean and not physically threatening. It appears nonviolent. Its violence cannot be, as our culture demands, quantitatively measured; nor is it visually apparent. And we have been robbed of our ability to believe what we cannot see. We frame it as virtual violence; but it is real.

Here, in fact, would be a good place to veer off into a consideration of one of the more popular ways we manage this violent invasiveness—the use of psychotropic drugs. This is not the subject of this piece, but I cannot help suggesting that in using the technology of antidepressant drugs we may only exacerbate the problem by introducing a further invasion. Peter D. Kramer (1993), in one of the early books on the phenomenon of the widely used drug Prozac, reports that some of his patients said they felt "more like themselves" on the drug. Kramer acknowledges the odd cultural paradox of using medication to "reinforce cultural norms and encourage conformity" while rewarding those behaviors that we call nonconformist (p. 254). Prozac, and its offspring, are not simply antidepressants, but drugs that act on the entire personality. Whether these regimens are good, bad, or other for us—or for the culture—is not the topic of this examination. The point I wish to drive home here is that we are so accustomed to accepting the use of "mood elevators" and all their pharmaceutical relatives that we rarely think of them as an external elements that act on our internals. We don't think of them as invasive. Antidepressants are a virtual cure to a virtual illness. Because when the ailment is unseen we perceive it as virtual.

A CLEAN INCURSION

Two orders of violence are produced by living with this type of invasively violent technology. The first is that produced by technology. This is the loss of identity individuals experience when their privacy is taken away by being so completely interlinked. This is what McLuhan has termed "the violence *of* the media" (Sanderson & Macdonald, 1989, p. 92, italics added). Deprivation of identity, as McLuhan—and any sociologist—will say, easily produces, in an effort to recover identity, various levels of violence.

The second order of violence is that produced by cultures. It is the revenge of people violated by their technology wrecked not on the technology—the technology would not care, in fact, technology seems to benefit from being interconnected—but on each other. As members of the culture suffer the violent and invasive acts of technology, new technologies are invented that are specifically designed to produce violence. The modes we develop to perpetrate this violence both mirror and reverse, in a McLuhanesque sense, the manner in which our technologies do violence to us. As we become so extended and connected by the enormous tangled web of networks that will rule 21st-century life this mass of connections ultimately deprives us of any identity at all. This is a flipping over of the technology because the massive connections were intended to provide us with a richer context for self-definition. Once this happens, we are able to manufacture—without any hint of hypocrisy or discomfort—smart technology that we then use to inflict actual violence. The significant omission, of course, is the element of the physical. Because we suffer psychically, emotionally, and spiritually, the technology we produce to inflict violence becomes less and less physically violent. So we are left with an end product that can be unspeakably violent, although because we see no evidence of traditional violence we call it humane. A terrifying paradox.

This technology, as we all know by now, is what we have begun calling *smart technology*. It is with this smart technology that our technological expertise has finally caught up with our language. We long ago stopped calling weapons by names that indicated their enormously volatile possibilities. Missiles became peacekeepers, we worked on the neutron bomb (it's only neutrons, after all, not people), and lethal injection was a humane—almost pleasant—way of perpetrating a planned, premeditated killing. But now, although much of our technology is not physically violent, it produces an enormous assault on our identities, our ways of thinking about the world, our spirits, and our emotional stability. The peacekeeper missile is still a nuclear weapon that will cause an incomprehensible explosion accompanied by immeasurable devastation. Lethal injection is not unpleasant to anyone except the human being strapped down to the gurney (and his family and friends)—we see no physically violent effects. The environment is not assaulted, as it was with the electric chair, when singed skin filled the air with an acrid aroma, a human individual being killed jerked and strained at heavy leather straps, and blood occasionally leaked through the odd orifice. Just as the names we have given our newer technologies do not refer to any physical violence, we have finally been able to develop technologies that inflict their violence quietly, calmly, under the surface where it is all but invisible. It would be virtual, save that in the end, someone actually dies.

We find ourselves in a world populated by brilliantly intelligent technology. It seemed to begin during the first Gulf War. This was our first all-television war—not only did we see all of it on television, but much of it actually took place on TV monitors. President Bush, General Schwartzkopf, and all their buddies provided clips of smart ordnance finding its way down air vents, through passage ways and into just the very building we wanted to blow up. A chilling nanosecond of snow as the camera on the bomb became inoperative was followed by a confident-looking information officer or an incredulous-looking commentator explaining that no animals were harmed in the making of this film and that the building we had just not seen disappear was an unmanned weapons factory. Either way, our part in the "war" was clean, nonviolent, aimed solely at the inert, and above all—humane and moral.

Although smart bombs were not the first smart technology—we had, after all, taught a computer to play chess—they were the first to get major airtime and they *were* among the smartest. (Chess-playing computers had not, after all, been able to beat world chess champions—yet.) In the intervening years, all kinds of smart technology has found its way into our world. Web sites want to send you a cookie when you log on; a cookie being an invading spy in your hardware that reports back to the Web site of origin where you've been surfing. New Educational Testing Service tests taken on computer determine the difficulty of the questions you are given by the percentage of your correct answers thus far. The military develops smarter and smarter weapons until the scenario that opens *The Terminator*—where the smart machines simply get sick and tired of our idiotic ways and start a war to get us out of the picture—doesn't seem so far fetched any more.

We have become inured to the violence done to us and by us. The machines by which we inflict violence become more and more electronic and less and less physically violent. The machines that, in McLuhan's eyes, suck away our identities seem virtually, not actually, invasive. Yet, because the entire nervous system is extended they are far more psychically invasive than almost any other medium. Smart technology has cleaned up our act. Our privacy threatened and our identities on the line we have had to invent modes of violence that we can stomach. The panopticon is here and now. Because, as McLuhan points out, "electronic surveillance of every human being, every human action, is now a reality" (Sanderson & Macdonald, 1989, p. 24) the violence we inflict must be clean. We don't want even the mediated and far away, but bloody, violence of Vietnam. We want Gulf War I, with its clean, managed, and manageable violence.

THE DEATH PENALTY

Sanitizing violence is the name of the game for 21st-century technology. No example could be better than lethal injection. The drugs used to kill by lethal injection all have legitimate medical use. And none are even given in what we would call overdoses. The potassium chloride that stops the heartbeat is given in a similar dose to what an anesthetist might use when surgery requires the cessation of pumping blood. In fact, after the administration of this drug, a short window of time remains where it is possible to revive the person being executed. Throughout history, modes of execution have seen wide variations. They usually reflect the prevalent reasons a culture uses to justify killing its own citizens. Capital punishment has been seen as the work of god, a severing of human bonds, a deterrent to crime, and a punishment, both political and social. Methods used to accomplish execution have paralleled these desires and we have seen everything from the brutal to the presumably painless. Currently, the United States is among a minority of countries that kills its own citizens and we do it with a completely antiseptic flare. We also do it in a way that reflects the everyday violence of the media that McLuhan pointed out.

Just as everyday citizens are assaulted by a complete interface with digital technology, connected in every possible way—and some impossible ways—with other human beings all over the globe, people convicted of capital crimes suffer a similar fate. A large part of what is required for capital punishment to exist is the desire to remove the offending individual from the parameters of society. This is done, they are locked away in segregated units and kept under tight control by the state. But then we double back and observe them relentlessly, almost obsessively. A person about to be executed is watched, his or her privacy eliminated totally. The death watch begins a day or two before the execution and notes are made by corrections officers about the inmate's behavior at increasingly small intervals. Here is an example from the final hours of Karla Faye Tucker, who was killed by the state of Texas on February 3, 1998. It is an odd combination of antiseptic observation and poignant commentary.

6:00	Tucker awoken and given clean clothes to wear
6:06	Declined the opportunity to shower
6:14	Declined to watch television when asked if she wanted to watch the news
6:27	Sitting on bunk writing a letter
7:30	Standing at cell door with a smile on her face talking with Warden Dessie Cherry
7:40- 8:00	Talking with attorney David Botsford by phone
8:06	Escorted to visitation room
8:10	Given a cup of water and her personal Bible
8:11	Visiting with her husband, Dana Brown, sister Kari Weeks, and her father Lawrence Tucker
8:27	Accepted a soft drink and cheese crackers purchased by her husband. Stated she was starting to feel a little weak (from not eating)
8:29	Warden Cherry offers Tucker medical assistance, but she declines. Continues visit.
9:00	Visit described as calm and quiet.
10:20	Tucker reading to her family from the Bible
11:50	Dana Brown saying a prayer
11:54	Tucker is crying for the first time
11:55	Tucker and family members have their hands to the screen for closeness.

So while we attempt to sever this person from his or her connection to the human race, we increase surveillance and invasion to overwhelming proportions. This seems a peculiar and bizarre reflection of what happens to the culture as digital technology inserts itself further and further into our lives. We are far beyond punching time clocks now. Management can trace not only when people come in and leave, but how they spend every minute of their working day. Why shouldn't a condemned woman be watched obsessively as her government prepares to kill her? The invasive violence done to us is extended to our prey.

Our idea of violence has been peculiarly twisted by our relationship with technology. We think of lethal injection as a humane way to kill people. Not only does such a concept conflict with every past attitude about capital punishment, but it is, of course, not true. In the past, capital punishment was intended to achieve three things: the victim must die, he must die in disgrace, and in that single moment of horror his death must deter other potential criminals from trodding the same path. Lethal injection accomplishes only the first item on this list. The guillotine, the gas chamber, and the electric chair are all stops along a search for the most humane form of execution (which necessarily excludes the second item: one cannot be humane to and disgrace someone at the same time). Because we are culturally buying into the idea of and seeking out "humane" forms of execution we work to convince ourselves that if we do not perceive physical brutality then it is not violent.

INFORMATIONAL VIOLENCE

Violence is no longer simply an exertion of physical force; McLuhan, and many others, make clear that invasion of the psyche, deprivation of privacy, and the wearing away of ones sense of identity are our 20th-century violence. A culture that endures this type of violence wants its infliction of violence on others to be equally bloodless, equally smoothed over. So much so that such cultures cease thinking of these acts as acts of violence and rather think of them as humane acts of conscience. So we say that no matter why we kill, we must do it in a humane fashion. And in a culture where everyone is violated every minute of the day killing no longer strikes us as violence as long as it is done cleanly. It is simply business as usual.

McLuhan pointed out that "violence exerted by private individuals tends to have limited results, whereas the violence exerted by groups knows no bounds" (Sanderson & Macdonald, 1989, p. 92). Capital punishment, high-tech wars, massive invasion by the Internet are all violence perpetrated by the culture. All on scales that defy the imagination. A past example of massive institutional violence, the Holocaust, also defied the imagination. But it was perpetrated entirely by hand—no computers tracked the more than 6 million exterminated, many were killed at close range, and even after the development of Zyclon B for the gas chambers someone was still in close physical proximity to the crime. Standardization and official sanction changes violence to policy.

One similarity of past acts of mass violence to current electronic violence is the sheer volume of information gathered and maintained. Fascism is a forerunner of electronic database management. Although it can be difficult to coerce people, information is far easier to manage. The more information provided, the cleaner—and more moral—an act appears. The government controlled the press during the first Gulf War far more strictly than it ever had during any previous armed conflicts. During the second go-round it preempted information gathering by "embedding" reporters with units and at least attempting to force all others off to the side of the road. The state controls information provided at executions. Rather than hide what is happening as many other countries do, departments of corrections all across the United States provide press releases, Web sites, and even press packets for these events. Information makes events routine, it indicates that the official body carrying out the act has formulated a way of framing the event.

THE SPECTACLE OF BRUTALITY

The smarter and more invasive our technologies are, and the more information piled on us, the more we are severed from our identities. The reversal, or faux flip, occurs when we begin to take on the identity of the technology, and of imagined others as Sherry Turkle (1995) discussed. Where a personality once lay we have planted false perceptions of connectedness. Instead of Marx's false consciousness, we have false connections. Where once we were connected all around the world in class consciousness, we now suffer from false identification with others.

Here, in the overwhelming sea of information in which we must swim daily, we begin to see a resonance with Jacques Ellul's (1965) proposition that the more educated audiences—or at least those who suffer from the effects of information overload (as we certainly all do)—are more susceptible to propaganda. And who is in charge of the propaganda machine? The U.S. government? Bill Gates? Bud Selig? Alan Greenspan?

Violence in a culture with smart technology is manifested differently from violence in cultures with technologies of average intelligence. The message is almost always that violence has been cleaned up: psychically, emotionally, physically, and above all—morally. Virtual violence is not violence sayeth the machine. The McLuhanesque message, the change in scale, pace, or pattern, is the massive alteration of our relationship with technologies and concepts of destruction. It is a two-step procedure. Invasive technology first inures us to physical violence in the world. (We long ago stopped reacting, for instance, to pleadings from charities to support those wide-eyed starving children around the world. We are numb to the type of violence that has produced their condition.) In the second step, the irritation caused by the perpetual connections, the constant invasion of our psyches by electronic technology, constructs us in a world where sanitized brutality can no longer be perceived of as violence. If something is cleanly done and properly framed it is not violent. The idea of violation simply no longer exists. The manner of our transport to this point is Huxlian—it is far closer to soma than to war. But the end vision is Orwell's—we will live in a state of constant psychic invasion and violation.

The quote that propelled me into thinking about this issue, "the spectacle of brutality used as a deterrent can brutalize," is no longer relevant. The spectacle of brutality is passé, used only in action films. It has become, in fact, so brutal that it can be accomplished only with Hollywood technology. And it is no longer used to brutalize, it is used to entertain. Genuine brutality is now psychic invasion, separation from emotional identity, and a choking off of spiritual grounding. Technological brutality is invisible but felt keenly—the phantom pain of overstimulation.

Is it too late to respond? Does a social activist have a chance of effecting change. Or has the window of possibility for cultural change closed? How smart does technology have to be before it begins pulling the wool over our eyes? When intelligent technology tells us that it is altering the scale, pace, or pattern of human interaction a particular way—or not at all—will we have the gumption, the will, or the smarts to recognize a con when we see it?

REFERENCES

Ellul, J. (1965). *Propaganda*. New York: Vintage Books.

Kramer, P. (1993). *Listening to prozac*. New York: Viking.

McLuhan, M. (1964). *Understanding media: The extensions of man*. Cambridge, MA: MIT Press.

Sanderson, G., & Macdonald, F. (1989). *Marshall McLuhan: The man and his message*. Golden, CO: Fulcrum.

Tenner, E. T. (1996). *Why things bite back*. New York: Alfred A. Knopf.

Turkle, S. (1995). *Life on the screen*. New York: Simon & Schuster.

17 UNDERSTANDING McLUHAN IN THEOLOGICAL SPACE

Robert Lewis Shayon

University of Pennsylvania

A personal encounter with Marshall McLuhan has intrigued me for a quarter of a century. It led me into deeper reflections on the significance and character of the man and his media theories. In 1966, I discovered that McLuhan was superstitious.

That's a loaded word in academic discourse. Ever since the Enlightenment enthroned reason in philosophers' minds, superstition has been a bad thing—a throwback to primitive, outmoded ways of thinking—from which intelligent, educated people are liberated. Then and now *superstition* summons up visions of ignorance and irrationality.

This picture is at odds with the image of McLuhan who had a doctorate in English from Cambridge and taught for many years at the University of Toronto. But my personal encounter with McLuhan illuminates my assertion.

The year was 1966—2 years after the publication of *Understanding Media: The Extensions of Man* (1964). I was on the faculty of the Annenberg School for Communication at the University of Pennsylvania. Dean George Gerbner and I decided to invite McLuhan to participate in a panel, "From Gutenberg to McLuhan."

McLuhan's visit was a hit. But what happened before the panel was more significant than anything that happened during the visit. We had a dinner at the Faculty Club for panel participants and faculty. When McLuhan arrived, he took one look at the table and refused to sit down. Thirteen places were set. We had to recruit a secretary to join us before he would dine. No one commented on the incident, but we were all surprised to discover that Marshall McLuhan, the great guru, was superstitious!

Terrence Gordon, who published his biography of McLuhan in 1997, writes: "After his conversion [to Catholicism in 1937] McLuhan became partial to numbers divisible by three (the Trinity) and remained so all his life. He also avoided 13" (p. 75). Big deal. So what? A much more intriguing question provokes our historical curiosity: can we establish some connection between his media theories and his "irrational" beliefs?

Having recently re-read *The Gutenberg Galaxy* (McLuhan, 1962) and *Understanding Media*, I conclude that McLuhan was a Christian apologist disguised as a media scholar, secretly, perhaps unconsciously, preaching the kingdom of heaven. All through these two basic works, if read carefully with this notion in mind, are hints that the core of his theories about the media are fashioned under the shadow of revelation rather than reason.

In Gordon's (1997) biography is one such clue in his mention of "figure-ground," analysis, a favorite probe in McLuhan's "intellectual toolbox." "Ground" is the total "gestalt" environment, the "field" against which any phenomenon ("figure") may be understood and interpreted (p. 307).

Gordon tells of a visiting scholar who was frustrated by McLuhan's answers to his questions about the figure-ground theory. He wasn't quite sure whether the sage wasn't operating on a "theological level" *which he never stated but only assumed*. He wrote to McLuhan: "Am I entirely wrong in intuiting that the basic model in your mind, the unstated ground of all your figures, is the Bible?. . . It does not seem to me that you open the possibility anywhere in your thinking (or rather in your published work) to what one might call 'theological space'" (p. 312).

Gordon notes that "Though difficult to detect in McLuhan's publications, the connection between his faith and his media studies emerges clearly in his correspondence and his private papers" (p. 75). McLuhan himself wrote in a letter: "At one time, when I was first becoming interested in the Catholic Church, I studied the entire work of G.K. Chesterton and the entire group from the pre-Raphaelites and Cardinal Newman through to Christopher Dawson and Eric Gill. All this is really involved in my media study, *but doesn't appear at all*" (p. 75, italics added).

Another hint that theology was the unstated background to all of McLuhan's media theories, is the fact that, in 1979, he was excited about an upcoming Christianity and Culture forum at the University of Toronto's St. Michael's College. Gordon writes that "for a long time he had wanted to extend the notion of 'the medium is the message' to Christ, and had promised to deliver a talk in the St. Michael's series entitled 'The Eucharist and Contemporary Media'" (p. 286). The talk was never delivered; McLuhan died a year later.

From my own reading in his major works, buttressed by the aforementioned clues in Gordon's biography, I venture this "probe" or speculative suggestion—Marshall McLuhan's essential insight was apocalyptic in the Fourth Gospel sense—he lifted the veil on our serious human situation and made us see it as it really is—a spiritual crisis.

McLuhan, being a reasoning man, trained in the rational print mode, doesn't quite put it in scriptural terms. He hides or suppresses it by a modern liturgy of a scholarly media vocabulary; but we can touch (tactile sense) the borders of the divine garment, if we involve ourselves by creative, in-depth perception.

The heavenly strain may have been latent for a long time. McLuhan was raised a Baptist, but the theme began to emerge after his conversion to Catholicism; later it manifested itself in his expressed wish to speak on the extension of "'the medium is the message' to Christ" and the "Eucharist and Contemporary Media." These theological intentions may have foreshadowed his readiness to "come out" publicly in his writings.

Practically no references to Christianity appear in *The Gutenberg Galaxy. Understanding Media* is even less explicitly given to Christian allusions, but the religious underground, like hot spring waters, can be detected in many places.

The ascetic strain in Christian tradition (Jesus' advice to the rich man seeking eternal life to "sell all that you have, and give to the poor and follow me,") is reflected in McLuhan's sympathetic comment on the 1960s mood of suburban beatniks: "They reject a fragmented and specialist consumer life for anything that offers humble involvement and deep commitment" (McLuhan, 1964, p. 321).

The strong antimaterialism of early Christians is reflected in McLuhan's pervasive criticism of the values of American television content as, for example, when he speaks of "the aggressive lunge . . . for the remaking of Western man, *via TV*, [which] has become a vulgar sprawl and an overwhelming splurge in American life" (McLuhan, 1964, p. 322).

His notions of the totality of the tribal, transpersonal mode of perception, as opposed to the individualization of the literate, eye-oriented, print mode may show the influence of the Biblical stress in the New Testament on the sense of oneness ("I and my Father are one"). He also brought the concept of original sin to his study of media. He sees modern man as a sinner because of his failure to understand that human society is the result of its dominant, eye-oriented technology. He will obtain redemption when he achieves the proper balance between sense ratios.

His Christian values belong to the age of print—which in his view was outmoded; perhaps that is why he avoided asserting them. He found it difficult to reconcile his Catholicism with his revolutionary media views.

His final word on television, however, is violent—contrary to early Christian values. Gordon (1997) quotes McLuhan's remark to a friend or colleague while watching TV: "Do you really want to know what I think of that thing? If you want to save one shred of Hebrao-Greco-Roman-Medieval-Renaissance-Enlightenment-Modern-Western civilization, you'd better get an ax and smash all the sets" (p. 301). One cannot fail to recall Jesus' agitated diatribe against the money-changers when, in uncharacteristic fashion, he overturned their tables and whipped them out of the Temple in Jerusalem.

McLuhan exhibits all the marks of a Judeo-Christian reformer. He thinks we are in a time of spiritual trouble. He wants to save us in our ordeal. Like Paul on Mars Hill in Athens, observing the altar of the Greeks to "the unknown god," he points us to the true God. McLuhan, in speaking to contemporary readers, translates this to—You are ignorant of media. You must understand the true nature of media. Once you do you will be saved. Understanding media is a long, hard road. You cannot change your life by changing any one aspect of it. You must change it totally; lay it all on the altar. "The aspiration of our time for wholeness, empathy and depth of awareness is a natural adjunct of electric technology. . . . There is a deep faith to be found in this new attitude—a faith that concerns the ultimate harmony of all being" (McLuhan, 1964, pp. 5-6). Is this not an expression of religious faith?

McLuhan counsels patience, as did Paul. We must maintain an "even course toward permanent goals, even amidst the most disrupting innovations." In this way we shall all come into the light—the whole light of electric technology.

You must judge for yourself the persuasiveness of my probe. It deliberately avoids the more complicated dimensions of McLuhan's ideas of media. I have narrowed my focus to the allegedly "superstitious" or "irrational" religious ground of his thinking. I believe that, when reading his complex, rather dazzling writings, the proposition that this Canadian tap-dancer of the mind on the stage of the universe of media, was essentially and emotionally a Roman Catholic apologist, may help us better to understand Marshall McLuhan and his media theories.

We can see McLuhan afresh as more than a media analyst—even a Biblical prophet calling us back from idols to the worship of the true God. What he is really saying is that we must temper our preference for human reason with a larger respect for intuitive, "irrational" ways of thinking and living. This and this alone is McLuhan's true message. Only by forsaking the idols of reason and turning to the revelation of the true God, can we find redemption and salvation—the kingdom of heaven.

All the other varied aspects of McLuhan's notions, are merely important, significant glosses camouflaging the hidden, essential preaching of the prophet. McLuhan left us a rich treasure mine. We must continue to explore it. But we must recognize and acknowledge his major religious insights—"Having eyes, ye see not; having ears ye hear not," and, "the kingdom of heaven is within you."

If we wish to honor Marshall McLuhan, this is his message that we should take with us into the 21st century.

REFERENCES

Gordon, W. T. (1997). *Marshall McLuhan: Escape into understanding*. New York: Basic Books.

McLuhan, M. (1962). *The Gutenberg galaxy: The making of typographic man*. Toronto: University of Toronto Press.

McLuhan, M. (1964). *Understanding media: The extensions of man*. New York: McGraw-Hill.

SECTION V

Communication and Culture

18 CHILDREN OF THE MECHANICAL BRIDE

ADDITIONAL ABSTRACTIONS OF HUMAN STEREOTYPES

Barbara Jo Lewis
Brooklyn College of CUNY

A mind loaded in a 6-foot robotic vacuum cleaner, a human brain in a 72-foot armored dreadnought, another mind controlling a humanoid body composed of magnetic rings—these are some creatures of mid-century American science fiction that illustrate the musings of Marshall McLuhan in his 1951 book, *The Mechanical Bride*. McLuhan wrote the book in a cold-war era but warned of a more insidious danger lurking *within* both the democratic and communist regions: technological man. He suggested that the mechanization of society cannot occur without the mechanization of its members, and he warned that in a new, post-war social contract, we may lose our free will. This was a time when the notion that humans could be programmed to respond as machines—take the Japanese Kamikaze pilots or the Hitler Youth—was deeply disturbing.

The term *cyborg* did not exist when McLuhan (1951) wrote of "Superman" (p. 102). First used in 1960 in *Astronautics Magazine* (Clynes & Kline, 1960), cyborg referred to a hypothetical augmented human constructed for life in space. This is precisely the sort of hybrid McLuhan suggested would develop from an interface between man and machine; an interdependent intermingling of the two.

In "Superman" McLuhan wondered if our answer to a machine world might be to become a machine. Conceived in 1935, a time of confrontation with different cultures, Superman became a figure of rescue for a plagued world: a character who fell from the skies, a benevolent alien protecting humans from each other.

Likening Superman to the medieval angel, for both "exert . . . energy of superhuman kind" (p. 103), McLuhan observed that humans have long fantasized about becoming similar to such beings. For instance, humans have historically imagined the synthesis of the natural with the unnatural (e.g., in Egyptian synthetic figures, the more-than-human aspects of Egyptian gods were suggested by depicting them with the other-than-human attributes of animals). It is the putting together of two different entities, two different orders of being, that is shocking. The indwelling of an unnatural form, in an interface of human and machine, becomes the extension of McLuhan's commentary. We cope with the futility that humans feel in relation to great power, by imagining Clark Kent—that which is not the fittest—coupled with great mechanical power. McLuhan suggested that we create these heroes to protect ourselves from what we fear. If we fear the other, then we take in the other, absorbing and assimilating it.

In *Superman*, the character chooses to cross back and forth between his two forms: that of Clark Kent, the inept human, and Superman, the super hero. But in contemporaneous science fiction, the crossover becomes permanent, and perhaps illustrates the more dire aspects of McLuhan's commentary on our increasing mechanization.

SON OF SUPERMAN

Often, the metamorphosis is precipitated by some definitive event permanently altering the biological body. This theme is illustrated in Keith Laumer's (1965) novel *A Plague of Demons*. CBI agent John Bravais has undergone alterations to become a PAPA (a Power Assisted Personal Armament), a "coordinated development in bioprosthetics, neurosurgery, and myoelectronics" (p. 8) to become a new weapon—the Invulnerable Man.

Yet despite our efforts to make a Superman from the materials found on our earth, that is, not to rely on that which may fall from the skies, we fail. Bravais is taken over by the aliens who defeat and decapitate him. He wakes to find his brain encapsulated within a 72-foot dreadnought, slave to an alien *over-mind*. "It is far cheaper and more efficient to use the well-designed human brain to power the war machine than building a mechanical brain." But a recurring stir of "phantom-memories—faint echoes of a forgotten dream of life . . . of flesh and blood, soft and complex, infinitely responsive" (p. 112) awakens the somnolent Bravais, freeing him from the *over-mind*.

Although his body has been disposed of, the human hero reasserts his humanity by stating "I am a man. A man named Bravais" (p. 11). With the aliens waging war on hundreds of worlds, Bravais vows that he will "fight for home, wherever I find the enemy" (p. 159). The propaganda of the war machine found a receptive populace of post-war patriots. Uncle Sam Needs You and Bravais rallies to the cause.

But it is almost as if he is the revenge for Superman. Where Superman is an alien protective of humans, Bravais is a human taken over by aliens who assail his fellow humankind. Bravais is a son of McLuhan's fantasy because he represents an extreme end product of societal mechanization.

DAUGHTER OF WONDER WOMAN

McLuhan was not speculating within a cultural void. Earlier writers had already envisioned the hybrids he fears; they described figures whose metamorphosis, once initiated, took on an uncontrolled and exponential growth. Once initiated, the human-machine synthesis quickly exceeds human control. In "Love-Goddess Assembly Line" (p. 93), McLuhan likens a dancing chorus line, filled with "Bodies by Fisher" articulating "smooth, clicking routines," to the clockwork rigidity of a machine. Each member of this line becomes a "replaceable part . . . Maxfactorized, streamlined . . . parts of a vast machine" (p. 96).

This vision of mechanized pleasure had been treated earlier in C.L. Moore's (1944/1995) novella, *No Woman Born*, where Deirdre, a celebrated dancer, has been resurrected after a theater fire. Her flesh has been irreparably charred, but her brain has been extracted and encased within a body composed of metal bracelets fitted inside and sliding on each other, moving with a litheness not quite human. As the engineers were unable to work out a static facsimile of her beauty, they based her new form on her likeness in motion. Muscles of magnetic currents hold her together with her "radiant mind poised in metal, dominating it, bending the steel to the illusion of her lost self" (p. 31). The characterization of Deirdre's ego as an imposed force on the movement of her golden-ringed body suffices to humanize her. Moore's point, and possibly, hope, is that a mechanical body can become personalized, humanized to the point of being a duplicate, in both mannerisms and mood, of the human body it replaces.

Here the machine is appearing as more human and more alluring than the original flesh. But this machine also possesses concealed superhuman capabilities; it is able to leave stasis in a movement too swift to be followed by human eyes, and so become a "tesseract of human motion, a parable of fourth-dimensional activity . . . the room shimmered [in] sudden, violent heat" (p. 60). This action, called *blazing*, disconnects Deirdre from humanity. She has been exiled in metal, and is forgetting what flesh feels like. She calls herself a baroque, a creation that could never be duplicated, and she fears isolation, fears being alone in her metal housing with her humanity slowly draining out of her, leaving her with that "strange little quiver of something . . . unDeirdre . . . which had so briefly trembled beneath the surface of familiarity" (p. 39).

Lacking the sensory perceptions of touch, taste, and smell, though now endowed with wondrous powers, Deirdre is tormented with longings for her once-biological self. Deirdre is a daughter of McLuhan's fantasy in that her social roles changed when her body was recrafted.

THE SIX MILLION DOLLAR COUPLE

Citing Norbert Wiener's conviction that humans are destined to rely on the mechanized brain, McLuhan (1951) warned of the misapplication of applied science in "The Voice of the Lab" (p. 90). He asked if we are to sink into a "serfdom," physically, intellectually, and emotionally bound by the promised superiority of the electronic brain. Perhaps the solution is an alliance between the two forms. McLuhan cited a headline from The Needham Market: Test-Tube Babies Will Produce Robots (p. 92).

So how do we define humanness in our current technological state? How much humanness must be in the machine to maintain its human rights? A contemporary novel demonstrates that McLuhan's fears are on-going concerns. In the novel *The Modular Man*, author Roger Allen (1992) probes alternatives to biological humanness. David Bailey has been severely injured while riding in a robotic taxi—a transitional passenger vehicle that already implies the loss of a controlling self. Mortally injured, Bailey hurriedly completes an experimental machine—a 6-foot robotic vacuum cleaner. To retain his consciousness, he mindloads his human essence into this container. He has been reduced to dealing with life from a remote perspective, the equivalent to a household tool.

In this world, mindloading is a criminal procedure, and therefore Bailey the Vacuum is placed into a police property room. Here, he robotically proceeds to clean all the evidence shelved in the room, thereby removing fingerprints and other incriminating dirt from evidence of other crimes. Thus the result of our mechanized explorations: something that cannot be controlled even in the middle of a police station. Dusting off fingerprints becomes a metaphor for the utter loss of individuality that McLuhan warned of, the price one pays for making oneself into a stereotype in response to manipulative messages from "The Voice of the Lab."

Bailey has become the "ultimate cyborg. You could say there is nothing left of Bailey but the idea of Bailey. Is he alive? Can he be, with no organic tissue left?" (p. 22). What happens to a man when his place in the physical world has been so inexorably altered? Can he be recognized as human? Bailey asks, "am I a man? . . . And if I judge myself a man, call myself a human, then by what criteria. . . . How much have I lost?" (p. 207). The novel ends with the query "maybe it's not a question of what 'human being' means, but what it means to be a human being" (p. 265).

The question of how one retains biological humanity is again put forth in this novel. Bailey's companion, Suzanne, has had all four limbs amputated. Her head has been englobed by a teleoperator helmet containing sensors to run a remote body. She can "never touch, never taste, never eat or drink or cry, any more than any other machine could"(p. 39). The Baileys could have sprung full-blown from McLuhan's brow. Indeed cyborg literature develops the same psycho-fantasies articulated by McLuhan—its figures the end products of the processes he described theoretically.

All four of the creatures I have introduced to you ache for their organic selves, even while recognizing the wondrous capabilities of their new mechanized forms. They might have observed, along with McLuhan, that "nothing beats the taste of Coca-Cola."

REFERENCES

Allen, R. (1992). *The modular man*. New York: Bantam Books.

Clynes, M.E., & Kline, N.S. (1960, September). Cyborgs and space. *Astronautics Magazine*, pp. 26-27, 74-75.

Laumer, K. (1965). *A plague of demons*. New York: Warner Books.

McLuhan , M. (1951). *The mechanical bride*. New York: Vanguard Press.

Moore, C.L. (1995). No woman born. In *Women of wonder: The classic years*. New York: Harvest Original. (Original work published 1944)

19 WHY PRINT IS "COOL" AND ORALITY IS BODY TEMPERATURE

Raymond Gozzi, Jr.

Ithaca College

McLuhan's metaphors of *hot* and *cool* media were controversial from the start. Already in his introduction to the second edition of *Understanding Media* (McLuhan, 1964, p. viii) he is defending their use against complaints ("The section on 'media hot and cool' confused many reviewers. . . ."). In the 30 years since, it is safe to say that these metaphors have not become widely accepted (see Gozzi, 1992, 1999).

In this chapter, I propose an explanation for the difficulties of the hot and cool metaphors: The metaphors are not used in a structurally appropriate manner. The primary dimension suggested by the *hot–cool* continuum is one of activity, both physical activity and emotional activity. *Hot* things are active, *cool* things are still. Emotions are *hot*, reasoning is *cool*. These metaphorical uses are extensions of our physical body experience.

Embodied experience structures many of our concepts and metaphors using what Johnson (1987) calls *image schemas*. The *hot–cool* image schema produces the common attribution of *heat* to anger, love, emotional arguments, rage. The same image schema produces the metaphorical attribution of *coolness* or *coldness* to aloofness, separation, reserve, emotional disengagement, reason, calculation (see Table 19.1).

TABLE 19.1   Activity Dimension of Hot–Cool Metaphor from Body-
Based Image-Schema

HOT	COOL
Moving	Still
Excited	Calm
Emotional	Intellectual
Angry	Aloof
Passionate	Rational
Engaged	Calculating

McLuhan went against this common image schema by claiming that
print was *hot* and television was *cool*. It would have been more structurally
consistent with the activity dimension to reverse these. Print, which is still,
silent, and inactive, might better be described as *cool*. Then television, which
is moving, noisy, and active could be considered *hot*. If we are going to use
a *hot–cool* metaphorical spectrum, the active electronic media fit better at the
hot end, and quiet print at the *cool* end.

MCLUHAN'S DIMENSIONS OF HOT-COOL METAPHORS

McLuhan, however, did not apply this image-schematic dimension to his *hot*
and *cool* metaphors. Instead he used three dimensions of his own to define
and use the metaphors: "definition," "sense dominance," and "participation."

In the definition dimension, a *hot* medium was "high definition," meaning it was "full of information." A *cool* medium, on the other hand, was
"low definition," with less information presented, needing to be filled in by
the user. I point out that there is no metaphorically necessary connection
between the amount of information contained by a medium and the
metaphors of heat and cold. And, as Zettl (1990) points out, the same medium may be relatively full of information at one time, and leave gaps at other
times. I suggest separating the dimension of "high and low definition" from
the *hot* and *cool* metaphors altogether.

McLuhan's second dimension was a "sensory" dimension. He claimed
that a *hot* medium emphasized *one* sense and gave it predominance over oth-

ers. *Cool* media allowed for an interplay of different senses. However, this reliance on just one sense seems completely arbitrary. It is also not particularly useful in an age when media are converging and routinely engage more than one sense.

McLuhan's third dimension was participation. A *hot* medium, being full of information, excluded people and was low on participation. By contrast, a *cool* medium invited participation, as people filled in the gaps left by its sparse information. However, participation was not carefully defined, and seemed to be used in different ways. With a more careful definition of participation I think this dimension could comfortably fit with the *hot* and *cool* metaphors.

Thus, there are many reasons the *hot* and *cool* metaphors have not "caught on," and are not in widespread use at present.

REALIGNING THE METAPHORS

Even with the difficulties just cited, these metaphors are fascinating, and reflect real and potential insights into media. In this spirit, I would like to propose a realignment of the *hot* and *cool* media metaphors. Rather than use *hot* and *cool* as completely relative terms, I would like to anchor them in the experience of the body, and propose a mediating third term: *body temperature*. This accords with Johnson's (1987) claim that our conceptual and metaphorical "structures typically depend on the nature of the human body, especially on our perceptual categories and motor skills" (p. xi).

Table 19.2 displays a partial list of McLuhan's *hot* and *cool* metaphors for media.

TABLE 19.2   McLuhan's Hot and cool Metaphors for Media

HOT	COOL
Radio	Telephone
Movies	Television
Photography	Cartoons
Phonetic alphabet	Hieroglyphics
Print–typography	Manuscripts

It should be noted that if telephone and television were moved to the hot column, and the phonetic alphabet and print were moved to the cool column, there would be a grouping with print and writing at the *cool* end and electronic media at the *hot* end. In other words, it would not take much change to produce the *hot–cool* spectrum that accords well with the activity dimension of the metaphors based on body experience.

However, McLuhan is also interested in the user's participation with the medium. To bring in this dimension, one needs to distinguish types of participation. I claim that *hot* media invite emotional participation, *cool* media invite intellectual participation, and *body temperature* media invite physical participation.

Into the new category of *body temperature media* I would put oral communication (not exactly a medium), where people participate with their whole bodies; telephones, where people speak and gesticulate into the medium, and listen to it actively; photographs, where people rush to get into the picture; and manuscripts, including handwritten letters, where people write them themselves. The revised table of media is shown in Table 19.3.

In this schema, electronic media generally tend toward the *hot* end, and print and writing media toward the *cool* end of the spectrum. This listing of media provides a better structural fit with the common image schema of hot and cool in our body experience.

Personal computers are in an intermediate position, which is changing as the technology develops. With graphic user interfaces, and connection to the Internet, personal computers are becoming less like print, and more like electronic media (see Gozzi, 1997).

TABLE 19.3   Hot–Body Temperature–Cool Spectrum of Media and Types of Participation

HOT	BODY TEMPERATURE	COOL
Emotional participation	Physical participation	Intellectual participation
Television	Telephones	Print
Radio	Photographs	Phonetic alphabet
Internet	Manuscript	Cartoons
Personal computer	Letters	

REWRITING HOT AND COOL HISTORY

This metaphorical reversal of print and television's temperatures will require a rewriting of the metaphorical history of media according to new *hot* and *cool* criteria. I can only suggest the bare outlines of such a rewrite here (see Table 19.4). Orality, to begin with, is *body temperature*, with its limited range of variations toward hot and cool. Oral cultures are relatively homogeneous, with firm boundaries between acceptable and unacceptable thought and behavior.

The arrival of writing metaphorically cools down the *body temperature* oral culture. It adds social distance, intellectual abstraction, and creates a sense of separate individuals. When alphabetic writing came in to ancient Greece, for example, it helped produce the *cold* calculating strategies of the rhetoricians, who were willing to detach language from its speaker and take any position in a debate. In politics the *cold* strategies of alphabetic Greece led to exploitation and empire which embroiled Athens and all of Greece in the fateful Peloponnesian Wars.

With *cool* print in Renaissance Europe, the *cold* rational abstractions of science and instrumental logic, were applied ever-more expansively to all areas of *body temperature* life. The resulting impersonal society of industrialism, furthered by the *cool* medium of print, fostered social anomie and hyperindividualism.

Into the *cold*, rational, individualistic society of the West burst the *hot* electronic media in the 20th century. These media engaged people's emo-

TABLE 19.4   Re-Writing Hot & Cool History

---

1. Oral cultures are body temperature.
    - Direct participation
    - Limited range of expression, thought
2. Writing introduces a cool medium.
    - Class separation, aloofness, individuality
    - Abstraction, impersonal calculation in culture
3. Print accelerates cool tendencies.
    - Industrialism, rationality, science, technology
4. Electronic media heat up industrial society.
    - Emotionality, fanaticism, mythic thought
    - Instantaneous transfer of information, money
    - Melting and blurring of boundaries

---

tions, not their rationality, and upset the delicate balances of *cold*, abstract structures that had relied upon *cool* print and its associated cognitive and emotional habits of disinterested calculation.

It was this volatile injection of *hot* media that threatened to *melt* the *cool* structures of Western society that so engaged McLuhan's attention. McLuhan described very well the increasing fluidity of thought and society in the electronic era. He instinctively understood that formerly discrete *cool* categories were blurring their boundaries as they melted in the glare of *hot* electric media.

McLuhan noted the increasingly mythical thought evident in the electronic age. This is consistent with a departure from print's *cold* rationality and logic, toward a more *body temperature*, oral culture, provoked by *hot* electronic media.

McLuhan claimed that traditional educational practices, linked to print, were obsolete. He advocated that education become more integrative, dealing with the whole person, instead of trying to develop only rational skills (McLuhan, Hutchon, & McLuhan, 1980). In the new metaphorical terms used here, he wanted to move education away from its *cold* emphasis, and warm it up, make it more fully human, bring it closer to *body temperature*.

Tracing out the implications of our metaphors as guides for the future, we would expect society and culture to become more feverish in the glare of the *hot* electronic media. We would expect more emotionalism and more fanaticism (as predicted by Nystrom, 1977). We would expect many people to get burned who get too close to the media (as often happens to political figures already).

These predictions of a *hotter* society point to the necessity for developing and preserving *cool* institutions, which can ecologically balance the heat produced by electronic media. Schools, literacy programs, mediation centers, antiviolence training, and yoga and meditation centers are examples.

In summary, I believe it is quite possible to think coherently about the history of media using metaphors of *hot* and *cool*. It is unfortunate that McLuhan's uses of these metaphors violated a widespread body-based image schema. As a result, the metaphors produced confusion instead of understanding. If, however, we realign these metaphors with their commonly understood structure, we may recover a useful vocabulary for understanding media.

REFERENCES

Gozzi, R., Jr. (1992). Hot and cool media. *ETC: A Review of General Semantics*, *49*(2), 227-230.

Gozzi, R., Jr. (1997). Metaphors converging on the internet. *ETC: A Review of General Semantics, 54*(4), 479-486.

Gozzi, R., Jr. (1999). *The power of metaphor in the age of electronic media.* Cresskill, NJ: Hampton Press.

Johnson, M. (1987). *The body in the mind.* Chicago: University of Chicago Press.

McLuhan, M. (1964). *Understanding media* (2nd ed.). New York: New American Library.

McLuhan, M., Hutchon, K., & McLuhan, E. (1980). *Media, messages, and language.* Skokie, IL: National Textbook .

Nystrom, C. (1977). Immediate man: The symbolic environment of fanaticism. *ETC: A Review of General Semantics, 34*(1), 19-34.

Zettl, H. (1990). *Sight sound motion* (2nd ed.). Belmont, CA: Wadsworth.

20 MARSHALL McLUHAN MEETS COMMUNICATION 101

McLUHAN AS EXILE

Gary Gumpert
Queens College
and *Communication Landscapers*

I'm not sure how to approach this chapter on the subject of Marshall McLuhan because I don't know whether to capitalize on my actual relationships with him or simply to stress gathered academic insights, but I will try to both briefly mention a personal and professional relationship and articulate my insights because my persona as a scholar (or persona seeking scholarhood) was so influenced by him.

Thirty-five years ago I was a graduate student in Detroit, Michigan and in order to support my quest for a degree, I was hired as a television director/producer at Wayne State University and WDET-TV. As part of my graduate assistantship, I was assigned to direct a lot of different television programs including concerts, recitals, lectures, quiz programs for the library, dramas—in short, it was a wonderful opportunity to experiment and play with the exciting and creative medium of television at a time when cameras were bulky, studio conditions less than ideal, and electronic editing was not available. It was a time when ingenuity, imagination, and clever adaption was necessary because videotape was not yet commonplace. All productions were done live from beginning to end without stopping and thus the only means of recording was a kinescope—a film made directly from the television screen.

It was under these circumstances that Lee S. Dreyfus, my supervisor and senior professor (later I would work with him at the University of

Wisconsin in Madison and later yet he would become governor of Wisconsin), asked me to attend a lecture at the Merrill Palmer Institute being presented by a Canadian named Marshall McLuhan. I had no idea who this person was, nor why I was suddenly thrust into this lecture hall. I don't remember a word that was said, except that the circumstances and the aura around this unique charismatic personality remains vivid.

He spoke and the air bristled. His tall demeanor dominated the room. The question period was intense and surprisingly, often hostile. There was something about the man that brought out the argumentative personality hidden in all of us. He spoke, but appeared, at times, not to listen. I was recently reminded of a descriptive comment made by Lee Dreyfus, one that McLuhan apparently enjoyed, about himself: "Listening to Marshall McLuhan is like attempting to drink from a fire hydrant." I was unaware that in 1951 he had already published *The Mechanical Bride: Folklore of Industrial Man* (McLuhan, 1951) . Later I would find out that behind the contemporary and modernistic façade, McLuhan was a classical scholar who earlier had written on the works of Ezra Pound, T.S. Eliot, James Joyce, and Thomas Aquinas, among others. I was aware that I was in the presence of an extraordinarily magnetic character who always spoke, but seldom listened. I was unaware of the circumstances that would soon follow and that would, to some extent, shape and perhaps slightly change the course of my life.

Several days after the Merrill Palmer Institute lecture, I was asked or informed by Lee Dreyfus that I would be directing and producing[1] a 30-minute television program with Marshall McLuhan about his work. The production was being sponsored by the National Association of Educational Broadcasters "Project in Understanding New Media." And several weeks later Marshall McLuhan and I were sharing a bottle of scotch in my apartment on the Wayne State University campus. Once his cigar was in hand, planning would begin and last several weeks. Letters and telephone calls between Detroit and Toronto became an obvious necessity. I had begun to panic. My first responsibility was to find out what McLuhan was about . . . and that was no easy task. I didn't have much else to go on except for the dialogue that evolved over the next few months, correspondence and telephone calls between us, and the script of a previous television program called *The Teenager* in which he had been involved with the Canadian Broadcasting Company.

On May 10, 1960, I received the following letter:

---

[1]There are some questions as to who was actually producing the program. Many years after the production, the outline for the program indicates that Marshall McLuhan was the producer, although I functioned at that time with the presumption that I was producing the program.

> There is a brutal amount of data to be handled and I would prefer to
> have a kinescope that would have be played over and over, rather than
> to sacrifice basic aspects of the Gutenberg effect. I will write a complete
> dialogue for the various shots, as soon as you and I have a had a chance
> to go over the script.
>   My theme is quite simple, in this respect at least; that I see the entire
> Gutenberg 500 years as repetition in all levels of life and culture of the
> basic matrix of the Gutenberg press itself. The Greeko-Roman world,
> from the phonetic alphabet forward, was in the same way a repetition of
> the technology of that alphabet as applied to the papyrus and to-day our
> world shows the beginnings of a repetition in all human transactions of
> the basic electric circuit. I mention this because if we can consider the
> 500 years of Gutenberg dominance as located between two other tech-
> nologies it should help to define our problem. (McLuhan, personal
> communication, 1960)

Producing and directing this television program was not going to be an
easy task. There would never be a "complete dialogue for the various shots."
    What emerged was an outline of images and ideas that would stimulate
and prod the McLuhan free-flowing associations. Translating McLuhan into
visual terms, disciplining him to adhere to the limitations of television's time
and space, without inhibiting his creativity, was going to be difficult. Here I
was, a footnote in graduate study about to produce a television program
with someone who suddenly exploded into the foremost media guru of the
1960s. A reproduction of the first page of the outline/script (see appendix)
indicates the enormity of the task. In the first 4 minutes, minus 1 minute for
the opening credits, the concepts preliterate, postliterate, and Gutenberg
would be introduced.
    On June 4, 1960, Harley Parker from the Royal Ontario Museum,
Robert Shafer, associate professor of education at Wayne State University,
Marshall McLuhan, and a television crew got together and we produced a
program the budget of which was $365 (which included a $75 directorial fee
for myself) plus one negative kinescope and print for $250 adding up to a
grand total of $650. The result was *The Gutenberg Galaxy*, a less than pol-
ished, but fascinating 30-minute program one kinescope copy of which
today resides in a crevice somewhere in my overgrown study, and the impact
of which I am unable to judge. The title of that program would later be the
title of a volume published in 1962 by the University of Toronto Press
(McLuhan, 1962).
    I'm not sure why Marshall McLuhan became a media happening and
hit. But certainly, hostile academic reception kept pace with his popularity.
The cover of *Newsweek* announced "The Message of Marshall McLuhan"
(1967). *Mademoiselle* interviewed him and he spoke about "speed, women,
and his native Canada" (1967). *Glamour* featured "The Brave New World of

Marshall McLuhan" (1966). *Life* wrote a story about the "Oracle of the Electric Age" (Howard, 1966). *Harper's Magazine* featured a Richard Schickel (1965) story on "Canada's Intellectual Comet." He made the cover of the *Saturday Review* (Culkin, 1967) and he was the featured interview in the March 1969 issue of *Playboy* (McLuhan, 1969). He was everywhere and commensurate with this rise were the accompanying intellectual attacks. He was an intellectual sitting icon. Benjamin DeMott (1966) ended his *Esquire* article:

> How much can be said for an intellectual vision whose effect is to encourage abdication from all responsibility of mind?
> Or: what good is this famous McLuhancy if it makes men drunk as it makes them bold? (p. 73)

In 1968, Eliot Fremont-Smith reviewed two books for *The New York Times* written by McLuhan: *War and Peace In The Global Village* (McLuhan & Fiore, 1968), *Through the Vanishing Point* (McLuhan & Parker, 1968), and a volume entitled *McLuhan: Pro & Con* (Rosenthal, 1968). The review was devastating. It ends with the following:

> Whatever else it is, McLuhanism has become its own little industry—a trifle passe perhaps, a trifle tedious, but clearly thriving still. Yet it need no longer be intimidating. Indeed, he may wake up one morning to find it has all blown away, like so much swamp gas. (Fremont-Smith, 1968, p. 45)

Thirty years after his meteoric rise, academics have attempted to exorcize him from the hall of scholarship—perhaps because he became too important and too popular at the same time, perhaps because his aphorisms ran out of control. His epigrams offended and had begun to breed. His popularity bred contempt.

The heart of McLuhan's message was not complex. He raised some basic questions. Do human beings think and perceive the world differently because of the media which exist in their environment? Do media alter the way we use our senses?

In 1963 he sent me a letter in which he said:

> I have begun to direct a new [graduate] Center here [Toronto] ... for the "Study of the Extensions of Man." That includes all technologies whatever, from speech and clothing to computers. Have a new book ready on this subject, which should be out in the Spring. [he was referring to *Understanding Media* (McLuhan, 1964)]. The advantage of the concept of the *Extensions of Man* is that everybody can see at once that any extension modifies the existing sense ratios, whether in the individual or

> the society. It also becomes easy to see why the extension is the crux in effecting change, and not the "content" The "content" is always another medium which had its impact earlier. (McLuhan, personal communication, 1963)

Imbedded in those few words are both the obvious and the not so obvious. They need to placed within the context of a time of extraordinary and swift technological change. The shifts and changes in communication that have occurred in the last 150 years are awesome—photography (from black and white to color to Polaroid to digital), motion pictures (from black and white to color), telegraphy, the typewriter (from the manual introduced by Remington in 1874 to electric typewriters to word processors), telephony (from the party line to the beeper and cellular phone), sound recording (from acoustical to stereo to digital, from disc to tape to CD), radio (from wired to wireless, from AM to FM and short wave, from home to car to ear), typography and high-speed printing, television (from live to film to tape to disc), xerography (and copies galore), facsimile, high band and broad band satellite transmission, the computer and its countless variations of digitalizing information pushing us into the Internet, cyberspace, and virtual reality.

My experience in producing *The Gutenberg Galaxy* and studying McLuhan (and company) altered me. The ideas became imbedded in my scholarship. This was not a deliberate process, it happened over time. You interiorize the exterior. You become what you learn. You absorb and preach. You teach. It is almost an unconscious process And at the same time I have become puzzled by the McLuhan enigma. Why has McLuhan, the communication theorist, not been integrated in the contemporary communication curriculum aside from a fairly small coterie of true believers and critical scholars? I suppose that the same question could be asked about the work of Harold Innis, Eric Havelock, and Walter J. Ong who seem to have been relegated to the realm of the respected esoteric. But why was the popular McLuhan so exorcized from the study of communications? Why is his spiritual presence absent? Why has the fascination eroded into denial? Why is it politically incorrect in some academic sectors to state the word according to McLuhan? I witnessed the anger and resentment outside the communication domain as he became popular, but all but a little nagging part of my cerebellum thought that "the word" was being passed on . . . but where and how?

The important 1998 Fordham University McLuhan Symposium answered the question in part, but there have been few such precious pockets of adoration and critique. I would still ask why McLuhan has not been absorbed into the standard communication pedagogy? Why is McLuhan excluded from the undergraduate communication curriculum?

I asked a number of colleagues to respond to a set of totally unscientific questions. "Are you aware of any courses in your curriculum that are substantially, or in part, devoted to an analysis of McLuhan's work? Are you

aware of any introductory courses in your curriculum that simply introduces his ideas . . . or the notion that he existed?" The unidentified (to protect the innocent) responses were interesting and chilling:

> I spend one of 15 sessions in my graduate course on McLuhan and they
> write a critical essay on him. I argue that he remains seminal, no matter
> how many critics are out there, and of course many of his ideas are
> flawed, but perhaps no one else raised better questions than did
> McLuhan.

> He was fun in the 1960s but now needs interpretation. I will not use
> *Understanding Media* in an undergraduate course. The students won't
> "get it."

> In my introductory course on Communication, Rhetoric and Society
> . . . I do mention that Canadian, especially in the context of a discussion
> on form and content. I also use Postman's *Amusing Ourselves to Death*
> and *Technopoly* and he too mentions McLuhan.

> No courses focus on his work. I am sure that the text in our
> "Introduction to Mass Media" class mentions him.

> The only mention of McLuhan is a brief mention in the "Theories of
> Mass Communication" graduate course.

> My quick reaction to your question is actually a sad one. I have a feel-
> ing that much of the curriculum is tied in to what's hot, what's in the
> journals and texts at any given point in time. It strikes me that McLuhan
> hasn't been "hot" or "cool" (excuse me for that) for a long time. This
> may or may not have anything to do with the quality of his observa-
> tions/assertions. It may be more of a marketing function. . . . I'm over-
> generalizing. His work is still used and used credibly. And I think as
> "mediated communication" takes on all sorts of modified forms, shapes,
> constructions, there should be heightened attention to the
> McLuhanesque frames of observation. . . . I think he came to be identi-
> fied with a time and that time passed. Critical studies, economic analy-
> ses seem to have become the primary frames through which analysts
> have chosen to examine the field in recent years/decade. Where it was
> once "cutting edge" to invoke McLuhan's name. Today, it's probably
> considered quaint. . . . I'm saddened because its disappointing to think
> that we are so politically correct so that certain approaches are "in" and
> others are "out."

> No courses that I know of have been devoted to McLuhan's work.
> There is a required Theories of Communication course that covers
> McLuhan, but it is just an introduction.

There we have it, perhaps a complete quantitative analysis of the reactions should follow, but the responses are not unexpected. By the way, one does not have to be quoting McLuhan to be eligible for entry into the club of awareness. An innate sense of understanding will do. But what accounts for the current state that has cleansed McLuhan from the communication discipline? Let me suggest a few notions. I'm sure you will have other ideas. I'm going to disregard the nagging, but preposterous notion that McLuhan had nothing to say that is relevant to the broad study of communication. Absurdity is to be dismissed.

1. The field of communication has had an antitechnology bias built into its historical structure—particularly in the United States. In 1960, rhetoric and public address were the only legitimate areas of study. All else was peripheral and McLuhan was somehow always linked to a "mass media" popular culture orientation—one with little intellectual respectability. Among the communication scholar traditionalists who shaped curriculum and research, it was fashionable to look at "popular culture" and the "mass media" with disdain—and McLuhan was pushed into that convenient niche.

2. The turf orientation of the communication discipline has no room for the interdisciplinary and infectious nature of McLuhan's ideas, particularly within the structural chaos that characterizes contemporary communication study. The territorial preoccupation of communication scholars has created a series of nonpermeable fiefdoms that isolate ideas rather than stimulate the potentially rich thoughts which emerge out of interdisciplinary study.

3. The last reason, which I cannot support with evidence, is that the deterministic aspect of McLuhan's ideas are particularly appalling and threatening to communication traditionalists who maintain that the creation of thought is either divinely inspired or the result of complete self-will.

In the summer 1994 issue of the *Chronicle of Higher Education,* Langdon Winner wrote an article in which he grappled with the issue of technological innovation:

> what most conventional ideas about technology lack—is any notion of technological development as a dynamic social and cultural phenomenon. This is not an arcane topic. Every thorough-going history of the building of technological systems points to the same conclusion: Substantial technological innovation involve a re-weaving of the fabric

of society—a reshaping of some of the roles, rules, relationships, and institutions that make up our ways of living together. (Winner, 1994, p. B1)

Winner's analysis stresses the complex interrelationships of innovation and states that "the technology is never the sole cause of the changes one sees. But it is often the occasion and catalyst for a thorough redefinition of the operating structures of society and of the daily experiences of people in their work, family, life, and communities" (p. B1).

About 9 years after the production of *The Gutenberg Galaxy,* Marshall McLuhan came to deliver a series of lectures at Queens College in New York. It was a difficult experience for him. He was just recovering from a severe illness and his treatment by a number of critics and faculty members could only be described as severe. His teaching duties required that he cut short his visit to New York, much to our disappointment, but he promised to return, at his own expense, to fulfill his contractual obligations to the college. A week prior to his return he sent me a letter that I should have looked at much more carefully, because it was very revealing.

> I am looking forward to being back with you on Wednesday and would like you to ask your classes to pass in as many written suggestions as they can muster. I mean suggestions about how to improve *Understanding Media* and my other things. My plan is to revise some of them for new additions. Had even thought of putting at the end of chapters the heading "The Moral": and their [there] inserting both banal and relevant comments as if I were reviewing my own book. You see, I consider the actual *processes* set up by media as immense involuntary things for which private views are childish and impertinent. On the other had, it is impossible for any individual to grasp very much of the total process in any one instance. Therefore I regard my work as entirely tentative, an initiation for others to pitch in and enlighten *me.* It is very discouraging, therefore, when reviewers merely report their private opinions about what they consider to be my private opinions. This futile action carries the whole drama into absurdity. It is merely the newspaper or book-man piggybacking on another medium. (McLuhan, 1971, personal communication)

This was a more hesitant McLuhan. Someone who had grown sensitive to the constant attacks that he had, to some extent, brought on himself as a result of his style and popularity. But he continued, perhaps in a more thoughtful manner, more removed from the spotlight of his former commercial success, to order and refine his own ideas and theoretical approach. And I think it's time that communication scholars carefully look at Herbert Marshall McLuhan as a compelling and influential scholar from whom we can continue to learn today. It time that communications scholars looked at themselves carefully and broadened their narrow vision dispensing and emerging from the arrogance of their pedagogical playpens.

APPENDIX: REPRODUCTION OF PAGE 1 OF THE "GUTENBERG GALAXY" SHOOTING SCRIPT

SUPER:
"GUTENBERG GALAXY"

MARSHALL MCLUHAN

ROBERT SHAFER

HARLEY PARKER

MCLUHAN INTRODUCES HIS
COLLEAGUES AND SUBJECT,
HE STEPS DOWN TO AN EXHIBIT
OF PRIMITIVE SCULPTURE
(PRELITERATE)
AND TELEVISION SET
(POSTLITERATE)

MCLUHAN MOVES BACK TO CHAIR
GRAPHIC: IGLOO
FILM: EGYPTIAN SCRIBE

ANNCR:
The Gutenberg Galaxy;
A voyage between two
worlds—with Marshall
McLuhan, for the National
Association of Educational
Broadcasts, Robert Shafer,
associate professor of
education at Wayne State
University and Harley
Parker from the Royal
Ontario Museum.

                    1:00   1:00
MARSHALL:
Point of travel through five
centuries of print culture.
Polarization.

Define Gutenberg.

Contrast the two artifacts
                    2:00   3:00
Discussion which leads to
shape of Igloo.

Discussion of this aspects
leads to the Egyptian scribe
                    1:00   4:00
Transition from preliterate.

Scribe visualizing

Sound on clay

REFERENCES

The brave new world of Marshall McLuhan. (1966, July). *Glamour*, pp. 100-101, 133-135.

Culkin, J. M. (1967, March 18). A schoolman's guide to Marshall McLuhan. *Saturday Review*, pp. 51-53, 70-72.

DeMott, B. (1966, August). Against McLuhan. *Esquire*, pp. 71-73.

Fremont-Smith, E. (1968, September 4). The tedium is the message. *The New York Times*, p. 45.

Howard, J. (1966, Feb. 25). Oracle of the electric age. *Life*, pp. 91-92, 95, 96, 99.

McLuhan, M. (1951). *The mechanical bride: Folklore of industrial man*. New York: The Vanguard Press.

McLuhan, M. (1962). *The Gutenberg galaxy*. Toronto, Canada: University of Toronto Press.

McLuhan, M. (1964). *Understanding media: The extensions of man*. New York: McGraw-Hill.

McLuhan, M. (1969). Marshall McLuhan: A candid conversation with the high priest of popcult and metaphysican of media. *Playboy*, pp. 53, 54, 56, 59-62, 64-66, 68, 70, 72, 74, 158.

McLuhan, M., & Fiore, Q. (1968). *War and peace in the global village: An inventory of some of the current spastic situations that could be eliminated by more feed-forward*. New York: Bantam.

McLuhan, M., & Parker, H. (1968). *Through the vanishing point: Space in poetry and painting*. New York: Harcourt & Row.

The message of Marshall McLuhan. (1967, March 6). *Newsweek*, pp. 53-57.

Rosenthal, R. (Ed.). (1968). *McLuhan: Pro and con*. New York: Funk & Wagnalls.

Schickel, R. (1965, November). Canada's intellectual comet. *Harper's Magazine*, pp. 62–68.

Understanding Canada and sundry other matters: Marshall McLuhan. (1967, January). *Mademoiselle* , pp. 114-115, 126-130.

Winner, L. (1994, Summer). *Chronicle of Higher Education*, p. B1.

21 EARLY MEDIUM THEORY, OR, ROOTS OF TECHNOLOGICAL DETERMINISM IN NORTH AMERICAN COMMUNICATION THEORY

Donna Flayhan

State University of New York—New Paltz

INNIS AND McLUHAN: FROM MARGINS TO CENTER

Although much of the Canadian scholarship on Harold Innis and Marshall McLuhan deals with similarities in their work as representative of a Canadian school of communication, what is most significant is how their approaches differ from all other North American communication scholarship throughout the United States and Canada.

The marginal cultural positions of Innis and McLuhan are important, yet we should not celebrate them because they represent some sort of Canadian mind, or Canadian school, but because they offer significant insights into the study of communication, consciousness, and culture thus differing radically from other scholars of the day: They also differ radically from one another.

The main differences between the ideas of Innis and McLuhan are a consequence of their different methods, paths of investigation, ways of looking. Innis' empirical, historical, "dirt research,"[1] method led him to investigate

---

[1]*Dirt research* is a term that Innis used to describe his multileveled method of empirical investigation.

the *cultural* implications of communication technologies concerning access to information, power, empires, and monopolies of knowledge. McLuhan's theoretical, literary, "probe,"[2] method led him to discuss the effects of communication technologies on *consciousness*—changes in sense ratios, sensory balance, and alterations of the central nervous system.

Some current Canadian scholars argue that Innis and McLuhan, as scholars on the margins, produced a uniquely Canadian theory of history and communication technologies. This argument also takes the form of discussing them as representative of the Canadian mind (Kroker, 1984; Robinson & Theall, 1975; Stamps, 1995). Although such discussions are interesting, they tend to overlook the point that Innis and McLuhan were marginal within Canada, too. Innis and McLuhan's marginal positions as Canadian scholars in North America is important, yet most significant are their marginal theoretical positions in all of North American scholarship resulting from their unique insights into forms of communication, culture, and consciousness.

Innis and McLuhan did indeed share a marginalized and unique perspective developed as scholars on the margins—both geographically (Canada as opposed to the United States) and *intellectually*: Their cultural, historical, theoretical research on media forms stand in stark contrast to the dominant functionalist and behavioralist studies of media content effects research of the time. The insights offered by Innis and McLuhan are a consequence of broad, interdisciplinary, qualitative approaches to scholarship at a time when most research in North America was specialized, quantitative, and concerned mainly with methods (Hardt, 1992).

Studies of media in North America in the late 1940s, 1950s, and most of the 1960s, were products of their post-World War II industrial boom environments (Carey, 1989). The post-World War II climate in North America was marked by new technological innovations and rapid economic growth. This climate infected universities, putting many scholars in the position of administrative research at the service of government and corporations. Funding flowed into communication studies as administrative research, the transmission view of communication, behavioral effects research, sales research, studies for private industry, studies for the military, and the development of methods on methods in the absence of theory all flourished (Adorno, 1971; Carey, 1989; Hardt, 1992).

Thus, the most striking aspect of the work of Innis and McLuhan is that they stood aside from the social scientific craze of specialization and quantification sweeping Canada, the United States, and Britain (Hardt, 1992). It is that marginalization that allows the scholarship of Innis and McLuhan to

---

[2]*Probe* is the term used by McLuhan to refer to "the product of his thinking" (Ong, 1982, p. 135).

be so insightful and useful to us today. Like the Frankfurt School and the British and American Cultural Studies traditions, these early medium theorists offer communication scholars a chance to recapture the vital scholarship that, as Innis predicted, flourished along the margins of the social scientific center of communication studies for too many decades. It is time to bring medium theory to the center of communication theory and cultural studies.

HAROLD INNIS: FROM ECONOMIC HISTORY TO COMMUNICATION THEORY

Harold Innis was an economic historian who adapted his meticulous methods for studying economic monopolies to the study of information monopolies. Perhaps more accurately, Innis' methods adapted him to the study of information monopolies and biases of communication.

Innis was an empirical, historical theorist. That is what led him from the study of economics to the study of communication technologies. Unlike McLuhan, one cannot point to a theorist who pushed Innis toward the study of communication technologies. This is because he came to the centrality of communication through empirical investigation. This brilliant historian paid most of his attention to the particular, yet because he abhorred narrow specialization, he was able to make incredibly insightful generalizations from the vast array of particulars with which he familiarized himself. Innis' references to his style of research as "dirt research" suggests the primal toil it involves. Yet, Innis was also a generalist and a theorist who made larger connections.

INNIS' LATER WORK: COMMUNICATION

In 1948, Innis presented what became the first chapter in *The Bias of Communication*, "Minerva's Owl," to a group of scholars at Oxford. In the speech, he presented a complete list of (known) dominant forms of communication in the West for the past 3,000 years—all in one sentence.

In *Empire and Communication* (Innis, 1950) and *The Bias of Communication* (Innis, 1951), Innis expanded his argument that social and political power are exercised through monopoly control over a given medium of communication, which in turn leads to monopolies of knowledge, monopolies of knowledge that can in turn be broken by the development of new media.

Innis' ideas and fears in regard to monopolies of knowledge and the bias of communication reveal much about his ideas regarding the role of forms of communication in shaping history, the ways people think, and what counts for knowledge in a given society.

Innis argues that new forms of communication helped marginal groups to challenge monopolies of knowledge. Yet he does not make the claim that new media will "set us free." His historical specificity allows him to avoid the trap of the technological sublime—the hope for technological salvation. McLuhan will not be so fortunate.

Innis emphasized the importance of communication and made a plea for time in the space-biased empire of electronic media. His main theoretical concern was with cultural consequences of forms of communication: the role played by communication technology in empires either supporting or challenging monopolies of knowledge. Innis was also concerned with the interaction between existing social structures and the time and space bias of various forms of communication. Although Innis' method of dirt research led him to his important theoretical insights regarding biases of communication, his inclusion of too much of the dirt in his summaries leave his theoretical insights scattered among the particles.

We may have to dig through the dirt to find the insights in Innis' work but the mining is well worth the effort, indeed it was mining Innis that inspired McLuhan to make an abrupt break in his academic work.

McLUHAN'S EARLY WORK: MEDIA CONTENT

In contrast to Innis, McLuhan came to study forms of communication via revelation, not empirical investigation. Innis came to the study of media forms through historical empirical investigation. McLuhan read Innis. Thus, the continuity between Innis' early and later work stands in stark contrast to the abrupt break between McLuhan's earlier and later work

If we look at *The Mechanical Bride: Folklore and the Industrial Man* McLuhan's (1951), pre-Innis work, we see straight critical cultural theory (New Criticism) of mass-produced messages. In 1951, McLuhan was not looking at the invisible structures of media that permeate our lives or even our nervous systems, he was looking at advertisements as a literary critic. His own opening description puts it plainly:

> Most of the exhibits in this book have been selected because of their typical and familiar quality. They represent a world of forms and speak a language we both know and do not know. Amid the diversity of our inventions and abstract techniques of production and distribution there

will be found a great degree of cohesion and unity. This consistency is not conscious in origin or effect and seems to arise from some sort of collective dream . . . unfolded by exhibits and commentary as a single landscape. A whirling phantasmagoria can be grasped only when arrested for contemplation. (McLuhan, 1968, p. v)

Here and throughout the book, we see traces of the later McLuhan: his use of mystical explanations (the "language we both know and do not know" "seems to arise from some sort of collective dream"); his annoying habit of naming an era after his own ideas (the second half of the title— *Folklore of Industrial Man*); and on the pages of *The Mechanical Bride* his refusal to write in standard scholarly prose (advertisements combined with thought-provoking statements, not arguments). Yet, aside from these similarities in style, the theoretical approach in *The Mechanical Bride* has no hint of McLuhan's later work in medium theory with a bias for the study of forms of communication.

The Mechanical Bride was a straight content analysis presented in an uncommon format. The later McLuhan often defended the choice of arrangement and presentation of his ideas in unorthodox academic forms as an intentional representation of the new style of the Post-Gutenberg Era, yet his form preceded his theory in *The Mechanical Bride*.

The content analyses within *The Mechanical Bride* were done with the intention of enlightening the targets of advertisements (audiences), an idea based on the assumption that progressive change occurs through formal education. This is an idea that McLuhan would come to reject entirely. The later McLuhan would argue that it is the unconscious effect of forms of electronic communication on our central nervous systems that will free alienated Industrial (Gutenberg/Literate) Man. This argument is the polar opposite of the rational critique of media content that he is arguing for as the route to freedom from alienation in 1951.

McLUHAN'S LATER WORK: MEDIA FORMS

McLuhan's later work was heavily influenced by his reading of Innis. McLuhan (1962) writes in *The Gutenberg Galaxy*, "Harold Innis was the first person to hit on the *process* of change as implicit in the *forms* of media technology. The present book is a footnote of explanation to his work" (p. 50).

McLuhan grasped many of the theoretical insights broadcast throughout Innis' major works on communication. For Innis, the bias of a medium often has an impact on the ways people think and what counts as knowledge in a society. McLuhan turned the effect of media influencing the ways people think into a symptom of deeper changes (effects)—media induced alterations in our "sense ratios."

Whereas Innis wanted to strike a balance between the space and time bias *externally* with ideas of empires and monopolies of knowledge, McLuhan wanted to strike a balance *internally* between the senses (particularly visual and aural senses). This twist in medium theory can be explained in part when we examine the influence of Henri Bergson on McLuhan's thought during his conversion to medium theory.

McLuhan's explanation of changes experienced in the 1960s as a consequence of electronic media altering human sense ratios gained enormous publicity in 1967 (Rosenthal, 1968). Part of the explanation can be found in two main influences on McLuhan's thought before his 1962 publication of *The Gutenberg Galaxy*: Innis and Bergson.

Bergson repeatedly deals with issues related to the collective unconscious. Bergson's major premise that "the brain is part of the material world; the material world is not part of the brain" is both accepted and rejected by McLuhan (Bergson, 1911, p. 4). It is accepted in regard to the brain being part of the material world, but rejected in that McLuhan sees the technological world as an "outering" of the central nervous system. Thus, McLuhan actually turns Bergson's premise on its head when he melds it with his trajectory of medium theory. McLuhan gives us a theory that goes like this: Our thoughts and ideas (brains) are mere content (thoughts as symptoms) reflecting changes in forms of media that alter our sense ratios and the balance of our central nervous system. The central nervous system equilibrium will be brought about by electronic media, according to McLuhan (1964) in his *Understanding Media*:

> a general cosmic consciousness which might be very like the collective unconscious dreamt of by Bergson. The condition of "weightlessness," that biologists say promises a physical immortality, may be paralleled by the condition of speechlessness that could confer a perpetuity of collective harmony and peace. (p. 80)

Thus, our brain is a mere reflection of the material world, but in contrast to Bergson, McLuhan's material world is a mere reflection and extension of the central nervous system. In *The Gutenberg Galaxy*, McLuhan's (1962), first book-length venture into medium theory, the influence of Innis and Joyce dominates over the influence of Bergson and predates his concern with sense ratios. The main site of analysis in *The Gutenberg Galaxy* is the historical role of the printing press and book literacy in the West. As Neil Compton (1968) stated in "The Paradox of Marshall McLuhan," "If *The Gutenberg Galaxy* is a maddening and undisciplined contribution to the study of the role of printing in Western culture, it is also virtually the only work of its kind. Until one of us writes a better book we should be grateful to have this one" (p. 117).

The use of Innis in *The Gutenberg Galaxy* predates McLuhan's total fascination with the central nervous system that would come to dominate his discussions of television. In his soft determinist days, McLuhan (1962) wrote:

> The key facts are at the end of the passage. Literacy gives people the power to focus a little way in front of an image so that we take in the whole image or picture at a glance. Non-literate people have no such acquired habit and do not look at objects in our way. Rather they scan objects and images as we do the printed page, segment by segment. Thus they have no detached point of view. They are wholly *with* the object. They go emphatically into it. The eye is used, not in perspective but tactually, as it were. Euclidean spaces depending on much separation of sight from touch and sound are not known to them. (p. 37)

Here we see a nice extension of Innis and a reasoned argument based on actual experiences due to the bias of the media.

McLuhan's style of scholarship in *The Gutenberg Galaxy* is useful and similar to the medium theory work on consciousness being carried out by Walter Ong and Eric Havelock. Even as late as 1967, useful traces of insights regarding the impact of orality and literacy on internal structures of consciousness occur in McLuhan's work. In *The Medium is the Massage*, McLuhan writes:

> Visual space is uniform, continuous, and connected. The rational man in our Western culture is a visual man. The fact that most conscious experience has little "visuality" in it is lost on him. Rationality and visuality have long been interchangeable terms, but we do not live in a primarily visual world any more. . . . Until writing was invented, man lived in acoustic space: boundless, directionless, horizonless, in the dark of the mind, in the world of emotion, by primordial intuition, by terror. Speech is a social chart of this bog. (McLuhan & Fiore, 1967, pp. 45-48)

In these passages we see a thoughtful, theoretical, soft determinist analysis. Yet, unlike the work of Walter Ong and Eric Havelock, McLuhan ultimately falls into the trap of mistaking the dominance of electronic media as a return to primary orality and tribal solidarity.

As McLuhan moves further away from detailed discussions, he moves closer to the technological hope encouraged by the technological sublime. Although *The Gutenberg Galaxy* is a fine stimulus in the development of medium theory (current medium theorists, such as Elizabeth Eisenstein,

Eric Havelock, Joshua Meyrowitz, and Walter Ong looked to it as a source of ideas for their more detailed research), overall McLuhan falls into the trap of the technological sublime: he often predicts a return to a golden age via electronic media while ignoring all that stands between.

CONCLUSIONS ON INNIS AND McLUHAN

One of the major flaws in McLuhan's later work on electronic media is that he completely overlooks questions of power, domination, capitalism, drive for profit, and human agency in his theorizing and fails to detail his arguments. McLuhan (1964) demonstrates his oblivious state in the following quote:

> After three thousand years of explosion, by means of fragmentation and mechanical technologies, the Western world is imploding. During the mechanical ages we had extended our bodies in space. Today after more than a century of electric technology, have extended our central nervous system itself in a global embrace, abolishing both space and time as far as our planet is concerned. (pp. 45-48)

For Innis, space bias is always connected to notions of empire, and the term *space bias* indicates a medium's inherent characteristics that allow for, and exert pressure toward, increased centralized control over space by some group over others. This is precisely the case with electronic media. A space bias in the dominant medium of the time combined with the drive for profit fosters and aids imperialism. But for McLuhan, as the quote just cited indicates, electronic media do not have a space bias but abolish space. A space bias indicates increased centralized control over vast geographical areas. In contrast, McLuhan's annihilation of space is also an annihilation of the space bias—imperialism. McLuhan's idea of the annihilation of space and time ending centralized control and nationalist divisions is similar to claims made by many postmodernists.

For Innis, the question of who controls which forms of communication and when is central to his analysis of multiple social forces, empire, monopolies of knowledge, and forms of communication. For McLuhan, the question of who controls which forms of media and when are irrelevant—there is no human agency in McLuhan's medium theories. In McLuhan's later writings, media are completely extracted from their historical contexts (although the initial insights come from the specific contexts originally observed in *The Gutenberg Galaxy*). What Innis identified as biases of media in particular historical contexts, McLuhan generalized into laws of media. This lack of historical specificity and human agency in McLuhan's later work is consistent with his underlying theoretical assumption that the effects of media are wholly unintended and uncontrollable.[3]

The role of the human being in McLuhan's theory is strictly that of historical object. Human beings in McLuhan's *Gutenberg Galaxy* could not even comprehend their condition, never mind alter it. McLuhan (1962) explains, "Until now a culture has been a mechanical fate for societies, the automatic interiorization of their own technologies" (p. 40). Yet now with electronic media, McLuhan thinks we can comprehend our condition, not in order to analyze and alter it, but to go with its flow. In a response to Ashley Montagu's discussion of aspects of nonliteracy, McLuhan (1962) makes this statement:

> What Montagu opens up here concerning the intense practicality of the non-literate applies perfectly as gloss to Joyce's Bloom or Odysseus, the resourceful man. What could be more practical for a man caught between the Scylla of a literary culture and the Charybdis of post-literate technology to make himself a raft of ad copy? He is behaving like Poe's sailor in the *Maelstrom* who studied the action of the whirlpool and survives. May not it be our job in the new electronic age to study the action of the new vortex on the body of the older cultures? (p. 77)

Human beings experiencing "postliterate technology" can comprehend their situation but do not really need to because the study of the media is not predicated on Marx's notion that the point is to change them, or even the academic idea that we theorize to understand, but on the Madison Avenue idea of "Why ask Why?" or "Just do It." We can now understand the impact of media forms on human beings, according to McLuhan, but we do not really need to do so since we are moving in the right direction. Although this was a minor theme in *The Gutenberg Galaxy*, it became the hallmark of McLuhan's later work.

Whereas Innis encourages scholars to act as human agents to exert pressure on the media that exert pressure on us so that we may strike a balance, McLuhan most often encouraged us to sit back and enjoy the ride. Yet both scholars offer unique insights into the influence of forms of communication

---

[3]In *The Medium Is the Massage,* McLuhan does devote an entire page to the single line, "there is absolutely no inevitability as long as there is a willingness to contemplate what is happening" (McLuhan & Fiore, 1967). This one line and the few others that some scholars delight in finding in his work, however, cannot and do not negate the major assumption that underpins nearly the entire contents of his post-1964 writings: that we are *objects* of history on an electronically mediated path to wholeness.

on consciousness and culture. If we work to resurrect Innis from the dirt and pull McLuhan down from the cosmos, we can move in interesting new directions.

REFERENCES

Adorno, W. (1971). *The culture industry*. London: Routledge.
Bergsen, H. (1911). *Matter and memory*. New York: The Macmillan Company.
Carey, J.W. (1989). *Communication as culture: Essays on media and society*. Boston: Unwin Hyman.
Hardt, H. (1992). *Critical communication studies*. New York: Routledge.
Innis, H.A. (1950). *Empire and communications*. New York: Oxford University Press.
Innis, H.A. (1951). *The bias of communication*. Toronto: University of Toronto Press.
Kroker, A. (1984). *Technology and the Canadian mind: Innis/McLuhan/Grant*. New York: St. Martin's Press.
McLuhan, M. (1951). *The mechanical bride*. New York: The Vanguard Press.
McLuhan, M. (1962). *The Gutenberg galaxy: The making of typographic man*. Toronto: University of Toronto Press.
McLuhan, M. (1964). *Understanding media: The extensions of man*. New York: McGraw-Hill.
McLuhan, M. (1967). *Verbi-voco-visual explorations*. New York: Something Else Press.
McLuhan, M. (c1988). *Laws of media: The new science*. Toronto: University of Toronto Press.
McLuhan, M., & Fiore, Q. (1967). *The medium is the massage: An inventory of effects*. New York, Bantam.
Ong, W.J. (1982). *Orality and literacy*. London: Methuen.
Robinson, G.J., & Theall, D. (Eds.). (1975). *Studies in Canadian communications*. Montreal: McGill.
Rosenthal, R. (1968). *McLuhan: Pro and con*. Funk and Wagnalls.
Stamps, J. (1995) *Unthinking modernity*. Montreal & Kingston: McGill-Queen's University Press.

22 RETRIEVING McLUHAN FOR CULTURAL STUDIES AND POSTMODERNISM

Paul Grosswiler
University of Maine

The work of Marshall McLuhan often has been ridiculed and rejected in U.S. communication theory, and its relevance to critical media studies in the cultural studies and postmodern traditions largely has been ignored. It is the purpose of this chapter to help retrieve McLuhan and his work for their continued importance to critical, cultural, and postmodern media and social theories. This retrieval, however, runs against both the history of cultural studies' negative assessment of McLuhan and scholarly critiques of postmodernism. In this chapter, I hope to respond to that history and those critiques in arguing for McLuhan's continuing central position in critical communication theory.

British cultural studies had responded negatively to McLuhan for nearly 40 years, led by Raymond Williams, as has U.S. cultural studies, reflected in the work of James Carey (Carey, 1968, 1981, 1987, 1989; Carey & Quirk, 1989; Williams, 1967, 1992). But this critical field has come nearly full circle with one cultural sociologist, John B. Thompson (1995), applying Harold Innis and McLuhan as one of three foundations in his study of media and social practices. British cultural studies scholar Nick Stevenson (1995) has strongly called for a historical reappraisal of McLuhan, and Canadian cultural studies scholar Jody Berland (1992) has incorporated McLuhan's spatial analysis in her research on cultural technologies. Carey (1998) wrote that whether McLuhan was a technological determinist is not important to assess his and Innis' insights.

Postmodern media and social theories and McLuhan have gone hand in hand in the writings of many media scholars, some of whom have warmly regarded McLuhan and his theories (Baudrillard, 1981, 1983; Fekete, 1994; Jencks, 1986; Poster, 1990). Canadian Glenn Willmott (1996) regards McLuhan as a double-coded figure who lived postmodernism. Willmott paints McLuhan as a modernist who helped usher in ideas of postmodernism and embodied postmodernism. Other postmodernists have applied McLuhan's theories at other times under others' names (Lowe, 1982; Poster, 1984, 1994; Wolff,1993), but McLuhan still retains the stigma of a technological determinist among many postmodernist writers and critics (Aronowitz & Giroux,1991; Best & Kellner, 1991; Kellner, 1989a, 1989b).

Much of this recent scholarship runs counter to decades of negative scholarly assessment of McLuhan, which was more dismissive in the United States than Canada or Europe, representing part of a new reassessment of McLuhan that was not possible during his lifetime. Finding McLuhan's theories resurfacing today among a diverse group of theorists in cultural studies and postmodernism illustrates McLuhan's continued relevance to critical communication approaches. Cultural studies, with its methodological openness and defiance, embodies McLuhan's spirit, and even as postmodernists label McLuhan a technological determinist and attempt to move beyond him, much of his analysis seems ever more applicable and relevant in light of their concerns.

CULTURAL STUDIES RECLAIMS McLUHAN

Cultural studies has become a contested terrain in recent years, with factions arguing for various elements of the field since its inception in Marxist-based British cultural studies, the liberal pluralism of some brands of American cultural studies, and its more recent manifestations in various postmodern versions stemming from diverse methodologies and theories. McLuhan's presence has gradually resurfaced in this variety of cultural studies first through unattributed adaptation of his orality–literacy typology (Fiske, 1987a), followed by juxtaposition of McLuhan and Williams (Brantlinger, 1990), and the identification of McLuhan as one of the progenitors of cultural studies (Hartley, 1992). Cultural studies further reclaimed McLuhan through comments on the "reach" or effects of television as a technical media system constitutes a global village (Silverstone, 1994), as well as the equation of the global village with capitalist postmodernity (Ang, 1994, 1996).

Thompson (1990), analyzing the ways media have changed social interaction and experience in modern societies, credits McLuhan and Innis for emphasizing the effects of media forms on social interaction, writing that they "argued, rightly in my view, that different technical media help to create different environments for action and interaction; they argued that the form of the medium itself, quite apart from the specific content of the messages it conveys, has an impact on the nature of social life" (p. 225). Thompson finds the theme more interesting than the ways McLuhan and Innis develop it. Rather than pursue the broad conclusions drawn by Innis and McLuhan, Thompson (1990a) examines how technical media have "transformed the nature of social interaction, have created new contexts for action and interaction and new arenas for self-presentation and the perception of others" (pp. 226-227).

More recently, Stevenson's (1995) exploration of the relationship between mass communication and social theory boldly calls for a thorough reappraisal of McLuhan to revisit both his contributions and his shortcomings:

> I am to move against the grain of his most vocal detractors and forcibly suggest that his work be critically re-evaluated by students of the media. I will defend a version of McLuhan's writing that does not rest well with culturalism or postmodernism: that McLuhan's emphasis on technical media is important for distinguishing between different modes of cultural transmission (oral, literate, electric) and that these media structurate intersubjective social relations. (p. 115)

Stevenson finds McLuhan and Jurgen Habermas to be the only theorists to consider the impact of media other than television, as social theory neglected the importance of the media until the television age was well under way. Looking at theories that focus on the technological means of communication as one of three paradigms of communication research—in addition to critical approaches of British Marxism and the Frankfurt School, and audience research—Stevenson suggests that McLuhan's "distinctive analysis" has been neglected by social theorists. Three of McLuhan's ideas, including implosion, hybridity and time and space restructuring, offer a substantial contribution to social theory (Stevenson, 1995). In implosion, "cultural hierarchies" and the public and private spheres have merged, "The globe has imploded vertically, temporally and horizontally. Humanity, McLuhan goes on, has collapsed on itself, returning to the village-like state characteristic of oral societies" (Stevenson, 1995, p. 123).

Stevenson also emphasizes McLuhan's concept of hybrid media, or "hybridized cultural forms" (p. 123). This concept favors "spatial constellations" rather than "linear patterns of development," enabling researchers to study media effects on other media as McLuhan "fruitfully suggests" a medium's historical development should be compared to other types of cultural production (p. 124). This shows a clear appreciation of McLuhan's mosaic, or field approach. In summary, Stevenson (1995) finds McLuhan "continues to offer challenging perspectives to those who are concerned to map out the contours of our culture" (p. 142).

Reconsideration of McLuhan is well under way in Canadian cultural studies, including the work of Berland. She argues that social theorists—except for Innis and thinkers influenced by him—have long thought of space as "static and secondary" as a cultural and social force (Berland, 1992, p. 39). Recently, social theory is challenging this view; however, for more than four decades since Innis, Canadian communication theory has focused on the media's space, and time effects.

Berland (1992) calls the mediation between the production of texts, spaces and listeners of popular music "cultural technologies" (p. 39). In this term, Berland seeks to present popular culture as a mediation between technologies, economics, spaces, and listeners. Drawing both on Innis' theory of media temporal and spatial bias, and on McLuhan's focus on technology, Berland argues that by examining audiences and media effects in terms of technological and social changes, Canadian communication theory diverges from mainstream media research. The latter configures the audience as a group of individuals with different moods, tastes and choices. McLuhan, on the other hand, argued that the media produce "a continuous sensory and spatial reorganization of social life" (Berland, 1992, p. 43).

McLUHAN AND POSTMODERNISM

In McLuhan's published work, the term *postmodernism* is not found, and his writing discusses none of the prominent postmodernists, except to assert that pop-art was non-art, denying art's definition as a special object being inserted in a special space (McLuhan & Parker, 1968). Yet, postmodern thinkers have rallied around McLuhan, adapted McLuhan, and drawn from McLuhan. Postmodernists themselves disagree about the nature of postmodernism, its origins and its history, but McLuhan and postmodernism appear fused by many critical theorists. Brooding about a decisive, global change, the fading of modernism and the emergence of a postmodern era in the mid-1970s, Fredric Jameson (1988) mentions "MacLuhanism" (*sic*) as one of the "straws in the wind" along with postmodern literary and art theory, and the rise of computers and information theory, that "seem to confirm the widespread feeling that 'modern times are now over' and that some fundamental divide . . . or qualitative leap now separates us decisively from what used to be the new world of the mid-twentieth century" (p. 17). In Jameson's critique, postmodernism coincides with the global multinational capitalism that emerged after World War II, following the "modernism" of the era of monopoly capitalism or imperialism. Postmodernism, then, is seen as a cultural "dominant" that affects social arenas beyond those of aesthetics or culture alone (p. 67).

James Curtis (1978) identifies "McLuhan and other postmodernists" who shocked scholars by seriously considering mass culture (p. 92). For Curtis, modernism is equated with art movements of the first half of the 20th century, whereas postmodernism, although continuous with modernism, differs in one of several ways, by focusing on popular culture. Other postmodernist scholars, such as architect Charles Jencks and philosopher Jean Baudrillard, herald McLuhan as a harbinger of postmodernism, and both adapt and extend his work. Perhaps the most celebrated and vilified of these is Baudrillard.

As postmodernists vary their readings of McLuhan, descriptions and evaluations of modernism and postmodernism also vary from theorist to theorist. Even the argument over the definition of "postmodernism" is an example of postmodernism, as no authority is positioned to make a definitive ruling that will go without challenge, as Jencks (1986) notes. Art historian John Walker (1983), contrasting positive and negative responses to the notion of postmodernism, notes that on the positive side, postmodernism recognizes a rich diversity and pluralism of cultural styles and forms globally, and it accepts a multitude of pasts and embraces tradition and history. It acknowledges that "at any one moment in time various generations are alive" and "the present contains within it a multitude of pasts." Conversely, negative interpretations include "stylistic anarchism," "unhealthy obsession with the past," "a mannerist phase," "shallow and superficial," and "the sign of a divided, decadent society" (Walker, 1983, p. 84).

Walker offers a thematic typology of modernism as an aesthetic ideology that dominated Western culture for 125 years until the 1960s. He then compares thematic typologies of modernism and postmodernism. First, modernism embraces the new age of machines and technology and develops new forms of expression. Second, modernism completely breaks with the past to advocate the "tradition of the new," which values novelty and originality. Third, modernism rejects decoration and ornamentation, preferring geometric forms that suggest simplicity, uniformity, order and rationality. Fourth, modernism rejects local styles, favoring a single universal style. And fifth, modernism describes itself as art of the future, frequently inspired by socialism. Artists perceive themselves as engineers of a "brave new world" (Walker, 1983, p. 82).

Walker describes postmodernism in the arts as a "half-way house" between the past and an unclear future. First, postmodernism rejects one universal style in favor of a plurality of styles and hybrids. Also, postmodernism revives historical and traditional styles in quotations and parodies. Third, postmodernism permits ornament and decoration. Fourth, postmodernism values complexity, contradiction and ambiguity, rejecting simplicity, order and rationality; the blending of high and low culture, fine and popular art is favored in offering multilayered readings. Finally, postmodernism values references in art to other works (Walker, 1983).

McLuhan's arts and media theory straddles these categories of modernism and postmodernism. McLuhan is opposed to the modernist desire for a modern style that reflects a new age of technology—but he does embrace a new age of technology in which form determines function, rather than form following function. He also would reject the modernists' desire for a "complete break with the past" and the value of novelty and originality. Within his dialectic, the deeper past is always being retrieved as the recent past is being obsolesced. Modernism's values of simplicity, clarity, uniformity, order and rationality equate quite strongly with McLuhan's concept of visual or typographic culture, a historically bounded culture that is being discontinuously changed by electronic or acoustic culture. Modernism's rejection of national styles in favor of an international style is similar to McLuhan's idea that nationalism has become irrelevant in electronic culture, while a global village is being created. He does find, however, that in this global village minority voices are difficult to ignore. The modernist idea that the artist knows best and is producing the art of the future is an idea that McLuhan pursues in calling the artist the "antenna of the race" who is the sole guard against the onslaught of media technology.

McLuhan shares more assumptions and themes of postmodernism. He embraces a "plurality of styles" and "hybrid styles." In fact, McLuhan assumes that the pluralism of acoustic space is textually richer; the whole notion of "hybrids" is central to the creative power of McLuhan's critical media universe. The retrieval of history and tradition, through "retro-style," "quotations," "collage," "recyclings," "parodies," and "pastiches of old styles," is a theme that permeates McLuhan's mosaic thinking, perhaps made most clearly in his works *From Cliché to Archetype* (McLuhan & Wilson, 1970) and *Through the Vanishing Point* (McLuhan & Parker, 1968). Another strongly stated postmodern theme in McLuhan is the value of "complexity and contradiction," as well as ambiguity, which replace simplicity, purity, and rationality. This is the centerpiece of acoustic space in McLuhan's thought. Also, McLuhan strongly favors the postmodern "mixtures of high and low culture, fine art and commercial art" that are "capable of yielding multi-layered readings," which are again central to acoustic space. The postmodern concern with design as "languages" resembles McLuhan's concern with media forms as "languages" through which different statements and meaning are constructed. And, finally, the postmodern idea of "inter-textuality," that "every literary text or work of art relates to, alludes to, or comments on . . . various other texts or works" also brims with McLuhan's mosaic method of looking at media in relation to other media and seeing social and media change as interrelated (Walker, 1983, p. 82).

Although Walker makes no allusions to McLuhan, Jencks (1986), one of postmodernism's major proponents and defenders, finds McLuhan's theories useful in distinguishing between modernism and postmodernism, which, he says, began in 1960. Jencks defines postmodernism as a "paradoxical dualism, or double coding, which its hybrid name entails: the continuation of Modernism and its transcendence." The "double coding" of combining modern techniques with traditional techniques in order to reach the public as well as a high-culture minority is at the centre of Jencks' notion of postmodernism. Transcending modernism through the double coding of irony or humor symbolizes a loss of innocence and a desire to move beyond modernism's stylistic restrictions, as well as representing the failure of modernism, Jencks contends. His 30 indicators of postmodernism emphasize symbolism, ornament, humor, technology and the relation of the artist to current and past cultures (Jencks, 1986).

McLUHAN AND POSTMODERN THEMES IN CULTURAL STUDIES

Cultural studies approaches to postmodernism are probably as varied as its approaches to cultural studies itself. But a number of themes that are central to postmodern theory can be identified in reviewing cultural studies theorists' writing about postmodernism. Stevenson (1995) contrasts the postmodern theories of Baudrillard, whose "rejection of ideology, truth, representation, seriousness, and the emancipation of the subject" embrace many issues of postmodernism, to the postmodern theories of Jameson, whom Stevenson finds to be the "most sophisticated" postmodernist today (p. 162). In general, Jameson calls postmodernism the "cultural expression" or "logic" of "late capitalism." Fine and popular arts have been merged as the economic sector takes over the cultural sphere. Modernist culture has lost its subversiveness and contemporary cultural forms, like punk rock, are co-opted by the capitalist economic system.

For Jameson, the main themes of postmodernism include the absence of context and the uncertainty of interpretation; a growing concern with discourses; the end of the notion of individual style or the "death of the subject"; and a fragmentation of social meanings yielding "discursive heterogeneity" that best represents modern culture by parody or "pastiche," which Jameson calls a "blank parody" because the fragmenting of cultural styles has eroded social norms (Stevenson, 1995, p. 163).

The themes of postmodernism identified by Jameson and some other themes that rise among a group of cultural studies scholars include: the death of individualism, as well as the end of Enlightenment thinking; fragmentation leading to parody and beyond to pastiche, with the loss of text and context, and, more positively, the gaining of intertextuality; the focus on discourse and codes (Ang, 1996; Brantlinger, 1990; Collins, 1994; Fiske, 1987b; Hartley, 1992; Silverstone, 1994), the retrieval in postmodern thought of premodernism; the pointlessness of political action; and the concept of the "other."

By mediating the identity of the individual, as well as social forms, political and economic systems, and the media and arts themselves, with technology, as a dialectical interplay of the human and media extensions in history, McLuhan's theories posit an extremely fluid and changing concept of "human nature" that leaves identity largely as a construct of the dominant medium and society. As an effect of the technologies of printing and the alphabet, which removed the individual from the corporate community, the subject has a historical beginning that is being challenged by the rise of electronic media culture. In McLuhan's analysis, the individual has been socially organized as a construct by print culture, and is being dissolved by electronic culture—the death of the subject.

The death of the Enlightenment can be compared to the death of McLuhan's Gutenberg Galaxy. McLuhan clearly has challenged print culture logic, reason, linearity, and its very mode of consciousness, which, again, are historically bound within the rise and fall of print culture. Along with postmodernists, McLuhan has argued of the passing of modernism, of the Enlightenment, of visual culture.

Fragmentation is a concept that McLuhan, unlike most postmodernists, associates with visual culture. Continuity, homogeneity, mechanization and fragmentation are all aspects of writing and print culture, according to McLuhan. However, if fragmentation is understood more in terms of McLuhan's mosaic of unrelated elements in interplay, then fragmentation is really a different idea more along the lines of synaesthesia, discontinuity, anti-linearity. Of course, McLuhan relies heavily on parody as well as humor, and intertextuality. He, too, as a formulist, moves beyond the text, or content, of media, although as an interdisciplinarian he contextualizes this low-content analytic tool.

If "discourse" means a way of thinking, a paradigm, or a logic that characterizes a period and then discontinuously halts and is replaced by an unrelated way of thinking, then McLuhan does focus on discourse. The modes of consciousness created by oral culture, print culture, and electronic culture, deriving from an unconscious system of rules, as in Foucault's epistemes, to McLuhan are periodic discourses that change radically from period to period.

Other themes also reflect McLuhan's ideas. The concept of retrieving premodern forms strongly resembles the phase of retrieval of McLuhan's mosaic method and his tetradic laws. For McLuhan, the cultural capital of accumulated eras is by definition brought into play in electronic media culture, as the media make previous cultural products available and as the new media environment retrieves aspects of earlier environments even as it obsolesces some aspects of the most recent media environment. Even as this retrieval occurs, another postmodernist characteristic of McLuhan's thought is the merging of mass and high culture, a point made by Jameson.

Regarding political action, McLuhan is ambivalent. On the one hand, he argues that the new electronic media had stripped individuals of many of their rights and that the effects of the media were beneath consciousness, so political action would be futile. On the other hand, McLuhan argues that the artist represented the best response to new media as a make-aware agent instead of a make-happen agent. Through art, then, action is possible. Finally, the concept of the "other" can be seen reflected in McLuhan's contrast of Western and traditional cultures, as well as the collision within the West of the Enlightenment visual culture against the postmodern electronic media culture. For the alienated and fragmented visual culture, the alien other is the acoustic culture. However, this otherness is supposed to be resolved by the emergence of an acoustic electronic culture.

McLUHAN AND BAUDRILLARD

Although McLuhan shares many general themes with a wide range of postmodernist theorists in the arts and cultural studies, the closest comparison may be drawn between McLuhan and Baudrillard. Baudrillard (1981) meditates on McLuhan both admiringly and menacingly in his critique of Marxism's analysis of mass media. Baudrillard himself has been labeled a "new McLuhan" who "out-McLuhans McLuhan" in describing the importance of the medium and the irrelevance of content as Baudrillard revises McLuhan in postmodern terms (Kellner, 1989a).

Baudrillard both lauds McLuhan's theorem that "the medium is the message" and criticizes McLuhan, asserting that "he exalts the media and their global message with a delirious tribal optimism," and his theorem is "not a critical proposition" (p. 172). Baudrillard finds "mass mediatization" to be the "quintessence" of the media, which consists of "the imposition of models" (p. 175). McLuhan's "medium is the message" formula, he argues, transfers meaning onto the medium as technological structure. It is not the content of the press, television or radio that is "mediatized"; rather it is the "forced socialization as a system of social control" (pp. 175-176).

According to Douglas Kellner (1989a), Baudrillard followed McLuhan by interpreting modernity, or McLuhan's print culture, as the explosion of commodities, mechanization, technology and market relations. Postmodern society, or McLuhan's acoustic culture, is the implosion of all boundaries, regions and distinctions between high and low culture, appearance and reality. Baudrillard later collapses the medium and the content into the "simulations" and "simulacra" of "hyperreality," that still draws McLuhan into its base, as illustrated in *Simulations* (1983). Kellner (1989a) notes that by the late 1970s, Baudrillard sees media, especially television, as "key simulation machines which reproduce images, signs and codes which in turn come to constitute an autonomous realm of (hyper)reality" (p. 68). The media comprise a "hyperreality" that is "more real than real," subordinating the "real" to representation and leading to a "dissolving of the real" (Kellner, 1989a, p. 68).

Baudrillard has done McLuhan's theories a disservice even as he has embraced them in the way that he has reduced them to a few uncritical theorems, and then altered and extended them to unrecognizable form as he outdistances McLuhan. For example, in reciting "the medium is the message" as an incantation, Baudrillard ignores the process that underlies this idea. This implies that media forms have psychological, social, political and economic effects—not just television or electronic media, or even books and newspapers, but every medium of communication, from clothes to cars and numbers to money—as they collide with former media in a complex process in which human autonomy is the key. McLuhan was trying to distance communication theory from its emphasis on content and its blindness—or deafness—to media forms. As Berland has noted, the content of a new medium is an old medium. As some cultural studies scholars have also written, this connects to McLuhan's notion of "rearviewmirrorism," or the fact that new media look backward for content and meaning. McLuhan's theorem, then, clearly still posits a difference between medium and message, and does not erase the message, as Baudrillard does.

By declaring the death of the medium and the message, Baudrillard also ignores the important historical context provided by McLuhan. The mediated and the real, which Baudrillard asserts have collapsed in a hyperreality of mediated communication, have never been stable or separate in human experience, as all media, again using McLuhan's inclusive notion of media as a wide range of cultural products and social practices, have always altered, determined and negotiated the real. The spoken word itself is a technology, much as is television. By positing the end of history and the end of media and reality in hyperreality, Baudrillard has ignored that McLuhan's dialectical historical process is ongoing, and television, about which McLuhan wrote very little, is perhaps the newest dominant medium but not the end of media, or history, or ideology.

REORIENTING CULTURAL STUDIES AND POSTMODERNISM

With the arrival of a multimedia culture, the call to resistance, as well as to adjustment, would lead invariably to the artist, broadly defined by McLuhan as the voices of the humanists and scientists in all fields who can mediate the effects of these new technologies and who can help us think things out before we put them out. In media studies, McLuhan's "early warning system" today no doubt would include cultural studies and postmodernist scholars and activists who would both accede to and resist the social and media forms they study.

McLuhan's major contribution to cultural studies would be his insistence on studying media forms and message production as well as their effect on individuals and cultures. Cultural studies scholar James Lull (1995) described quite well, although unintentionally, I think, the quandary that cultural studies has created in largely abandoning its Marxist roots and focusing on audience decoding of messages. A gulf exists between the hegemonic media production of messages and the individual and social act of making meaning out of these hegemonic texts in ways that can resist if not reject dominant meanings. Studies of Madonna's fans reading her as a subversive text, for example, neglect to answer the question of how to change the media that produce Madonna in the first place (Fiske, 1987a). McLuhan's focus on form and encoding, as well as the formal effects on reading texts, could help reorient cultural studies to include production as well as consumption. McLuhan would argue that the tension between media production and media consumption cannot be resolved. With the rise of multimedia culture, the need to continue to make cultural meaning in the face of diminishing odds and opportunities also becomes more important.

Multimedia culture could offer that opportunity to both produce meaning and make meaning as an act of autonomy and resistance, unless we sell our rights to corporate media. The outcome, applying McLuhan's open-ended method, also is open-ended. It is not an end run for technological determinism. Apologists of the existing information order will need to find another standard bearer. Technological determinism also has been attractive to some postmodernist scholars. Exemplified by Jean Baudrillard, postmodernism could seem resigned in the face of the collapse of media and reality into this high-definition, high-participation "hyperreality" of multimedia. With the dissolution of the individual as an effective social actor, postmodernism can call upon post-Marxism to help neutralize media and social activism.

McLuhan's sense of postmodernism, however, has much greater historicity than this. McLuhan's method would argue that we live in a world of post's, as well as pre's, as part of an ongoing process that does not reverse modernism but transcends it in becoming and reversal. The danger of the postmodern critique is that it abandons the possibility of even the need for social action. Much of this political philosophy has also abandoned Marxist principles as these principles become part of the modernism that has succumbed to its successor. McLuhan's take on postmodernism, although he appears not to have used the term often, is more along the line of the humanist, positive postmodernism reflected in the works of Jencks (1986) and Walker (1983), involving the retrieval of past cultures, of the simultaneous existence of many cultures and pasts, and an acceptance of that abundance and diversity. Willmott (1996) regarded McLuhan as a double-coded figure himself, living postmodernism. He painted McLuhan as a modernist who helped bring about the ideas of postmodernism and embodied postmodernism. Willmott (1996) argued that McLuhan was part of a "radical culture" articulated by the New Left and its rejection of technocratic authority in favor of cultural utopianism (p. 200).

Reclaiming McLuhan's legacy could help channel media analysis for a rich and diverse reading of the postmodern world. Intensifying the postmodern trends in media and culture would serve greater human self-expression and creativity, which are, in the end, at the heart of McLuhan's media and culture universe. The human is the measure of McLuhan's method, where Arthur Kroker's (1984) label of him as "technological humanist" most properly applies. In addition to enriching cultural studies and postmodernism, McLuhan's media theories can help retrain their critical focus, retrieving the human being from technological structures. Ultimately, his ideas forecast the potential reversal of a highly technological media culture into a human one.

REFERENCES

Ang, I. (1994). In the realm of uncertainty: The global village and capitalist post-modernity. In D. Crowley & D. Mitchell (Eds.), *Communication theory today* (pp. 193-213). Stanford, CA: Stanford University Press.

Ang, I. (1996). *Living room wars: Rethinking media audiences for a postmodern world.* London: Routledge.

Aronowitz, S., & Giroux, H. A. (1991). *Postmodern education: Politics, culture, and social criticism.* Minneapolis: University of Minnesota Press.

Baudrillard, J. (1981). Requiem for the media. In *For a critique of the political economy of the sign* (pp. 164-184). St. Louis: Telos Press.

Baudrillard, J. (1983). *Simulations.* New York: Semiotext(e).

Berland, J. (1992). Angels dancing: Cultural technologies and the production of space. In L. Grossberg, C. Nelson & P. Treichler (Eds.), *Cultural studies* (pp. 38-50). New York: Routledge.

Best, S., & Kellner, D. (1991). *Postmodern theory: Critical interrogations.* New York: Guilford.

Brantlinger, P. (1990). *Crusoe's footprints: Cultural studies in Britain and America.* New York: Routledge.

Carey, J. (1968). Harold Adams Innis and Marshall McLuhan. In R. Rosenthal (Ed.), *McLuhan: Pro and con* (pp. 270-308). Baltimore, MD: Penguin.

Carey, J. (1981). McLuhan and Mumford: The roots of modern media analysis. *Journal of Communication, 31,* 162-178.

Carey, J. (1987). Walter Benjamin, Marshall McLuhan, and the emergence of visual society. *Prospects: An Annual of American Cultural Studies, 12,* 29-38.

Carey, J. (1989). Space, time, and communication: A tribute to Harold Innis. In *Communication as culture: Essays on media and society* (pp. 142-172). Boston: Unwin Hyman.

Carey, J. (1998). Communication, culture and technology: An internet interview with James Carey. *Journal of Communication Inquiry, 22,* 123.

Carey, J., & Quirk, J.J. (1989). The mythos of the electronic revolution. In *Communication as culture: Essays on media and society* (pp. 113-141). Boston: Unwin Hyman.

Collins, J.M. (1994). By whose authority? Accounting for taste in contemporary popular culture. In D. Crowley & D. Mitchell (Eds.), *Communication theory today* (pp. 214-231). Stanford, CA: Stanford University Press.

Curtis, J.M. (1978). *Culture as polyphony: An essay on the nature of paradigms.* Columbia: University of Missouri Press.

Fekete, J. (1994). *Moral panic: Biopolitics rising.* Montréal-Toronto: Robert Davies Publishing.

Fiske, J. (1987a). British cultural studies and television. In R. C. Allen (Ed.), *Channels of discourse* (pp. 254-289). Chapel Hill: University of North Carolina Press.

Fiske, J. (1987b). *Television culture.* London: Methuen.

Hartley, J. (1992). *The politics of pictures: The creation of the public in the age of popular media.* London: Routledge.

Jameson, F. (1988). *The ideologies of theory: Essays 1971-1986* (Vol. 1). Minneapolis: University of Minnesota Press.

Jencks, C. (1986). *What is post-modernism?* New York: St. Martin's Press.

Kellner, D. (1989a). *Jean Baudrillard: From Marxism to postmodernism and beyond.* Stanford, CA: Stanford University Press.

Kellner, D. (1989b). Resurrecting McLuhan? Jean Baudrillard and the academy of postmodernism. In M. Raboy & P.A. Bruck (Eds.), *Communication: For or against democracy* (pp. 131-146). Montréal: Black Rose Books.

Kroker, A. (1984). *Technology and the Canadian mind: Innis/McLuhan/Grant.* Montréal: New World Perspectives.

Lowe, D.M. (1982). *History of bourgeois perception.* Chicago: University of Chicago Press.

Lull, J. (1995). *Media, communication, culture: A global approach.* New York: Columbia University Press.

McLuhan, M., & Parker, H. (1968). *Through the vanishing point: Space in poetry and painting.* New York: Harper & Row.

McLuhan, M., & Wilson, W. (1970). *From cliché to archetype*. New York: Viking Press.

Poster, M. (1984). *Foucault, Marxism and history: Mode of production vs. mode of information*. Cambridge, MA: Polity Press.

Poster, M. (1990). *The mode of information: Post-structuralism and social context*. Chicago: University of Chicago Press.

Poster, M. (1994). The mode of information and postmodernity. In D. Crowley & D. Mitchell (Eds.), *Communication theory today* (pp. 173-192). Stanford, CA: Stanford University Press.

Silverstone, R. (1994). *Television and everyday life*. London: Routledge.

Stevenson, N. (1995). *Understanding media cultures: Social theory and mass communication*. London: Sage.

Thompson, J. B. (1990). *Ideology and modern culture*. Stanford, CA: Stanford University Press.

Thompson, J. B. (1995). *The media and modernity: A social theory of the media*. Stanford, CA: Stanford University Press.

Walker, J. A. (1983). *Art in the age of mass media*. London: Pluto Press.

Williams, R. (1967). Paradoxically, if the book works it to some extent annihilates itself. In G. E. Stearn (Ed.), *McLuhan hot and cool* (pp. 88-191). New York: Dial Press.

Williams, R. (1992). *Television: Technology and cultural form*. Hanover, NH & London: Wesleyan University Press.

Willmott, G. (1996). *McLuhan, or modernism in reverse*. Toronto: University of Toronto Press.

Wolff, J. (1993). *The social production of art* (2nd ed.). New York: New York University Press.

23   HE DIDN'T DO IT

SOME CAUTIONS ON THE CURRENT McLUHAN REVIVAL

Frederick Wasser ·
Brooklyn College

Harris Breslow
Calumet College

McLuhan wrote his seminal work in the early 1960s. As has been made clear in this collection, he wrote eclectically and inspired different people to hear him saying various and often contradictory things. We want to make our remarks, not to further explicate or smooth out the contradictions of McLuhan, but because we think that his central themes lead directly to a powerful research program. This research program has yet to be fully implemented. This is because researchers continue to be distracted by the relationship between the subject and language and by the content of media. Therefore, we begin with a note of caution. McLuhan, himself, was often distracted by these relationships. But we argue that as we develop his legacy, we must always be true to the central insight that media are physical and that their physical features frame the social relations they engender. Our insistence contrasts with those who align McLuhan with the linguistic turn. Every one of us can find remarks that McLuhan made that lend plausibility to the linguistic turn, however these remarks are neither necessary nor desirable for the central mission of a McLuhan-inspired media studies.

Although McLuhan's writings are prophetic, they are very much the products of his time. He had to fight, on the one hand, against the prevailing trend of contemporary media analysis, which strove to be a rigorous social science, conducted with the theoretical presumptions of positivism. On the other hand, he had to get the literary types to stop talking about content. In both cases, the struggle was against isolating factors of analysis, whether these factors were the observations of individual audience member's behavior or of the text. McLuhan followed Harold Innis' pioneering opposition to this fragmentation of the data (McLuhan, 1964). He urged us to treat media effects as all-encompassing phenomena. Effects were the results of the way society combined the available media. Therefore, Innis and McLuhan insisted on considering which medium dominated a particular societal media combination. They concluded that the domination of one medium in a given society had very different implications for the social and cultural organization of that society than if it was dominated by another medium.

McLuhan used all the available tools at hand to fight against the fragmenters and isolators. He used anything that supported a holistic approach to media, ranging from Edward Sapir and Benjamin Whorf's unifying claims for language (see Carey, 1967) to Mumford's history of technology (McLuhan, 1964/1994). Fortunately, by now the dominant paradigm of the social sciences has broken down and has been supplanted by what may be called critical and cultural research. This is due in no small part to McLuhan. James Carey (1967) points out that much, if not all, of the critical cultural work has tried to understand media effects as sociocultural in nature, and to embed these effects within language. Critical and cultural theorists and researchers have done much to deconstruct the artificial distinctions—the borders—heretofore erected between environment, language, meaning, and behavior. As a result, cultural theorists have become unable to describe that part of social formations that exists outside of language. Although we laud these efforts for the complexities of which they inform us and allow us to explore, we note that one unfortunate consequence of this activity is that there are now few accepted conceptual and methodological tools that would allow one to understand and explore the differences among media effects in terms of their material differences.

We can restate this in terms of emblematic thinkers—it is time to realize that McLuhan's struggle was premised more on Innis/Mumford than on Sapir/Whorf. McLuhan read Innis through the inflection of Mumford. Innis saw the course of empires and civilization determined by the oscillation between time and space biased technologies. The early Mumford (1934/1967) of *Technics and Civilization* gave an importance to the history of technology that it had not had before. An important component of Mumford's history was the three-part division of periods of technology, according to the primary means of distributing energy in each period. The first is wood, wind, and water; the second is coal; and the third is electricity. McLuhan fused the two works together in his own work and came up with his own scheme of media history and change.

Technology, rather than language, serves McLuhan as an adequate description of the limits placed on human behavior and experience. Carey

(1967) concluded that McLuhan followed the Sapir/Whorf hypothesis that "largely reduces the structure of perception and thought to the structure of language" (p. 16). However, Carey goes on to note that McLuhan severely modifies Sapir/Whorf by interpreting the grammar of language as a sensual mixture and by extending "grammatical analysis" to modes of communication such as print and television which are not normally treated as types of language. McLuhan's commitment to physical features transformed Sapir/Whorf into language as an analogy for technology rather than reducing the structure of thought to the structure of language. McLuhan's intentions are not those of a linguistic determinist. Although on several occasions McLuhan refers to language as a medium, this is a mistake even within his own rather eclectic philosophy. Linguistic determinism leaves analysis stranded within the relationship between subject and language. It never gets outside. This is our critique of structuralism. But McLuhan's breakthrough is precisely that he adopts an external approach to media by stressing their physical and technical natures. Unfortunate references to language as medium should be set aside.

McLuhan's privileging of the physical analysis of media was a continuous search for the balance between figure and ground. Hence we applaud the recent efforts to read McLuhan in the German dialectical tradition (see, e.g., Grosswiler, 1998; Stamps, 1995). McLuhan set for himself two tasks: to describe the radical shift of the figure/ground balance following the introduction of the printing press and to describe a new balance with the new electronic age. McLuhan (1962) convincingly used contemporary literary witnesses such as Shakespeare and Erasmus to demonstrate the radical shifts of the printing press. However, he had fewer literary witnesses to the new electronic age balance. James Joyce was one of the very few McLuhan cited for this task. However, Joyce's early twentieth century witnessing is of little value regarding the mid-century arrival of television and newer media. In compensation for the lack of literary evidence, McLuhan's comments turn increasingly to his own intuitions about the formal properties of the new media machines, rather than the entire apparatus of production, transmission and delivery. The formal nature of his comments about television and their future thrust tend to sound overly liberating and utopian.

Baudrillard (1981) who follows McLuhan for approximately 90%, provides the necessary corrective to the remaining 10%. Baudrillard, building on McLuhan (and Innis), realizes that the age of the mass media arrives when the audience does not respond. He goes further to argue that the masses even chose to remain silent in this age.

This parallels McLuhan's (1954a) own comments that, "today when it is no longer possible to be sure of what being a member of society may involve, the 'author' has to bestir himself as much as any pollster" (p. 125). McLuhan already understood that the authorship that is based on intimate ties with the community and its responses had been radically disrupted by the printing press and subsequent developments. Thus, witnesses to the rise of typographic man—Erasmus, Shakespeare, and so on—are in a different trajectory from contemporary witnesses. The earlier witnesses already have sensibilities trained in the integration of the communication cycle. They easily occupied a dual position within their society because they were in direct contact with their readers or audience. Erasmus was experiencing the first generation effects of the printing press on his own activities as a scholar and educator. He knew through his own life the divisions that the printing press was creating between men of letters and the reading public. To an even greater degree, Shakespeare was living through the full-blown transformations of the printing press a century after its introduction to England. He was negotiating the new ambiguities of writing stage drama that was distributed both as performance and as printed folio.

Even as late as Walter Scott or Charles Dickens, the writer was in this direct relationship with the audience and thus could be treated as a dual figure (although this was fast becoming a romantic myth and certainly lack earlier organic relationships). This was because the audience could still hope to respond in the same medium as the artist. But now the audience has become ciphers. The *avant* artist responds by leaving the work open-ended to be completed by the unknown audience. The mass medium artist completely packages the work, leaving nothing to chance and designing everything according to the latest fragmentary data available, the ratings, the box office, whatever.

This has changed the nature of witnessing entirely. McLuhan did not think this through. He continued to claim that James Joyce bore witness to the new electronic person, the same way that Erasmus bore witness to the typographic era (McLuhan, 1954b).

The one who now occupies the dual position is the distributor. This is because the audience no longer responds in communication but in behavior. The distributor is in direct position to receive this feedback. "How big was our box office yesterday?" "What do the overnight numbers show?" How many hits did our web site get?" It may be a hollow relationship but it is the enabling one for the current media environment.

McLuhan (1964/1994) inadvertently acknowledges this when he momentarily gives up his attempt to re-institute a Thomist quest for sense ratios in the audience and muses that "media as extensions of our senses institute new ratios, not only among our private senses, but among themselves, when they interact among themselves" (p. 53). We read this as call for the study of media institutions, for a close study of media as apparatuses of physical production, distribution and reception. In short, it is a call for the study of "media ratios." This model of media ratios is the payoff for McLuhan's investigation of sense ratios. He did not overtly create a theory of media ratios but both *The Gutenberg Galaxy* (McLuhan, 1962) and *Understanding Media* (McLuhan, 1964/1994) are permeated with the understanding that media exist in relationships with each other and that they form a cohesive media environment that determines and limits the social sphere.

The artistic witness is that person who experiences, in his or her own work and life, the changing sense and media ratios. In the switch to the typographic era it was the writer who fully experienced the media ratio change as a sense ratio change first. When *Playboy* asked McLuhan why the artists are privileged to perceive the media environment that is invisible to ordinary folk, he answered: "Because inherent in the artist's creative inspiration is the process of subliminally sniffing out environment change. It's always been the artist who perceives the alterations in man caused by a new medium" (E. McLuhan & Zingrone, 1995, p. 237). However, in the age of mass media, the act of witnessing itself changes since the central act is now distribution. McLuhan's insistence that we consider the medium rather than the content is recognition of this change.

We conclude that the logic of Innis/McLuhan provides the basis for a study of media transitions by understanding technologies of distribution. One key feature of the contemporary mass apparatus is the increasing flexibility of media usage and the nature of merging both media equipment and the environments in which we use this equipment. We can broadly label these developments as "media convergence." We can now receive almost any media text when and where we want, often in the form we want it. This is true whether the formal nature of the text is aural, or visual, in real time or not. In this era we must renew Innis and McLuhan's project of describing mass media in terms of their existence as material apparatuses, particularly as these apparatuses reveal themselves in acts of distribution. Their understanding of the social and technological differences, which exist among the mass media, was framed in terms of the divergence in the social and material relationships. Just as these relationships are far broader than that of reader to message/text, our notions of witnesses to this relationship must move beyond a concern with artists and now encompass and embrace distributors.

REFERENCES

Baudrillard, J. (1981). *For a critique of the political economy of the sign.* New York: Telos Press.

Carey, J. W. (1967). Harold Adams Innis and Marshall McLuhan. *The Antioch Review, 27*(1), 5-39.

Grosswiler, P. (1998). *Method is the message: Rethinking McLuhan through critical theory.* Montreal: Black Rose Books.

McLuhan, E., & Zingrone, F. (Eds.). (1995). *The essential McLuhan*. Ontario: House of Anansi Press.

McLuhan, M. (1954a). New media as political forms. *Explorations, 3*, 120-126.

McLuhan, M. (1954b). Notes on the media as art forms. *Explorations, 2*, 6-13.

McLuhan, M. (1962). *The Gutenberg galaxy: The making of typographic man*. Toronto: University of Toronto Press.

McLuhan, M. (1964). Introduction. In H.A. Innis, *The bias of communication*. Toronto: University of Toronto Press.

McLuhan, M. (1994). *Understanding media: The extensions of man*. Cambridge MA: MIT Press. (Original work published 1964)

Mumford, L. (1934/1963). *Technics and civilization*. New York. Harcourt Brace.

Stamps, J. (1995). *Unthinking modernity: Innis, McLuhan and the Frankfurt School*. Montréal and Kingston: McGill-Queen's University Press.

SECTION VI

Extensions

24 WAY COOL TEXT THROUGH LIGHT HOT WIRES AND THIN AIR*

Paul Levinson

Fordham University

McLuhan's distinction between hot and cool is one of his most celebrated, misunderstood, and useful tools for understanding the impact of new media. Gerald Stearn's (1967) anthology of often sharply critical commentary on McLuhan's work—with contributions by such notables as Tom Wolfe, George Steiner, and Susan Sontag—is aptly titled *McLuhan: Hot & Cool*. Haskell Wexler (1969) named his acclaimed movie about media and politics *Medium Cool*. In *Annie Hall*, Woody Allen (1973) waits in a movie theater line and pulls McLuhan out of the shadows to correct a professor pompously holding forth that television is "hot": "You know nothing of my work," McLuhan helpfully offers, "you mean my whole fallacy is wrong." The professor was perhaps misinformed by Jonathan Miller's (1971) *Marshall McLuhan*, the "Modern Masters" book, which blithely states that "the term 'hot,' then, applies to those messages that have gaps in their information structure, requiring an act of positive inference from the recipient" (p. 97)—or precisely the opposite of McLuhan's usage.

Like most of McLuhan's probes, the hot–cool thermometer can provide an immediate rush of presumed comprehension, followed by long periods of

---

*A slightly different version of this paper was published in Levinson, P. (1999). *Digital McLuhan: A guide to the information millennium*. London & New York: Routledge.

frustrating, even maddening, attempts to fit together readings that apparently defy integration. Such frustration, alas, has been the first and last stop for
many academic and casual readers of McLuhan, who fail to reap the rewards
that a sustained and fully reasoned pursuit of hot and cool can provide. Chief
among these benefits are assessments and predictions for our wider culture—
weather reports, to invoke the ecological analogy favored by McLuhan.

Of course, one often gets an initial sense of the temperature by just putting a finger up to the wind. The results are far from immediately clear or
well organized—and this is the case for McLuhan's taking the temperature
of media—but they may put us in better touch with what is actually going
on in the world than a host of statistical surveys and abstract ideologies.

McLuhan's invocation of hot and cool derived from jazz slang for
brassy, big band, music that overpowers and intoxicates the soul (hot) versus wispy, tinkly sketches of sound that tickle and seduce the psyche (cool).
The brassiness of the big hot band bounces off us, knocks us out—we neither embrace it nor are immersed in it—in contrast to the cool tones that
breeze through us and bid our senses to follow like the Pied Piper.

McLuhan's first full-blown presentation of this dichotomy and its application to communications media appears in *Understanding Media*
(McLuhan, 1964), which builds on his discussion of high-definition versus
low-definition media in his typescript *Report on Project in Understanding
New Media* (McLuhan, 1960). His idea was that hot media have loud,
bright, high-profile deliveries of information that accost and sweep over our
soon satiated senses, whereas cool media have blurry, soft, low-profile
demeanors that invite our involvement to complete or bring to life the quiet
evening. The now classic media players in McLuhan's performance of this
script include hot, big screen, Technicolor motion picture theaters versus
cool, small screen, black-and-white TV; hot printed prose in novels and
newspapers versus cool poetry and graffiti; true-to-life photography versus
the spare, suggestive lines of political cartoons; and the fuller dimensions of
sound and music on radio, hi-fi, and stereo versus the irresistible tin ear of
the telephone.

Furthermore, and more importantly, McLuhan saw such hot coals and
cool winds as regulating the temperature of the cultural environments they
inform and in turn draw energy from. The 1930s, running on radio and
motion pictures, were a hot age. Vivid colors, sharp hairdos, keen wit and
articulation were in. By the 1960s, television had cooled down the culture to
the point that faded jeans, long hair, and an inchoate getting in touch with
one's feelings were essential for anyone with a sense of style.

But on further reflection, how exactly can television, which conveys
both images and sounds, be cool in comparison to radio and its sound only?
And whereas prose in a textbook may be less participational than poetry,
surely prose in a love letter provokes the most involvement of all.

The latter example touches the heart of this chapter. Online communication—e-mail, group discussions, digital text in cyberspace and cell-phones—is by all standards the most fully interactive medium in history, and much more ephemeral, sketchy, wide-ranging, fast-moving than print fixed on any paper. Online text thus seems cool to the point of approaching Kelvin's zero. Yet it is clear that older forms of print—newspapers, magazines and books—are among McLuhan's favorite examples of hot, high-definition packages.

Does this mean that McLuhan's hot and cool taxonomy is broken, stretched beyond serviceability, an obsolete wreck on the shoals of the digital age?

We'll see here why this is certainly not the case—we'll see, indeed, how and why text rendered electronically inevitably acquires and radiates a coolness that far exceeds that of television, and is in synch with the success of such cool recent forms as rap music and Quentin Tarantino movies.

To understand this process, we first have to more carefully examine what the hot–cool distinction means—how it in fact operates—and what constitutes a medium, or agent of a hot–cool impact.

BARE BONES OF THE MEDIA THERMOMETER

McLuhan thinks television with its sounds and pictures is cool, less complete, in comparison to imageless radio, and for that matter to most words printed on a page lacking sound as well as image. How can that be?

Because the coolness of a medium, its invitation to fill in the details, comes not from the number of senses it engages, but from the degree of intensity of its engagements. The sound on most television today has far less clarity, depth, and range than the output of radio, "walkmen," and CDs. This flows from television's origin as a talking-head medium, in contrast to radio (at least after Sarnoff in 1915; see Dunlap, 1951), tape players, and CDs as conveyors of music. And the images on TV—even years after television grew colors, trebled its original size, and developed a memory via VCR—are still less overwhelming than the pictures in movie theaters, and less easily retrievable, more fleeting, than words printed on the pages of a book.

Thus, television began and remains as a cool medium, despite its cutting a wider sensory swath than some of its rivals. We might say that the expanse of a medium—whether gauged by the number of senses it appeals to, or the number of people it reaches—works as a multiplier or accelerant of its coolness (or hotness), provided that the components of the expanse all have an equivalent media temperature. More skin, less cover, is generally more cool, more inviting.

Of course, comparisons of media temperature, like comparisons of any individual factor, are easier to ascertain to the extent that other factors are the same. Television is most obviously cool in comparison to the movie theater, because of its equivalent audiovisual array. The postage-stamp speaker in the telephone's earpiece most clearly sets off its coolness in comparison to radio's heat (however, the inherent interactivity of the telephone also figures prominently in its coolness), just as the brevity of poetry trumps most prose in coolness in an immediately apparent way. Sound to sound, words-on-a-page to words-on-a-page, make the best comparisons.

Such clear-cut peas-in-a-pod are useful starting points in any exploration, elaboration, and application of the hot–cool taxonomy of media. The key is not to get stuck in them—to be ready to investigate the possibility, as we just did above, that television is cool not only in comparison to its audiovisual sibling the movie theater, but in contrast to radio and print as well. Hotness and coolness, in other words, are more than relative measurements of one medium to another: They are rather properties of a medium's usage by humans, properties that to some degree persist regardless of the presence of one or another medium in the environment.

But neither should we conclude from this that television or any given medium has some sort of eternal, unchanging, metaphysical claim on coolness (or hotness). To the contrary, media constantly undergo evolution under pressure of human usage and invention, and this can at any time register a profound change of temperature. Television, as indicated above, has become hotter since its introduction in the late 1940s, now offering color, 2-foot or larger screens, and retrievability via VCRs, DVDs, and on-demand services. That it continues to function as a cool medium means that such changes, these "hotting ups," to use McLuhan's parlance, have not been hot enough to burn through and transform TV's cool packaging (i.e., the incompleteness of presentation that one still receives from watching a full size, color, high-definition Sony with a VCR attachment in one's living room).

Similarly, the printed word cooled down considerably in the twentieth century, under the autumn breeze of paperbacks, McLuhan's books themselves, and deliberate attempts to air-condition the pages and format of magazines such as *Wired*. But as unlike the 19th-century tome and periodical as today's sleekest, multidimensional media of print may be, they nonetheless share the fixation of words to paper that has been the defining characteristic of writing since its inception, and renders it hot in comparison to more fleeting media ranging from speech to television.

The advent of writing on screens, however—our crossbreeding of a new medium that seems an almost 50/50 hybrid of hot text and cool TV—is a different matter. Will the traits only cancel each other out, leaving life on the computer and cellphone screen neither hot nor cool, just lukewarm water, remarkable for neither its high profile nor its invitation? We already know that is not the case. But then, which trait, which temperature, will ultimately be dominant? Or will the result be a medium with patches of each?

The answer hinges on how media perform as the content of other media. Every medium is like a Chinese box or a nesting doll—a medium within a medium within a medium, going back to thought itself—and when we experience any given medium, we hear the voices, see the faces, feel the breath, of all the media that have come before. What makes each new medium different, then, is the specific way it commends to our attention the prior media that it may encompass. When shown in a movie theater, film is a hot, bigger-than-life, theatrical experience, complete with laughing, gasping, sobbing, and applauding audiences. When shown on TV, the same film becomes content for a very different medium, at once icier, isolational, and more in need of the warmth of our participation. And when shown via a VCR, with the capacity it gives us for stopping and contemplating, for replaying, for moving quickly ahead, that same film becomes part of a significantly different medium yet again— it becomes, in Nikita Khrushchev's remarkably apt description on seeing a video tape of his "Kitchen" debate with Richard Nixon in July 1959, "like reading" (McGee, 1959).

This suggests that, however hot the legacy of the printed word, it will yield to the cooler currents of words in motion on screens, since those infinitely refreshable and thus indefinite screens are the proximate media that deliver the words.

But this triumph of cool entails a factor that goes beyond the properties of the personal computer or cellphone and its Web applications. Not only do hot and cool not operate in a vacuum for individual media—not only are these media characteristics best observed in comparison of one like medium to another—but they also have an effect on the overall culture, which in turn selects media of appropriate temperature.

Indeed, for McLuhan, the most important result of the rise of television as a cool medium is that it chilled down our culture, our attitudes, our interpersonal behavior, leading us to prize the whispered invitation to the marching-band announcement.

Elements of hot culture which dominated the first half of the 20th century of course continued to have impact, but the general lowering of temperature in the age of television made the advent of cool computers no coincidence. Our culture was waiting for them.

CULTURAL CONSEQUENCES

The terms *hot* and *cool* were already laden with connotation well beyond their jazz origins when McLuhan first started applying them to media in 1964. And their popularity has continued to expand.

To be cool has long been desirable—not only that, but "way cool" for at least the past decade. But hot is no small potatoes either. Certainly, at least one automobile company thinks so—"Toyota's hot, hot, hot!"

Cool connotes a profound, effortless synchronicity with the universe as it actually is and will likely be, speaks softly of deep pools, of being in tune with the future. Hot is fast cars indeed, fast food, life in the fast lane, encounters quick, overwhelming, intense—hot buns, hot abs, hot babes and hunks, *embrassez-moi*, run me over and leave me senseless.

The cultural ideal, apparently, is to be either hot or cool in the appropriate environment, that is, in situations or eras that most reward or require one or the other.

This is often not easy. In his two pertinent chapters in *Understanding Media* ("Media Hot and Cold," "Reversal of the Overheated Medium"), McLuhan (1964) not only indicates how the temperature of a medium or constellation of media can determine the heat of the larger culture, but how hot cultures often provoke the emergence of cooling media, and vice versa, in a thermostatic or balancing function. McLuhan developed this notion from his fellow Canadian and mentor-in-media Harold Innis' view that cultures do a see-saw act between time-binding or preservational media and space-extending or disseminative media (Innis, 1950, 1951). McLuhan later expanded this view into his "laws of media" or "tetrad" theory. Given such flux, one can often get caught with one's pants down—or at very least, dressed inappropriately for the media occasion.

Peter Cook and Dudley Moore's classic *Bedazzled* (Donen, 1967) portrays this problem beautifully. Moore strikes a Faustian deal with the devil to make seven wishes come true. He asks in one of them to become an Elvis-like rock star. Alas, his joy is short-lived, for by the time this movie takes place, hot Elvis has been replaced by cool Mick Jagger as the rock icon. Poor Moore/Elvis is out of synch with the temperature of the times. (And Jagger continued as an icon of coolness into the 1990s—at least for baby boomers like Bill Gates—as evidenced by Microsoft's use of the Stones' "Start Me Up" as theme music for its Windows 95 TV commercials.)

McLuhan had a field day plumbing for hot and cool vectors in American politics. Adlai Stevenson's literacy was an early victim of the television age, which favored the cipher that was Eisenhower. But JFK's wit and poetry played perfectly to the camera: surveys conducted after the Kennedy–Nixon debates showed Kennedy won the debate on television, while Nixon carried the day in the same debate heard on hot, serious, articulate radio. Eight years later, however, Hubert Humphrey's in-your-face ebullience made him a much hotter candidate than Nixon, who had learned to somewhat disguise his face and his logic from the camera. But TV had the last laugh on Nixon in Watergate, in which his earnest denials of guilt, reasonable enough in print and voice, came across as a cartoon villain's shifty-eyed protestations on television. A classic political cartoon by Herblock from that era pictured Nixon crouched against the side of an overturned desk in the White House, ammunition ready, shouting "Come and get me, copper!"

Most of these hot-and-cool interpretations have a degree of plausibility, and the examples ring true. Yet surely other factors played a role in the rise and fall of those political fortunes. McLuhan, in any case, did not live to see the strongest challenge to hot-and-cool exegesis of politics in the 1980s, when Ronald Reagan, who by most standards was a hotter candidate than the inarticulate Jimmy Carter and low-key Walter Mondale, outpolled his rivals in two elections.

The success of Reagan's old-time warmth in a cool age could be explained by recourse to hot elements in the 1980s—say, the heating up of television described above, or even the temperature of early personal computers, much more dependent on fixed, rigid (i.e., hot) programs than the more open architecture that followed. One could also seek elements of coolness in Reagan's style—his trademarked capacity for saying little or nothing so eloquently, honed by his work in television commercials in the 1950s.

But the better lesson for hot–cool cultural assessment to be drawn from the Reagan years is that hot and cool as a tool of analysis has its limits when applied to politics. Indeed, we might construct a general principle from this: the further away from its media origins, the more tentative, conflicted, attenuated the hot–cool analysis becomes. Applied to music, movies, and clothes (which, as McLuhan noted, are in many cases more a medium of personal communication than a means of protection from the elements), it works fine.

It has its innings in politics too. Although George H. W. Bush's victory over the practically tongue-tied Michael Dukakis in 1988 was another hot success, Clinton in most respects was certainly cooler than the first-President Bush in 1992 and Bob Dole in 1996. George W. Bush, the son, was less articulate than Al Gore, but the results of the 2000 election were a dead heat, and thus tell us nothing about hot-and-cool advantages in politics.

As an example of where hot and cool eddies in overall culture have least impact, we might consider the enterprise of science. Although cultural expectations no doubt direct scientific research and govern initial interpretations of findings, the evidence of external reality sooner or later cuts through prevalent beliefs—otherwise, we would not have scientific revolutions on the level of Copernicus, Darwin, and Einstein. The key factor here is an external reality which, although filtered to us via our perceptions, beliefs and media, exists to a large extent independent of them. Fritjof Capra (1975) may have given *The Tao of Physics* a popular spin—a song that continues playing today in books like Tipler's (1994) *Physics of Immortality*, which claims the future already exists and governs our present—but the real progress in science still comes from the hard edges of experiment and observation. Reality bites, whether the temperature is hot or cool.

That our popular culture has undergone a pervasive cooling since the 1950s, however, there can be no doubt. Soft colors, soft voices, software—all offer quiet basins of attraction that pull forth our participation. A signal irony here is that television, which led the way to the shady side of the street, is obviously not intrinsically an interactive medium. McLuhan saw this lack of interactivity as the source of one of television's most important effects: Stimulated to participate by a medium that does not permit it, viewers develop an insatiable need to reach out and touch someone, to get in touch—to reach through the light-through medium—and to be in as much literal physical contact with others as possible. Everything from touchy-feely groups to the Beatles "I Wanna Hold Your Hand" to the sexual revolution follows or at least gets impetus from this.

But what happens when a medium issues a soft invitation to interaction that *can* be accommodated—more, pursued as never before—via the medium itself? What happens when the participational possibilities are hardwired into the very system that tempts us with its low-profile, incomplete presentation?

We get electronic text and its consequences.

TEXT INTERACTIVE

Although television received most of the credit for the cool age, it was not the first low-profile medium in the communications revolution, and perhaps not even the most important. That priority goes to the telephone, an 1876 invention that was child and perhaps partial catalyst of a cool age of Impressionism in painting, poetry, and music.

The relatively poor quality of telephone sound—it delivers but a gloss of the full human voice—made it from the outset a quintessentially cool medium. But it had a reason far more profound to elicit interaction: namely, that the telephone is essentially, regardless of the quality of its sound, an interactive instrument. Indeed, it is a medium whose ringing can barely be gainsaid. The hope, however slim and unrealistic, that the caller will at last be providing the means for fulfilling my career, my fantasy, my need to be recognized by everyone or someone in the world, is almost always irresistible. Few if any other activities can take precedence. Communication theorists have long joked about couples afflicted by "telephonus interruptus" in their lovemaking, and the joke is often but truth.

So powerful, then, is the interactive pull, the tug of a live human being on the other end, that telephone would have been a cool medium regardless of the intensity and clarity of its sound. Indeed, we might speculate that telephone remained cool—the quality of its sound has not dramatically increased in the past 100 years—because it was locked into a keenly satisfying cool loop by virtue of its interactivity. Rather than a low profile that engendered interactivity, the interactivity of the telephone sealed its low profile, made any kind of higher profile unnecessary.

In contrast, noninteractive cool television, as discussed earlier, rapidly evolved to some degree of heat in its colors, size, clarity, and retrievability. This may also account for the enormous influence of TV on our culture, in contrast to the telephone. Television, for all its ephemerality, was something to see, to focus on. Telephone traffics in evanescent information—the answering machine only somewhat counters this—and as such it may have been too cool, may have operated too pervasively and unconsciously in our culture, to exert major discernible influence on it.

But what consequences ensue when visual text—prose, an archetypal hot medium—becomes the content of cool telephone?

The early take on personal computers—early but still prevalent in the 1990s among media critics such as Neil Postman (e.g., in his speech at the New School for Social Research in honor of John Culkin, one of McLuhan's disciples, in February 1994)—was that they were some kind of souped up television screen, likely to have similar impact on the cognitive process (namely: either none or deleterious). More enlightened users—and I immodestly include myself among them—thought that computers could be more appropriately considered new kinds of books. (As an aside, the Supreme Court apparently agreed, striking down the Communications Decency Act in 1997 on the grounds that the Internet is more like a print medium than a broadcast medium, and therefore entitled to fuller First Amendment protections; see Greenhouse, 1997.) In any event, when connected to the worldwide telephone system, the personal computer immediately transcends both TV and the book: it becomes a special type of telephone, not only retaining its powerful cool interactivity but amplifying it. It actually has not two but three parents—books, telephone, and television—and the last two are cool. Online text thus comes by its coolness naturally, by a score of two to one.

The onlining of text—the immersion of hot print in the cool interactive milieu of the global telephone network, outfitted with screens—has been a baptismal breakpoint in the history of writing, and per force of our human existence. The fixed, linear specificity of first alphabetic writing and then print had long been one of its defining characteristics, rendering it a hot medium par excellence. Socrates was an early complainer about this heat, worrying in the *Phaedrus* that the written transcript, unlike verbal dialogue, provides but one unvarying answer to its questioners. He yearned for "an intelligent writing which . . . can defend itself, and knows when to speak and when to be silent" (Plato's *Phaedrus*, sec. 275-276). Of course, living authors of even the most hidebound texts could always in principle be questioned as to their meanings, and text in the form of personal letters has always been intrinsically interactive—a sort of highly delayed, asynchronous telephone conversation, looked at in retrospect. But time is inextricably of the essence in human affairs, and the degree of delay in written questioning of living authors and personal letter writing—the time usually consumed for response and re-response in such asynchronous interactions—can deprive this interactivity of much of its impact. Perhaps this is why I. A. Richards (1929) wisely counseled in his *Practical Criticism* to let texts speak for themselves, insofar as this was possible, since an author questioned years after the act of writing might well be no longer reliable as guide to what was intended in that act.

Text rendered online, however, has the capacity for instant interactivity. Indeed, as early online users of American bulletin boards and commercial systems and the French "Minitel" discovered by the mid-1980s, text as a vehicle of synchronous immediate conversation could be more provocative than verbal exchanges. The same is true today with texting on cellphones. McLuhan's concept of cool can help us understand why: Verbal conversations on the phone come in packages that usually tell the conversing parties who they are, their general emotional state from tone of voice, and so on. These details can be seen as heating elements carried over from in-person conversations, in which an enormous amount of hot, high-profile detail is available: Their retention on the phone serves to heat up, or slightly "de-ice," the telephone environment. But they can be missing entirely in an online text community, when participants in a conversation have only each other's written words by which to know each other.

No wonder that inhibitions are down when fingers do the limbo on keyboards and mice in the middle of the night; no wonder that total strangers are propositioned and relationships virtually consummated in online chats now going on the world over. No wonder that thumbs can often say more than tongues on cellphones. Text on telephone is even cooler, more seductive, than speech—it is often addictive (in a psychological sense) precisely because its mode of presentation prevents us from ever getting enough of it.

A dollop of asynchronicity can heighten the impact of this potent mix. Conversationalists on Usenet lists see their comments responded to in minutes, hours, almost never longer than a few days. The Western Behavioral Sciences Institute in the early 1980s found such a tempo ideal for intellectual dialog: The combination of the more time allowed for considered response, the endurance of the record, and the global situation of participants made online seminars far more productive than the typical in-person meeting. Online courses since conducted for academic credit have recorded similar, consistent results: asynchronous interactivity, when paced in minutes and hours and days online rather than days and weeks and months offline, engenders a level of participation in quality and quantity that often exceeds that of the typical in-person classroom, in which only one person (usually the teacher) can speak at any one time (see, Levinson, 1995, for details). A cool middle ground is achieved, one that maximizes participation because it is free of two sets of inhibiting factors—those that characterize the in-your-face-in-person meeting, and those attendant to the molasses inter-activity of traditional street-mail letter-writing and the noninteractivity of taking books out of a library. Online learning thus improves on place-based, book-paced (which also could be spelled book-paste) education. It conveys some of the benefits of the older tutorial system that mass education had itself largely supplanted (except in tutorial systems still in operation in Oxford and Cambridge, and more recently established in the British Open University system)—with the key difference that online education is in prin-ciple global in reach, in contrast to the inevitable locality of in-person edu-cation, whether on the tutorial or mass level.

McLuhan (1960) would no doubt have been an advocate of cool online education. "My entire syllabus," he writes in his *Report on Understanding New Media*, "proceeds on the principle that low definition (LD) is necessary to good teaching. The completely expressed package offers no opportunity for student participation. . . . LD media like telephone and television are major education instruments because they offer inadequate information" (pp. 14-15). Although his expectations have been fulfilled for television only partly and for voice telephone not at all, the online course conducted via personal computers that send and receive text via telephones connected to "computer conferencing" facilities on central computers and the Internet has become an ideal forum for cool "good teaching"—as defined not only by McLuhan, but education theorists ranging from Dewey to Piaget to Montessori, who have all emphasized the importance of the teacher as facil-itator (not lecturer) and the active student learner (see Perkinson, 1982, for more on the philosophy and history of nonpassive education).

Unsurprisingly, the cool impetus of text interactivity has picked up energy and mass as it has evolved. The evolution of hypertext and its links—predicted decades ago, albeit on centralized mainframe systems that never quite came to be, by Ted Nelson (see, Nelson, 1980/1990 for a summary of his 1960s work)—offers the online user a myriad of possible hidden knowl-edge connections. You could click on McLuhan, were you reading this doc-ument in online hypertext, and who knows where that might lead you. You would likely be linked to online repositories of McLuhan's work, to the extent they exist, but you would also likely have access to work relevant to McLuhan that does not even exist as yet at the time of this writing. On the one hand, you can rest assured that a huge amount of knowledge is little more than a keystroke or two away; on the other hand, neither you nor I nor anyone can ever know at any time just what the extent of that knowledge is, because it is constantly being re-arranged, added to, linked to new links ad infinitum in possibility. The Web and its hyperlinks thus comprise a quintessential case of a cool system—a sea breeze wending its way through every leaf in the hothouse of knowledge, not only cooling but also pollinating as it moves along.

No wonder that the Web and its pages are catnip to anyone with a taste for intellectual inquiry. The deeply cool procedure of every reader creating his or her own book, different with each navigation of the hypertext Internet, has already connected with other cooling aspects of our popular culture. What is *Pulp Fiction* (Tarantino, 1994)—and *Reservoir Dogs* (Tarantino, 1992) before it—if not a hypertext movie, a presentation of disparate though intricately related swatches of narrative, with the viewer invited to put them together to tell his or her story? Rap music and its open, riffing structure offers similar invitations. In both cases, we see hot media—like text before the Internet—cooling down under the influence of a major plunge in temperature in our cultural environment. (See Benzon, 1993, for some interesting speculation on the synchrony of rap music and computer culture.) Indeed, the integration of phone calls into talk radio has cooled down that hot broadcast medium as well, and has also begun to break down the noninteractive bastion of what we can now see as the old-fashioned voyeuristic coolness of TV.

At the same time, we can see McLuhan's thermostatic or reversal principle coming into play, as the pervasive coolness of electronic texts creates a need for some scraps of detail, some warmth of image, lest we shiver unduly online. The icons of Windows and their progeny on online services are too ambiguous, cartoonish, to provide much heat in this regard. But the picturing of Web pages with literal photographs—still or in motion, with or without sound—the quest to know just what the authors of pages look like, to have explicit visual renditions of places and events described, is a dash for some shelter, a clutch for some fig leaves, an assertion of some familiar, reliable sources of comfortable hearth and detail, as the cool winds of change blow ever stronger around us.

REFERENCES

Allen, W. (1973). *Annie Hall* [Motion picture].
Benzon, W. (1993). The United States of the blues: On the crossing of African and European cultures in the 20th century. *Journal of Social and Evolutionary Systems, 16*(4), 401-438.
Capra, F. (1975). *The tao of physics.* New York: Bantam.

Donen, S. (1967). *Bedazzled* [Motion picture].

Dunlap, O. E., Jr. (1951). *Radio & television almanac*. New York: Harper.

Greenhouse, L. (1997, June 27). Court, 9-0, protects speech on Internet. *The New York Times*, pp. A1, 20.

Innis, H. (1950). *Empire and communications*. Toronto: University of Toronto Press.

Innis, H. (1951). *The bias of communication*. Toronto: University of Toronto Press.

Levinson, P. (1995). *Learning cyberspace: Essays on the evolution of media and the new education*. San Francisco, CA: Anamnesis Press.

McGee, F. [Writer]. (1959, July 24). *Time and again*, Khrushchev-Nixon "kitchen" debates, rebroadcast on MSNBC-TV, July 24, 1997.

McLuhan, M. (1960). *Report on project in understanding new media*. Washington, DC: U.S. Department of Health.

McLuhan, M. (1964). *Understanding media*. New York: Mentor.

Miller, J. (1971). *Marshall McLuhan*. New York: Viking.

Nelson, T. (1990). *Literary machines*. Sausalito, CA: Mindful Press. (Original work published 1980)

Perkinson, H. (1982). Education and learning from our mistakes. In P. Levinson (Ed.), *In pursuit of truth: Essays on the philosophy of Karl Popper*. Atlantic Highlands, NJ: Humanities Press.

Postman, N. (1994, February). *John Culkin memorial talk*. Presented at the New School for Social Research, New York City.

Richards, I. A. (1929). *Practical criticism*. London: K. Paul, Trench, Trubner.

Stearn, G. E. (Ed.). (1967). *McLuhan: Hot and cool*. New York: Dial.

Tarantino, Q. (1994). *Pulp Fiction* [Motion picture].

Tarantino, Q. (1992). *Reservoir Dogs* [Motion picture].

Tipler, F. (1994). *The physics of immortality*, New York: Doubleday.

Wexler, H. (1969). *Medium Cool* [Motion picture].

25 THE GLOBAL VILLAGE VERSUS TRIBAL MAN

THE PARADOX OF THE MEDIUM AND THE MESSAGE

Susan B. Barnes

Rochester Institute of Technology

As more people begin to use the Internet as a medium of communication, a central paradox emerges—does the Internet bring people together or tear them apart? This paradox can be viewed in a variety of ways. For example, Kenneth Gergen (1991) and Mark Poster (1990) examine how global electronic media fragment concepts of self. From an interpersonal communication perspective, Gerald Phillips (1995) used this paradox to try to understand whether or not the Internet would bring people together into a global community or isolate them into small narrow-minded virtual tribes. All of these various approaches illustrate how global media are connecting us together, while simultaneously fragmenting individual experience. However, when we apply McLuhan's most famous paradox—the medium is the message—to this issue, we realized that all of the previous approaches tend to focus on the content rather than the form of the medium.

Paradox is a technique found in many of McLuhan's books. According to Kroker (1997): "To read McLuhan is to enter into a 'vortex' of the critical, cultural imagination, where 'fixed perspective' drops off by the way, and where everything passes over instantaneously into its opposite" (p. 89). For example, in the *Medium is the Massage* (McLuhan & Fiore, 1967), McLuhan spoke of technology in highly contradictory terms—electric technology simultaneously contains possibilities for domination and emancipation.

McLuhan asserts that electric technology ushered in a new era of technological change. It was the end of "visual uniform culture" based on mechanical technologies and the beginning of a new tribal culture that would require man to face the challenges of electric simulation of consciousness. Depending on how we face the challenges, electric technologies could dominate or emancipate. Similarly, they could bring us together or separate us.

Presently, technologies that substitute a language of codes and the electric processing of information for "natural" or face-to-face experience are double-edged. Therefore, we need to pay critical attention when new electronic media are being introduced into a culture. McLuhan's most famous paradoxical statement, *the medium is the message*, challenges us to ignore the content of the messages being sent through a medium and critique the biases embedded in the medium itself. By examining media in terms of paradoxes, we are forced to think about media in new ways. Kroker (1997) describes this process as follows:

> When McLuhan spoke of electronic technology as an extension, or outering, of the central nervous system, he also meant that modern society had done a "flip." In order to perceive the "invisible ground rules" of the technological media, we have to learn to think in reverse image: to perceive the subliminal grammar of technology as metaphor, as a simulacrum or sign-system, silently and pervasively processing human existence. (p. 94)

Media are so pervasive in our lives that people have difficulty understanding the impact that technology has on our view of the world. The particular use to which a technology is put, like the particular content that a medium may carry, functions as a distraction and smoke screen. According to McLuhan (1964): "'the medium is the message' because it is the medium that shapes and controls the scale and form of human association and action. The content of uses of such media are as diverse as they are ineffectual in shaping the form of human association. Indeed, it is only too typical that the 'content' of any medium blinds us to the character of the medium" (p. 24).

WHY THE MEDIUM IS THE MESSAGE

The medium influences the content and what can be created and transmitted through it. For example, the messages transmitted through broadcast television are controlled by media corporations. Average people do not have access to the creation or dissemination of mass messages. In commercial broadcasting, advertising revenues pay for the programming. As a result, advertising is both a major part of the message content and an influence on the type of programming presented. For example, in *Amusing Ourselves to Death*, Postman (1985) argues that television is essentially an entertainment medium. Information viewed on commercial television is generally received within the context of amusement, therefore, it is difficult to take seriously. The recreational characteristic of the medium shapes the form and meaning of information presented on and received from television. Because the television medium alters the way we receive information, it consequently influences how we perceive the world.

Stated another way, media become the message because they directly shape the form of information and how it is understood. McLuhan and Zingrone (1995) describe this as follows:

> The perception of reality now depends on the structure of information. The form of each medium is associated with a different arrangement, or ratio, among the senses, which creates new forms of awareness. These perceptual transformations, the new ways of experiencing that each medium creates, occur in the user regardless of the program content. (p. 3)

McLuhan utilizes the metaphor of the human body to explain media biases. Oral cultures primarily perceive information through the ear, in contrast, literate cultures perceive it through the eye. A shift in perception from the ear to the eye, will change the way people understand the world. Following this idea, studies by Havelock (1963) and Ong (1982) illustrate how the shift from oral to written cultures have changed perception. For example, Ong (1982) describes the human lifeworld in orality versus literacy as follows:

> In the absence of elaborate analytic categories that depend on writing to structure knowledge at a distance from lived experience, oral cultures must conceptualize and verbalize all their knowledge with more or less close reference to the human lifeworld, assimilating the alien, objective world to the more immediate, familiar interaction of human beings. A chirographic (writing) culture and even more a typographic (print) culture can distance and in a way denature even the human, itemizing such things as the names of leaders and political divisions in an abstract, neutral list entirely devoid of a human action content. (p. 42)

Currently, we are going through another media shift from print to electronic media. Using the body metaphor, McLuhan (1964) argues that the printed book is an extension of the eye, in contrast, electronic media are an extension of the nervous system. McLuhan asserts that "rapidly, we approach the final phase of the extension of man—technological simulation of consciousness, when the creative process of knowing will be collectively and corporately extended to the whole of human society, much as we have already extended our senses and our nerves by the various media" (p. 19). The Internet and the World Wide Web now appear to be the embodiment of McLuhan's final vision of electronic technology. They extend our nervous system through a global electronic network that connects people together into a "global village."

ORAL, LITERATE, AND ELECTRONIC CULTURES

To date, communication researchers describe three primary media environments: oral, literate, and electronic. In *The Gutenberg Galaxy*, McLuhan (1962) describes how the differences between orality and literacy influence cultural attitudes. Moreover, he speculates on the shift from literate to electronic culture.

> But today, as electricity creates conditions of extreme interdependence on a global scale, we move swiftly again into an auditory world of simultaneous events and over-all awareness. Yet the habits of literacy persist in our speech, our sensibilities, and in our arrangement of the spaces and times of our daily lives. Short of some catastrophe, literacy and visual bias could bear up for a long time against electricity and "unified field" awareness. (pp. 28-29)

Although shifts from one predominant medium to another influence attitudes, cultures with a long literate history will be more resistant to the changes brought about by electronic media as auditory bias. In the past, cultures were shaped by the fact that they were either primarily oral or literate. For example, Havelock (1963) argues that Plato's *Republic* was written during the Greek transformation from orality to literacy. He states that Plato's discussion of forms "announced the arrival of a completely new level of discourse which as it became perfected was to create in turn a new kind of experience of the world—the reflective, the scientific, the technological, the theological, the analytic" (p. 267). Havelock describes forms as follows: "What the theory of Forms was properly designed to affirm was the existence of abstract properties and relations of physical objects and so forth" (p. 270). Therefore, Plato's concept of forms can be compared to the abstract characteristics of written language. According to Havelock, Plato's *Republic* is an argument in support of the written method of communication that symbolically abstracts the object into language rather than the oral method of delivering information utilized by the "Poets." Plato is rejecting the "oral-style of thinking perpetuated in Homer in favor of the keen analysis or dissection of the world and of thought itself made possible by the interiorization of the alphabet in Greek psyche" (Ong, 1982, p. 28).

Writing establishes text as a continuity outside of the mind that follows a new linear organization of events in time. Texts can be referred to and reviewed. In contrast, oral utterance vanishes as soon as the word is spoken. Oral communicators use redundancy and repetition to keep both the speaker and hearer focused on key ideas. As a result, redundancy characterizes oral thought and speech. Moreover, orality is a more natural pattern for thought and speech than writing. According to Ong (1982): "Sparsely linear or analytic thought and speech is an artificial creation, structured by the technology of writing" (p. 40).

The artificial creation of writing distances knowledge from lived experience. Written culture can separate knowledge from human activities. Ong (1982) asserts: "Oral cultures know few statistics or facts divorced from human or quasi-human activity" (p. 43). In contrast, conceptual situations in oral cultures tend to remain close to the concrete human lifeworld. The separation of facts from actions creates new ways for people to view the world, a perspective based on abstract statistics is very different from one directly connected to human activity. Ong (1977) states: "Since writing came into existence, the evolution of the word and the evolution of consciousness have been intimately tied in with technologies and technological developments. Indeed, all major advances in consciousness depend on technological transformations and implementations of the word" (p. 42).

Today the Internet represents another transformation—the shift from printed to digital media. However, the Internet is a mixture of both orality and literacy. Derrick de Kerckhove (cited in Kelly, 1996) states: "It's the only medium we've ever known where language appears orally and written at the same time" (p. 149). According to McLuhan (1962), orality and literacy foster different types of cultural attitudes. McLuhan asserts that nonliterate tribal cultures create an auditory space for human interaction that supports a feeling of tight community and co-existence, giving us a "possessive world of total interdependence and interrelation that is the auditory network" (McLuhan, 1962, p. 22). In contrast, literate cultures depend on visual space. The visual space of the alphabet breaks apart sight and sound and meaning. As a result, alphabet-oriented cultures create "numerous specializations and separations of function inherent in industry and applied knowledge" (p. 35). This separation leads to a sense of individualization that is further developed through the technology of the printing press.

In opposition to the individualization created by the alphabet and print-based culture, electronic media (radio, television, and computer) return us to a tribal base. A world interdependent on CNN's global news broadcasts, the

Internet's worldwide e-mail, and MTV's continuous flow of music videos. McLuhan argued that the main effect of the electric process is to retribalize the structure of psychic and social awareness. "Millions of people sitting around the TV tube, CNN-style, absorbing the modern equivalent of shamanistic lore from the authorized source is closely analogous to the old tribal relations of tyrannous instruction and control" (E. McLuhan & Zingrone, 1995, p. 4).

As the Internet develops, the World Wide Web is quickly turning into a television-oriented mass medium. In contrast to the original alphabet-centered Internet, the Web presents information in a multimedia format of sight, sound, color, and motion. Thus, two very different types of media environments are created by computer networks—one that resembles printed texts and the other that is closer to television. The current hybrid nature of the Internet makes it a more difficult medium to understand than many older media.

ORALITY, LITERACY, AND THE INTERNET

Ong (1977) identifies a law of media that helps to explain what is happening on the Internet: *A new medium reinforces the older one and then transforms it.* Applying this idea to television, Ong (1977) states: "A new medium of verbal communication not only does not wipe out the old, but actually reinforces the older medium or media. However, in doing so it transforms the old, so that the old is no longer what it used to be" (pp. 82-83). For example the oral nature of television and radio, "alerts us to the curious ways in which electronic, secondary orality, though derivative from and permanently dependent on writing and print, reproduces some noetic structures characteristic of early or primary (preliterate) orality" (p. 229). Although television is primarily an oral medium, television's orality is based on writing and print, therefore it is a "secondary orality." The printed word is "essential for the manufacture and operation of the equipment and for its use as well" (Ong, 1982, p. 136). Additionally, printed scripts are used to develop television programming and written time logs structure the length of programming versus commercials on both television and radio. Ong (1982) describes secondary orality as follows:

> Secondary orality is both remarkably like and remarkably unlike primary orality. Like primary orality, secondary orality has generated a strong group sense, for listening to spoken words forms hearers into a group, a true audience, just as reading written or printed texts turns individuals in on themselves. But secondary orality generates a sense for

groups immeasurably larger than those of primary oral culture—McLuhan's "global village." Moreover, before writing, oral folk were group-minded because no feasible alternative had presented itself. In our age of secondary orality, we are group-minded self-consciously and programmatically. (p. 136)

Applying Ong's law of media to the Internet, in the beginning, communication through the Internet was presented to computer users as the electronically mediated printed word. The electronic print simultaneously reinforces and transforms texts. Both the typographic and electronic word share the same alphabet system, however unlike fixed pages of print, electronic words can be changed on the computer screen. "What happens when text moves from page to screen? First, the digital text becomes unfixed and interactive. The reader can change it, become writer. The center of Western culture since the Renaissance—really since the great Alexandrian editors of Homer—the fixed, authoritative, canonical text, simply explodes into the ether" (Lanham, 1993, p. 31). When the printed word becomes electronic, the text is no longer fixed and static. The permanence of the printed word is transformed into an ever changing array of characters that scroll across the computer screen.

Despite the difference between printed and electronic words, early Internet users tended to follow the thinking patterns of a print-based mindset. Many of the people who were early adopters of computer media were highly literate people. They were educated with the written word and began to use the Internet to communicate with each other in correspondence that resembles older forms of print-based writing. For example, electronic mail generally follows a standardized format that is similar to other written correspondence. Many e-mail systems require a person to enter information into a "To" and "Subject" line. The "From" and "Date" lines are programmed into the software. The overall result is the transmission of a message that resembles older forms of typed or written memorandums.

Although the structure of e-mail resembles older written media, many people write messages that imitate the informality of the spoken word. E-mail messages are brief, not grammatical and use colloquial vocabulary. Lee (1996) states that "deviations from formal grammar usually signify efforts to visualize talk" (p. 287). For example, e-mail writers will type phrases such as: "Hi! . . . uh, wait just a sec, there's somethang I gotta do." Thus, e-mail alters traditional written language into one that imitates oral speech. In opposition to Ong's description of secondary orality that uses the written word to shape oral language, e-mail attempts to incorporate oral features into the writing process. Similar to secondary orality that is a hybrid between orality and literacy, e-mail is also a hybrid medium. From this perspective, it could be argued that e-mail is also a form of secondary orality. But, as more people use the Web, which can integrate voice and audio software into online correspondence, the Internet will more clearly fit Ong's description of secondary orality.

As previously mentioned, cultures with a literate history will tend be more resistant to the changes brought about by electronic media Following this trend, people corresponding through the Internet are inclined to follow print-based behavior. For example, people participating in online discussions tend to fragment themselves into small isolated special interest groups. Internet observers have described these groups as small societies or tribal cultures. For example, Mandel and Van der Leun (1996) argue that the network is a society of tribes. They state: "In the Net, as in the world, people tend to gravitate to groups and associations that, as individuals, they perceive will be comfortable or in their interests" (p. 34). Thus, people on the Internet separate themselves into specializations instead of coming together into a large mass group.

The tendency for people to gravitate toward small online groups with people who share similar interests and points of view, has led some critics to fear that the Internet will isolate us from each other. Instead of forcing people to be aware of diverse perspectives and cultures, individuals will stay confined in their own small corners of cyberspace. This scenario assumed that the tendency toward specialization and the drawing of boundary lines associated with print culture is now seeming intensified.

Currently, print-based literacy is a requirement for online communication. Although a number of visual symbolic elements, including graphical interfaces, emoticons, and avatars, have been added to electronic discourse, the written word is still a primary form of human-to-human communication through the Internet. A person must be able to read and write before he or she can communicate online. This further supports the tradition of print-based culture.

INTERNET, EDUCATION, AND LITERACY

Although electronic media have become a major method for distributing information in American society, our schools are primarily print-based. Commercial mass media are generally kept out of the classroom and the media literacy curriculum has not been widely accepted. McLuhan is an unsung pioneer of the media literacy movement and he, along with Hutchon and his son Eric, wrote a textbook titled *Media, Messages, and Language: The World as Your Classroom* (McLuhan, Hutchon, & McLuhan, 1980). As the title suggests, he proposed to bring the world back into the classroom for study. McLuhan's ideas about media literacy were further fleshed out by John Culkin, at Fordham University and then at the New School.

Presently, a problem with the endorsement of media literacy is conflicting points of view about what it is supposed to teach. Christ and Potter (1998) state: "In building a [media literacy] curriculum, there is the tension between the often competing goals of training students for specific tasks that could help them get a job and educating students in a liberal manner to be prepared for our complex society" (p. 9). In the United States there is a conflict between training students to be practitioners in the media industries and educating students to become media literate citizens. In many approaches to teaching media literacy, students are taught to read messages but they are not taught to write them. Herein lies the conflict in media education.

When students are taught to create media messages, the goal tends to focus on industry skill training. In contrast, educators who take the critical approach tend to emphasize the reading or decoding of the media message. A combined approach would be to create media messages that are critical of the media. But, this can be difficult because many students tend to emulate what they see on the media without consciously realizing what they are doing. For example, when teaching digital media courses, I find that students can create a work that *looks* like an advertisement or MTV style video without fully understanding the thinking processes that occur during the creation of these types of commercial works. The visual illusion is present, but the message is missing. When asked about the message, students can not explain what message their work is trying to communicate because they have only paid attention to the visual *look and feel* of their project. As a result, a critical examination of their work reveals a confused message that is covered by a visual facade.

A critical examination of any medium requires traditional literacy skills. Postman (1979) argues this point in *Teaching as a Conserving Activity*, proposing a thermostatic view of education where schools would counterbalance cultural biases: "*The school stands as the only mass medium capable of putting forward the case for what is not happening in the culture*" (p. 27). He argues for a school curriculum that is concept-centered and grounded in writing and print media. Specifically, he argues that the teaching of logical linguistic statements should counterbalance television's curriculum of emotional picture stories.

Currently, television has been blamed for the decline in literacy skills in the United States and schools are beginning to focus on this crisis (Healy, 1990). Concerns over traditional literacy tend to overshadow the idea of integrating media literacy into the curriculum. This occurs because traditional literacy is associated with democratic citizenship, whereas mass media messages tend to be associated with business practices.

However, at the same time that educators are dealing with these curricular issues, the computer is being introduced into classrooms. Advocates for computer-based education are associating this medium with citizenship arguments rather than media literacy perspectives. Learning computer skills are placed in a category similar to basic reading, writing, and math. But, today's definitions of computer literacy generally refer to operating a computer (reading skills), rather than programming one (writing skills). In an information society, employers require people to know basic literacy skills and most require computer skills. As a result, rhetoric describing computers in education tend to associate computer skills with basic requirements for equal job opportunities (see Clinton & Gore, 1993).

However as computers enter the school, three issues need to be addressed: access to technology, literacy skills, and knowledge control. In the United States, government and industry are encouraging educators to integrate computing into the curriculum by donating machines, setting up grant programs, asking schools to connect to the Internet, and placing computers in public libraries. The goal is to provide access to information and focus on developing high-tech literacy for an information economy. Former President Bill Clinton made the following statement in his 1997 State of the Union Address:

> We must bring the power of the Information Age into all our schools. Last year I challenged America to connect every classroom and library to the Internet by the year 2000, so that, for the first time in history, a child in the most isolated rural town, the most comfortable suburb, the poorest inner-city school will have the same access to the same universe of knowledge. I ask your support to complete this historic mission. (cited in Harrison, 1997)

Bringing the Information Age into all our schools by connecting classrooms to the "information highway" makes an assumption about the nature of education. The information highway metaphor implies moving information from one place to another. When applied to education, however, it seems to assume that access to information *is* education. More and more, this notion is filtering into educational discourse. There seems to be a growing misunderstanding between delivering a message and the goals of teaching and learning. Sending the same message to every classroom in America sounds like it equalizes education, but it does not mean that every student will be able to understand the information they receive. Although, a first-, second-, or third-grade student will be able to click on an icon with a mouse and access information, reading and comprehending the information requires traditional literacy skills. Moreover, mastery of traditional literacy skills creates a power balance in an information society. Danny Goodman (1994) states:

> Even if the most compelling applications should become available at no or low cost tomorrow, there would still be a significant division between

the literate and illiterate members of our society. These groups, in my opinion, are the true "haves" and "havenots" on the information super-highway. If a person can't read text that comes down the off-ramp, then it's not text or information: it's visual noise. (pp. 105-106)

Lost in the techno-rhetoric of the information highway is a basic under-standing of literacy. Somehow visions of "information access" overshadow the reality that there are estimates that 40% to 50% of the American popu-lation is currently illiterate. By the year 2000, many people had access to the Internet. But, how many people were able to read the information? Moreover, how many were able to understand it?

Phillips (1994) argues that traditional literacy skills are a requirement for computer use. The people who are currently illiterate will have to become literate before they will have the basic skills to work with a computer. He states:

The written word is immutable for computers, too. The program either works or it doesn't. In case of failure, we follow the law of RTFM [Read The Freaking Manual] or call in a consultant. It is virtually impossible to conceptualize computer software or hardware of any level of com-plexity that does not have a written manual somewhere early in the process. (p. 53)

Similarly, Harrison (1997), a California seventh- and eighth-grade teacher, argues that even if computer/Internet literacy were mandated in the schools, the proper curriculum path would not start with the Internet: "It might be something like: Reading/writing literacy, typing/keyboarding/gen-eral computer literacy, a variety of computer application programs, comput-er mechanics and ethics—*then* the Internet" (p. 32). However, when the World Wide Web fully integrates sound and video into the information accessed through the Internet, media literacy will become another skill requirement. Although politicians and school administrators focus on acquiring equipment to make students computer literate, a larger problem that needs to be addressed is teacher literacy.

Before the Internet can be successfully integrated into the curriculum, teachers need to become fully literate in these new technologies. In a world full of computers, television, movies, and visual advertising, schools prima-rily teach reading and writing. Most teachers do not know how to produce a web page, television show, radio program, advertisement, or motion pic-ture. Despite the fact that we live in world full of multimedia symbols, as Kubey (1998) notes, teachers do not receive formal training in media litera-cy and must often arrange for and pay to attend media literacy workshops by themselves. As a result, the creation of multimedia teaching materials is dominated by people who work for media corporations. It is a skill that people learn primarily on the job or by attending specialized industry training programs. Therefore, most teachers are not in control of their classrooms' multimedia content, computer companies are.

Prior to the widespread introduction of personal computers in classrooms, the school was not considered to be a commercial marketplace. But now, media corporations and software companies are viewing education as another opportunity for them to sell multimedia content products. For example, after attending the recent *Digital Diploma Mills Conference*, Langdon Winner (1998) observed that corporate penetration into higher education is greater than he expected. He states: "Among the most powerful forces are those in the corporate sector that see education as a huge, largely untapped market for the new goods and services. . . . New firms, the University of Phoenix and the Home Education Network, for example, have already taken a substantial bite of the growing market for distance learning and look forward to huge profits in the future" (no page). As people become pressured to learn new skills required for working in a digital information society, opportunities for commercialized education expand.

While media literacy critics argue about the purpose of media education, media corporations have already jumped on the digital technology bandwagon and are offering courses and programs to train people to work in an information society. Winner (1998) fears that this trend will create an education split between people who receive quality, face-to-face education from a traditional university and those who are educated through a hybrid organization that is part business and part university. Obviously this type of two-tiered educational system also creates a social split—one that could turn the majority of the population into consumers rather than producers of information.

MASS MEDIA MESSAGES ARE CONTROLLED BY CORPORATIONS

Mass media separates society into owners and consumers of information. Phillips (1994) states: "Our society presently maintains two intellectual oligarchies: those who own information and those who can process it. Consumers of information are useful for they often produce income for the providers. They are, however, dependent on those who own, produce and process it" (p. 56). Following the commercial pattern of mass media, software companies are trying to turn students into information consumers by marketing educational products to schools.

Educational software products package information or knowledge into multimedia presentations. It is argued that multimedia presents information in a more exciting format that enables students to interact with the materials at their own pace. However, prewritten software packages have been criticized for forcing students to respond to a series of canned prompts. Students internalize these prompts and program themselves to answer the questions rather than effectively learning the material being presented (Tuman, 1992). In an information age, people need to learn how to make meaning, rather than consume information. As knowledge is packaged as a commodity, Lyotard (1979) asserts:

> The relationship of the suppliers and users of knowledge to the knowledge they supply and use is now tending, and will increasingly tend, to assume the form already taken by the relationship of commodity producers and consumers to the commodities they produce and consume— that is, the form of value. Knowledge is and will be produced in order to be sold, it is and will be consumed in order to be valorized in a new production: in both cases, the goal is exchange. Knowledge ceases to be an end in itself, it loses its "use-value." (pp. 4-5)

A concern about introducing computers in the schools is that the needs of business and industry will start to dominate the curriculum. Selling knowledge products will overshadow the educational process of teaching and learning. For example, the use of preprogrammed software packages shifts control of information from the teacher to the software company. Moreover, hypertext databases accessed through CD-ROM or the Internet are information products. Tuman (1992) states: "In the midst of all the enthusiasm about hypertext it is too easy to overlook the fact that it is fundamentally a system for retrieving digitized information . . . that has vast economic potential for anyone who has the resources to collect such information and the legal right to distribute it" (pp. 78-79). Hypertext enables companies who own the rights to atlases, encyclopedias, dictionaries, handbooks, and so on, to sell this information to people as they need it. As the Internet becomes more commercial, individuals and schools should expect to pay access fees and charges for downloading information.

Currently, there is a push in the United States to wire all of our classrooms with Internet access. But the technology, rather than the content, is the focus of this movement. A question that needs to be asked is: Who will control the information? Today, global mass media messages are increasingly dominated by fewer and fewer media conglomerates. For this reason, technology writers, such has Philip Elmer-DeWitt (1995) have described the Internet as an antidote to mass media because individuals have access to this technology for creating and distributing messages. Presently, content on the

Internet is *not totally* controlled by media corporations. Both individual and corporate points of view are expressed online. One reason why average people can participate in Internet discourse is because the messages are distributed in a written form. However, the print-oriented Internet is quickly turning into the television-like World Wide Web. The Web incorporates sound, video, animation, graphics, and advertising into messages displayed on a computer screen.

Although some schools are beginning to teach web page design, these skills are not easy to learn. For example, to create a web page, in addition to traditional literacy, a person needs to know some HTML programming and how to use at least three software programs, including word processing, image processing, and a browser. Moreover, sophisticated Web sites require people to learn animation, audio, and object-oriented programming skills. Quickly, content development for the Web is becoming a specialized skill that is beyond the scope of today's basic educational system. Following the trend of older mass media, content on the Web is becoming an industry related skill that could also become controlled by media corporations.

Today, the symbolic form of Internet communication resembles older media—the printed word and television. But in contrast to the way people receive the content, the underlying symbol system of the computer is binary math. Underneath the symbolic facade of print or television, all information, including text, pictures, graphics, sound, and video, are converted into a digital symbol system that is understood by a computer. Therefore, the true symbolic form of Internet information is mathematical.

DIGITAL VERSUS OLDER MEDIA

Any examination of the structure of the Internet as a medium of communication requires exploration of the digital characteristics of this medium. Digital computers abstract all symbols into a binary, on/off, yes/no mathematical code. As Paul Levinson (1997) points out in his book *The Soft Edge*, this is the same type of code that was used by the original electric medium—the telegraph. But unlike the telegraph, in addition to codifying language into a binary form, the computer also abstracts all human symbol systems into a digital code that can then be distributed through a network. In the digital process, all information processed by computers must be reduced down into a binary code that is called machine language.

The languages that computers understand are different from human languages. Ong (1982) notes that they "do not grow out of the unconscious but directly out of consciousness. Computer language rules ('grammar') are stated first and thereafter used" (p. 7). Conversely, English evolved as people used it, "but its creation through centuries was not self-conscious and rational, as the creation of programming languages is" (Bolter, 1984, p. 125). The rules of grammar developed in natural languages are first used and then abstracted into stated words. In contrast, "computer languages are codes whose purpose is to represent the logical structure of problems to be solved" (p. 124). They are far removed from the ambiguous, emotional, and vocalized languages that people speak everyday.

Since the early development of computer languages, designers have been trying to make programming languages more natural and easy for people to use. Presently, computers utilize a hierarchy of languages. On the lowest level is machine language and it "is fundamentally the only command code that the computer understands, a code more of less built into its hardware. Consisting of 1s and 0s like everything else in the computer, machine language is extremely cumbersome" (Bolter, 1984, p. 128). To make the computer easier to program, engineers developed a more readable code, called assembly language, that incorporated fixed names, such as ADD, SUB, MUL for add, subtract, and multiply. Programmers would write in this assembly language and then they would use a translator to convert the code into machine language.

"The next step was to develop codes that removed the programmer further from his machine, allowing him to write in a more mathematical language" (Bolter, 1984, p. 128). These new languages were called *high-level languages* and they were translated into machine instructions by using a *compiler*. High-level languages include: FORTRAN and PASCAL. As high-level languages evolved, the BASIC language was developed at Dartmouth College for students to learn about computers. BASIC uses English-like keywords and syntax and it was later adopted by computer developers for use on personal computers. Users could write programs by typing the BASIC commands into the computer keyboard. This type of human–computer interaction is called a command-line interface. But, it still requires users to learn, remember, and type computer instructions.

To bring computers to average people, graphical interfaces were developed that add another level to the programming hierarchy. "User-friendly" graphical interfaces, such as Macintosh and Windows, were created to make operating a computer easier for everyone. Instead of memorizing and typing in computer commands, users could point and click on visual icons to execute commands. Levy (1994) contends: "Before 1984 the concept of ordinary human beings participating in digital worlds belonged to the arcane realm of data processing and science fiction. After Macintosh, these digital worlds began to weave themselves into the fabric of everyday life" (p. 8). In addition to making general computers easier to operate, graphic interfaces, such as Netscape and Microsoft's Internet Explorer, make it easier to access information from the Internet.

A difference between graphical interfaces and older text-oriented command-line interfaces is that graphical systems can easily display both text
and graphics. The digital codification of information in graphical systems
alters the relationship between words and images. In contrast to printed
texts that codify information as fixed sequences of discrete letters represented by symbols and sounds, graphical computers reduce all information into
the mathematical binary system of 1s or 0s. Text, pictures, photographs, and
graphics can all be stored as binary information. As a result, the digital codification of information alters the relationship between written words and
images. According to Lanham (1993): "Digitized communication is forcing
a radical realignment of the alphabetic and graphic components of ordinary
textual communication" (p. 3). The graphical user interface's ability to display graphics as easily as words on computer screens is an additional factor
in the icon/alphabet ratio change.

Today, the increased use of icons in texts adds visual thinking to the
reading process and challenges the stability of language as the major medium of written communication. Rudolf Arnheim (1969), a pioneer in visual
thinking research, states: "in order to evaluate the important role of language
more adequately it seems to me necessary to recognize that it serves as a
mere auxiliary to the primary vehicles of thought, which are so immensely
better equipped to represent relevant objects and relations by articulate
shape. The function of language is essentially conservative and stabilizing"
(pp. 243-244). Lanham (1993) suggests that this stabilizing function is
undermined by the way language and icons are mixed in digital communication: "The digitalization now common to letters and shapes creates a mixed
text of icons and words in which 'static and immobile' and dynamically
mobil cognitive style toggle back and forth into a new bi-stable expressivi-
ty" (p. 77). Suzanne Langer (1957) describes the differences between visual
and verbal thinking as follows:

> Visual forms—lines, colors, proportions, etc.—are just as capable of
> articulation, of complex combination, as words. But the laws that gov-
> ern this sort of articulation are altogether different from the laws of syn-
> tax that govern language. The most radical difference is that visual forms
> are not discursive. They do not present their constituents successively,
> but simultaneously. (p. 93)

The change in the icon/alphabet ratio observed by Lanham, is a characteristic of electronic text that is created by the merging of icon and word in
graphical interface technology. He states "the Apple world, born in personal computers not mainframes, has from the beginning been dominated by
the play impulse. It colored motive, style, mood, personality type. Apple's
graphics-based computers were built on, assumed, a transformed

alphabet/icon ratio" (Lanham, 1993, p. 47). Obviously, this type of symbolic transformation will begin to influence traditional literacy skills. Moreover, a change from using printed textbooks to electronic computer screens as an educational medium will ultimately influence our perceptual understanding of the world. In the future, the shift from printed to digital media could have as profound an effect on culture as the shift from orality to literacy did.

As human–computer interaction evolves, new types of interfaces are being developed, including virtual reality, sophisticated Web browsers, and voice recognition software. Both virtual reality and Web browsers rely on visual rather than textual commands. Moreover, sound is an important element in all of these interface technologies. For many years, developers have been working on creating systems that replace visual computer commands with spoken commands. Currently, speech recognition software runs on devices called digital signal processors (DSPs). According to Penzias (1995): "The rapid progress in DSP technology, and in the algorithms that direct this handy hardware, have combined to make 'computers you can talk to' an emerging reality" (p. 106). For example, speech-processing programs exist that will translate a real-time conversation between two people speaking different languages. Moreover, programs have existed for several years that enable computer users to verbally execute computer commands rather than use a keyboard or mouse.

Visual interfaces and voice recognition tools will make it easier for people who are alphabet illiterate to operate computers. For example, fast-food chains such as McDonalds already place pictures on their cash registers instead of numbers. Workers do not need to know the price of a hamburger, they just press the pictures and give the customer the change displayed on the screen. Computer devices that enable people to do jobs without understanding how or why erode traditional literacy skills. According to Phillips (1994), a new type of techno-orality is emerging that enables people to compute without knowing about computing. However, he argues that "as techno-orality forces a decay of literacy, it sews the seeds of its own destruction" (p. 64).

Computer technology rests on a literate foundation. Phillips' position follows Ong's argument that secondary orality is built on a foundation of the printed word. Computer technology, like television, radio, and the telephone, is dependent on the written word for the manufacture and development of hardware and software. Replacing traditional textbooks with computers could undermine the traditional literacy process because average students will not want to learn how to read and write when they can point, click, and speak commands into the computer to access television-like multimedia documents. Instead of bringing literacy to all people, user-friendly interface designs could further divide society into illiterates, partial literates, and techno-literates. Eventually, the techno-literates could become a small group of people who will work for computer companies that write the software and design the interfaces for the masses.

OBSERVATIONS ABOUT DIGITAL MEDIA

As Steve Talbott (1995) points out, digital computers add another level of abstraction to the symbolic process. Writing is an abstraction of speech and on the computer writing is further abstracted into math. In contrast to arguments that computer generated virtual realities will enable people to interact in more "natural" ways, he believes computer-generated worlds are abstract mathematical worlds that further remove us from real people, events, and objects. In fact they add another symbolic layer to the process of symbolization.

Currently, educational computer proponents Papert (1993) and Negroponte (1995) argue that learning by interacting with computer simulated models is superior to learning by reading a book. This argument is reminiscent of Dewey's (1916) argument that learning through experience is the best method of education. Applying this to the computer, Papert (1993) argues that the computer supports experiential learning and problem solving. As a result, computers enhance the learning process and should replace books in education. However, Papert does not seem to realize that like books computer programs are also abstract representations of objects and events. Children who experience the world through computer-generated constructions are actually learning in an *abstract not a concrete* environment (see Talbott, 1995).

Papert's argument is another example of how people focus on the message rather than the medium. Although computers may be a more physically interactive medium than a book, they add another level of abstraction to the learning process because students are working with simulated objects rather than real ones. While we gain interactivity, we simultaneously lose touch with the real world. Although simulation can aid in the understanding of complex scientific concepts, it can not replace experiences with nature and actual objects. Moreover, simulated microworlds are mathematical models designed to represent an event, therefore, they might not always be an accurate representation.

Finally, digital symbol systems cannot be understood by human beings. In contrast to the telegraph's Morse code, which people can learn to read and write, computer code remains in the domain of the machine. Although there are layers of software languages above the machine code that people can read and write, the actual binary symbols are for the most part beyond human comprehension. Depending on an individual's computer literacy skills, people interact with computer generated symbolic interfaces which include various programming languages, command-line text-oriented interfaces, graphical interfaces that combine icons and words, voice recognition, and virtual environments that do not require written language at all. When people program the computer, translation software is used to convert the programmer's language into machine code. As a result, digital media are dependent on machines to symbolically write the digital content.

Looking at electric media in terms of being able to read and write, we can see a trend emerging. Print-based media require people to know how to both read and write to be considered literate and our educational system attempts to provide equal access to traditional literacy skills to all citizens. In contrast, access to television does not require literacy training to understand basic messages. To go beyond basic messages, media literacy programs are designed to help people to learn how to become critical viewers. But, most people will never have an opportunity to "write" television because these messages are controlled by people working in media organizations. In general,"television literacy" eliminates the process of writing.

Similarly, "digital literacy" eliminates the need to write programs to interact with computers. But there is a difference between mass media and the computer. People working in media corporations arrange the symbolic forms of television programs. In contrast, machines control the symbolic form of computers. Although we can argue that people control the machines, people are not directly manipulating the underlying digital mathematical symbols that run the computer. Herein lies the central difference between computers and all previous forms of communication technologies. People are abstracted out of the symbol making process because there is a step in the digital process that remains strictly in the domain of the machine.

Humans do not have access to all of the symbolic manipulations taking place in a digital computer. What then is the message of digital media? When humans turn over symbol making to their machines, what does that say about human relationships to technology? Are our machines now superior to people? Are we equal? Moreover, what does this tell us about our relationships to symbols? Are we moving further away from direct physical interaction with people and objects?

Today, we need to put the information aside and pay closer attention to the structure of digital media. Although digital media unify symbolic code and the global distribution of messages, they remove people from the underlying symbolic process. To compensate for this feature, layers and layers of software programs are put on top of the digital symbol system. Software is available for people with a wide range of literacy skills, but controlling the machine requires sophisticated digital literacy skills. Although schools attempt to provide equal access to print-based literacy, providing equal access to digital literacy is impossible. As a result digital media tend to separate us into social classes like the ones described by Arthur Kroker (1993), which include the dispossessed, working class, technocrats, and command-ers. On one extreme, the dispossessed, like the homeless, will be outside the system. On the other, the commanders who are presidents of technology corporations will control the system.

Although the symbol system of digital media unifies the codification of human messages and makes it easier to distribute them on a global level, it simultaneously separates humans from the symbol making process. As a result, people become machine dependent. A social stratification begins to emerge when we examine who has access through digital skills to control the machines. Moreover, if we turn control of our symbolic processes over to machines and a priesthood of "digital commanders," we could turn into a techno-oral culture where people do not need to learn print-based literacy skills. Instead of interacting with electronic words people will be able to interact with verbal voice commands and in three dimensional virtual reali-ty. Utilizing these types of oral and visual interfaces could make written lan-guage irrelevant.

A consequence of a shift from language to math as a primary form of cultural symbolization could eliminate the need for written language in daily life. A new type of techno-orality could emerge where machines translate speech into digital codes to facilitate both human to human and human–machine communication. The skills of both traditional and digital reading and writing could remain only within a new corporate "priesthood" that is controlled by a small group of commercial interests.

CONCLUSION

Our failure now to examine the possible consequences of a shift from writ-ten to digital media in both eduction and society at large could have serious social consequences. Techno-orality could foster a social structure that iso-lates the highly literate from the illiterate. Moreover, bridging the gap between the techno-literate and illiterate will be far more complicated than learning how to read and write an alphabet-oriented language. Phillips (1994) sums up my primary argument as to why the Internet and digital technologies are more likely to separate us rather than bring us together.

> It is important to maintain technical skill to develop new systems and adapt to new problems, but in each generation, the complexity of design and engineering reduces the number of people able to manage the tech-nology. The result has been a corporate oligarchy, with a few manufac-turers maintaining a global dominance. (p. 70)

REFERENCES

Arnheim, R. (1969). *Visual thinking*. Berkeley: University of California Press.

Bolter, J.D. (1984). *Turning's man: Western culture in the computer age*. Chapel Hill: The University of North Carolina Press.

Christ, W.G., & Potter, W.J. (1998). Media literacy, media education, and the academy. *Journal of Communication, 48*(1), 5-15.

Clinton, W., & Gore, A. (1993). *Technology for America's economic growth: A new direction to build economic strength*. (Electronically distributed, Archive CNI-BIGIDEAS: file whouse.paper at listserv@cni.org)

Dewey, J. (1916). *Democracy and education*. New York: Macmillan.

Elmer-Dewitt, P. (1995, Spring). Welcome to cyberspace. *Time*, special issue, pp. 4-10.

Gergen, K.J. (1991). *The saturated self: Dilemmas of identity in contemporary life*. New York: Basic Books.

Goodman, D. (1994). *Living at light speed*. New York: Random House.

Harrison, T. (1997, June). A chicken in every pot, a net link in every classroom. *Computers & Society, 27*(2), 32-34.

Havelock, E. A. (1963). *Preface to Plato*. Cambridge, MA: Harvard University Press.

Healy, J.M. (1990). *Endangered minds: Why children don't think and what we can do about it*. New York: Simon & Schuster.

Kelly, K. (1996, October). What would McLuhan say? *Wired, 4*(10), 148-149.

Kroker, A. (1997). Digital humanism: The processed world of Marshall McLuhan. In A. Kroker & M. Kroker (Eds.), *Digital delirium* (pp. 89-113). New York: St. Martin's Press.

Kroker, A. (1993). Codes of privilege. *Mondo 2000, 11*, 60-67.

Kubey, R. (1998). Obstacles to the development of media education in the U.S. *Journal of Communication, 48*(1), 58-69.

Langer, S. K. (1957). *Philosophy in a new key: A study in the symbolism of reason, rite, and art*. Cambridge, MA: Harvard University Press.

Lanham, R.A. (1993). *The electronic word: Democracy, technology, and the arts*. Chicago: The University of Chicago Press.

Lee, J.Y. (1996). Charting the codes of cyberspace: A rhetoric of electronic mail. In L. Strate, R. Jacobson, & S.B. Gibson (Eds.), *Communication and cyberspace* (pp. 275-296). Cresskill, NJ: Hampton Press.

Levinson, P. (1997). *The soft edge: A natural history and future of the information revolution*. New York: Routledge.

Levy, S. (1994). *Insanely great: The life and times of Macintosh, the computer that changed everything*. New York: Viking.

Lyotard, J. (1979). *The postmodern condition: A report on knowledge*. Minneapolis: University of Minnesota Press.

Mandel, T., & Van der Leun, G. (1996). *Rules of the net*. New York: Hyperion.

McLuhan, E., & Zingrone, F. (1995). *Essential McLuhan*. New York: Basic Books.

McLuhan, M. (1962). *The Gutenberg galaxy*. Toronto: University of Toronto Press.

McLuhan, M. (1964). *Understanding media: The extensions of man*. New York: Signet Books.

McLuhan, M., & Fiore, Q. (1967). *The medium is the massage.* New York: Simon & Schuster.

McLuhan, M., Hutchon, K., & McLuhan, E. (1980). *Media, messages, and language: The world as your classroom.* Skokie, IL: National Textbook.

McLuhan, M., & Powers, B.R. (1989). *The global village.* New York: Oxford University Press.

Negroponte, N. (1995). *Being digital.* New York: Alfred A. Knopf.

Ong, W.J. (1977). *Interfaces of the word: Studies in the evolution of consciousness and culture.* Ithaca, NY: Cornell University Press.

Ong, W.J. (1982). *Orality and literacy: The technologizing of the word.* New York: Methuen.

Papert, S. (1993). *The children of the machine.* New York: Basic Books.

Penzias, A. (1995). *Digital harmony: Business, technology & life after paperwork.* New York: HarperBusiness.

Phillips, G.M. (1994, April) A nightmare scenario: Technology & literacy. *Interpersonal Computing and Technology: An Electronic Journal for the 21st Century,* 2(2), 51-73. [Available at http://www.helsinki.fi./science/optek/]

Phillips, G.M. (1995, March 15). Cliches. Electronic message to Interpersonal Computing and Technology Discussion List. IPCT-L@GUVM.GEORGE-TOWN.EDU.

Poster, M. (1990). *The mode of information.* Chicago: University of Chicago Press.

Postman, N. (1979). *Teaching as a conserving activity.* New York: Dell

Postman, N. (1985). *Amusing ourselves to death.* New York: Penguin Books.

Talbott, S. (1995). *The future does not compute.* Sebastopol, CA: O'Reilly & Associates.

Tuman, M. C. (1992). *Word perfect: Literacy in the computer age.* Pittsburgh: University of Pittsburgh Press.

Winner, L. (1998). Tech knowledge review: Report from the Digital Diploma Mills Conference. NETFUTURE, Issue #72. [Available at: http://www.oreilly.com/~stevet/netfuture/]

THE HYPERTEXT HEURISTIC

McLUHAN PROBES TESTED
(A CASE FOR EDIBLE SPACESHIPS)

Michel A. Moos

EDIBLE PAPER

In the spring of 1967, at the height of McLuhan mania, with McLuhan's face on the cover, *Newsweek* had this to report about the experience of actually reading him: "At Columbia, a coed likens reading McLuhan to taking LSD. 'It can turn you on,' she says. 'LSD doesn't mean anything until you consume it—likewise McLuhan'" (McLuhan, 1967, p. 53). As the fastest-selling nonfiction paperback on university campuses, *Understanding Media* (McLuhan, 1994) was indeed being consumed in large quantities. Here was reading not as some inert, passive exercise in spectation but as an interactive experience that you underwent—that in fact consumed *you*. What was this if not hypertext in action, capsules of insight packet-switched by you, assembling into koans of awareness and revelation. What better interface for hypertext than this, a delivery system that meshes with "some intricate web of trails carried by the cells of the brain" (Bush, 1945, p. 106). Was this not text fully activated, equipped with all the capabilities the superlative *hyper* confers, an ultimate bio-plug-in, turning the participant-reader on through language to a greater awareness of the media forms that surround him? Was this not language deployed as micro-machine, as nanomotor, as one of the new smart drugs or "final prostheses" (Virilio, 1993, p. 123) that operate remotely within the human organism? Was this not semiosis operating at last as a science?

However much potency psychotropics are estimated to contain within "the entire poststructuralist pharmacopeia" (Moulthrop, 1994, p. 301), perspectives such as these may be helpful in assessing McLuhan's contribution to media studies as well as to the futures of critical theory and artificial intelligence alike. To this end I have been looking at the relationship of McLuhan's writing to the emergent electronic form of writing known as *hypertext*. I am concerned here with one technical problem, that of the source code of McLuhan's message—the actual writing—and how the anachronicities and culture lags between media allow a relatively timeworn, obsolescent medium like the book to produce effects a cutting-edge medium like the computer can only hint at. The ideas behind hypertext are interesting because from its inception hypertext represents an attempt to free thought from the strictures of printed communication without abandoning a written record of the line of thought itself. In an age of electronically mediated attention structures, it also opens directly onto the question of how you edit your consciousness.

NEURONICS

The dream of key words and patterns functioning as quasi-magical entrances to a networked reality is nothing new; what is new is the use of electricity to transform the archive of knowledge into a transparent labyrinth. Whereas the recent application of electricity to a textual problem is what properly denotes hypertext, the issues with which hypertext grapples are part of a fundamental navigational puzzle intrinsic to language itself. Questions of associative linking relate ultimately to the ways in which the brain sends, receives and processes verbal messages. In this respect, the literary critical and theoretical groundwork for hypertext can be traced to Russian Formalism and Jakobson and Halle's (1971) theory of language that formulated a basic principle of structural linguistics, namely that language, like other sign systems, has a binary character. Building on aspects of de Saussure's (1986) distinction between the "syntagmatic" and "associative" plane of language, and supported by early evidence from the clinical study of aphasia, Jakobson describes language function in terms of two operations:

selection and combination. The dichotomy is elaborated by Jakobson along two semantic lines that he terms *metaphor* and *metonymy*; it can also be seen to correspond to binary oppositions such as langue–parole, paradigm (or system)–syntagm, code–message in structural linguistics and semiotics, and condensation–displacement in psychoanalysis. Although it is not my intent to take a semiotic approach to hypertext, it is worth noting the extent to which these attempts at formal discourse analysis anticipate the cybernetic prospects of artificial intelligence research. To view all cultural phenomena as sign systems and culture in toto as "a comprehensive semiotic modeling system" (Lucid, 1977, p. 5) is already an approach much in line with projects investigating "possible automation of the basic processes of human knowledge" (Ivanov, 1977, p. 35).

For our purposes, the example of semiotics is useful in alerting us to a procedural redundancy, namely that language is already a hypertext. Language or, as McLuhan (1994) calls it, "this technical extension of consciousness that is speech" (p. 79), is already a montage of consciousness in that it presents elements of reality in selective combination. To reduce language function to coordinates such as selection and combination is to highlight this basic real-time mapping problem of language consciousness. It is a means of bringing language's basic figure ground relationship into relief, this sense of the infinite background of (linguistic) possibility out of which the momentary expression gets crafted. Where we may not be very aware of performing these operations in the act of speaking, it is an experience which in many ways defines the act of writing. Walter Benjamin (1969) touches on this point when he cites interruption as "one of the fundamental devices of all structuring," noting that it is "the basis of quotation. To quote a text involves the interruption of its context" (p. 151). This begs the question: If the text being quoted has had its context interrupted, then can text into which the quotations are inserted be viewed finally as a mosaic of infinite con-texts delimited solely by the timeline of the medium itself, whether speech, writing, or further contexts generated in the acts of reading and listening? Hypertext aims to make this view of textuality explicit.

One can see from this, first, the extent to which hypertext is a writer's problem and, second, the degree to which the hypertextual rub lies squarely between speaking and writing: hypertext being essentially an attempt to wed the speed of association afforded through thinking in speech with the resources of memory provided by a culture of writing. But if speed and memory (i.e., association and retrieval) are central to the motivation and design of hypertext, there is also a lengthy tradition that teaches the study of language itself as a means of increasing these parameters. Whereas the term hypertext refers to computer software, early hypertext software was not electronic but neuronic, relying on the arts of language to program the mind of man for eloquence and wisdom, and was known broadly as rhetoric.

GRAMMAR NOT/AND DIALECTICS

In his doctoral dissertation, *Thomas Nashe and the Learning of His Time*, in order to account for Nashe's variegated style and to situate him in relation to his 16th-century contemporaries, McLuhan found it necessary to embark on a full-scale study of medieval and ancient rhetoric (Gordon, 1997). This survey of the entire rhetorical canon from Cicero to Nashe, which became by extension an investigation of the shifting modes of education through the centuries, came to be the central subject of the thesis. McLuhan discovered that while education had for all this time continued to be based on the elementary division of the seven liberal arts known as the trivium, an internecine struggle had been raging from the outset, a pitched battle for no less than authoritative control over the spoken and written word. Whatever unifying dynamic may originally have held grammar, rhetoric, and dialectic (also called logic) harmoniously together as an analogical mirror of the Logos, soon yielded to feuding and rivalry amongst the practitioners, so that grammarians and dialecticians have since squared off into the warring camps of two radically opposed intellectual traditions. The motives of the partisans are complex, yet the trend that emerges is a gradual suppression of grammar and rhetoric by dialectics. McLuhan relates "the techniques by which grammatica was eliminated from humanistic studies" in a 1978 memo: "The strategy of eliminating the study of language is via abstraction. What is eliminated is the ground of corporate utterance by concentrating on the figures of speech and thought. This amounts to transforming percepts into concepts and reducing literary experience to logical schema" (Kuhns, 1997). Dialectics fosters abstract compartmentalizations leading in time to a Cartesian worldview, to the segregation of the disciplines, to an insistence on categorical explicitness, and to the empirical hairsplitting of transcendental metaphysics. The pervasiveness of structuralism within the university today represents a renewed and far-reaching assertion of dialectics over the humanities; it in part explains phenomena such as the active suppression of McLuhan within the ivory tower over the last 30 years (Marchand, 1998). Insofar as computers are sophisticated truth-function evaluators, dialectics necessarily underpins literary models of hypertext currently in development.

If McLuhan indeed deploys an alternative model for hypertext, he does so partly as a proponent of grammatica; in chronicling the prevailing forces that shape the history of the trivium, it is against the ascendant hegemony of dialectics that he traces an unbroken, if increasingly marginalized, tradition of grammarians leading eventually to Nashe. As the art of exposition and interpretation of phenomena, grammar has also a claim to be viewed as an important basis of scientific method but is marked by a refusal to segmentalize knowledge or restrict domains of enquiry, a predilection for the reasoning of proportion and analogy, and valuation of the concrete, or rhetorical, models of language.

HYPERTEXT PERFORMED: THE MODEL OF ORATORY

The position of the grammarians and rhetoricians is distinguished at heart by adherence to a tradition of Ciceronian humanism that preserves ancient rhetoric's unity of eloquence and wisdom. The clash of grammar and dialectics at once involves both the ends to which knowledge should be put as well as the methods in which it is acquired. The crux of the hypertext problem arises when strategies for organizing knowledge begin to suggest their own pragmatics:

> The Sophists . . . gave oratorical displays on all the themes of art, science, and philosophy. To manipulate this encyclopedic knowledge it became necessary to organize it around basic "commonplaces" or loci of argument; and in order to retain this knowledge "Hippias' system of mnemonics was of great importance." Naturally, the Sophists made logic subordinate to rhetoric or persuasion, since their end was political. And this it was which raised against them the opposition of Socrates, Plato, and Aristotle, who were all agreed that dialectics should control rhetoric, that knowledge was superior even to prudential action. (McLuhan, 1969, p. 226)

With the Socratic turn from forensics to speculation and definition, hypertext is already on the scene. The trivial arts are technical responses to an information storage problem. Just as hypertext today represents a technological manipulation of the archive, rhetoric is a techne treating the possibilities of discourse as applied knowledge. McLuhan (1997) ingeniously calls the figures of rhetoric "postures of mind" and notes that "writing made it possible to card-catalogue" them (p. 9). Yet mnemonics is present already in oral culture as a sort of "writing," in the techniques of spatialization (locus, topos) behind verbal formulaics, in the making of "places" in which tropes and arguments are stored for use (Ong, 1967, pp. 84-5). The doctrine of the commonplaces strives to be panoptic, as Richard Lanham (1991) observes, tending from "smaller-scale figures like epitheton and proverb toward the larger-scale design of a full memory theater" (p. 170). Ironically, then, proto-hypertext is realized not in text at all, but in the heightened speech of oratory which stages a web of spoken meanings to be apprehended in real time against a backdrop of collective recall. Each of the commonplace figures or postures that writing eventually inventories ideally represents a link, node, or pathway in the living library of a cultural habitus. Portrayed by the orator, these "stances" dramatize an ethical and moral consensus, paths urging the right course of action.

SPEED AND MEMORY: HYPERLANGUAGE

If an alternative route to hypertext lies in grammatical art, the 16th-century philosopher, Francis Bacon was a notable exponent. As one 19th-century commentator remarks ("Lord Bacon," 1838), in terms mindful of the ongoing dispute, "Though Bacon did not arm his philosophy with the weapons of logic, he adorned her profusely with all the richest decorations of rhetoric." He quotes Bacon taking "all knowledge to be my province," and adds, "The knowledge in which Bacon excelled all men, was a knowledge of the mutual relations of all departments of knowledge." Central to the practice of grammatical art is another weapon, not logic, but wit: "In wit, if by wit be meant the power of perceiving analogies between things which appear to have nothing in common, he never had an equal." Notably, the effect of Bacon's style is felt as a sort of compression: "He had a wonderful talent for packing thought close and rendering it portable" (p. 193). This portability of thought is not the overt handiness of the book as object but an internal mobility of language through which thought itself advances. Bacon figures prominently in McLuhan's thesis, who considers this mode of delivering knowledge "part of a scientific technique of keeping knowledge in a state of emergent evolution" (Gordon, 1997, p. 105). McLuhan (1951) develops the implications of the aphoristic style as it resurfaces in the work of Harold Innis:

> How exciting it was to encounter a writer whose every phrase invited prolonged meditation and exploration. Innis takes much time to read if he is read on his own terms. That he deserves to be read on his own terms becomes obvious as soon as that experiment is tried even once. So read, he takes time but he also saves time. Each sentence is a compressed monograph. He includes a small library on each page, and often incorporates a small library of references on the same page in addition. If the business of the teacher is to save the student's time, Innis is one of the greatest teachers on record. (p. ix)

McLuhan's defense of Innis' methodology is remarkable for being essentially a description of a page of hypertext. The praxis stands as implicit critique of currently evolved hypertext models simply because it supplies levels of compression which are actual and not virtual. Whereas with standard hypertext, each reference or link only exists for the reader if he activates it, the Innis or McLuhan page incorporates an active reference library on the page itself. Here is hypertext not as a database you access in your computer but as a mode of thinking that reaches back into your own "headset" and accesses you. The page has screenal interactivity built into its surface insofar as it draws on the reservoir of language's verbal functionality. The current paradigm is inverted since, rather than seek to automate the inert record, here the project is to tap into the reader, to access and activate his "inner storehouse," the vast evocative spaces of language as collective phenomenon or corporate ground, what de Saussure (1986) posits as "the form of a totality of imprints in everyone's brain" (p. 19). The effect is to enable those very functions computer hypertext regards as constitutive yet still strives to define, namely, integration of the reader into the writing process and real-time access to the archive. Indeed, as temporal dilation and compression across the interface shows ("he takes time but he also saves time"), the two features are analogues of each other. Thus, Innis "expects the reader to make discovery after discovery that he himself had missed" (McLuhan, 1951, p. vii).

In its lineaments, the technique can be likened to putting speech back into writing. McLuhan (1951) describes it as the presentation of "insights in a mosaic structure of seemingly unrelated and disproportioned sentences and aphorisms," as a "paratactic procedure of juxtaposing without connectives," and "the generating of insights by the method of 'interface,'" noting that "it is the natural form of conversation or dialogue rather than of written discourse" (pp. vii-viii). In its rehabilitation of the literary form it is aligned with the poetry of the Symbolists and the early-century art forms cubism and surrealism, and related to such experiments as automatic writing, William Burroughs' literary application of collage in his use of cut-ups, Kerouac's spontaneous prose, or the fractal grammatology of Joyce's *Finnegans Wake*. Yet we do not think of these forms as hypermedial. What makes the multiphasic writing McLuhan practices hypermedial per se is fractural stress on the arrangement of verbal information such as exceeds the density of spoken exchange, in other words, a design that specifically addresses problems of compression and selection as they confront the scholar and researcher. Deliberately assembled with degrees of interpenetration and multilevel montage to surpass the monology of print, McLuhan's probe prose is a studied response to the challenge of analyzing electronic environments as well as to the archival quandary of bibliocentric information. If the litany of objections to McLuhan's approach belies its academic viability, as research method it would appear to be backed by neurology:

> The brain depends upon elegance to compensate for its own small size and short lifetime. As the cerebral cortex grew from apish dimensions

through hundreds of thousands of years of evolution, it was forced to
rely on tricks to enlarge memory and speed computation. The mind
therefore specializes on analogy and metaphor, on a sweeping together
of chaotic sensory experience into workable categories labeled by words
and stacked into hierarchies for quick recovery. (Wilson, 1984, p. 60)

Analogy and metaphor are a mandate for grammatical art. The unity of
eloquence and wisdom, of knowledge compressed in verbal meaning,
describes a mental circuit hyperadapted to overcoming the brain's own processing limitations, a shorthand means of capturing information in residual
patterns. Rather than attempt to make writing function hypertextually, here
text is used to stage language as a hypersite for the deployment of insight, its
own noetic "writing" synthesizing a concentrated imaginative awareness of
experience. The value of hyperlanguage as alternative hypertext emerges
more clearly when contrasted with the more familiar electronic versions of
textual automation.

THE MICRODOT LIBRARY: SUBLINGUAL OPERATORS

The precursive vision of electronic hypertext was put forward by the engineer, Vannevar Bush in his 1945 article, "As We May Think." There he
describes an imaginary, automated system to link together all of humanity's
knowledge and introduces a machine that would supposedly enable such a
feat, which he calls the "memex" (viz., memory extender), a sort of microfilm editing desk with fantastical powers. Bush writes in response to what is
already at the time a daunting proliferation of information and our dwin-
dling capacity to handle it. He cites "a growing mountain of research"
spawned by the spread of specialization, and the fact that "publication has
been extended far beyond our present ability to make real use of the record."
In the face of information overload, the machine Bush imagines would
house an increasingly large chunk of "the inherited knowledge of the ages."
He estimates that using the power of microfilm, "A library of a million volumes could be compressed into one end of a desk" (pp. 101-103). Yet compression is only one part of the problem. If photocells and thermionic tubes
promise to put the record at hand, there is the more important question how
to consult it effectively—"the task of establishing useful trails through the
enormous mass of the common record" (p. 108). Bush's solution, which he
considers the essential feature of memex, is "a provision whereby any item
may be caused at will to select immediately and automatically another" (p.
107). Working with a maze of available materials that can be moved through
rapidly in many alternative sequences and repeatedly excerpted and spliced,

what emerges is recombinant text, a new trail or series of text passages held together by its pertinence to the interests of the memex user. In the final section of the article, Bush envisions the revolution memex might visit on data production, storage and retrieval:

> Wholly new forms of encyclopedias will appear, ready-made with a mesh of associative trails runnning through them, ready to be dropped into the memex and there amplified. The lawyer has at his touch the associated opinions and decisions of his whole experience, and of the experience of friends and authorities. The physician, puzzled by a patient's reactions, strikes the trail established in studying an earlier similar case, and runs rapidly through analogous case histories, with side references to the classics for the pertinent anatomy and histology. (p. 108)

Do these new "encyclopedias" herald the esemplastic hypertext theorized by postmodernism or is this just a virtual recreation of the archive, its multiplication according to its image, the production of instant copies? Does the memex author function as Foucault's (1979) "principle of thrift in the proliferation of meaning" (p. 159) or as its opposite? Can the resultant document be compared to Barthes' (1988) "tissue of quotations drawn from the innumerable centres of culture" (p. 146)? Does not the mass of data at the user's disposal restore the onus of iterative searching and is not memex in fact a souped-up filing cabinet? Certainly as a reference tool electronic rearrangement of the archive is invaluable and in this respect of database consolidation Bush's vision has been faithfully pursued, foremost in professions he examples; LEXIS and NEXIS brought the legal and medical professions online early on, and database management, or information technology as it is called, now engulfs the business sector where it has been used to transform accounting into marketing. But this is advanced library science, not interactive critical theory.

Hypertext systems have from the outset been conflated with information retrieval systems. Bush himself would later be puzzled by this (Nyce & Kahn, 1989). The latent, implicit idea behind memex as a machine intended for personal use is that of operationalizing language: to perform written composition "at a speed sufficient to create the sense of a mind actively engaged in learning and in self-expression" (McLuhan, 1997, p. 10)—the sense imparted while speaking or reading. But Bush never states this. He explicitly goes much further, wanting to marry machine logic to the preverbal impulses of thought. When Bush (1945) comes to "the heart of the matter of selection," contrasting "the artificiality of systems of indexing" with the way the mind "operates by association," language has already been dissolved on both sides of the memex user's transparent screen. It is against the "speed and flexibilty with which the mind follows an associative trail" that

Bush pits the capabilities of memex. We are well below the level of verbal sequences when the criterion to be emulated is "some intricate web of trails carried by the cells of the brain." Such a microtext is not text anymore at all but a series of engrams governed by sublingual operators, the discretization of language into its own neurophysiological processes, a readout to be deciphered only by other machines. Wittingly or no, this was of course de Saussure's diremptive coup, the reduction of language to values emanating from a nominally linguistic system—association in memory outside the context of discourse. Bush neglects to mention that "selection by association" may be mediated by an interior monologue, that memex, the "device for individual use," the "private file and library" could also already be language (pp. 106-107). In the imperceptible slide to information retrieval systems, it may be well to remember that "all discourses are information, but not all information is discourse" (Kittler, 1986, p. 157). The informatic "mesh of associative trails" no longer resembles nor refers to the network of discursive relations Bush sought only to interpenetrate. Mutual clarification is to be had by considering the ways in which these two competing bases for hypertext, the one reliant on chip architecture, the other on the amplitude of verbal combinatorics, have played out in the intervening decades.

WORLD WIDE WORD

Theodor Nelson (1981) coined the word *hypertext* some 20 years later, now that the integrated circuit had made processing power a reality. Nelson revived Bush's plans for associative indexing when he called for a computerized text system based on "nonsequential writing" that would allow students to explore academic material along a variety of paths. The term *hypertext* designates this "text that branches and allows choices to the reader, best read at an interactive screen" (p. ii). There is a parallel development in literary theory dating from the late 60s and early 70s, when the French poststructuralists began to theorize scenarios of textual interaction that look a lot like hypertext. Giving close reading a new name, Jacques Derrida deconstructs key literary and philosophical works into echoing traces of intertextual resonance. Deleuze and Guattari's (1987) rhizomic assemblage of smooth and striated spaces describes a literary machine whose sole purpose is to be plugged into other machines. And there is Roland Barthes' (1970) ideal text, an open-ended, infinitely branching network of signifiers that generate meaning via links between series of textual fragments he calls lexia (pp. 12, 20).

Lately, regarding these developments, two notable advances have occurred. The first is that a number of postmodern theorists, struck by the similarity of the French poststructuralist ideas to those of computer theoreticians such as Nelson and Andries van Dam, now maintain that hypertext represents the site of a convergence between contemporary critical theory and technology. Various claims of poststructuralist criticism can apparently find resolution via the implementation of an interactive, screen-based environment of textual exchange. George Landow (1992), for instance, believes that "critical theory promises to theorize hypertext and hypertext promises to embody and thereby test aspects of theory. . . . Using hypertext, critical theorists will have, or now already have, a new laboratory, in addition to the conventional library of printed texts, in which to test their ideas" (p. 3). The second advance, occurring at roughly the same time, is that a physicist named Tim Berners-Lee, while at the European Particle Physics Laboratory in Switzerland, sat down and in an astounding burst of creativity wrote the specifications for a global system which we all now know by the acronyms HTTP and HTML. Aptly enough, Berners-Lee called this code hypertext and indeed, with Mosaic's swift addition of pictures and sound, the World Wide Web appears to make real the dreams of hypertext visionaries such as Bush and Nelson.

Yet, if we look closely at these recent trends, an aporia arises in the space between postmodern critical theory's speculative hypertext and the Web's brushfire of real-time interconnectivity. On one hand, the idea that with hypertext one now has a means of testing postmodern theory remains precisely that—so much postmodern theory—until one actually has the specimen in question: either an adequate hypertext interface or at least a writing sample that embodies the requisite tropes of interactivity. It is the opposite of the position the software pirate often finds himself in: we have the manual but not the actual program it refers to. On the other hand, to the extent that the Web instantiates hypertext, it must be noted that this is a distributed hypertext. The original problems that Bush and Nelson address, those of compression and selection across a wide field of available data, have not been solved. The existence alone of the Web merely accounts for the fact that information has gone online and therefore been made more readily accessible. In order for it to go *hyper*, it would have to be able to coalesce into useful segues and overlays, much as music producers currently massage disparate sound samples into cogent tracks. For the solitary user, the Web exists as a relatively untapped pool of hyperpotential, awaiting the powerful thrust of browsers and the torqued search engines of an organizing intelligence. Thus, on one hand, we have critical theory's hypertextual desire for writing that transcends the monoplanar tedium of scholarly procedure and, on the other, the economically charged environment of the information superhighway, a vast docuverse of globally dispersed communication.

REVERSE ENGINEERING

What is perplexing in all of this digital revolutionizing is the overall drive to want to plug text directly into other media. Richard Lanham (1990), for instance, looks forward to the idea that "Word, image, and sound will be inextricably intertwined in a dynamic and continually shifting mixture" (p. 13). Whether it is the design of hypermedia by the literary advocates of electronic writing or by the software entrepreneurs of the Web, textual discourse is merging directly with the audiovisual resources of a hypergraphic environment. Yet as language leaves the page for the screen and is scattered into real time, the first thing to disappear is the specific density or "voice" of thought that exists only as the speaker-to-speaker or reader-to-writer frequency. If hypertext represents a technological response to the effects of the microchip on the verbal organization of knowledge, plugging text directly into other media simply obliterates the "train of thought" that text represents, the very scale and mode of thought processing we recognize as language, to say nothing of sites conducive to critical theory.

But what if, instead of trying to plug text into electronic media, one actually attempted to plug electronic media into text? By which I do not mean adding graphics, video and flash animation to web pages. But rather, what if it were possible to actually have all these other media present in the text itself, right there in the verbal strategies on the page? McLuhan, I think, literally does this.

He shows how to take the low-tech interface of the page and reverse engineer it so it can handle other inputs, so that you can, in effect, plug other media into it. The "heuristic probes" (McLuhan, 1997, p. 73) which make up his work are often hard to unpack because they are not metaphors but paradigm confrontations, precisely in Thomas Kuhn's (1970) sense of breaks in ways of thinking and ideas that do not map to one another. Because, as we all know, each medium creates its own paradigm or environment in the user, these probes are like the adapter cables necessary to "run" other media in a text-based operating system. They are the applications that allow cross-platform dialoguing in order for critical theory to be able to handle the programming languages of other media.

To view McLuhan's writing as hypertext is to see how textual discursivity can branch out and interconnect with other media and other forms of information while still being what it is: analytic thought recorded in writing for the reader to follow. McLuhan's (1997) hypermedialization of the book depends discursively on other media precisely because the literary form, short of becoming "some quaint codification of reality" (p. 12), must depend for its survival, or relevance, on developing interconnections with other media, on making contact with—in the sense of talking about—"the diverse and discontinuous life of forms" (p. 19) that are the media themselves. It is for these reasons that McLuhan's discursive style of "academic free association" (Forsdale, 1989, p. 170) perhaps best enacts the sort of hypertextual experience the literary poststructuralists are dreaming of. The form the argumentation takes, the bold connections and parallels drawn without preamble—what are ironically referred to as assertions—could well be the report of a trail blazed by this ideal hypertext user, able to interact with vast bodies of knowledge and experience. The sudden, unexpected leaps and bounds of his prose could be the links and paths an erudite hypertextualist might forge were he plumbing an electronic archive of western civilization for relevant inference.

Like electronic hypertext, McLuhan's hypertext is a reply to the marginalization of the book as an effective tool for critical inquiry. Yet where the progress of electronic hypertext is governed by the thresholds of the microprocessor, McLuhan sets about retooling the instruction set of that obsolescent processor known as print. Alphabet and print, "by arresting the movements of speech and thought in a visual code" (McLuhan, 1961, pp. 9-10), do much to attenuate the simultaneous awareness and interaction of the spoken form. We recognize this unwieldiness of the literary form in the cumbersome burdens of proof fostered by linear rationality, in a critical apparatus mired in procedures that are largely curatorial, in research agendas whose methodologies are for the most part administrative. The mosaic writing McLuhan develops is an algorithm that solves for these speed and memory bottlenecks. It optimizes language on the page with better compression techniques, enlarged memory storage, and enhanced program logic. Obviously the resultant document will be edited differently and will be radically reconfigured. Of course it will contain entirely unexpected ratios of composition, expressive parameters, and retrieval tactics. But the new computer programs are not self-explanatory either. It is McLuhan's prerogative to have seen that the type of discourse brought into being by the book is by no means the only form of discourse the book may carry, that in terms of the thought structures text is capable of conveying, one may redesign the written line so it becomes tractable for exploration, participation and analysis, so that in essence, paperware functions as software.

INFONAUTS ALL: THE DAILY HYPERME

A primary advantage, therefore, to come from considering McLuhan's writing as hypertext is that it obviates the persistent tendency to disparage his prose as scattershot and abstruse. It seems incredible that we still have the obligatory caveats about the "recondite prose style" (Dery, 1995, p. 8) or "sheer sloppiness of his books" (Edmundson, 1997). Why not judge McLuhan's work on criteria it sets for itself, rather than holding it up to inadequate protocols it specifically sets out to replace? Understanding how McLuhan's discourse delivers hypertext in its own discursive terms may help to do this. The structure of McLuhan's analysis can answer what critical theory looks and feels like in hypertext, what it is like to think critically in a hypertextual mode. McLuhan (1997) not only considers this multilayered prose a "serious art form" (p. 71) but a necessary mutation if cultural criticism is to keep pace with the increasing complexity of the objects it purports to describe.

A second advantage to accrue from all of this is the way a hypertextual conception of McLuhan's writing opens into the substance of his work. The model for hypertext has always been the active, associational matrix of the mind itself. Hypertext's driving vision is to deliver the reader from the doldrums of passive reception and enmesh him in "the active, independent, autonomous construction of meaning" (Paulson, 1988, p. 139). If McLuhan aptly simulates this experience, conveying a dynamic of total involvement, it is because he connects with what is already an extant hypertext network. Language itself of course, is already a hypermedium whose symbolic functionality allows one to access and motivate the shared knowledge-base of its users. But on another level, too, McLuhan demonstrates that hypertext need not await the building of a multimedia hyperscape out there on the servers. When McLuhan (1994) speaks of "the technological extension of our central nervous system that we call the electric media" (p. 352), he refers to the global hypermedia network already installed in its users by the delivery systems of electronic communication. Cyberspace is a dimension of experience all global villagers already possess. The simultaneous multiplanar compression adumbrated by hypertext is a daily event, a pastiche of random factors that cut our consciousness moment to moment. Contemporary consciousness is a hypertext around us. What makes McLuhan's writing heuristic is precisely the extent to which it actively interfaces with these active nodes of our experience. A heuristic is, specifically, an exploratory problem-solving technique that utilizes self-educating techniques such as feedback to improve performance. A heuristic program is therefore a cybernetic model, one that self-modifies or learns to learn. This is the unifying ecological aspect of McLuhan's (McLuhan & Nevitt, 1972) argument, the need for "simultaneous awareness of the interplay of the total field of processes" (p. 233), which he generates hypertextually by venturing, as he says, "to interlace or link complex events in a way that reveals the causal processes of change" (McLuhan, 1951, p. viii).

A heuristic is also a construct that can be tested. Seeing McLuhan's work as a hypertext heuristic points the way to that rarest of endeavors in the humanities, the undertaking of pure research. As details of the present picture McLuhan described come to fruition for us now in that rearview mirror we call the future, the heuristic tools he devised reveal themselves as powerful reagents catalyzed by time. Contrivances such as the difference between public and mass, the participation gradient of media hot and cool, the corporate image or form whose parts are interpenetrating, the content of media forms being other media, and their colonizing effects studied as tetrads—these jargon-free, counterintuitive heuristic devices provide valuable feedforward in deciphering "the cultural logic of late capitalism" (Frank et al., 1997, p. 15), what we loosely refer to as *postmodernism*. Phenomena as diverse as the rise of the new attention economy; the vulnerability of people's personas online; the triumph of the news leak; the fact that guests take lie detector tests on daytime talk shows; and metaphenomena such as alternative identity; hyperdemocracy and the erosion of representative government; separatism and balkanization in the face of corporate supranationalism; downsizing, decentralization and disintermediation; the interchangeability of business and culture and the blurring line between branding and programming; cooptation of irony by the televisual nexus; the proleptic simulation of real events by media occurrences; the apparent rise of violence—these vectors of the zeitgeist are able to be charted using many of McLuhan's probes, not least of all because they bear many of them out.

FEEDFORWARD

In revisioning, then, the place of language as it impacts on the tasks of textual discursivity, and the possibility of text as a hypermedium, McLuhan's understanding is of language as but one physiological rectifier of the white noise over and against which media are what they are, now only one of many protocols for formatting consciousness amidst the background flow of existence. As the partially connected artificial intelligences of electronic mediation carve up available bandwidth, "we are all of us persons of divided and sub-divided sensibility through failure to recognize the multiple languages by which our world speaks to us." To this end, language retains a limited, specialized function as perceptual probe or "instrument of exploration and research" (McLuhan, 1997, pp. 114, 134). If current hypertext gambits to set technology against the power of thought appear as blatant attempts to cinematize the book, if the cybernetic challenge to simulate consciousness seems too facile a by-product of "well-computed binarism" (Derrida, 1981, p. 167), there is this other "technology of thinking" (Deutsch, 1966, p. 10) that rallies "all the ancient traditions of language as science" (McLuhan & Nevitt, 1972, p. 150), a factive script mining "the special poetic ways of modeling the world that constitute the highest level of the sign systems of verbal art" (Ivanov, 1977, p. 35). Granted, this hypertext is not distributed many-to-many in real time as the chat rooms of cyberspace, yet it has the advantage of being installed on what is still—*pace* Microsoft—the most ubiquitous platform and originary shareware: language. Its "concentrated relevance" (McLuhan, 1944, p. 273) may yet prove useful in the development of human powers of insight and action.

And what of edible spaceships? Deep into *Understanding Media*, discussing that other all-pervasive medium of exchange, McLuhan (1994) traces money's gradual transformation from a store of work and skill to programmed knowledge, "a steady progression toward commercial exchange as the movement of information itself." He then notes that this trend once more approaches the nonspecialized character of tribal money. Surely this is just the sort of lateral connection the custodians of dialectical inquiry abhor. But McLuhan goes further still, offering one of his infamous improbable examples: money in tribal society "can be eaten, drunk, or worn like the new space ships that are now designed to be edible" (pp. 137-138). For a moment, the acid criticism seems almost justified; even his editors must have balked at such untethered spacewalks of meaning. Could this really be a laconic hyperlink to potent registers of awareness? Does the reader gloss over this image as static or does he pause to fathom its hypergonic possibilities? Does he notice the fantastic voyages of miniaturization, the new forms of wealth created by the "spinning canopy of information" (McLuhan & Nevitt, 1972, p. 275), the waning of distant goals and objectives, "the previous environment swallowed by the new environment and reprocessed for whatever values are digestible"? (McLuhan, 1997, p. 87) Is this not, as Bruce Sterling (1997) muses, money as a "very large, very slow, highly distributed computer" (p. 196) that society uses to process itself, so many bits and bytes as current and currency of perception? However, given the constraints of compression and selection here in force, such experiments await further absorption in the vagaries of the *hyperreal*.

REFERENCES

Lord Bacon: His character and writings, Part 3 (Unsigned contribution). (1838, March). *Southern Literary Messenger, 4*(3), 190-196.

Barthes, R. (1970). *S/Z*. Paris: Editions du Seuil.

Barthes, R. (1988). The death of the author. In S. Heath (Ed. & Trans.). *Image, music, text*. New York: Noonday.

Benjamin, W. (1969). *Illuminations: Essays and reflections* (H. Arendt, Ed., H. Zohn, Trans.). New York: Schocken. 1969. (Original work published 1955)

Bush, V. (1945, July). As we may think. *The Atlantic Monthly, 176*, 101-108.

Deleuze, G., & Guattari, F. (1987). *A thousand plateaus: Capitalism and schizophrenia* (B. Massumi, Trans.). Minneapolis: University of Minnesota Press. (Original work published 1980)

Derrida, J. (1981). *Dissemination* (B. Johnson, Trans.). Chicago: University of Chicago Press. (Original work published 1972)

Dery, M. (1995). The medium's messenger. *21*C*, *2*, 8-12.

Deutsch, K. W. (1966). *The nerves of government: Models of political communication and control.* New York: The Free Press.

Edmundson, M. (1997, November 2). TV guide. *The New York Times Book Review.*

Forsdale, L. (1989). Marshall McLuhan and the rules of the game. In G. Sanderson (Ed.), *Marshall McLuhan: The man and his message* (pp. 169-178). Golden, CO: Fulcrum.

Foucault, M. (1979). What is an author? In J. V. Harari (Ed.), *Textual strategies: Perspectives in post-structuralist criticism.* Ithaca, NY: Cornell University Press.

Frank, T. et al. (1997). Introduction. In T. Frank & M. Weiland (Eds.), *Commodify your dissent: Salvos from The Baffler* (pp. 13-17). New York: W. W. Norton.

Gordon, W. T. (1997). *Marshall McLuhan: Escape into understanding. A biography.* New York: Basic Books.

Ivanov, V. V. (1977). The role of semiotics in the cybernetic study of man and collective. In D. P. Lucid (Ed. & Trans.), *Soviet semiotics: An anthology* (pp. 27-38). Baltimore, MD: Johns Hopkins University Press.

Jakobson, R., & Halle, M. (1971). *Fundamentals of language* (2nd ed.). The Hague: Mouton. (Original work published 1956)

Kittler, F. (1986, Spring). A discourse on discourse. *Stanford Literature Review, 3*(1), 157-166.

Kuhn, T.S. (1970). *The structure of scientific revolutions* (2nd ed.). Chicago: University of Chicago Press. (Original work published 1962)

Kuhns, B. (1997). *The war within the word: McLuhan's history of the trivium.* Internet list posting, March 18, 1997.

Landow, G.P. (1992). *Hypertext: The convergence of contemporary critical theory and technology.* Baltimore, MD: Johns Hopkins University Press.

Lanham, R.A. (1990). *Electronic texts and university structures.* Unpublished manuscript.

Lanham, R.A. (1991). *A handlist of rhetorical terms* (2nd ed.). Berkeley: University of California Press.

Lucid, D.P. (1977). Introduction. In D. P. Lucid (Ed. & Trans.), *Soviet semiotics: An anthology* (pp. 1-23). Baltimore, MD: Johns Hopkins University Press.

Marchand, P. (1998, April 4). Rebooting McLuhan. *The Toronto Star*, p. M1.

McLuhan, M. (1944, April). Poetic vs. rhetorical exegesis: The case for Leavis against Richards and Empson. *Sewanee Review, 52*(2), 266-276.

McLuhan, M. (1951). Introduction. In H. A. Innis, *The bias of communication* (pp. vii-xvi). Toronto: University of Toronto Press.

McLuhan, M. (1961). The humanities in the electronic age. In A. Lucas (Ed.), *Thought 1961: Papers from the Learned Societies of Canada* (pp. 5-14). Toronto: W. J. Gage.

McLuhan, M. (1967, March 6). The message of Marshall McLuhan. Special report. *Newsweek*, pp. 53-57.

McLuhan, M. (1969). An ancient quarrel in modern America. In E. McNamara (Ed.), *The interior landscape: The literary criticism of Marshall McLuhan* (pp. 223-234). New York: McGraw-Hill.

McLuhan, M. (1994). *Understanding media: The extensions of man.* Cambridge, MA: MIT Press. (Original work published 1964)

McLuhan, M. (1997). *Media research: Technology, art, communication* (M. A. Moos, Ed.). Amsterdam: G+B Arts International.

McLuhan, M., & Nevitt, B. (1972). *Take today: The executive as dropout.* New York: Harcourt Brace Jovanovich.

Moulthrop, S. (1994). Rhizome and resistance: Hypertext and the dreams of a new culture. In G. P. Landow (Ed.), *Hyper/text/theory* (pp. 299-319). Baltimore, MD: Johns Hopkins University Press.

Nelson, T. H. (1981). *Literary machines.* Swarthmore, PA: Author.

Nyce, J.M., & Kahn, P. (1989). Epilogue. Innovation, pragmaticism, and technological continuity: Vannevar Bush's memex. *Journal of the American Society for Information Science, 40*(3), 214-220.

Ong, W.J. (1967). *The presence of the word: Some prolegomena for cultural and religious history.* New Haven, CT: Yale University Press.

Paulson, W. R. (1988). *The noise of culture: Literary texts in a world of information.* Ithaca, NY: Cornell University Press.

Saussure, F. de (1986). *Course in general linguistics* (C. Bally, A. Sechehaye, & A. Riedlinger, Eds.; R. Harris, Trans.). La Salle, IL: Open Court. [Accumulated store (p. 122) is rendered "inner storehouse" in the Wade Baskin translation (New York: McGraw-Hill, 1966), p. 123.]

Sterling, B. (1997, November). The missing link. *Wired, 5*(11), 196.

Virilio, P. (1993). The law of proximity (L.E. Nesbitt, Trans.). *D: Columbia Documents of Architecture and Theory, 2,* 123-137.

Wilson, E. O. (1984). *Biophilia.* Cambridge, MA: Harvard University Press.

27 REMEDIATION

UNDERSTANDING THE NEW MEDIA[1]

Jay David Bolter

Georgia Institute of Technology

Richard Grusin

Wayne State University

"REMEDIATING" McLUHAN[1]

The term *new media* is now common for describing such digital technologies as the World Wide Web, games and educational programs on CD-ROM and DVD, interactive television, virtual reality systems, and so on. As the name suggests, the rhetoric of "new" media tends to be revolutionary; the enthusiasts assume that new media should break radically with their predecessors, especially their electronic predecessors such as television and radio. On the other hand, if we look past the rhetoric to the current designs and uses, we see continuity as well as change. For example, the World Wide Web, perhaps the most popular of the new media, draws heavily on earlier media for its forms as well as its content. Everywhere on the Web we find pages that seek to look or function like advertising brochures, book covers, tech-

---

[1]Portions of this article are taken from Jay David Bolter and Richard Grusin, (1999), *Remediation: Understanding New Media,* published by the MIT Press.

nical reports, encyclopedias, newspapers, television broadcasts, soap operas, phone sex lines—that is, instances of earlier media or genres identified with earlier media.

In this respect, the Web is typical of new media, all of which borrow from and reshape earlier forms. Why is this borrowing so general? The conventional wisdom is that the early phase of a new medium is characterized by borrowing, because designers and their audiences have not yet grasped the possibilities that the new medium offers. Thus, the argument goes, early film resembled stage production—actors paraded before a fixed camera—until directors learned to create their own filmic language of edits and changing point of view. Likewise, television passed through a phase in which it borrowed from stage production, vaudeville, and film until it developed its own language (Auslander, 1999). The personal computer supposedly followed a similar trajectory. Among the first popular applications were word processing and desktop publishing, which appropriated the assumptions and goals of printing and typewriting.

We are not claiming that that this observation is wrong; new media in their early phase do borrow from older media. The question, however, is whether the borrowing ever ends. Even when a new medium supposedly finds its own language (a modernist and essentialist notion), the new medium is still entering into relationships of rivalry and homage with other media. In our media-saturated culture, a medium seldom, if ever, reaches a state of purity, in which its forms and meanings are essentially unrelated to the those of its predecessors and contemporaries. Instead, new media construct their meaning from the ways in which they borrow from older media and from each other.

In *Digital Mosaics*, media theorist Steven Holtzman (1997) calls this borrowing by the familiar name *repurposing*. Like other theorists, he argues that repurposing has played a role in the early development of new media but will be left behind when new media find their authentic aesthetic:

> In the end, no matter how interesting, enjoyable, comfortable, or well accepted they are, these approaches [repurposing] borrow from existing paradigms. They weren't conceived with digital media in mind, and as a result they don't exploit the special qualities that are unique to digital worlds. Yet it's those unique qualities that will ultimately define entirely new languages of expression. And it's those languages that will tap the potential of digital media as *new* vehicles of expression. Repurposing is a transitional step that allows us to get a secure footing on unfamiliar terrain. But it isn't where we'll find the entirely new dimensions of digital worlds. We need to transcend the old to discover completely new worlds of expression. Like a road sign, repurposing is a marker indicating that profound change is around the bend. (p. 15)

Repurposing is a Hollywood or advertising term for the reuse of the same plot, characterization, or visual imagery in different media, in order to make more money from the same intellectual property. Thus, the story of *Jurassic Park* began as a novel and then became a movie, which in turn spawned a computer game, toys, and other branded merchandise. Despite Holtzman's claim, repurposing in this sense is not a marker that profound change is "around the bend," but rather an indication that change has already occurred. The media that receive the repurposed content have often reached some maturity. The entertainment industry does not usually repurpose its expensive brands into unknown or untried media, but rather into media whose market value is already established. When he repurposed *Jurassic Park* from novel to film, Spielberg was not taking a chance on an untried medium. Even the trend now to create computer games out of Hollywood properties is not a particularly daring move, for narrative computer games have been around since the 1970s and visual narrative games since the 1980s. *Dragon's Lair* was an early example (Herz, 1997, p.147).

At the beginning of *Understanding Media*, McLuhan (1964) remarked that "the 'content' of any medium is always another medium. The content of writing is speech, just as the written word is the content of print, and print is the content of the telegraph" (pp. 23-24). This suggests a subtler process than mere repurposing and one that is ongoing: it does not necessarily cease at some arbitrary point at which the new medium forges a new language. Much of *Understanding Media* is devoted to exploring how a new medium competes with its predecessors. With his later notion of the tetrad, McLuhan provided an even more general explanation of technological interaction by describing how an artifact or technology works through the amplification, obsolescence, retrieval, or reversal of older forms. But the tetrad is a very general analytic tool indeed. What the artifact affects in these four ways can be anything from another technology (the automobile renders the wagon obsolete) to a practice (cash money obsolesces barter) to a belief or attitude (perspective enhances the private point of view) to a figure of speech (metaphor reverses into allegory) (McLuhan & Powers 1989).

We want to narrow the focus and consider not all technologies, attitudes, beliefs, and rhetorical modes, but rather the techniques and cultural practices through which one medium is related to other media. This is not to deny that the tetradic relationships can apply here. One medium can appear to amplify some aspect of another or render another obsolete, as graphic design on the Web both amplifies and obsolesces graphic design for print. One medium can retrieve some aspect of a prior technology, as photorealistic computer graphics might be said to retrieve linear perspective, after the technique had been rejected for decades in modern art. Such effects are gestures of homage and rivalry: the designers and audiences in the new medium pay homage to a previous medium by appropriating and amplifying its characteristics, and at the same time they make tacit or explicit claims that the new medium surpasses other media and renders them obsolete or reverses their characteristics. These gestures are not passing or incidental. New media need their predecessors in order to make these claims and therefore constitute their own cultural meaning.

We use the term *remediation* to describe the relationship of formal and cultural interdependency that exists between two media or among several. Media and cultural critics tend to play down this interdependency, because, like Holtzman, they are caught up in the rhetoric of the new, which they inherit from modernism. Even McLuhan, who is so aware of this interdependency, can occasionally succumb to the rhetoric of the new. He writes, for example, of the revolutionary nature of television: "The mode of the TV image has nothing in common with film or photo, except that it offers also a nonverbal gestalt" (McLuhan, 1964, p. 272). In fact, the TV image has so much in common with film and photography that its cultural meaning is unthinkable in the absence of these other technologies, and soon television's cultural meaning will be unthinkable apart from its interaction with computer graphics and the monitoring function of the Internet.

WHAT IS A MEDIUM?

We propose this admittedly circular definition: A medium is that which remediates. It is that which appropriates the techniques, forms, and social significance of other media and attempts to rival or refashion them in the name of the real. A medium in our culture can not operate in isolation, because it must enter into relationships of respect and rivalry with other media. There may be or may have been cultures in which a single form of representation (perhaps painting or song) exists with little or no reference to other media. However, such isolation does not seem possible for us today, when we cannot even recognize the representational power of a medium except with reference to other forms. If someone were to invent today a new device for visual representation, its inventors, users, and economic backers would inevitably try to position this device over against film, television, and the various forms of digital graphics. They would inevitably claim that it was better in some way at achieving the real or the authentic, and their claim would involve a redefinition of the real or authentic that favors the new device. Until they had done this, it would not be apparent that the device was a medium at all.

In the past 60 years the digital computer has undergone exactly this process of "mediatization." The programmable digital computer was invented in the 1940s as a calculating engine (ENIAC, EDSAC, etc.), and by the

1950s the machine was also being used for billing and accounting in large corporations and bureaucracies. At that time, proponents began to understand and promote the computer as a new writing technology: that was in fact the message of the "artificial intelligence" movement, which began as early as 1950 with A. M. Turing's (1963) famous essay "Computing Machinery and Intelligence." The important cultural contribution of artificial intelligence was not that the computer could be a new kind of mind, but rather that it could be a symbol manipulator and could therefore remediate earlier technologies of arbitrary symbol manipulation, such as handwriting and printing. However, as long as computers remained expensive and rare, available only to a limited group of experts in large institutions, their remediating functions were limited. In the 1970s, the first word processors appeared, and in the 1980s the desktop computer. The computer could then become a medium, because it could enter into the social and economic fabric of business culture and remediate the typewriter almost out of existence. Although the computational device itself, even the "user-friendly" word processor, was not a medium, that device together with its social and cultural functions did constitute a new medium. Furthermore, in the 1980s and 1990s the digital computer took on new technical and social functions and was constituted as a second medium, or series of media, for visual or sensory representation.

The cultural work of defining a new medium goes on during, and in a sense even before, the invention of the device itself. The technologists working on the device may have some sense of where it might fit in the economy of media, what it might remediate—as 15th and 16th-century printers did in their project to remediate the manuscript and as the inventors of photography did in the 19th century. Or they might be working on a device for a different purpose altogether, and they or someone else might realize its potential for constituting a new medium. In some cases, the potential might emerge only slowly as the device evolved and changed (as with radio and the telephone). All sorts of cultural relationships with existing media are possible: the only thing that seems impossible is to have no relationship at all.

TECHNOLOGICAL DETERMINISM AND THE CULTURAL CONTEXT OF MEDIA

The media relationships that McLuhan (1964) defines in *Understanding Media*—speech as the content of writing, writing of print, and print of the telegraph—are all forward-looking. Writing comes after and to some extent supercedes speech as the main carrier of culture, the telegraph supplements but also supercedes some aspects of print. In each case, a new medium appropriates or incorporates older ones, as if moving towards the goal of ideal communication. Admittedly, the situation for McLuhan is not that straightforward, since electronic media of radio and television do constitute a sort of recorso to an era of oral rather than visual primacy.

In *The Soft Edge*, Paul Levinson (1997) adopts an explicitly evolutionary explanation of the relationships among media. He uses the term *remedial medium* to describe specific instances in which our culture uses one medium to reform or improve on another. For Levinson, media in general develop in an "anthropotropic" fashion—that is, to resemble the human. Remediation becomes an agent in this evolution, as our culture invents media that improve on the limits of prior media. Thus, writing makes speech more permanent; the VCR makes TV more permanent; hypertext makes writing more interactive; and so on. The development Levinson describes is almost invariably progressive. We would argue, however, that the interplay of media is not necessarily progressive, because, for one thing, the measure of progress is culturally determined and can therefore change historically. Media do not become more natural or more human, although over time we may become more used to their modes of mediation. For example, we are now so accustomed to the filmic conventions of the so-called Hollywood style that color films from the 1950s to the present seem more natural than films of earlier decades. The conventions simply do not jump out at us. Furthermore, it is not always the case that newer media remediate older ones. The process of reform and refashioning can be mutual. For example, newspapers, such as *USA Today*, and television news broadcasts, such as CNN Headline News, imitate Web sites, even as Web sites are fashioning themselves after their printed or televised counterparts. And one medium can borrow or appropriate from several others at the same time: as we have already suggested, the World Wide Web borrows from many media forms, including print, television, and film.

Any description of media that, like McLuhan's or Levinson's, suggests teleological goals seems open to the charge of technological determinism. Indeed, any description that focuses on the formal or "essential" properties of media seems to reduce culture to the role of the passive recipient of technologically imposed change.[2] In the 1970s, Raymond Williams (1975) was thinking in the first instance of McLuhan when he made his influential argument against the notion that new technologies "are discovered, by an essentially internal process of research and development, which then sets the conditions for social change and progress"(p. 13). Williams was protesting

---

[2]McLuhan has of course been the subject of such charges for decades. Levinson (1997) is certainly aware of the problem and distinguishes between hard and soft determinism.

against a view that was popular in the 1960s and 1970s and remains so today. Whether they are blaming or praising technology, politicians, futurologists, and print and electronic journalists fall easily into the rhetoric of technological determinism. Enthusiasts for cyberspace such as John Perry Barlow credit the Internet with creating a new culture, while conservative politicians speak as if the Internet had itself called forth a new form of pornography. Meanwhile, Williams and others have convinced almost all historians, social scientists, and humanists, with the result that technological determinism has been one feature of traditional Marxism rejected by postmodern theory and cultural studies. Whenever it is made, the charge is now considered fatal: Nothing good can come of technological determinism, because the claim that technology causes social change was regarded as a justification for the excesses of technologically driven capitalism in the late 20th century.

For Williams, McLuhan was not only a determinist concerning the impact of media on culture, but also an essentialist. McLuhan had isolated media from their social contexts, as if media could work directly on some abstract definition of human nature. Each medium seemed to have an essence that altered the human sensorium. Williams (1975) objected that "in [McLuhan's] work, as in the whole formalist tradition, the media were never really seen as practices. All specific practice was subsumed by an arbitrarily assigned psychic function, and this had the effect of dissolving not only specific but general intentions. . . . All media operations are in effect dissocialised; they are simply physical events in an abstracted sensorium, and are distinguishable only by their variable sense-ratios" (p.127). In *Understanding Media*, McLuhan (1964) did often claim that media change us, and he continues to influence popular versions of technological determinism today. Although he was regarded as a radical in the 1960s, McLuhan has now been adopted as a patron saint of the information industry. If in the 1960s, his phrase "global village" sounded like a justification of social protest and "flower power," communications giants today happily borrow the phrase in their advertising. The idea that new electronic technologies of communication will determine our social organization is clearly not threatening to corporations that market those technologies.

On the other hand, McLuhan also notices intricate correspondences involving media and cultural artifacts. Although Williams is right that McLuhan returns repeatedly to the claim that media bring about cultural change, the chapters of *Understanding Media* are filled with contemporary as well as historical examples, from popular as well as literary culture. Many of McLuhan's correspondences point to the ways in which one medium remediates others (especially print, radio, film, and television). Often the remediations involve the social practices that accompany media: for example, how a contemporary American family views television or film. We can let go of the premise of cause and effect and still examine the interrelationships among media for which McLuhan argues. We need not be afraid of McLuhan's "formalism," as long as we remember that technical forms constitute only one aspect of technologies that are simultaneously social and economic. McLuhan's notion that media are extensions of the human sensorium can even be regarded as an anticipation of Donna Haraway's cyborg. McLuhan did bring to our attention the fact that media take their meaning through interactions with the senses and the body, although feminist writers since the 1970s have elaborated this idea in ways that McLuhan did not envision. In short, we can reject determinism and still appreciate McLuhan's analysis of the remediating power of various media.

We also need to keep in mind the other half of Williams' critique. Williams (1975) also warned against the notion of "determined technology [which] has a similar one-sided, one-way version of human process. Determination is a real social process but never . . . [functions] as a wholly controlling, wholly predicting set of causes" (p. 130). Williams argued that social forces "set limits and exert pressures, but neither wholly control nor wholly predict the outcome" (p. 130). In an effort to avoid both technological determinism and determined technology, we suggest that social forces and technical forms be treated as two aspects of the same phenomenon—that digital technologies themselves should be regarded as hybrids of technical, material, social, and economic facets (Latour, 1987, 1993). Thus, virtual reality is not only a head-mounted display and computer hardware and software. It is also the sum of the entertainment and training uses to which this hardware and software is put, and it is the institutional and entrepreneurial capital devoted to these uses. Finally, virtual reality enacts a subjective, point-of-view aesthetic that our culture has come to associate with new media in general. These facets of the cultural meaning of virtual reality are so closely associated that it is unproductive to try to tease them apart. Like a quark, no one facet can exist in isolation: Any argument forceful enough to detach one facet from its network of affiliations would necessarily bind that facet into some other cultural network. Because our digital technologies of representation are simultaneously material artifacts and social constructions, there is no need to insist on any aspect as cause or effect.

The cultural studies of popular media (e.g., *Media Culture* by Douglas Kellner, 1995) have been right to insist on close ties among formal and material characteristics, "content," and economic and social functions. Indeed, the various elements of media are so tightly bound that they can never be entirely separated. For example, to say that the commercial funding of American television is the cause of its insipid content (or induces individuals to identify with dominant ideologies or whatever) is already to separate the technical form of television (as the creation and distribution of programs on television sets) from its economic expression. In fact, commercial financing is an integral aspect of the medium of American television, as are its social uses (such as TV dinners, occupying the children, defining shopping habits). We do not mean that it would be impossible to design a different system, say public financing, but rather that, in the unlikely event that it were ever established, public financing would redefine American television as a technology and medium. This in turn does not mean that the mode of financing *causes* American television to be what it is, but rather that the character of a technology such as television is articulated through a network of formal, material, social and economic practices. Any change in one of these elements alters the network itself.

Relationships of remediation among media involve all the elements in this network. In the case of film, for example, when we look at what happens on the screen (in a darkened theater), we can see how film refashions the definitions of immediacy that were offered by stage drama, photography, and painting. However, when the film ends, the lights come on, and we stroll back into the lobby of, say, a suburban mall theater, we recognize that the process of remediation is not over. We are confronted with images in a variety of media (posters, computer games, and videoscreens) as well as social and economic artifacts (the choice of films offered and the pricing strategy for tickets and refreshments). These various elements do not simply provide context for the film; they take part in the constitution of the medium of film as we understand it in the United States today. We should be able to recognize the hybrid character of film without claiming that any one aspect is more important than the others. This is the claim implicit in most cultural studies analyses of popular media: that film and television embody or carry economic and cultural ideologies and that we should study media principally in order to uncover and learn to resist their ideologies (Kellner, 1995). Although it is true that the formal qualities of the medium reflect their social and economic significance, it is equally true that the social and economic aspects reflect the formal or technical qualities.

THE WORLD WIDE WEB AND COMPUTER GAMES AS REMEDIATORS

We use the term *remediation*, therefore, to describe the process by which one medium can seek to take over and remake the form and at the same time the cultural and even economic function of other media. Although this process has a long history, it has perhaps never been more clearly manifest than in new media today.

As we have already indicated, the World Wide Web is a vigorous remediator, refashioning practically every available medium, including print, graphic design, photography, film, radio, and television. In its earliest period, from 1990 to 1993, the Web was conceived and implemented to remediate printed or typed text. Its inventor, Tim Berners-Lee, believed that a global hypertext system would be more efficient way for scientists and others to exchange their drafts and papers and technical reports. When in 1993 programmers at National Center for Super Computer Applications (NCSA) created the first graphical browser (Hafner & Lyon 1996), which could display static graphics on the web pages along with text, they enabled the Web to remediate graphic design for print. This paradigm, the Web as an instantaneous global system for graphic design and display, has since prevailed. In his printed book, *Creating Killer Websites*, David Siegel (1997) is one of the most eloquent advocates of this paradigm for the Web: eloquent, that is, through the visual rhetoric of his illustrations as much as in the verbal rhetoric of his text. Siegel's own Web site (www.killersites.com August 27, 1998) remediates his book. The opening page of the site reproduces the book's cover. McLuhan's characterization (that one medium provides content for another) fits Siegel's site perfectly, in the sense that Siegel's printed book, at least its cover, is literally the content of the web page. Siegel offers his principles of graphic design as a philosophy for constituting web pages and Web sites as a whole. For Siegel explicitly, and for thousands of web designers implicitly, a Web site should take its formal significance from graphic design for print. Web sites can not only borrow, but improve on that form. It is true that the Web does yet not offer the visual precision of well-designed magazines or books, but revisions of the underlining control language (html) are giving the designer greater control over each pixel on the screen. Furthermore, the web interface possesses qualities that static print does not: animation and point-and-click interactivity. These qualities challenge the ability of a printed graphic to hold the reader's attention or answer his questions. Finally, and not insignificantly, Siegel and other web designers are trying to appropriate for the Web the cultural and economic functions of commercial design for print. Indeed, they are succeeding in convincing our culture that the Web is the place to locate some of the most interesting new designs and that web designers should be respected and remunerated accordingly.

The integration of text and graphics has also made possible effective news web sites, such as *The New York Times* on the Web (www.nytimes .com August 31, 1998) and CNN Interactive (www.cnn.com August 31, 1998), which both complement and compete with their printed or televised counterparts. The sites, such as the Times on the Web, whose counterparts are printed papers, can easily appropriate the text and graphics from the earlier medium; what these sites offer in addition is ease of access and rapid and repeated updating. Sites like CNN Interactive have a harder task, for they must remediate the apparent liveness of a televised broadcast. CNN Interactive does offer some digitized video and audio, but it remains largely a site that must be read. Nevertheless, the site can claim to deliver a more immediate and timely experience by permitting the user to navigate through a series of menus to exactly the story that she is interested in. Although the site can not be live in quite that sense that CNN Headline News claims to be, it can refashion the liveness that has always been a characteristic of television, and that is one of the qualities that distinguish television from film (Flitterman-Lewis, 1992). The site is live both in the sense that it is updated frequently (every few minutes during active periods) and in the sense that it is interactive and responsive to the user's queries.

As these examples suggest, borrowing and refashioning imply competition, a sense of doing better than the medium from which one is borrowing. The Web purports to be better than graphic design and better than television at providing an authentic, timely, and immediate experience. For the Web, as for other new media such as CD-ROM multimedia, the claim of immediacy is based largely on the quality of interactivity that the computer can provide and that books and television cannot.

If we turn now to CD-ROM (and soon DVD) multimedia games, we again find the same strategy at work—remediation in order to provide the user with a more immediate and compelling experience. In this respect, one genre of computer game stands out: so-called "interactive film," which explicitly borrows from and refashions our experience of the cinema. An excellent example of this genre is *The Last Express*, whose creator Jordan Mechner (1997) has completely absorbed the style of the traditional Hollywood film. His mis-en-scène and "camera shots" are entirely consistent with the Hollywood style. The game appropriates not only the visual style, but also the narrative structure of film, so that the player clearly feels herself to be in a film of mystery or detection, in a plot that recalls Hitchcock or Graham Greene. The action takes place aboard the Orient Express on the eve of the World War I. The player is assigned the role of an American expatriate who boards the train to discover that his friend has been murdered. He must then assume the identity of his friend and continue his journey on the train. At the beginning, the American character (and of course the player) knows nothing about the plot in which he is implicated by the discovery of his friend's murder. In typical Hitchcock fashion, he must learn the truth while avoiding arrest by the police and whatever danger killed his friend. He must learn in real time as the train moves across Europe—by walking up and down the corridors, meeting people who seem to know him, and eavesdropping on conversations that may provide clues.

The Last Express borrows from film in order to compete with film. It tacitly claims to provide a more engaging narrative than traditional film because in the game the narrative outcomes are, at least partly, under the player's control. Enthusiasts may speak of the realism and accuracy of a game like *The Last Express*. But the player's sense of involvement, the sense of immediacy of experience, does not come from the game's resemblance to "real life." It comes instead from the player's feeling of being "in" a Hitchcock movie. It is hard to imagine any player enjoying this game who has not read Greene or seen Hitchcock or at least participated in our culture's fascination with the mystery genre in novels and films.

In addition to such resonant examples as *The Last Express*, there must now be hundreds of less innovative games, many based explicitly on Hollywood film originals. Some of these, such as *Blade Runner*, use three-dimensional graphics to recreate the atmosphere and cinematic style of the original film; others string together segments of live-action film, as does *Star Trek Borg: The Interactive Movie*, which is shot entirely from the first-person, point-of-view perspective of the player as a character. Just as photorealistic computer graphics has defined reality as being in a photograph, interactive films define it as being in a movie. In games such as *Star Trek Borg*, the player-as-character is directly addressed by fellow characters in the scenes, and her choices change the course of events. Conventional filmed scenes establish the narrative line, while the player's action at various decision points will determine which filmed scenes will be presented next. Although at present, the interaction between the player and the filmed scene is clumsy, the goal of this genre is to close such gaps and give the player the sense that she has fallen "into a movie."

If interactive computer games now remediate cinema, current cinema also provides perhaps the best example of what we may call "retrograde remediation": the refashioning of a newer medium by an earlier one. State-of-the-art computer graphics has become part of the definition of a Hollywood blockbuster. In such films as *Jurassic Park*, *The Lost World*, or *Terminator II*, the visual technology is highlighted: the computer compositing and the animatronics are the stars of the film. In many other films, for example *Titanic*, the visual technology is almost as important, but it is effaced. The viewer is not supposed to notice the digital interventions. In either case, the purpose of the remediation is the same—to "rescue" film from the computer graphic revolution. Filmmakers and the Hollywood industry are seeking to show that traditional film can absorb the new digital technologies without changing its fundamental character as linear narrative and can continue to be vital without introducing the key quality of point-and-click interactivity that computer games offer.

TRANSPARENT IMMEDIACY AND HYPERMEDIACY

In contemporary culture, both producers and consumers of media seem to regard authenticity or immediacy of experience as the ultimate measure of any medium. To fulfill a desire for the authentic, "live," point-of-view television programs show viewers what it is like to accompany a policeman on a dangerous raid or to be a skydiver or a race-car driver hurtling through space. Filmmakers routinely spend tens of millions of dollars to film "on location" or to recreate period costumes and places in order to make their viewers feel as if they were "really" there. "Webcams" on the Internet pretend to locate us in various natural environments—from a backyard bird feeder in Indianapolis (www.wbu.com/feedercam_home.htm January 24, 1998) to a panorama in the Canadian Rockies (www.banffgondola.com/ Janaury 24, 1998). In all these cases, what we may call a logic of "transparent immediacy" dictates that the medium itself should disappear and leave us in the presence of the thing represented: sitting in the race car or standing on a mountaintop.

On the other hand, these same old and new media often refuse to leave us alone. Many Web sites are riots of diverse media forms, including graphics, digitized photographs, animation, and video—all set up in pages whose graphic design principles recall the psychedelic 1960s or Dada in the 1910s and 1920s (gertrude.art.uiuc.edu/ludgate/the/place/urban_diary/intro.html August 31, 1998; http://www.hotwired.com/rgb/opp/ August 31, 1998). Hollywood films, such as *Natural Born Killers* and *Strange Days*, mix media and styles unabashedly. Televised news programs feature multiple video streams, split-screen displays, composites of graphics and text—a welter of media that is somehow meant to make the news more perspicuous. Even webcams, which operate under the logic of immediacy, can be embedded in a hypermediated Web site (wct.images.com/jukebox August 31, 1998), where the user can select from a "jukebox" of webcam images to generate his or her own paneled display. There is a logic of "hypermediacy" that operates alongside that of transparent immediacy.

Furthermore, as this webcam jukebox suggests, these two seemingly contradictory logics not only co-exist in digital media today, but are mutually dependent. Transparent immediacy depends on hypermediacy. In the effort to create a seamless moving image, filmmakers combine live-action footage with computer compositing and two- and three-dimensional computer graphics. In the effort to be up to the minute and complete, television news producers assemble on the screen ribbons of text, photographs, graphics, and even audio without a video signal when necessary (as was the case during the Persian Gulf War). At the same time, even the most hypermediated productions strive for their own brand of immediacy. So, for example, directors of music videos rely on multiple media and elaborate editing to create an immediate and apparently spontaneous style: they take great pains to achieve the sense of "liveness" that characterizes rock music.

The desire for immediacy leads digital media to borrow avidly from each other as well as from their analog predecessors, film, television, and photography. Whenever one medium seems to have convinced viewers of its immediacy, other media will try to appropriate that conviction. The CNN Interactive Web site is hypermediated—arranging text, graphics, and video in multiple panes and windows and joining them with numerous hyperlinks; yet the Web site borrows its sense of immediacy from the televised CNN newscasts. At the same time, as we have noted, the televised newcasts are coming to resemble web pages in their hypermediacy. The team of web editors and designers, working in the same building in Atlanta from which the television news networks are also administered, clearly do want their technology to be better than television. Similarly, one of the most popular genres of computer games is the flight simulator. The action unfolds in real time, as the player is required to monitor the instruments and fly the plane. The game promises to show the player "what it is like to be" a pilot, and yet in what does the immediacy of the experience consist? As in a real plane, the simulated cockpit is full of dials to read and switches to flip. As in a real plane, the experience of the game is that of working an interface, so that the immediacy of this experience is pure hypermediacy.

TRANSPARENT IMMEDIACY AND HYPERMEDIACY: HOT AND COOL?

In *Understanding Media*, McLuhan (1964) identifies ours as the age of "cool" media, which he opposes to the "hot" media of the former age of print. We too are offering a way of characterizing the cultural history of media in terms of a dichotomy. The concept of *remediation* allows us to understand the current cultural moment, in which new digital media embody the two competing logics of mediation, transparent immediacy and hypermediacy. Furthermore, remediation did not begin with the introduction of digital media; we can identify the same process throughout the last several hundred years of Western visual representation.

Throughout this period the two logics of remediation have been at work. A painting by the 17th-century artist Pieter Saenredam, a photograph by early 20th-century realist Lewis Hine, and a computer system for virtual reality are different in many important ways, but they are all attempts to achieve immediacy by ignoring or denying the presence of the medium and the act of mediation. All of them seek to put the viewer in the same space as the objects viewed. The illusionistic painter employs linear perspective and "realistic" lighting, while the computer graphics specialist mathematizes linear perspective and creates "models" of shading and illumination. Furthermore, the goal of the computer graphics specialists is to do as well and eventually better than the painter or even the photographer. Like immediacy, hypermediacy also has its history: a medieval illuminated manuscript, a 17th-century painting by David Bailly, and a buttoned and windowed multimedia application are all expressions of a fascination with media. Today as in the past, designers of hypermediated forms ask us to take pleasure in the act of mediation, and even our popular culture does take pleasure. Although some hypermediated art has been and remains an elite taste, the elaborate stage productions of many rock stars are among many examples of hypermediated events that appeal to millions.

At first glance these two visual styles of logic might seem to correspond with McLuhan's characterizations of the differences between hot and cool media. In particular, our distinction between the "transparent immediacy" of perspective painting, photography, film, or virtual reality and the "hypermediacy" of illuminated manuscripts, photomontage, multimedia CD-ROMs, or the World Wide Web would seem to reproduce McLuhan's distinction between "hot" media, which involve only one sense at a time and thus work to erase the signs of their mediation, and "cool" media, which engage multiple senses in an interactive fashion that calls attention to their mediated staus. Although there is a correspondence, our distinctions do not map neatly onto McLuhan's. Some media that we would designate as striving for transparency are in McLuhan's sense cool in that they strive for involvement, interaction, instantaneity, and immediacy. This is particularly true of a medium like virtual reality. Similarly, media that operate under the logic of hypermediacy have elements that McLuhan would ascribe to "hot" media in that they are hardly seamless but usually characterized by the fragmentation that McLuhan identified with the mechanical, industrial age of print: for example, the fragmented hypermediacy of the World Wide Web.

The differences between our taxonomy and McLuhan's come primarily from a different interpretation of the relationship between media technologies and history. For us, transparent immediacy and hypermediacy are not tied to particular technologies, and thus particular historical moments. Instead, these two styles emerge in different forms at different historical moments and often, as we have seen, in different ways at the same historical moment within the same medium. Thus, one Dutch painter may pursue a hypermediated style, while an Italian contemporary pursues transparency: the same has been true in literature, photography, film, digital graphics, and other media. Where McLuhan identifies hot media with the mechanical, industrial age of print, and cool media with our electronic age (or with preliterate, tribal, oral cultures), we see transparent immediacy and hypermediacy at work both in our current digital era and throughout history. At different times or within different cultural formations, one style may predominate the other. We do not think, however, that these periods of predominance are simply the result of large-scale transformations in media technolo-

gies, but are rather the product of complex networks of social, technological, cultural, and economic forces.

BASEBALL AND THE REALITY OF MEDIA

One consequence of McLuhan's fondness for large-scale narratives of technological and historical change is that some of his speculations about large
or small changes in the cultural uses of media appear in retrospect to be off
the mark. One such speculation comes in his remarks about baseball in
Understanding Media, where McLuhan comments that television is not a
good medium for baseball, because television's seamless all-at-onceness
reveals baseball as the product of the specialized, linear one-thing-at-a-time-
ness of industrialized, mechanical print culture. Empirically, McLuhan was
responding to the fact that in the mid-1960s baseball was declining in popularity, but his explanation of this decline as a consequence of television did
not prove to be entirely correct. Baseball's popularity increased tremendously in the 1980s and 1990s, both at the park and on television (and increasingly on the Web). Why did McLuhan's analysis prove so off target here?

McLuhan did not anticipate the ways in which baseball would remake
itself in response to the demands of television. Artificial turf, more speed on
the basepaths and on defense, postseason playoffs, and the live ball: all of
these worked to speed up the game. Furthermore, television itself made
changes that helped baseball. Instant replays and split-screen shots made it
more apparent to viewers that baseball was not just a linear, one-thing-at-a-
time game. Rather, like football or basketball, baseball was a game in which
many other things were going on while the pitcher was standing on the
mound and the batter was waiting at the plate. McLuhan's analysis of baseball did not sufficiently take into account the fact that baseball and its mediation were not separate, but that baseball was the sum of its mediations. Put
differently, McLuhan's analysis of baseball did not seem to accept the fact
that "baseball" was not just the game on the field (or the game as televised
by 1960s media technology, which really extended initially from the hot
medium of radio); instead, as the available media changed, the game of baseball changed too (even as its rules stayed relatively constant).

What has changed since the 1960s is baseball's mediation in and through
the major league stadiums themselves. It was not long after McLuhan wrote,
for example, that the dead spaces between pitches, hitters, and innings disappeared; as baseball fans now know, recorded music and eventually giant
video screens filled the spaces between baseball's specialized, one-at-a-time
moments. More recently, the stadiums have become large, semi-public mediated spaces. A good example is Atlanta's Turner Field, whose plaza beyond

the outfield walls has been designed to have the feel and function of a town square. In this town square, however, the central visual feature is a giant television screen broadcasting the game that is currently being played on the field. Beneath this screen is a bank of television monitors displaying the television coverage of other games in progress at that moment in other parks. Just as these video monitors work to dislodge the spectators from the stationary points of view of their assigned seats, the stadium itself encourages spectators to be peripatetic. The game can be viewed from the Chop Shop, a restaurant and bar in dead center field. In the plaza and underneath the left-field stands are games where youths can pitch to or hit against video images of their favorite players. Furthermore the Coca-Cola Pavilion in the left-field corner of the upper deck has displays and activities for children. If, by some miracle, a player were to hit a home run into the pavilion (a feat even Mark McGwire has suggested is impossible), the Coca-Cola Company will pay the lucky fan who catches the ball $1 million. All of these changes illustrate how baseball has refashioned itself through the remediating effects of new media and cultural and economic practices.

FORMS OF REMEDIATION

Remediation is a defining characteristic of media in our culture today and therefore of new media. What might seem at first to be an esoteric practice is so widespread that we can identify a spectrum of different ways in which digital media remediate their predecessors. The spectrum depends on the degree of perceived competition or rivalry between the newer medium and the older one as well as on the remediating medium's presentation of itself as transparent or hypermediated.

At one extreme, an older medium is highlighted and re-presented in digital form without apparent irony or critique. Examples include CD-ROM (or DVD) picture galleries (digitized paintings or photographs) and collections of literary texts, such as Project Gutenberg (www.promo.net/pg/ August 31, 1998). In these cases, the electronic medium is not set in opposition to painting, photography, or printing; instead, the computer is offered as a new means of gaining access to these older materials, as if the content of the older media could simply be poured into the new one. The electronic version justifies itself by granting access to the older media. The digital medium wants to erase itself, so that the viewer stands in the same relationship to the content as she would if she were confronting the original medium. Ideally, there should be no difference between the experience of seeing a painting in person and on the computer screen, but this is an ideal that cannot be achieved. The computer always intervenes and makes its presence felt in some way, perhaps because the viewer must click on a button or slide a bar to view a whole picture or perhaps because the digital image appears grainy or the colors seem untrue. Transparency, however, remains the goal.

Creators of other electronic remediations seem to want to emphasize the difference rather than erase it. In these cases, the electronic version is offered as an improvement, although the new is still justified in terms of the old and seeks to remain faithful to the older medium's character. There are various degrees of fidelity. Encyclopedias on CD-ROM, such as Microsoft's *Encarta* or Grolier's *Electronic Encyclopedia*, seek to improve on printed encyclopedias by providing not only text and graphics, but also sound and video and feature electronic searching and linking capabilities. Yet, because they are presenting discrete, alphabetized articles on technical subjects, they are still recognizably in the tradition of the printed encyclopedia since the 18th-century *Encyclopédie* and *Encyclopaedia Britannica*. In the early 1990s, the Voyager Company published series of "Expanded Books" on CD-ROM, an eclectic set of books originally written for printed publication including *Jurassic Park* and *Brave New World*. The Voyager interface remediated the printed book without doing much to challenge print's assumptions about linearity and closure. Even the name "Expanded Books" indicated the priority of the older medium. Much of the current World Wide Web remediates older forms without challenging them. Its point-and-click interface allows the developer to reorganize texts and images taken from books, magazines, film, or television, but the reorganization does not call into question the character of a text or the status of an image. In all these cases, the new medium does not want to efface itself entirely. Microsoft wants the buyer to understand that she has purchased not simply an encyclopedia, but an electronic and therefore improved encyclopedia. So the borrowing might be said to be translucent rather than transparent.

The digital medium can also be more aggressive in its remediation. It can try to refashion the older medium or media entirely, while still marking the presence of the older media and therefore maintaining a sense of multiplicity or hypermediacy. This is particularly clear in the rock CD-ROMs, such as the Emergency Broadcast Network's (1995) *Telecommunication Breakdown* in which the principal refashioned media are music recorded on CD and its live performance on stage. This form of aggressive remediation throws into relief both the source and the target media. In the "Electronic Behavior Control System," old television and movie clips are taken out of context (and therefore out of scale) and inserted absurdly into the techno-music chant. This tearing out of context makes us aware of the artificiality of both the digital version and the original clip. The work becomes a mosaic in which we are simultaneously aware of the individual pieces and of their new, inappropriate setting. In this kind of remediation, the older media are presented in a space whose discontinuities, like those of collage and photomontage, are clearly visible. In CD-ROM multimedia the discontinuities are indicated by the window frames themselves and by buttons, sliders, and other controls, which start or end the various media segments. The windowed style of the graphical user interface favors this kind of remediation: different programs, representing different media, can appear in each window—a word-processing document in one, a digital photograph in another, digitized video in a third—while clickable tools activate and control the different programs and media. The graphical user interface acknowledges and controls the discontinuities as the user moves among media.

Finally, the new medium can remediate by trying to absorb the older medium entirely, so that the discontinuities between the two are minimized. The very act of remediation, however, ensures that the older medium cannot be entirely effaced; the new medium remains dependent on the older one in acknowledged or unacknowledged ways. We have already discussed the genre of computer games called "interactive films," in which the players become characters in a cinematic narrative. They have some control over both the narrative itself and the stylistic realization of it, in the sense that they can decide where to go and what to do in an effort to dispatch villains (as in the action-adventure game *Doom*) or solve puzzles (as in the tremendously popular *Myst*). They can also decide where to look, where to direct their graphically realized points of view, so that in interactive film, the player is often both actor and director. On the World Wide Web, on the other hand, it is primarily television rather than cinema that is remediated. There are numerous Web sites that borrow the monitoring function of broadcast television. These sites present a stream of images from digital cameras aimed at various parts of the environment: pets in cages, fish in tanks, a soft drink machine, one's office, a highway, and so on. Although these point-of-view sites monitor the world for the Web, they do not always acknowledge television as the medium that they are refashioning. In fact, television and the World Wide Web are engaged in an unacknowledged competition in which each now seeks to remediate the other. The competition is economic as well as aesthetic; it is a struggle to determine whether broadcast television or the Internet will dominate the American and world markets.

Like television, film is also trying to absorb and repurpose digital technology, as we have mentioned above. Digital compositing and other special effects are now standard features of the Hollywood films, particularly in the "action-adventure" genre. And in most cases, the goal is to make these electronic interventions transparent. The stunt or special effect should look as "natural" as possible, as if the camera were simply capturing what really happened in the light. Computer graphics processing is rapidly taking over the animated cartoon; indeed, the takeover is already complete in Disney's

Toy Story. And here too the goal is to make the computer disappear: to make the settings, toys, and the human characters look as much as possible like live-action film. Hollywood has incorporated computer graphics partly to hold off the threat that digital media might pose for the traditional, linear film. Again, this attempt shows that remediation operates in both directions: users of older media such as film and television can seek to appropriate and refashion digital graphics, just as digital graphics artists can refashion film and television.

Unlike other instances of hypermediacy, however, this form of aggressive remediation does create an apparently seamless space. It conceals its relationship to earlier media in the name of transparency; it promises the user an unmediated experience, whose paradigm again is virtual reality. Games like *Myst* and *Doom* are desktop virtual reality applications, and, like immersive virtual reality, they aim to inspire in the player a feeling of presence. On the other hand, like these computer games, immersive virtual reality also remediates both television and film: it depends on the conventions and associations of the first-person point-of-view or subjective camera. The science fiction writer Arthur C. Clarke claimed that: "Virtual Reality won't merely replace TV. It will eat it alive" (Rheingold, 1991). As a prediction of the success of this technology, Clarke is likely to be quite wrong, at least for the foreseeable future, but he is right in the sense that virtual reality remediates television (and film) by the strategy of incorporation. This strategy does not mean that virtual reality can obliterate the earlier, visual, point-of-view technologies; rather, it ensures that these technologies remain at least as reference points by which the immediacy of virtual reality is measured. Paradoxically, then, remediation is as important for the logic of transparency as it is for hypermediacy.

REMEDIATION AS REVERSAL

This paradox deserves some further consideration. We have used the term *immediacy* in two senses: one epistemological, the other psychological. In the epistemological sense, immediacy is transparency: the absence of mediation or representation. It is the notion that a medium could erase itself and leave the viewer in the presence of the objects represented, so that he or she could know the objects directly. In its psychological sense, immediacy names the viewer's feeling that the medium has disappeared and the objects are present to him or her, a feeling that the viewer's experience is therefore authentic. Hypermediacy also has two corresponding senses. In its epistemological sense, hypermediacy is opacity, the fact that knowledge of the world comes to us through media. The viewer acknowledges that he or she is in the presence of a medium and learns through acts of mediation or indeed learns about mediation itself. The psychological sense of hypermediacy is the experience that the viewer has in and of the presence of media: It is the insistence that the experience of the medium is itself an experience of the real.

The appeal to authenticity of experience is what brings the logics of immediacy and hypermediacy together. The desire for an authentic, "real," (apparently) unmediated experience lies behind and unites both strategies of representation and is the motive for remediation. In the case of transparent immediacy, the designer's strategy is to pretend that the medium does not exist. In the case of hypermediacy, the strategy is reversed. Hypermediated media forms do not try to erase the medium; instead, they frankly admit that the viewer is having a highly mediated experience and try to make that experience itself as compelling as possible. By highlighting the medium and multiplying signs of mediation, they can claim to provide the viewer with an authentic experience. That experience itself is unmediated in the sense that the medium is the subject of the experience. Because the experience of media is the experience of the real, hypermediacy passes into immediacy.

This passage from hypermediacy to immediacy is a good candidate for McLuhan's fourth tetradic form, reversal. Hypermediacy is the pushing of a medium to its extreme. On the Web, some sites are relatively transparent, but most follow the strategy of hypermediacy. Some sites are a pastiche of different forms, combining text, static graphics, animations, and even digitized video. Such Web sites recall and refashion a variety of other media, but they do not transparently represent any one of these media. They do not look like books, graphics displays, films, or television broadcasts, although they may borrow elements from all of these. The viewer certainly could not mistake such sites for "real life," as was supposed to be the case with some linear perspective paintings and photographs. Nor, as we have indicated, do these sites possess quite the same "liveness" of television, which is another form of immediacy. In their extreme juxtaposition of diverse media forms, web sites pass from hypermediacy back to its opposite: they offer the user the immediacy of the web experience itself, the point-and-click interactivity and (ostensibly) instant responsiveness which are the Web's main tools in remediating its predecessors.

The strategy of transparent immediacy can also reverse into its opposite. Attempts to make the medium disappear (from trompe-l'oeil painting to virtual reality) can lead the viewer or user to attend all the more closely to the medium itself: both to admire the painter's or programmer's work and to look for remaining flaws that give away the deception. In this way transparency can pass into hypermediacy. The crossing or chiasmus of these two strategies of remediation would certainly have appealed to McLuhan.

REFERENCES

Auslander, P. (1999). *Liveness: Performance in a mediatized culture.* London: Routledge.

Emergency Broadcast Network. (1995). *Telecommunications breakdown.* [CD-ROM]. New York: TVT Records.

Flitterman-Lewis, S. (1992). Psychoanalysis, film, and television. In E. Allen (Ed.), *Channels of discourse, reassembled: Television and contemporary criticism* (2nd ed., pp. 203-246). Chapel Hill: University of North Carolina Press.

Hafner, K., & Lyon, M. (1996). *Where wizards stay up late: The origins of the Internet.* New York: Simon & Shuster.

Herz, J. C. (1997). *Joystick nation: How videogames ate out quarters, won our hearts, and rewired our minds.* Boston, MA: Little Brown.

Holtzman, S. (1997). *Digital mosaics: The aesthetics of cyberspace.* New York: Simon & Schuster.

Kellner, D. (1995). *Media culture: Cultural studies, identity and politics between the modern and the postmodern.* London: Routledge.

Latour, B. (1987). *Science in action: How to follow scientists and engineers through society.* Cambridge, MA: Harvard University Press.

Latour, B. (1993). *We have never been modern* (C. Porter, Trans.). Cambridge, MA: Harvard University Press.

Levinson, P. (1997). *The soft edge: A natural history and future of the information revolution.* London & New York: Routledge.

McLuhan, M. (1964). *Understanding media: The extensions of man.* New York: New American Library, Times Mirror.

McLuhan, M., & Powers, B. R.. (1989). *The global village: Transformations in the world life and media in the 21st century.* New York: Oxford University Press.

Mechner, J. (1997). *The last express.* [CD-ROM]. Novato, CA: Broderbund.

Rheingold, H. (1991). *Virtual reality.* New York: Simon & Schuster.

Siegel, D. (1997). *Creating killer websites.* Indianapolis, IN: Hayden.

Turing, A.M. (1963). Computing machinery and intelligence. In E. A. Feigenbaum & J. Feldman (Eds.), *Computers and thought* (pp. 11-35). New York: McGraw-Hill.

Williams, R. (1975). *Television: Technology and cultural form.* New York: Schocken Books.

ABOUT THE CONTRIBUTORS

Susan B. Barnes is Associate Professor in the Department of Communication and Associate Director of the Social Computing Lab (social.it.rit.edu) at the Rochester Institute of Technology. She is the author of *Online Connections: Internet Interpersonal Relationships* (2001); *Web Research: Selecting, Evaluating, Citing*, with Marie Radford and Linda Barr (2002); and *Computer-Mediated Communication: Human-to-Human Communication Across the Internet* (2003). Dr. Barnes has presented and published numerous articles and book chapters on computer-related topics, including interpersonal computing, computers in organizations, virtual communities, and the history of graphical user interfaces. Currently, she is a personal technology consultant for the *Democrat and Chronicle*, Rochester, NY's city newspaper.

Jay David Bolter is Director of the Wesley New Media Center and Wesley Chair of New Media at the Georgia Institute of Technology. He is the author of *Turing's Man: Western Culture in the Computer Age* (1984); *Writing Space: The Computer, Hypertext, and the History of Writing* (1991; second edition 2001); *Remediation* (1999), with Richard Grusin; and *Windows and Mirrors* (2003), with Diane Gromala. In addition to writing about new media, Bolter collaborates to construct new digital media forms. With Michael Joyce, he created *Storyspace*, a hypertext authoring system.

With Blair Macintyre, he is building an Augmented Reality (AR) system to create dramatic and narrative experiences for entertainment and informal educational settings.

Harris Breslow received his PhD from the Institute of Communications Research, University of Illinois, in 1994. He is the author of "Civil Society, Political Economy, and the Internet," in *Virtual Culture: Identity and Communication in Cybersociety* (Steven Jones, ed., 1997). He has taught communication studies at York University. His research is concerned with conceptualizing culture as a spatial field of human conduct. Breslow is currently working on a spatial history of urban fears.

James M. Curtis received his BA in German from Vanderbilt University and his PhD in Russian from Columbia University. He is Professor Emeritus from the University of Missouri, where he was Professor of Russian for 31 years. His book, *Culture as Polyphony* (1977), was the first detailed analysis and defense of McLuhan's work.

Mark Dery <markdery@optonline.net> is a cultural critic. He is the author of *Escape Velocity: Cyberculture at the End of the Century* (1996) and *The Pyrotechnic Insanitarium: American Culture on the Brink* (1999) <www.levity.com/markdery>. His seminal essay, "Culture Jamming: Hacking, Slashing, and Sniping in the Empire of Signs" popularized the guerrilla media tactic known as "culture jamming"; widely republished on the Web, "Culture Jamming" remains the definitive theorization of this subcultural phenomenon. In *Flame Wars: The Discourse of Cyberculture* (1993), an academic anthology he edited, Dery coined the term "Afrofuturism" and kickstarted the academic interest in black technoculture, and cyberstudies in general. He is the director of digital journalism at New York University, in the Department of Journalism.

Bob Dobbs was born in Paris in 1922 and after World War II worked with international intelligence agencies for many decades. He surfaced in 1987 on CKLN-FM in Toronto and began whistleblowing. Two interpretations of Dobbs are circulating in the popular media: one is through the Church of the SubGenius; the other is on two CDs, *Bob's Media Ecology* and *Bob's Media Ecology Squared*, put out by Time Again Productions, early students of Marshall McLuhan. The best presentation of Dobb's work is in his book, *Phatic Communication with Bob Dobbs*. Today, he travels the world explaining his/our victory over the Android Meme, and the tracings of these activities were regularly published in *Flipside* magazine in the late 1990s. His present writings can be found in the Baedeker section at http://mcluhaninstitute.org.

Donna Flayhan is Associate Professor of Communication and Media at the State University of New York-New Paltz. Flayhan's research interests are in the areas of Media Ecology and Health Communication. Flayhan's most recent academic work in media ecology analyzes the role of cell phone technologies in sudden death situations. Her paper, "Cell Phone Technology and Sudden Death: Comfort or a New Form of Post-Traumatic Stress Disorder," was presented in an international workshop on Mobile Technologies and Health in Udine, Italy, in 2004. An earlier version of that paper was published in *Explorations in Media Ecology* (2003). Flayhan's health communication research is currently centered on a grant-funded investigation into the health effects of September 11 on residents of lower Manhattan.

Stephanie B. Gibson is Associate Professor in the School of Communication Design at the University of Baltimore, where she directs the graduate program in Publications Design. She has served on the boards of several national death penalty abolition organizations and is currently the chair of the board of the statewide organization Maryland Citizens Against State Executions.

Raymond Gozzi, Jr. is Associate Professor in the TV-Radio Department at Ithaca College, Ithaca, NY. His book, the *Power of Metaphor in the Age of Electronic Media*, was published in 1999 by Hampton Press as part of the Media Ecology Series.

Paul Grosswiler is the author of a book on McLuhan's media and social theories, *The Method is the Message: Rethinking McLuhan through Critical Theory* (1998). He was a Fulbright scholar in 2000 at Wuhan University in China, where he taught critical media studies and ethics. His work on McLuhan, media and culture, international mass communication, and new media has appeared in *Canadian Journal of Communication, Journal of Communication Inquiry, Harvard International Journal of Press/Politics,* and *Journal of International Communication.* He earned a PhD at the University of Missouri in 1990 and is Associate Professor of Journalism and Mass Communication at the University of Maine.

Richard Grusin is Professor and Chair in the Department of English at Wayne State University. He received his PhD from the University of California at Berkeley in 1983. He is the author of three books. The first, *Transcendental Hermeneutics: Institutional Authority and the Higher Criticism of the Bible* (1991), concerns the influence of European (primarily German) theories of biblical interpretation on the interpretive theories of New England Transcendentalists like Emerson, Thoreau, and Theodore

Parker. His more recent work concerns historical, cultural, and aesthetic aspects of technologies of visual representation. With Jay David Bolter, he is the author of *Remediation: Understanding New Media* (1999), which sketches out a genealogy of new media, beginning with the contradictory visual logics underlying contemporary digital media. Grusin's latest book, *Culture, Technology, and the Creation of America's National Parks* (2004), focuses on the problematics of visual representation involved in the founding of America's national parks. Currently he is working on the social, political, and aesthetic relationships among film and new digital media.

Gary Gumpert is Emeritus Professor of Communication at Queens College of the City University of New York and co-founder of Communication Landscapers, a consulting firm. He is president of the U.S. chapter of the International Institute of Communication. Professor Gumpert's publications include: *Talking Tombstones and Tales of the Media Age*; and three edited volumes of *Inter/Media: Interpersonal Communication in a Media Age* published by Oxford University Press. He is a recipient of the Franklyn S. Haiman Award for distinguished scholarship in Freedom of Expression. He is on the board of directors of the recently established Urban Communication Foundation, Inc., a not-for-profit organization supporting research on communication and the urban condition. His primary research focuses on the nexus of communication technology and social relationships, particularly looking at urban and suburban development, the alteration of public space, and the changing nature of community.

Neil Hickey is a contributing editor to the *Columbia Journalism Review*. Formerly, he was a New York bureau chief and senior editor of *TV Guide*. He has reported from Vietnam, the Persian Gulf, the Soviet Union, Eastern Europe, Northern Ireland, Cuba, the Baltics, Singapore, and elsewhere. Hickey began his career as a reporter and editor on Baltimore newspapers, and later was an editor/writer at Hearst's *American Weekly*, the national *Sunday* magazine, and at *True*, the Fawcett men's adventure magazine. He is anthologized widely, and is the author of a number of books, among them: *Adam Clayton Powell and the Politics of Race*, and *The Gentleman Was a Thief*, a biography of the legendary 1920s jewel thief, Arthur Barry. In 1995, he won the Everett C. Parker Award for Life Achievement for his coverage of telecommunications issues. Hickey was a naval officer for three years aboard a destroyer, during and after the Korean War. A graduate of Loyola (Maryland), he lives in New York City and Carmel, NY.

Marvin Kitman was the media critic at *Newsday* from 1969 until 2005. His eight books include *The Making of the President, 1789* and *George Washington's Expense Account* (re-issued by Grove/Atlantic in 2000); *I Am* *a VCR* (1988) and *The Marvin Kitman TV Show and Encyclopedia Televisiana* (1973). His articles have appeared in *Harper's, Penthouse, The American Bar Association Journal, Playboy,* and *The New York Times Book Review.* A graduate of the City College of New York, he is a winner of the Townsend Harris Medal (1992), Folio Award (1988), the Society of the Silurians Humorous Writing Award (1991), and Special Commentary Award (1993).

Neil Kleinman is Professor of Communication and Media and Dean of the College of Media and Communication at the University of the Arts, Philadelphia, PA. He is the author of a book on propaganda, *The Dream That Was No More a Dream,* editor of *The Mime Book,* and writes and lectures on intellectual property, the digital economy, and the influence of technologies on society. He holds a PhD from the University of Connecticut and a JD from the University of Pennsylvania. Formerly Dean of the College of Liberal Arts at the University of Baltimore, where he was also founding director of the Institute for Language, Technology, and Publication Design, co-director of the School of Communication Design, and director of the University's doctoral program in Communications Design, he taught writing, publication design, literature, and social and economic history. In 1997, he received the Yale Gordon College's Distinguished Chair for teaching, and in 1998, he received the University of Maryland System Regents Award for Distinguished Teaching.

Elena Lamberti teaches Anglo-American Literature at the University of Bologna. She has specialized in English and Canadian Literature, and has published extensively on English and Anglo-American Modernism (Ford, Joyce, Pound, Hemingway), as well as on Anglo-Canadian culture of the late 20th century (Coupland, Cronenberg, McLuhan). She is the author of the volume, *Marshall McLuhan: Tra Letterature, Arti e Media* (Bruno Mondadori, 2000), the editor of *Interpreting/Translating European Modernism: A Comparative Approach* (Compositori, 2001), co-editor of *Il Senso Criticio: Saggi di Ford Madox Ford* (Alinea, 2001), and of *Ford Madox Ford and "The Republic of Letters"* (Clueb, 2002). She is currently editing a book, *Memories and Representations of War: The Case of WW1 and WW2* (Rodopi, 2005).

Paul Levinson's eight nonfiction books, including *The Soft Edge* (1997), *Digital McLuhan* (1999), *Realspace* (2003), and *Cellphone* (2004), have been the subject of major articles in such publications as *The New York Times, WIRED,* the *Christian Science Monitor,* and *The Financial Times,* and have been translated into Chinese, Japanese, and three other languages. He has appeared on "The O'Reilly Factor," "Scarborough Country," "The CBS

Evening News with Dan Rather," "Jesse Ventura's America," "Inside Edition," CNN, ABC, the History Channel, CSPAN, Fox News, MSNBC, CNBC, NPR, the BBC, and the CBC, and numerous local TV and radio programs. His views on media, culture, and politics are quoted frequently in *The New York Times*, the *Washington Post*, the *Los Angeles Times, USA Today*, AP, Reuters, UPI, and dozens of newspapers and news services. He is the author of four science fiction novels, including *The Silk Code*, which won the 2000 Locus Award for Best First Novel. He is Professor and Chair of Communication and Media Studies at Fordham University in New York City.

Barbara Jo Lewis as Associate Professor with a joint appointment in the Television and Radio and Economic Departments at Brooklyn College of CUNY. Her research has explored evolving attitudes towards technology as reflected in the treatment of fictional technological figures (i.e., the cyborg, the clone) in popular media artifacts. She has also examined Super Heroes as presented in comic and computer art and considered the influence such characters and their actions might have on identity formation of their primary demographic, the adolescent. Presently she is considering the notion of violence and how various mass media artifacts reflect societal acceptance of such actions. Her work has been published in such journals as the *Speech Communication Annual* of the New York State Communication Association, the *Journal of Evolutionary Psychology*, and the *International Journal of Comic Art*.

Joshua Meyrowitz is Professor of Media Studies in the Department of Communication at the University of New Hampshire-Durham, where he has won the Lindberg Award for Outstanding Scholar-Teacher in the College of Liberal Arts. Professor Meyrowitz teaches courses in mass media, analysis of news, media criticism, and communication theory. He is the author of *No Sense of Place: The Impact of Electronic Media on Social Behavior* (Oxford University Press), which has won a number of awards, including the "Book of the Year Award" from the Broadcast Education Association and the Golden Anniversary Book Award from the National Communication Association. Dr. Meyrowitz's articles on media and society have appeared in numerous scholarly journals and anthologies, as well as in general-interest magazines and newspapers.

Michel A. Moos was educated at Yale and at Oxford Universities and has been a Woodruff Scholar at Emory University in Atlanta, where he lives. He edited *Media Research: Technology, Art, Communication* (1997), a collection of essays by Marshall McLuhan, and is a contributor to *Encyclopedia of Postmodernism* (2000). He currently runs a web design company.

Michael J. O'Neill, former editor of the *New York Daily News* and past president of the American Society of Newspaper Editors, is the author of several books including: *The Roar of the Crowd: How Television and People Power are Changing the World* (Random House, 1993), *Terrorist Spectaculars: Should TV Coverage Be Curbed?* (Priority Press, 1986), and "Preventive Journalism" in *Preventive Diplomacy* (Basic Books, 1996). He has written satiric pieces for *The New York Times, Wall Street Journal* and *Newsweek*. One of his essays was listed as among the "outstanding writing" published in Harvard's *Nieman Reports* "during the last half of the 20th Century." As a Washington correspondent specializing in foreign affairs he covered the Cuban Missile Crisis and accompanied Eisenhower, Kennedy, and Johnson on various foreign missions. He is a member of the Council on Foreign Relations.

Paul Ryan's video art work has been presented in Japan, Turkey, France, Germany, Holland, Spain, Equador, and throughout the United States including *The Primitivism Show* at the Museum of Modern Art and *The American Century Show* at the Whitney Museum of American Art. His articles have appeared in *Radical Software, Leonardo, Semiotica*, and *Terra Nova*. He authored *Cybernetics of the Sacred* (Doubleday, 1974) and *Video Mind, Earth Mind* (Peter Lang, 1993). NASA published his Earthscore Notational System. His design for an Environmental Television Channel was presented at a United Nations Conference. His conceptualization of a program for a Hall of Risk in Lower Manhattan was presented at the Venice Biennial. Mr. Ryan is currently a member of the Core Faculty in Graduate Media Studies at The New School.

Robert Lewis Shayon spent 14 years writing, directing, and producing programs for WOR-Mutual in New York and for the CBS Radio Network. While at CBS, he worked closely in the 1940s with Edward R. Murrow. He pioneered television shows promoting grassroots democracy such as "The Whole Town's Talking" (similar to today's town meetings on television). He was the first television critic for the *Christian Science Monitor* and spent more than 20 years as media critic for *Saturday Review* magazine. His book, *Television and Our Children*, was the first analysis of the subject. He is also the author of *The Crowd Catchers—Introducing Television, Open to Criticism*, a selection of his media columns analyzed in light of his critical theory, and a memoir, *Odyssey in Prime Time*. For 25 years he taught graduate students at the Annenberg School for Communication, University of Pennsylvania, and has lectured widely on telecommunications.

Denise Schmandt-Besserat is Professor of Art and Middle Eastern Studies at the University of Texas, Austin. Her major publications include *Before*

Writing (1992), *How Writing Came About* (1996), and *The History of Counting* (1999). Her research on the origins of writing and mathematics has been widely reported in such publications as *Scientific American, Time, Life, The New York Times* and *The Washington Post*. Her work has also been the subject of several television programs. Schmandt-Besserat has been on the editorial/advisory boards of *Archaeology Odyssey, Visible Language,* and *Written Communication* and served on the governing board of the Archaeological Institute of America. She has been a visiting scholar at numerous institutions internationally and received grants from many public and private organizations. Schmandt-Besserat has been cited Outstanding Woman in the Humanities by the American Association of University Women.

Lance Strate, one of the editors of this book, is Associate Professor of Communication and Media Studies at Fordham University, where he organized the Legacy of McLuhan Symposium held on March 27-28, 1998 (out of which this anthology emerged). He is President of the Media Ecology Association, and a Past President of the New York State Communication Association. He edits the journal, *Explorations in Media Ecology*, and is co-editor of the anthology *Communication and Cyberspace*, now in its second edition. He is currently working on a book entitled *Understanding Media Ecology*.

Donald F. Theall is University Professor Emeritus of Trent University where he was President from 1979-1987. Before that he founded the Graduate Programme in Communication at McGill University where he was Molson Professor and had been Chair of English. He was also founding President of the Canadian Communication Association. Currently he is directing a research project on the pre-history of digiculture and its role in the integration of media into the "new media." Theall was McLuhan's first graduate student, and the academic secretary of McLuhan's initial Ford-sponsored Culture and Communication seminars. He is author of *The Virtual Marshall McLuhan* (2001), *James Joyce's Techno-Poetics* (1997), *Beyond the Word* (1995), and *The Medium is the Rear View Mirror: Understanding McLuhan* (1971). He has written numerous articles on communication theory, history, censorship, the rise of cyberculture, literary theory and its history, aesthetics, and literature.

Edward Wachtel, one of the editors of this book, is Director of the Edward A. Walsh Digital Media Laboratory and Associate Professor of Communication and Media Studies at Fordham University. He has authored *Television Hiring Practices, 1980-1985: The Status of Minorities and Women* (1987), and co-authored *Fiber Optics in the Home: The Changing Future of*

Cable, Television and the Telephone (1989). His articles on media, perception, and art have been widely published in scholarly journals such as *Leonardo, The Structurist, Et cetera*, and *Explorations in Media Ecology*. He has contributed chapters to numerous books devoted to media studies, the philosophy of technology, and art and culture.

Frederick Wasser is currently Associate Professor in the Department of Television and Radio, Brooklyn College. His book, *Veni, Vidi Video: The Hollywood Empire and the VCR*, won the MEA's 2003 Marshall McLuhan Award. He is currently a contributing columnist to *Flow*, an online journal. He has published in *Cinema Journal, Critical Studies in Mass Communication, Journal of Communication*, and numerous others. His book chapter will appear in a forthcoming Hampton Press book, *Perspectives on Culture, Technology and Communication: The Media Ecology Tradition*. His interests include film and other media industries, media technology, media ecology, criticism, and political economy. Before embarking on a scholarly career, Wasser spent many years in various freelance jobs in the film and television industries in New York City, Salt Lake City, and Los Angeles.

Frank Zingrone is Professor of Communications and now Senior Scholar Emeritus at York University. He has taught at SUNY, Buffalo, MIT, Cambridge (MA), and the Universities of Toronto and York. He works in communications mainly as an investigator of media effects. Philosophically, he is part of the Innis/McLuhan axis. His work is parallel to McLuhan's, his mentor, friend and colleague. His latest book, *Addiction to Illusion: Discovering the Global Mind* (2005) follows *The Media Symplex: At the Edge of Meaning in the Age of Chaos* (2004) and *Essential McLuhan* (with E. McLuhan, 1995-96), in 10 editions and 8 languages. Besides editing *Who Was Marshall McLuhan*, with H.B. Nevitt (1994), he has published two volumes of poetry, *Traces* (1980) and *Strange Attraction* (2000). He has been featured in magazines, on CD-ROMs, film, television and radio, has lectured widely, and has written more than 50 articles.

AUTHOR INDEX

SUBJECT INDEX

A

ABC (televison network), 62
acceleration, *see* speed
Achilles, 26
acoustic, 4, 25, 98, 124, 142, 157, 158,
    242, 252, 255, 256, 285, 286, 287
    see also sound, orality
activism, 71, 72
adulthood, 37-38, 40
advertising, 37, 96, 101, 102, 240,
    245, 284-285, 288, 291, 319, 323,
    325, 329
affluence, 30, 69-70, 101
Afghanistan, 72
Agel, Jerome, 6, 77
Albania, 166-167, 173
aleph-bet, 31
Allen, Woody, 2, 269
alphabet, 6, 27, 29, 54, 97, 98, 139 fn,
    222, 229, 254, 277, 287, 289, 317

America Online, 62
American triumphalism, 71
Amin, Idi, 166, 167, 169, 170, 172
Amusing Ourselves to Death, 285
ancient, 4, 109-121
animated cartoon, 341-342
Annie Hall (motion picture), 2, 91, 269
anthropotropic, 328
anti-environment, 45, 47, 85
Antigonish Review, 8, 10, 44
anti-gravity, 63
aphasia, 306
archetype, *see* cliché-archetype
Aristotle, 26, 53, 155
art, 5, 26, 43-48, 49, 50-57, 63, 85, 89,
    109-121, 123-135, 137-149, 155,
    156, 158, 186, 250, 251, 252, 254,
    255, 257, 264, 311, 318
artifactual ecology, 52, 54
artificial intelligence, 306, 307, 319,
    327

Printed in the United States
37855LVS00005B/76-132

9 781572 735316